DYING TO FORGET

DYING TO FORGET

OIL, POWER, PALESTINE,

& the Foundations of
U. S. Policy in the Middle East

IRENE L. GENDZIER

COLUMBIA UNIVERSITY PRESS *NEW YORK*

Columbia University Press
Publishers Since 1893
New York   Chichester, West Sussex

cup.columbia.edu

Library of Congress Cataloging-in-Publication Data
Gendzier, Irene L.
Dying to forget : Oil, power, Palestine, and the foundations
of U.S. policy in the Middle East / Irene L. Gendzier.
pages cm
Includes bibliographical references and index.
ISBN 978-0-231-15288-4 (cloth : alk. paper) — ISBN 978-0-231-52658-6 (ebook)
1. United States—Foreign relations—Middle East. 2. Middle East—Foreign relations—
United States. 3. United States—Foreign relations—1945-1953. I. Title.
DS63.2.U5G429 2015
327.7305609' 044—dc23

2015016376

Columbia University Press books are printed on permanent
and durable acid-free paper.
This book is printed on paper with recycled content.
Printed in the United States of America

c 10 9 8 7 6 5 4 3 2 1

COVER IMAGE: Map no. 103.1(B) February 1956 / United Nations

COVER DESIGN: Martin Hinze

For Assaf J. Kfoury

Contents

Acknowledgments

This work has been under way since at least 2008. Research for it was undertaken while I was Professor in the Department of Political Science at Boston University. During this period, I was also fortunate to be an Affiliate in Research at the Center for Middle Eastern Studies, Harvard University, and a Research Affiliate of the MIT Center for International Studies.

I am grateful for the opportunity to thank those whose assistance and support have been indispensable to the research and writing of this book, for which I remain solely responsible. Individuals are identified by the positions they held at the time they provided assistance.

First to be listed are the archivists and librarians who generously shared their knowledge and made U.S. records and presidential papers accessible. It is difficult to exaggerate the importance of their assistance; quite simply, without it this work, as I conceived it, would not have been possible. Second is the list of individuals and institutions that invited me to share my findings and enabled me to benefit from the questions and criticisms that followed. Third are those whose generous assistance and moral support made a great difference to my understanding of various aspects of U.S. policy and Israeli and Palestinian development. Some shared their own work, which opened doors that proved significant to my research. Others offered critical insights based on their knowledge of different aspects of postwar U.S. foreign policy. Others were helpful in posting my articles and essays at online sites and in publications such as the Israel Occupation Archive (IOA), ZNet, *Le Monde Diplomatique*, and *Bidayat* (Beirut). Still others include present as well as former graduate students, many now successful professionals, who in sharing their own work enriched mine. Unnamed in the list below are the many whose support—whether from near or far—gave me the courage to persist in the effort to make sense of the policies and politics

Reflecting on the named and the unnamed is a reminder of the extent to which the production of knowledge takes place in a social context, no matter how solitary is the task of writing and research.

The archivists and specialists at the Harry S. Truman Library and Museum were quite simply indispensable. Jim Armistead, Archivist Specialist, who guided me through the papers of Max W. Ball, Clark M. Clifford, and Ralph K. Davies, was not only consistently helpful and instructive but supportive of my research. In addition, Elizabeth Carrington, Archivist at the Harry S. Truman Presidential Library, provided critical assistance in President Truman's correspondence with Jacob Blaustein. Archivist-Librarians Ted Benicoff, of the Seeley G. Mudd Manuscript Library, at Princeton University, and Scott S. Taylor, the Manuscripts Processor at the Georgetown University Library, Special Collections Research Center, were similarly generous in providing information on their respective holdings. Nicole Toutounji, UNICEF Photography, Division of Communication at the United Nations, informed me about the Archival Reference Services Unit and the online database of UN documents related to Palestine, including those bearing on 1948. Correspondence and additional findings from related research efforts are incorporated in the body of the text.

The Government Documents section of the Harvard College Library at Lamont, part of Harvard University, also proved to be an indispensable resource to which I repeatedly returned and on whose expert librarians I relied. Among them were John A. Collins, Reference Librarian, Research Services, Government Documents; Vida Margaitis, Government Documents, Harvard College Library; Odile Harter, Research Librarian at the Harvard College Library; and John Baldisserotto, Data Reference Librarian, Harvard College Library.

At MIT, Bethanie Pinkus helped me to locate the papers of Freda Kirchwey through Institute Archives and Special Collections, and I also turned to the collection at the Schlesinger Library of the Radcliffe Institute. At Columbia University, Jerry Breeze, Government Information

Librarian of Lehman Library, made it possible for me to examine the papers of James McDonald in the Rare Book and Manuscript Library in Butler Library.

Presentations, lectures, and workshops were offered at the Middle East Institute, Columbia University; Department of Political Science, Boston University; The Middle East Center, Harvard University; the Emile Bustani Seminar, MIT; Watson Institute, Brown University; University of Maryland; Kevorkian Center for Middle East Studies, New York University; Tamiment Center, New York University; Graduate Center for Middle Eastern and Middle Eastern American Center, CUNY; and a seminar in the Department of Political Science, American University of Beirut.

Among the many individuals whose work and, in some instances, personal assistance, made a difference are Andrew Bacevich, Nathan Citino, Peter Dimock, Alain Gresh, Rashid Khalidi, Philip Khoury, Michael Klare, Zachary Lockman, Karim Makdisi, David Painter, Robert Vitalis, the late Eric Rouleau, Sara Roy, Steve Shalom, Yair Svoray, Salim Tamari, Fawwaz Traboulsi, and Walid Khalidi, whose pioneering work on 1948 remains unparalleled. Noam Chomsky holds a special place in this study not only because of his support for this undertaking but because his own work on Israel and Palestine has long served as an example of his courageous search for truth, which remains a permanent source of inspiration.

Editor Anne Routon was witness to the different stages of this work in progress and remained patient and steadfast in her support, as did other members of the Columbia University Press editorial staff, including Whitney Johnson, Roy Thomas, Michael Haskell, and Ben Kolstad, for which I am grateful.

Introduction

Open Secrets

GAZA 2014 AND 1948

I completed this study in 2014 in the midst of the Israeli invasion of Gaza. Those familiar with the distant origins of the present conflict will recall the events of 1948.[1]

As in past Israeli invasions of Gaza, in 2008 and 2012, the 2014 war in Gaza was enabled by U.S. support. In the summer of 2014, the National Security Agency (NSA) disclosed that "Israeli aggression would be impossible without the constant, lavish support and protection of the U.S. government, which is anything but a neutral, peace-brokering party in these attacks."[2] Subsequent disclosures in the *Wall Street Journal* exposed the direct link between Israel and the Pentagon, thus bringing to light a relationship that embarrassed the White House, which did not contest it.[3]

The link between the events of 1948, when Israel was established, and the latest war in Gaza was highlighted by William R. Polk, former U.S. diplomat and author. As Polk wrote in August 2014, "the events of today were preordained," adding that "only if we understand the history can we hope to help solve this very complex, often shameful and sometimes dangerous problem."[4] Gaza was directly affected by that history in 1948–1949, when its population was vastly increased as a result of the influx of Palestinian refugees.[5]

The problem transcends Gaza, however, as journalist Rami Khoury pointed out in the fall of 2012 when he asserted that

> as long as the crime of dispossession and refugeehood that was committed against the Palestinian people in 1947–48 is not redressed through a peaceful and just negotiation that satisfies the legitimate rights of both sides, we will continue to see enhancements in both the determination and the capabilities of Palestinian fighters—as has been the case since the 1930s.[6]

The connection between Gaza and 1948 was made by other critics as well, including Donna Nevel, who pointed out that "the heart of the problem is not Hamas or who the Palestinian leadership is, it is the Israeli occupation, beginning with the expulsion of the Palestinians from their land in 1948 (what the Palestinians term the Nakba or 'catastrophe')."[7] The same view was echoed by journalist Steven Erlanger in the *New York Times* on August 16, 2014, when he reported that "Israelis can feel as stuck, in different ways, as the Palestinians themselves. Because of course this is really just another round in the unresolved Arab-Israeli war of 1948–49."[8]

What these varied commentaries left unsaid was that this was but another chapter in U.S. policy in this region. By 1948–49, it was the United States that felt "stuck," as it confronted its failed efforts to resolve the very same conflict. U.S. officials engaged in the Palestine question understood then, as now, that they needed to address the core issues of the conflict, including the origin and repatriation of Palestinian refugees, the absence of internationally accepted boundaries, and the fate of Jerusalem.

Despite its avowed support for consensus between Arab and Jew as the essential prerequisite for a resolution of the conflict in Palestine, U.S. policy subverted such a goal. Washington's support for Israel's policy of "transfer," which meant the coercive expulsion of Palestinians from their towns and villages to ensure a largely homogeneous Jewish population, was incompatible with this objective. It intensified the refugee problem that the United States repeatedly criticized, as it repeatedly announced its support for United Nations General Assembly (UNGA) Resolution 194 and its recommendation for the repatriation of Palestinian refugees.

This was not the product of caution or confusion. There was no conspiracy involved. There was no wavering at the top. The United States was not ambivalent about what policies to pursue. On the contrary, the decisions to stop pressuring Israel to take action on the refugee question and to lay low in opposing Israel's territorial expansion were unmistakable signs that there was a shift in priorities.

U.S. officials recognized the Israeli reliance on force to expand and control territory. They appreciated the political efficiency of the Israeli leadership and its military superiority as compared to that of surrounding Arab states. On the basis of such developments, and, notably, in response to Israel's ability to alter the regional balance of power, Washington calculated that Israel could be useful in the protection of U.S. regional interests. While successive U.S. administrations continued to identify the core issues in the conflict in terms of refugee repatriation, territorial expansion, and Jerusalem's status, they did not move to implement changes. On the contrary, the United States deferred to Israeli policy while insisting on the need for Arab-Jewish consensus.

More than sixty years later, as U.S. Secretary of State John Kerry attempted yet another effort to broker peace talks between Israel and the Palestinians, the Israeli daily *Ha'aretz* observed that everyone knows that "the condition for reaching a deal is through agreements on the real core issues of the conflict: the refugees, the status of Jerusalem, borders and security arrangements."[9] The same editorial added that "any attempt to avoid dealing with these issues, or investment of energy in other issues, is as if no negotiations are taking place."

Seldom were the reasons for the failure of such efforts as starkly stated in the U.S. media, or in many parts of academia. The habit of deferral and denial was deeply ingrained in both circles, where the "lingering effects of past struggles on present confrontations" were ignored.[10] Yet as Eugene Rogan and Avi Shlaim reminded readers in considering the war over Palestine,

> no event has marked Arab politics in the second half of the twentieth century more profoundly. The Arab-Israeli wars, the Cold War in the Middle East, the rise of the Palestinian armed struggle and the politics of peace making in all of their complexity are a direct consequence of the Palestine War.[11]

WHY THIS BOOK?

The role of the United States in the Arab-Israeli conflict is an inextricable part of history in this region. Confronting that role is indispensable to understanding both U.S. policy in the conflict and its course.[12] A knowledge of the foundation of U.S. policy in the Middle East in the postwar years is indispensable to an understanding of current U.S. policies in the Middle East in which oil, Palestine, and Israel play such significant roles.

The record of U.S. policy from 1945 to 1949 challenges fundamental assumptions about U.S. understanding and involvement in the struggle over Palestine that continue to dominate mainstream interpretations of U.S. policy in the Middle East. Coming to grips with the U.S. record and its frequently mythified depiction of the struggle over Palestine is critical. Those engaged in the creation of the Common Archive, a project of Zochrot, the Israeli NGO, in which Israelis and Palestinians have joined to reconstruct the history of Palestinian villages destroyed by Israel in 1948,[13] clearly understand the importance of this record. Palestinian historians have long written about this history, and Israel's "New Historians" have confirmed it in their challenge to the dominant Israeli narrative of the war of 1948.

The Middle East in 2014 is not a mirror image of what it was in 1948, when the struggle over Palestine was at its height. In the immediate postwar years, the United States defined its policy in the Near and Middle East in terms of assuring unimpeded access and control by U.S. oil companies of its great material prize, petroleum. Congressional hearings on the role of petroleum and the national defense envisioned petroleum as a weapon of war. It followed that ensuring the presence and stability of compatible regimes was an essential dimension of policy, as was containing and crushing those whose nationalist and reformist orientation rendered them suspect.

At once undermining and inheriting Britain's imperial mantle, the American state was widely viewed by political leaders in the area as an anti-imperialist power, albeit driven by petroleum and political ambition. Its footprints were found in widely divergent endeavors, including missionary and educational enterprises. But in the immediate postwar years, Washington was increasingly drawn into the Palestine problem, whose origins linked Europe's dark history with Zionist ambitions protected by the British mandate. The ensuing struggle over Palestine was accelerated in the years that followed as Washington became increasingly involved in its outcome, aware of the inevitable link between the fate of Palestine and U.S. oil and defense interests in the Middle East. The controversies over British policy, over partition, the war of 1948, the armistice agreements, and the Lausanne Conference in 1949 consumed Washington's Near and Middle East specialists and their representatives at the United Nations.

This history is not new. The subject has long evoked interest and criticism. What was taboo yesterday, however, is openly discussed today, as the weight of current wars compels a confrontation with events that can no longer be ignored.

Disclosures of previously classified information, as well as previously ignored sources, whether of Palestinian or Israeli origin, have further altered the record. Although U.S. sources have long been open, they have been inadequately examined, significantly contributing to the flawed history of U.S. postwar policy in the Middle East, including oil and the transformation of Palestine.

Main Themes

A number of key questions have long dominated scholarly accounts of postwar U.S. policy in the Middle East, and these questions compel consideration. Among them is the ongoing controversy over the bureaucratic origins of U.S. policymaking in the Middle East in the postwar years. Did the State Department or the White House make Middle East policy? Was policy determined by domestic or foreign policy considerations? Did domestic lobbying by Zionists or by oil company partisans shape policy?

How did the president fit into this context? Some lauded President Truman as unquestionably committed to the creation of a Jewish state.[14] Was he moved primarily by religious, humanitarian, and moral considerations that trumped other factors?[15] Some argue that cultural, psychological, and religious factors cannot be ignored in shaping U.S. policy.[16] On the other hand, works by Kenneth Bain, and more recently by Peter Hahn, Melvin Leffler, and John Judis, have, in different ways, demonstrated the extent of the president's ambivalence, if not overt hostility, to the idea of a religious state.[17] Without ignoring any of these factors, some historians also include the role of the Cold War as an influence on U.S. policy in Palestine.[18]

Analysts such as J. C. Hurewitz, who was a consummate insider, recalled another important dimension of early policy formation in his study on Palestine. He reminds us that the bureaucracy dealing with the Palestine question in 1943 was very small, and few officials were involved.[19] U.S. policymakers confirmed this when they faced the need to define U.S. policy. Within a very few years, however, the Palestine question assumed greater importance, as its connection with developments in the Second World War and the Holocaust, as well as its relation to the foundation of postwar U.S. oil interests in the Middle East, promoted more attention to the needs of policymaking in this area.

As the question of partition on Palestine assumed greater importance in Washington, another theme dominated, as it still does. This was the claim that U.S. policymakers were faced with the choice of protecting U.S. oil interests or deferring to partisans of partition and, later, Jewish statehood. The question became: Oil or Israel? This formula erred, as I will explain in the following chapters. The choice facing policymakers was not oil versus Israel but rather oil and Israel. In the years that followed, it was oil and Israel versus reform and revolution in the Arab world.

The Changing Landscape of Middle East Studies

The changing landscape of Middle East scholarship is apparent in the spate of publications, books, and articles appearing on U.S. foreign policy in the Middle East. Collectively, they attest to the changing nature of research and the increasing availability of U.S. and international sources that contribute to a "transnational" and "multiarchival perspective."[20] Particularly at this time of increased U.S. intervention in the Middle East, this expanded view and increased understanding by western, notably American, writers on the Middle East is something that Ussama Makdisi has eloquently pleaded for, particularly at a time of increased U.S. intervention in the Middle East.[21]

The new scholarship promises no agreement but provides the seeds for a more informed debate, although thus far it has not altered conventional accounts of the Middle East or U.S. policy in the region. Nor has it fundamentally challenged the media, who often portray the Middle East as a danger zone whose complexity and controversy defies understanding, as does its alleged predilection to violence, instability, and sectarian hatreds.

Those seeking to break with such caricatured depictions of states and societies in the Middle East discover that this is no easy matter. The familiar images of mad mullahs and jihad-prone fanatics allow for scant reflection on who or what is involved, let alone the conditions giving rise to the emergence of religious movements across the region. In such an intellectual environment, approaches that challenge long-standing narratives are often viewed as frankly subversive. As a result, they are marginalized in the media and often in academia, particularly in fields such as international relations that have long served to justify western supremacy.[22]

In this context, recent scholarship may indeed make a difference. But examining previously neglected sources of newly declassified government documents, of whatever origin, is not enough. What is required is not only new data but new ways of thinking about what we know, or have chosen to ignore. Considering why certain questions related to policy remain unanswered, or unasked, involves asking who benefits from the existing production of knowledge, and whose interests are served by censoring those who challenge it?

Consider the impact of the invaluable studies of the Israeli-Palestinian conflict produced by some of Israel's new historians, such as Ilan Pappé, Benny Morris, and Avi Shlaim, and the journalist and historian Simha Flapan. Their work is based on the release of classified Israeli documents that challenge fundamental Israeli myths concerning the events of 1948 and Israel's emergence as an independent state.[23] Such works have confirmed the accounts of Palestinian historians such as Walid Khalidi, Nur-eldeen Masalha, and Rashid Khalidi and have been critically appraised by others, such as Joseph Massad, who have written about the events of 1948.[24] Masalha has argued that the work of Israel's "New Historians" is indicative of "a marked desire among the younger generation of Israeli authors and academics to unearth the truth concerning the events surrounding the Palestinian refugee exodus of 1948. This new tendency breaks the wall of silence, myth, secrecy and censorship instituted by the older generation of Zionist leadership."[25]

In a penetrating essay on the new Israeli historiography, however, historian Joel Beinin points out that "much, even if not all the details of the information [Benny] Morris presents in *The Birth of the Palestinian Refugee Problem* and other works was always available in one form or another. It was actively rendered illegible in the Israeli historical narrative."[26]

This applies to the historical evidence concerning U.S. foreign policy in the Middle East as well. U.S. sources provide evidence that has long been available but in some instances has been all but invisible. Sources such as those included in the Foreign Relations of the United States (FRUS), U.S. Presidential Papers, and the records of the U.S. Joint Chiefs of Staff, for example, in conjunction with Israeli and Palestinian sources, strongly suggest the need to reconsider the dominant narratives of U.S. policy in the conflict between the Israelis and the Palestinians.

How the Present Work Differs

Building on the record of past scholarship and criticism of U.S. policy, this book differs from previous accounts in several significant respects. It situates the origin of the U.S. relationship with Israel in 1948 in the framework of postwar U.S. policy when petroleum dominated U.S. planning for the Middle East. Moreover, on the basis of U.S. sources, the present study maintains that the prevailing assumption with respect to U.S. policy toward Palestine, according to which U.S. officials feared that support for Zionism and partition of Palestine would undermine U.S. oil interests in the Arab world, proved to be a false assumption. The papers of Max Ball, director of the Oil and Gas Division of the Interior Department, and his exchanges with the representative of the Jewish Agency in the United States, Eliahu Epstein, confirm this fear, as do Israeli records of the same period. Ball operated outside the formal channels of policymakers, which does not negate the importance of his experience. It may explain, however, why that experience has been neglected in accounts of U.S. policy.

Evidence of the encounter between Max Ball and Eliahu Epstein in 1948 forms the basis of the "oil connection" discussed in this book. The encounter opened doors and broke barriers that had long been considered taboo. It revealed that major U.S. oil executives were pragmatic in their approach to the Palestine conflict and were prepared to engage with the Jewish Agency and later with Israeli officials, albeit operating within existing constraints. The relationship between Max Ball, his son and associate, and his son-in-law Ray Kosloff, who became the first Israeli adviser on oil matters, yields additional information on how this former U.S. official assisted Israel in its fuel policy after his retirement.

Second, I emphasize the extent to which U.S. officials who were part of the formal policymaking framework understood the secular roots of the conflict in Palestine, its significance for Zionist support, and its traumatic impact on Palestinians. They understood that Zionist objectives were incompatible with Palestinian Arab self-determination and independence, even as they persisted in calling for compromise among the parties. Well informed about the consequences of the struggle over Palestine by U.S. consuls, officials in Washington, including the secretary of state, undersecretary, and their colleagues operating in the United Nations and in the specialized agencies dealing with Palestine and the Near and Middle East, were prepared to reconsider partition in favor of trusteeship. The record of their views on the Palestinian refugee problem and, specifically, the Israeli response and rejection of responsibility for its creation, led to major clashes between Washington and Tel Aviv after Israel's emergence.

That record is known, but a more detailed examination of the evidence is required and is presented here. This examination complements some of the work of Israel's "New Historians," as well as Palestinian historians. More attention needs to be paid to the contributions of the U.S. consuls in Jerusalem, Thomas Wasson and Robert Macattee, as well as to the views of Gordon Merriam, who had broad experience including oil policy as well as working within the Policy Planning Staff, among other assignments; Mark Ethridge, the U.S. delegate to the Palestine Conciliation Commission; and Philip Jessup in his role at the United Nations. Reconsidering their analyses as well as those of the far better known and more authoritative figures in the policy establishment—such as Robert McClintock, Loy Henderson, Robert Lovett, George Marshall, and Dean Acheson—provides a clearer view of the nature and evolution of U.S. policy toward Israel and Palestine.

Third, the input of the chief of staff of the U.S. Air Force, the chief of naval operations, the secretary of defense, and the Joint Chiefs of Staff (JCS) also provides insight into U.S. policy in the Middle East. Within months of Israel's emergence, U.S. officials reassessed their views of the new state, in accord with presidential recognition of Israel. What followed was not only recognition of Israeli sovereignty but recognition of its strategic potential in Washington's postwar policy in the Middle East, which was designed to exclude the USSR and to protect U.S. oil interests and allied defense arrangements. This assessment undermined Washington's critical position on Israeli policy toward Palestinian refugee repatriation and territorial expansion. These vital factors in the conflict between Israel-Palestine and the Arab world thereby assumed a subordinate position in light of the priorities defined by the JCS and officials in the Department of State.

Here, then, is the logic of U.S. oil policy, which was responsible for the increasing deference to Israeli policies whose purpose was to ensure that Israel turned toward the United States and away from the USSR. This objective, in turn, was allied to Washington's principal goal in the Middle East—protection of its untrammeled access and control of oil.

These connections are crucial to understanding what many historians have taken to be signs of the cautious and contrary character, or weakness, of U.S. policy, which appeared to waver between criticism of Israel and silence in the face of the very policies it criticized. In this book, I focus on the consequences of these policies, the network of relations they promoted, their objectives, and their effect on Israel, Palestine, and the Arab world in 1949 and the years that followed.

Confronting this history is an exercise in uncovering the open secrets of past U.S. policy and in confronting the past, which remains embedded in the troubled present.

DYING TO FORGET

PART I

The Petroleum Order and the Palestine Question, 1945–1946

Part I introduces readers to the dominant role of petroleum in postwar U.S. policy and illustrates the manner in which it shaped U.S. policy in the Middle East, including Palestine.

Chapter 1 demonstrates the U.S. commitment to maintaining access and control over Middle East oil resources, as revealed in the pronouncements and practices of U.S. officials in the State Department and the network of allied agencies established to deal with petroleum policy. Against this background, which constituted Washington's ongoing commitment to U.S. oil interests in the Middle East, President Truman and the policymaking elite confronted postwar conditions in Europe that had profound implications for Palestine and the Middle East. Chapter 2 analyzes the Earl Harrison Report, the Anglo-American Committee Report, and the Morrison-Grady plans that followed, with special attention to the reactions of U.S. officials, including the dissenters among them.

1

The Primacy of Oil

DEFINING U.S. OIL POLICY

The U.S. preoccupation with Middle East oil was a trademark of policy planning in the period after World War II, although it was by no means limited to the Truman era, as the experience of successive presidential doctrines of the Eisenhower, Nixon, and Carter administrations, and those that followed, have demonstrated.[1]

U.S. policymakers crafted their vision of a petroleum order in "postwar"[2] 1945, an environment marked by the emergence of the United States as the undisputed power of the postwar world, with an economy "three times the size of the USSR's and five times that of Britain, commanding half of the world's industrial output and three quarters of its gold reserves."[3] By contrast, Washington faced the despairing plight of millions of Displaced Persons[4] across the boundaries of its allies and former enemies, whose populations would be haunted by the trials and judgments at Nuremberg and by the nameless atrocities committed in Hiroshima and Nagasaki. Postwar U.S. policy in the Middle East, and more particularly in Palestine, was to be defined by these diverse and incompatible forces.

In 1945 John Loftus, the special assistant to the director of the Office of International Trade Policy in the State Department categorically asserted that "a review of diplomatic history of the past 35 years will show that petroleum has historically played a larger part in the external relations of the United States than any other commodity."[5] In explaining its "unique and outstanding importance," Loftus underlined the "absolute importance of oil as a commodity in terms of the gross value of annual production; and in part from the extremely high relative importance of oil in the foreign trade of certain nations."[6] In light of these conditions, Loftus argued that it was desirable for U.S. companies to control petroleum production abroad. He offered a two-part justification for this position; the first rested on the "talent of the American oil industry for discovery and development"; the second, was that "oil controlled by United States nationals is likely to be a little more accessible to the United States for commercial uses in times of peace and for strategic purposes in times of war."[7]

Moreover, as Philip Burch reported, "the nation's major corporate interests, having reestablished good working relations with the federal government during the war years, remained very much in control of the key defense and foreign policy posts during the Truman administration."[8] According to Burch's calculation, "over 70 percent (22 out of 31) of Truman's chief defense and foreign policy officials had elitist links, the bulk of them with America's rapidly evolving business establishment."[9] Among Truman's select officials were figures such as "Forrestal, Lovett, Harriman, Stettinius, Acheson, Nitze, McCloy, Clayton, Snyder, Hoffman—a stratum unlikely to overlook the interests of American capital in redesigning the postwar landscape."[10] The business most closely involved in consideration of Middle East policy, including that applicable to Palestine, was the oil business.[11]

In May 1940, in the very period in which Council of Foreign Relations members were deliberating on the economic dimensions of postwar U.S. policy, the Roosevelt administration created the Office of Petroleum Coordinator. In the following year, FDR's Secretary of the Interior, Harold Ickes, was named Petroleum Coordinator for National Defense, and in 1942 that agency became the Petroleum Administration for War (PAW). On March 27, 1944, by Departmental Order 1245, the State Department established a Petroleum Division (PED) in the Office of Economic Affairs that oversaw "the initiation, development and coordination of policy and action in all matters pertaining to petroleum and petroleum products," and maintained contact with related agencies.[12]

The subsequent creation of the Petroleum Industry War Council (PIWC) attested to the growing bureaucracy that "was made up of 78 top-flight industry executives" who, in addition to their other responsibilities, met with PAW executives, "and at these meetings all the major problems and policies of the *worldwide oil situation* are on the table. The Council, working with the executives of PAW, is the powerhouse of industry-government cooperation."[13] These remarks were made by Max Ball, who was the special assistant to Harold Ickes, the deputy administrator in the Petroleum Administration for War.

As Ball emphasized in an essay in 1945, the international range of the PIWC's responsibilities as well as that of PAW "do not stop at the water's edge: the cooperation of the industry is not circumscribed by our national boundaries. Every gallon of petroleum products produced or used by the United Nations anywhere in the world is within the sphere of interest and activity."[14] Ball estimated that there were some thirty or forty government agencies dealing with oil. Among them were "the Geological Survey, the Bureau of Mines, various bureaus of the Treasury Department, the Department of Justice, the Interstate Commerce Commission, the Office of Defense, Transportation, Defense Plant Corporation, Defense Supplies Corporation, the War Manpower Commission, the Office of Price Administration, the War Production Board, and a host of others."[15]

In the spring of 1946, Ralph K. Davies, ex-Deputy Petroleum Administrator for War, recommended to the president that a coordinating body be put in charge of the multiple and diverse agencies dealing with oil-related questions. Davies, who had been responsible for creating the Office of Petroleum Coordination in May 1941, was now calling for its dissolution. But he was also calling for the establishment of a permanent office capable of coordinating the vast hierarchy of oil-related agencies. In that capacity, he recommended a new office that would "operate in a liaison capacity with the petroleum industry in all oil and gas matters of concern to the administrative branch of the Federal Government."[16]

The president did, in fact, follow Davies's advice, and on May 6, 1946, the Secretary of the Interior, J. A. Krug, announced the creation of an Oil and Gas Division within his department. Ralph K. Davies became its first director. Along with the National Petroleum Council, the Oil and

Gas Division was assigned to consult with the president on petroleum policy. Among the duties of the new division was to amass and analyze information relevant to oil and gas operations, including the availability of existing and future supplies of petroleum, on the basis of which the president would recommend policy. In December, Davies nominated Max Ball to be director, having searched for a candidate who would have both the "technical and practical training" as well as the leadership qualities required.[17] What Davies did not write on this occasion, although it was probably unnecessary to do so, was that Ball's outlook on the question of private versus government control of oil was entirely compatible with that of the major oil companies and contemporary federal agencies, including those in which Davies had been involved.

Under Harold Ickes and PAW, for example, Davies, VP of Standard Oil of California, was named deputy coordinator. The organization of the Office of Petroleum Coordinator was itself modeled along the lines of the petroleum industry.[18] An "industry committee organization" was set up to ensure government policy was favorable to the oil industry, with the Justice Department complicit in arranging "to relax its antitrust procedures by agreeing to rule beforehand on proposals for group action within the industry."[19]

Max Ball's intimate knowledge of the petroleum industry's operation at both the national and international levels was to have particular significance in his relations with representatives of the Jewish Agency prior to May 1948, and with the Israeli government after its independence. Ball's encounters with Eliahu Epstein, one of the principal representatives of the Jewish Agency in the United States, in the winter and spring of 1948 are discussed at length in part II. Suffice it to note here that these meetings contradict one of the axioms of postwar U.S. policy. U.S. officials and their oil company collaborators feared the adverse effect of U.S. government support for partition and Jewish statehood on their relations with the oil-rich regimes of the Arab world.

In a seminal report titled "A Foreign Oil Policy for the United States," issued in 1944, Herbert Feis, former adviser on international economic affairs in the State Department, argued firmly in favor of private ownership of oil and its global expansion, U.S. capital investment in the oil sector, and the staunch support of the U.S. government. According to the 1975 Senate Foreign Relations Subcommittee Report on Multinational

Corporations, Feis's report represented "the most systematic analysis of the major oil companies' position."[20] Feis maintained that

> the companies insist that private enterprise is the best medium for oil development, and that oil controlled by American corporate interests is equally available for the needs of national security with that owned wholly or in part by the United States government. Secondly, they urge that the American petroleum industry be encouraged to expand its plans for developing the world's oil resources. To this end, they urge that the government should seek to secure for American nationals access to the world's oil resources on equal terms with the nationals of all other countries; it should also accord diplomatic support as effective as that accorded to nationals of other countries.[21]

Feis called on Washington to adopt a policy capable of guaranteeing adequate supplies in the event of war while not depleting U.S. reserves. He insisted that the arrangements he favored would provide for "(a) the maintenance of storage, as at bases, and (b) the acquisition directly by the United States government of proven reserves that could be quickly developed."[22] He insisted that private ownership of foreign oil would preclude a U.S. military presence, which would be a challenge to "every near-by country."[23] And along the same lines, he was persuaded that such arrangements would eliminate the risk of involvement in local petroleum politics and, more generally, in the politics of the Middle East.

Well before 1946 and the creation of the National Petroleum Council, the petroleum industry enjoyed close relations with policymakers. The creation of institutions such as the National Petroleum War Service Committee "served as a liaison between the government and the oil corporations, helping to develop and supervise plans for supplying oil necessary for the war. In all these efforts care was taken to maintain the market percentages and power of the key companies."[24]

At its opening meeting in 1946, Interior Secretary Julius A. Krug "reassured the oil leaders that there was no intent to increase government power over them, and that the Council could do 'no greater good to the oil and gas industry than by educating people in the Government in the economies and the problems of the industry.' "[25] In addition, Krug held out the promise that "you men will help U.S. with the staffing of our Oil and Gas Division to the end that we will get the kind of people who understand the problems of the industry and who know how to do a good job."[26]

Earlier, Feis had advocated for the expansion of U.S. oil interests abroad, arguing that "the war has established the fact that American military action may take place anywhere in the world, and that, particularly in any struggle involving the Pacific, control over these oil fields (and the political status of this area) might be of direct concern to U.S."[27] Hence the importance of expanding U.S. oil operations, along with U.S. support. The Soviet press, reviewing U.S. and British oil expansion several years later, recognized the importance of Feis's recommendations. They viewed them as extending beyond economic considerations, suggesting instead that "they may be referred to as secondary enterprises of 'American world system of bases' and as American outposts expanding along British naval and air communications."[28]

In its April 11, 1944, report on "Foreign Petroleum Policy of the United States," the Inter-Divisional Petroleum Committee of the State Department reviewed the official justifications for relying on foreign sources of oil, repeating the claim that it was essential to conserve Western Hemisphere petroleum for "military and civilian requirements of strategically available reserves," while identifying the foreign policy implications of such a policy.[29] The excuse was hardly convincing. Domestic reserves were not exhausted, nor were they being preserved in some artificial manner. The explanation for focusing on Saudi Arabia rested on the profits it generated for U.S. oil companies.

The authors of the State Department committee position paper, "Foreign Petroleum Policy of the United States," identified the regions of prime importance for oil, namely, "the great developed oilfields of Russia, Roumania, Iraq, Iran and the Arabian Peninsula as well as the potential petroleum resources of Turkey, the Levantine Coastal areas, Afghanistan and Baluchistan."[30] But the primal zone of U.S. Middle East policy was to be the Middle East; as the Department of State report pointed out, it was in the areas encompassed by "Iran, Iraq, and the Arabian peninsula including Saudi Arabia proper and the Sheikhdoms of Kuwait, Bahrein, Qatar and Trucial Oman," that "United States policy must be formulated and implemented."[31] If there was a dissenting voice in such deliberations, it came from Great Britain, whose primacy in the Middle East was to be fatally undermined by U.S. policy.

The Place of Saudi Arabia in the Postwar Petroleum Order

The project of building a base in Saudi Arabia appealed to the Pentagon and the State Department before the end of the war. The plan was part of a far more ambitious global initiative that included building bases across North Africa and the Middle East. When it was negotiated at the end of the war, the agreement was for the accord with Dhahran to last three years. In practice, it was repeatedly extended. "During the Cold War, U.S. Air Force tankers operated out of the base to refuel the B-29s, B-36s, and B-47s that constantly circled Russia's perimeters."[32]

But before the accord with Dhahran was reached, the U.S. faced British opposition. According to Secretary of State Cordell Hull, "we now have reliable, but highly confidential information indicating that the British directed Ibn Saud to refuse."[33] The refusal was problematic, however, given Saudi recognition of its own interests. In the words of U.S. Secretary of War Henry Stimson, "both from a long and a short range point of view the most important military interest in Saudi Arabia is oil and closely following this in importance is the right to construct airfields, the use of air space, and the right to make aerial surveys in connection therewith," and these goals would not be abandoned.[34] Stimson had further evidence of Saudi requests to the U.S. for military aid. Indeed, the Saudi monarch requested "six transport aircraft, preferably C-47s, and four bombers," as well as the building of "a small arms plant capable of producing 45-calibre and 7.9 mm. cartridges."[35] Several months earlier U.S. Army sources in Cairo had made modest amounts of ammunition available to the Saudis. The list included "1,667 rifles with accessories and 350,000 rounds of .30 caliber ammunition which was delivered to the Saudi Government with the understanding that it would be stored in Jidda pending the Arrival of an American military mission composed of eight officers and four enlisted men who would instruct the Saudi Army in the use, repair and maintenance of the rifles, and of any other military equipment which might be delivered."[36]

In late 1944, the Saudi king called for the construction or repair of major roads, for a water supply survey, access to radio communication and copies of aerial surveys, as well as provision of medical training for select numbers of Saudis proficient in English. By the following March the United States was offering to train Saudi pilots and crew as well as to provide the necessary supplies and maintenance equipment, and on completion of its training mission, the U.S. would offer the Saudis the field and its installations, including planes. In addition, Washington was offering medical support.

In this context, access to base rights at Dhahran appeared all the more justified. In late November the U.S. Air Force was reported to believe that "the acquisition of an American military air field at Dhahran, for use in redeployment of our forces to the Far East and to increase the efficiency of present military air transport operations, is considered an immediate necessity."[37] The role of the military airfield at Dhahran was justified in terms of greater efficiency in military air transport. The U.S. Air Force pronouncement did not address the Arabian American Oil Company (ARAMCO) connection directly. It was, however, implicit in the statement of the Ad Hoc Committee of the State-War-Navy Coordinating Committee (SWNCC) that declared "the most important economic fact in connection with Saudi Arabia is the presence in that country of rich oil resources presently under concession to American companies. Although the War Department has an interest in Saudi Arabia because of its geographical location athwart the most direct air route to the East, it is the oil of Saudi Arabia which makes that country of particular interest to the armed services."[38]

The polite formulation had been stated more bluntly by Secretary of the Navy James Forrestal in December 1944, who recalled that "the operations of the Navy, including the Naval air arm, in peace as well as in war, are dependent to a large degree upon the availability of refined petroleum products."[39] Emphasizing the importance of undeveloped oil reserves in the "Mesopotamian Basin area of the Persian Gulf," Forrestal observed that it was in the strategic interest of the United States to promote development of these oil reserves as they constituted a source of incomparable wealth whose possession would allow Washington to exercise global influence.

Throughout negotiations with the Saudi monarch in the summer of 1945, U.S. officials recognized Saudi sensitivity to its sovereign status. William Eddy, former oil man then U.S. minister in Saudi Arabia, explained to the secretary of state that the king "insisted that the Saudi flag should fly over the inland posts, the emergency landing field and the isolated stations where navigational aids are to be located, though the operations, and control of technical services at these posts will belong to the United States Army."[40] Eddy concluded that such arrangements were advantageous in that they protected the U.S. military from "untamed tribesmen" who might otherwise think the foreigners represented an invading force.[41]

GORDON MERRIAM: PETROLEUM POLITICS

Among those deeply involved in the planning and coordination of U.S. policy involving oil and Palestine was Gordon Merriam, appointed by Truman to be chief of the Division of Near Eastern Affairs in the State Department in August 1945. His overall view of the status of the Near East revealed his uncritical appraisal of European imperialism. Identifying the Middle East, or rather the "Near East," as "a highly dangerous trouble-spot," Merriam pointed to the USSR as threatening Turkey and Iran; to France, as failing to put down independence movements in Syria and Lebanon; and to Palestine, where "disorder may break out at any time" between Arabs and Jews.[42] In this scenario, Merriam viewed Washington's role as the anti-imperialist protector offering assistance to those he described as "for the most part ignorant, poverty stricken and diseased."[43] In Merriam's view, the U.S. role was consistent with "our higher long-range political, economic and strategic purposes."[44] Those purposes were best met with a politics that included carefully targeted development plans.

In May 1945, Merriam warned of Arabs and Jews becoming increasingly "restive" with the attendant risks of violence spreading throughout the region. He suggested that "the expenditures of large sums in connection with the carrying out of a far-reaching development plan applied not only to Palestine, but also to neighboring countries," which he believed would alleviate violence and political pressures at home insofar as Palestine was concerned.[45] In the case of Syria and Lebanon, Merriam observed that although they were still under French mandatory rule, they had appealed to the United States for assistance in the form of military training missions. Merriam thought their predicament reflected a more general problem—the ineptness of Anglo-French rule. In that context, he counseled Washington to adopt a policy "based upon the political, educational and economic development of the native peoples and not merely upon the narrow immediate interests of British or American economy."[46] This anticipated later economic development programs directed at Palestinian refugees, which were organized under George McGhee.

Merriam understood that Washington's interest in the area was exclusively a product of its resources. In short, U.S. policy in the Middle East was oil policy, which was in the hands of a small elite group. As William Quandt pointed out years later, it represented men "mostly of similar backgrounds—middle-aged male WASPS, often the products of east coast colleges" who had unusual access to the secretary of state or even the president.[47]

In an interview he gave to Richard Parker, Merriam reflected on the origin of this policy, recalling that "we just sort of grew into it as one thing happened after another."[48] He observed that Loy Henderson had an oil man as adviser in the department: first Max Thornburg, who was VP of the Bahrein Petroleum Company owned by the two oil giants that owned ARAMCO, and then Charles Rayner, who was the executive of Socony-Vacuum and replaced Thornburg. But the crucial factor was the underlying relationship between policymakers and oil people.

> We were in close touch with our oil people, all the way through, and used to see quite a lot of them. We thought they were a very capable crowd. They did that without any help from us at all. They didn't need any. In fact we had no representation in Saudi Arabia at all until they were well along in their discovery and development. I think, the first representative we had in Saudi Arabia was Parker Hart. And that was not diplomatic representation, we just set up a consulate over in the oil field so the oil people could be serviced. We were in close touch with our oil people all the way through.[49]

J. Rives Childs, U.S. minister to Saudi Arabia, understood the relationship, pointing out that "the Arabian American Oil Company was in Saudi Arabia before the legation at Jidda or the Consulate at Dhahran," which explained why the Saudi king's minister had become accustomed "to dealing with ARAMCO as they would with representatives of a foreign government."[50] Characteristically blunt, Merriam underlined Saudi Arabia's importance and the urgency of ensuring that it remained in the hands of those "following the paths of democratic civilization rather than those of Eastern dictatorships."[51] Merriam's rationale for supporting Saudi tribalism and authoritarianism outlived him. It became the consistently unexamined apology for a key dimension of U.S. Middle East policy through succeeding decades.

> In Saudi Arabia, where the oil resources constitute a stupendous source of strategic power, and one of the greatest material prizes in world history, a concession covering this oil is nominally in American control. It will undoubtedly be lost to the United States unless this Government is able to demonstrate in a practical way its recognition of this concession as of national interest by acceding to the reasonable requests of King Ibn Saud that he be assisted temporarily in his economic and financial difficulties until the exploitation of the concession, on a practical commercial basis, begins to bring substantial royalties to Saudi Arabia.[52]

As Merrriam explained, the United States estimated that some $10 million per year was necessary to ensure "a reasonable security to American interest in the vast Arabian oil fields."[53]

Of U.S. companies, the most powerful was ARAMCO and its vast holdings in Saudi Arabia. ARAMCO constituted the center of an archipelago of petroleum wealth, and it was run as a replica of the State Department, with an allied intelligence organization, based on the OSS model that dealt with the intelligence and propaganda section of the Middle East. As Vitalis points out, "his was the institutional home of ARAMCO's vaunted Arabists and, not coincidentally, many of the early CIA operatives in Saudi Arabia."[54]

The easternmost part of this concession covers the Persian Gulf coast of Saudi Arabia between Kuwait and Qatar. Bahrein Petroleum Company, Ltd. is U.S.-owned but registered as a British company. Standard Oil Company of California and the Texas company jointly own both Bahrein Petroleum and the Arabian American Oil companies. Petroleum Development Ltd. (a subsidiary of the British controlled

Iraq Petroleum Company) holds current concessions for all of Qatar and the Trucial coast. There were indications as recently as 1941 that Petroleum Development Ltd. still held a concession for the exploitation of oil in the Sultanate of Muscat and Oman.[55] To this the Kuwait Oil Company must be added as it held "the concession for the whole of Kuwait." The company, in turn, was co-owned by the British controlled Anglo-Iranian Oil Company and the U.S. owned Gulf Exploration Company.

Other prime areas of oil production included Iraq. Franklin Delano Roosevelt (FDR), and later Truman, invited the Regent of Iraq, Nuri Pasha, to Washington for a two-day visit with his delegation. In diplomatic language, the secretary of state dwelt on the prospects of encouraging the "free flow of traffic and communications between our two countries."[56] In practice, this meant "direct access of American civil aviation to Iraq, and also the setting up of a direct radiotelephone and telegraph circuit with the United States so that messages would not have to pass through other capitals."[57] The reference was to London. Nuri Pasha pointedly asked the United States to "do everything possible in order to bring about an increase in the extraction of petroleum in Iraq."[58] The invitation was welcome as it opened the door for U.S. entry into the most sensitive zone of operations.

The Iranian situation differed, but Teheran also viewed the United States as being outside the imperialist camp. Iran turned to Washington for assistance first in 1942 against Soviet policies in the north of the country, and later against moves in the south. In 1944, Mohammed Mossadegh—the nationalist leader the United States and Britain would bring down in a coup in 1953—called for a bill to arrest oil negotiations with foreign states, citing evidence of postwar plans for the partition of Iran. By 1946, the year in which the expansion of ARAMCO was being planned, the advance of U.S. oil corporations in the Middle East involved Saudi Arabia, Iraq, and Iran, with differing degrees of power and penetration, to which access to the "Continental Shelf" of the Persian Gulf claimed by the British must be added.

The full power of American oil became manifest with the ARAMCO merger that was consummated on March 12, 1947. The date resonates in U.S. policy in the Middle East as, in addition to ARAMCO's expansion, it was the year of the Truman Doctrine, the Pentagon talks between the United States and the United Kingdom that frankly delineated the respective privileges of the nearly past and future imperial power, and the UNGA Partition Plan for Palestine, Resolution 181.[59] In sum, the events of 1947 profoundly shaped the coming decade of U.S. and Middle East policy with long-running consequences whose outlines were apparent to those familiar with regional history and international economic policies.

In 1947, legal agreement expanding the Caltex group, which was the original base of ARAMCO, to include Exxon and Mobil was signed and approved by the attorney general's office even though its antitrust implications were clear to those involved. In October 1946, the VP and general counsel of Mobil, George V. Holton, had informed the executive committee of Mobil of his assessment of the significance of the merger. According to the official account, "the arrangement would place practical control of crude reserves in the Eastern Hemisphere in the hands of seven companies. Five of them would be American owned and all of the latter have substantial reserves in the Western Hemisphere also."[60] On the basis of the same source, "our great oil interests" in Saudi Arabia, Bahrein, and, to a lesser extent, Kuwait, and given Britain's position in the Gulf, the State Department recommended the expansion of U.S. commercial interests while cooperating with Britain. To this end, it proposed that the United States "encourage and support U.S. missionaries in the Persian Gulf in their medical and educational work."[61]

At the end of 1947 the Iranian government requested, without success, that the Anglo-Iranian Oil Company (AIOC) increase the revenue share allotted to Iran.[62] Three years later, the example of the so-called 50:50 arrangement set by ARAMCO in Saudi Arabia was a preemptive move by the U.S. corporation designed to blunt similar actions on the part of the Saudis. But the story did not end easily in Iran; the overthrow of Premier Mohammed Mossadegh in 1953 was directly linked to the refusal of AIOC executives, supported by the United States, to accept the premier's repeated requests for a negotiation of differences that included recognition of Iran's legitimate demands for an increased share of the revenue of AIOC.[63]

Merriam's discussion of Washington's oil-centered policies gave no indication of the postwar political and economic landscape of the Middle East. It offered no indication of the economic impact of the Second World War on the region, including the vast zones of discontent affecting oil workers across North Africa and the Arab East.

As economists Owen and Pamuk pointed out in their contemporary economic history of the Middle East, the Mediterranean was cut off to Allied shipping as a result of German intervention, depriving the area of consumer goods as well as agricultural and industrial products. Further, Allied forces imposed demands for "accommodation, labor, food and, in the case of Palestine, the production of essential military supplies such as petrol cans, mines, and barbed wire."[64] Overall, with the stimulus of the Anglo-American Middle East Supply Center, industrial growth under state-led control increased, as did the numbers of workers affected.

The largest employer of urban wage labor in Palestine until World War II was the Palestine Railways; its Arab-Jewish workforce peaked at 7,800 in 1943. Consolidated Refineries in Haifa began production in 1940 and employed over 2,000 Arab, Jewish, and British manual and clerical workers. By 1944 there were 100,000 Arab nonagricultural wage workers, about 35,000 of whom were employed at British military bases along with 15,000 Jewish workers.[65]

With the end of the war came the fear of unemployment, and in London and Washington the alarming prospect of labor unrest and radicalization. In Egypt, as the end of war approached, an estimated 250,000 workers were fired, a situation aggravated by "sharp fluctuations in production and intensified mechanization in the textile industry. The cost-of-living index rose from 100 in 1939 to 331 in 1952, and real wages did not keep pace."[66] This increased opposition to Britain's continued occupation and further inflamed the population against the corrupt monarchy. The resulting mobilization of radical unions prompted state intervention by police and military, leading to "a nine-day strike in January 1946 that targeted both the government and continuing layoffs in the textile industry."[67] Further repression was aimed at student demonstrations against the occupation, and the National Committee of Workers and Students "called a general strike and demonstration on February 21, 1946," as "thousands of workers from Shubra al-Khayma joined a crowd estimated at between 40,000 and 100,000 in the Cairo demonstration."[68] It was an example, multiplied by many others, that was meaningful to observers of the Egyptian uprising in 2011, a period when U.S. media coverage paid little attention to the role of labor then, or earlier, in Egypt's history.

In Palestine, the spring of 1946 proved to be a period of exceptional labor militancy with strikes effectively shutting down the operations of the mandatory power. "Postal, telephone, and telegraph workers were responsible for touching off what became an unprecedentedly broad strike of white- and blue-collar government employees."[69] It was also important as an effort that joined Arab and Jewish workers.

There were earlier instances of Palestinian Arab labor organization, such as the strikes generated by the rise in the cost of living that spanned the period from 1936 through 1945, eroding workers' wages and leading to splits in the existing Palestine Communist Party. Among the groups to emerge was the National Liberation League, a movement made up mostly of "Christian intelligentsia and the nascent working class," whose program consisted of "working-class social demands, democracy, and national liberation" that echoed communist lines.[70] In 1945, the Arab Workers' Congress was formed from the coalition of two preexisting movements and became "the largest and most important Arab labor organization in Palestine," with a membership of some 20,000 in 1945. It was "the leading Arab union federation in Jaffa, Gaza, Jerusalem, and Nazareth."[71] In Haifa, it succeeded in organizing workers in the oil sector, the port, steel, and chemical works as well as dominating "the Arab trade union movement in Jaffa, Gaza, Jerusalem, Nazareth, and several smaller towns."[72]

In Lebanon, the same period witnessed the organization of Lebanese tobacco workers against the French monopoly, Regie de Tabacs. In defiance of the Regie and the Lebanese regime that supported it, Lebanese workers, men and women, responded by occupying the factory and warehouse in Mar Mkhayil in what turned out to be a bloody strike. Women were active as organizers and participants in the mobilization of labor in the tobacco industry, contributing directly to the series of nationwide actions that followed protests by "representatives and members of political parties, social associations, workers' unions and federations" outraged by the nature and extent of state repression.[73] The passage of labor legislation was a direct result of such developments.

In Iraq, it was the Iraqi Communist Party that organized the Schalchiyyah railway workers who struck in protest against low wages in an action that lasted from mid-April to May 1, 1945. Similarly, it was the Communist Party that mobilized the port workers of Basrah, obtaining approval for the licensing of their union in advance of an extended period of labor actions. The situation in the oil fields, grown more active since the war, generated a level of organizing in response to inferior wages that culminated in a strike of "about 5,000 oil workers, that is, the bulk of the hands at Kirkuk."[74] The strike began on July 3. In the days that followed, "as the strike spread and increased in intensity, command after command came from Baghdad to the local authorities insisting on conclusive counter-measures and the use of force if necessary."[75] It was not long in coming, but it failed to stem the strikes that followed. In the spring of 1948, a major strike against the IPC station near Haditha was organized by the Iraqi Communist Party, leading IPC to retaliate, which, in turn, led to the decision of the strikers to march on the capital.[76]

In Saudi Arabia where there was no industrial activity outside of the U.S. controlled petroleum sector, ARAMCO's production was increased to meet Allied wartime needs, such as fuel in the Far East. The result was a parallel increase in the total number of workers employed, from 2,882 in 1943 to 11,892 in 1945, with the latter including 7,500 workers of Saudi origin.[77] Such development eventually resulted in the expansion of ARAMCO's role in the kingdom, which magnified the number of foreign workers who, with native workers, were not only subject to exploitation but a form of segregation that evoked the experience of the American South.[78] The overall result was to strengthen the repressive tactics of ARAMCO and the Saudi regime, which, in turn, antagonized those dissenters, such as the future founder of OPEC, Abdallah Tariki, who went into exile, while Abd al-Aziz Ibn Muammar and others were meted out a harsher fate.[79]

Yet strikes occurred. In June 1945 the first strike against ARAMCO took place at the Ras Tanura refinery. The grievances involved food and harassment. The second strike occurred in July in Dhahran, and this time inferior salary and benefits were the basis of protests. This was followed by the revolt of Italian workers, and then "the entire labor force of 9,000 Arabs employed in Dhahran, Ras Tanura, and the outlying worksites defied the amir and resumed the strike against ARAMCO."[80]

The strike produced limited results insofar as workers' demands were concerned. What improved was the company's surveillance of Arab workers. Two years later, it was estimated that "despite all the training programs, about 85 percent of the company's 10,000 Saudi workers were unskilled laborers in the three lowest of ARAMCO's ten pay grades. Only 80 Saudis were classified as 'journeyman' or 'skilled craftsman,' and although a handful had been promoted to supervisor, 'No Saudis supervised American employees.'"[81] Additional evidence further confirms the contempt in which Saudi workers were held by their American superiors.[82]

Considering the USSR in the Middle East

It was in the context of a politically mobilized region, from Greece to Iraq, that the risks of radicalization impressed U.S. officials who feared Soviet influence and intervention, particularly in the aftermath of the war. As for Moscow, its policy in Palestine went through various phases that culminated in support for partition and, later, for Jewish statehood.

In the winter of 1940, Palestine's chief rabbi met with Moscow's Ambassador to London, Ivan Maisky, who was reputed to be highly esteemed by Molotov and Stalin for his British connections. The purpose of the meeting was to obtain transit visas for religious students in Poland who wished to emigrate to Palestine.[83] Beginning in October 1940, the Zionist movement sought contact with Soviet diplomats in the United States and the UK, as the efforts of Nahum Goldmann, then representative of the Jewish Agency in the United States, and U.S. Rabbi Stephen Wise demonstrated in meeting with Soviet Ambassador Konstantin Oumanski in Washington. They offered to have a delegation visit the USSR to open discussions on the situation of Polish Jewish refugees in Russia. This preceded the 1941 meeting in London between Ivan Maiski and the president of the World Zionist Organization, Chaim Weizmann. On that occasion, Weizmann discussed the future of Palestine with the Soviet ambassador, an exchange important in the context of the Zionist movement's relations with the USSR. Maiski was reported to have had no qualms in recognizing the necessity of the transfer of Palestinian Arabs to enable Jews to settle. "Weizmann estimated that one million Arabs have to leave [i.e., be transferred] for two million Jews to be settled in their place."[84] Other versions of this exchange place the figure that Weizmann offered as half a million enabling the settlement of two million Jews in their place.[85]

In 1942 Zionist leaders met in Washington with Soviet Ambassador Maxim Litvinov and in Ankara with the ambassador to the UK, Sergei Vinogradov. The meetings led to the visit of two Soviet officials from the Ankara embassy to Palestine, where they attended a convention in support of the Soviet war effort. It was preceded by the creation of an anti-fascist committee that in May 1942 became the League for Victory, or the so-called V League. Such contacts continued through 1943, the year in which Moscow opened embassies in Cairo, Syria, Lebanon, and Iraq and Maiski visited Jerusalem and two kibbutzim in its vicinity.

Shortly after the issuance of the Anglo-American Committee report in 1946, the head of the Middle East division of the Soviet Foreign Ministry, V. Dekanozov, who was also deputy minister of Foreign Affairs, sent Andrei Vyshinskii, the Soviet Foreign Minister, his response to the proceedings. His position entailed a rejection of both Britain's presence in Palestine and Jewish demands for immigration. In their place, he signaled approval of a UN trusteeship "until the formation of an independent and democratic Palestine."[86] Moscow appeared to back a binational arrangement in a unitary Palestinian state during this period, but it did not prevent Soviet officials from continuing to meet with Zionist envoys.

Moscow's inconsistency in no way prepared those in Washington keen to grasp the direction of Soviet policy as being in support for partition. For those fearful of Soviet influence in the Middle East, such as Loy Henderson, director of the Office of Near Eastern and African Affairs, the risks remained unchanged. He viewed Moscow as bent on an ambitious expansion of its power, determined to penetrate Turkey and the Mediterranean, Iran, and the Gulf and the Indian Ocean.

The Soviet presence in Iran was raised at successive international conferences, as the competition between Washington and Tehran over Iranian oil emerged. In the opinion of George Kennan, then US Charge d'Affaires in Moscow, "the basic motive of recent Soviet action in northern Iran is probably not need for oil itself but apprehension of potential foreign penetration in that area coupled with the concern for prestige. The oil in northern Iran is important, not as something Russia needs, but as something that might be dangerous for anyone else to exploit."[87] The Iranian rejection of Soviet demands, further strengthened by a vigorous U.S. response, led to the USSR's meddling in separatist movements from Azerbaijan to Kurdistan and the Caspian, and to its involvement in Teheran's polarized domestic politics.

In 1946, the U.S. looked on Iranian developments with an eye to their implications for the rest of the Middle East. It was Clark Clifford, Truman's special legal counsel who was to play a crucial role in support of Zionist objectives, who warned against the course of Iranian affairs in that year. In a special report, Clifford "argued that the United States should be ready to use force to guard its vital interests, warning that 'continued access to oil in the Middle East is especially threatened by Soviet penetration into Iran.'"[88]

Washington did not remain aloof from these developments, but its primary concern was Iran's resources that were largely in the hands of the Anglo-Iranian Oil Company. The 1953 Anglo-American coup to bring down the democratically elected government of Mohammed Mossadegh in 1953 was a turning point in U.S. policy in the Middle East.

In the eastern Mediterranean, Washington focused on the area of the Turkish Straits, fearing that it might become the Soviet point of entry into the region. Henderson conceived of Turkey as "the most important factor in the Mediterranean and Middle East" from a strategic perspective, which Soviet policy aimed to exploit.[89] Soviet attempts to renew the Turkish-Soviet Friendship Treaty (1925), on condition that Ankara accept joint defense of the Dardanelles and the Bosporus, antagonized Turkey and worried Washington and London. The fear in Washington was less of imminent Soviet intervention than of a desire on the part of the United States to ensure Turkey's availability as a future base from which to protect the Cairo-Suez region and petroleum in points east.

Likewise, if the Soviets could be denied control of the Dardanelles, their submarines might be bottled up in the Black Sea, thereby ensuring much safer lines of communication for Allied forces traversing the eastern Mediterranean. If wartime developments permitted, Turkish airfields might even be used to launch raids against vital petroleum areas within the Soviet Union and Romania. At the very least, fighter aircraft stationed in Turkey might protect Allied bombers as they ventured into Soviet territory from the bases at Cairo-Suez.[90]

While Washington's concerns were focused on Soviet ambitions in the region's industrial bases and oil fields, Ankara's tensions with the USSR affected Turkey's economic development, which shifted toward increasing free enterprise and open markets. Washington's influence was evident in this turn, as was its intention in arming and financing the Turkish military. From Washington's perspective, Turkey and Greece emerged "as the sole obstacles to Soviet domination of a region which was in turn the link to Asia."[91]

Henderson's views of the situation in Greece were consistent with his overall outlook on U.S. policy in the eastern Mediterranean. He supported the right-wing General Tsaldaris and claimed to have been instructed by Under-Secretary of State Robert Lovett to confront him with Washington's conditions for support—namely, that he appoint a coalition government. Eventually Tsaldaris was made deputy to Prime Minister Sophoulis, an arrangement that Henderson found unsatisfactory. On his return to the United States, Henderson suggested to Secretary of State Marshall that the United States ought to have a military adviser in Greece who was experienced in dealing with guerrilla warfare. Henderson's suggestion was apparently heard.

In Washington, congressional support for U.S. policy in Greece and Turkey was uncertain, but the importance of developments in the eastern Mediterranean came to define U.S. policy:

> The United States was replacing British economic and strategic power in the Middle East; it was preparing for a radically more costly approach to foreign economic policy; it was moving toward the resurrection and final reintegration of German and Japanese power in an anti-Soviet alliance, as well as an American-led world economy; it was transforming its intervention against Left revolution into a standard policy and response.[92]

2

The Palestine Question: 1945

". . . probably the most important and urgent at the present time."[1]

Far from the preoccupation with the radicalization of Arab labor, the State Department faced an altogether different problem. It was one that involved European Jewish refugees, the aspiration of the Zionist movement in Palestine, and British policy in the Palestinian mandate it controlled. Despite the State Department's description of the Palestine question as "probably the most important and urgent," Washington recognized Palestine as being a British responsibility, with the United States having only a limited role to play. As for the European displaced persons, Washington had no formal policy to deal with them either.

The State Department's Near East Division, it should be recalled, had only fourteen officers in 1943.[2] The newly created intelligence service, the Office of Strategic Services (OSS), had an archive on Palestine consisting of two articles, one on Arabs, a second on Jews.[3] William Roger Louis remarked on the lack of organizational structure in dealing with Palestine:

Within the American government there existed no standing interdepartmental committee to give sustained attention to Palestine, nor did the president delegate responsibility to coordinate the views of the State Department and the Joint Chiefs of Staff. In 1945–6 the State-Navy-War Coordinating Committee gave the problem only perfunctory attention. Intelligence reports contained information that could be gleaned from major newspapers. The Secretary of State took only an erratic interest in the matter. Dean Acheson as

Under-Secretary in effect presided over American Palestine policy and attempted to reconcile the views of the White house staff and the area specialists of the Foreign Service.[4]

The State Department's Office of Near Eastern and African Affairs, established in 1944, was modestly staffed. Writing of the early and mid-1940s, Evan Wilson observed that "Palestine came under the Division of Near Eastern Affairs, which was one of the six geographical or political divisions of the Department [State Department] and which had responsibility for our relations with the countries of the Near or Middle East, the Indian subcontinent and virtually all of Africa."[5] As Wilson explained, fourteen officers in the division were responsible for roughly thirty-nine Foreign Service officers, involving legations and consulates. The chief of the division was Paul H. Ailling, with Wallace S. Murray as adviser on political relations and Gordon P. Merriam as assistant and later chief of the division. In addition, a select number of academic figures, including Philip W. Ireland and William Yale, and Lt. Colonel Harold B. Hoskins functioned as advisers.

With the accession of Truman, certain changes took place in the Department of State. James F. Byrnes became secretary of state in June 1945, remaining in that position until 1947, at which point George C. Marshall replaced him. Dean Acheson became under secretary, and Loy Henderson was named director of the Office of Near Eastern and African Affairs.

The two offices that were to be involved in matters related to Palestine were the Office of Near Eastern and African Affairs, under Loy Henderson, and the Division of Near Eastern Affairs, under Gordon Merriam. Wilson contended, and Merriam was probably in agreement, that once Truman assumed the presidency, control over Palestinian affairs would move to the White House.

In policymaking circles, criticism of the inadequacy of planning was pervasive. George Elsey, assistant to the special counsel to the president from 1947 to 1949 and then administrative assistant to the president between 1949 and 1951, recalled the limited number of "experts" that Truman had at his disposal. According to Elsey, "there were no 'experts' on foreign affairs at the White House."[6] Some on the White House staff dealt with both the Department of State and the Department of

Defense, but not in their capacity as foreign policy experts. In addition, there were advisers of an informal kind who held no title but were known to have access to the president, such as David Niles, whom Henderson considered "one of the trump cards held by Zionists."[7] In Elsey's view, the president consulted the "Secretary of State and the Secretary of Defense, the Joint Chiefs of Staff, for the advice, the opinions, the information, and the recommendations that he needed in formulating foreign policy decisions."[8] From Elsey's perspective, the National Security Council became the center of foreign policy analysis in 1947.

In dealing with the Palestine question, some maintained that the White House was more attuned to domestic pressures than to Palestinian developments.[9] Presidential advisers such as David Niles were viewed by Nahum Goldmann, president of the World Jewish Congress and the World Zionist Organization, as "one of our best and most loyal friends in Washington."[10] Niles's office under President Truman has been described as "the centre of Palestine activity in the White House."[11] Along with Judge Samuel I. Rosenman, Niles had previously worked in the FDR administration. Max Lowenthal, who worked for Clark Clifford in 1947–48, was credited by Truman as "the primary force behind the American recognition of Israel."[12] Clark Clifford, who succeeded Rosenman as special counsel to the president from July 1946 to January 1950, was to play a key role as an insider sympathetic to Zionist objectives. "No personal aide was more influential than the pro-Zionist Clifford," writes Peter L. Hahn in a discussion of Truman's advisers.[13] He was viewed as "the chief architect of the administration's pro-partition position" and, along with Max Lowenthal, one of a number of conduits to Jewish circles.[14]

Secretary of the Interior Harold Ickes was alleged to have wanted to become chair of the Washington division of the Committee to Rescue European Jews in 1943, a front of the Irgun (the Jewish terrorist organization in Palestine) operating in the United States. In 1944 the head of the American Jewish Congress, Stephen S. Wise, wrote to Ickes to persuade him to withdraw from the organization.[15]

Gordon Merriam was put in charge of Palestinian Affairs when he was assistant chief of the Division of Near Eastern Affairs in the Department of State shortly after it was established. He attributed the absence of policy with respect to Palestine to the manner in which it came before the State Department. According to Merriam, "we also got into it (Palestine) because the British gave up their mandate in Palestine and we, and particularly the White House, had been giving all this free advice to the British about running Palestine and preventing them from moving aggressively, because by various White House pronouncements we made it impossible for the British to succeed in getting agreement between the Zionists and the Palestinians."[16]

As far as the State Department was concerned, Merriam was persuaded that "Mr. Truman and the White House were fighting us but we didn't know it. Because we were not on the same track at all, and we assumed all the way through that our advice was being considered by the White House, but it never was."[17]

Yet in late January 1945, Evan Wilson, Gordon Merriam, and Foy Kohler of the Division of Near Eastern Affairs of the State Department, along with Dr. Philip Ireland and Prof. William Yale of the Division of Territorial Studies were responsible for several studies dealing with Palestine that Under Secretary of State Stettinius took with him to the British Foreign Office.[18] Although the studies were not policy statements, they merit consideration. They represent an early pronouncement in favor of maintaining Palestine as a unitary state under a trusteeship arrangement.

In their opening memorandum on "Form of Government," the authors declared themselves to be in favor of Palestine as "an International Territory under Trusteeship with a Charter, granted by the International Organization"[19] They proposed that such a charter offer "principles for immigration, land transfers, and economic development" with Britain as trustee. In addition, representatives of the Christian, Jewish, and Muslim communities were to be represented in a Board of Overseers. Most important, they argued, was "that the Arabs and Jews in Palestine be recognized as national communities and be granted self-government in all areas where they are, respectively, predominant." The reasons offered for this position revealed the State Department's vision of a future Palestinian state.

This recommendation is made because: (a) it eliminates the conflicting commitments of the past; (b) it places Palestine outside the bounds of nationalist and imperialist ambitions; (c) it provides the means to solve basic economic problems; and (d) it would create conditions favorable to that cooperation between Arabs and Jews essential to the ultimate independence of Palestine.

A second memo focused on immigration and the need to adjust it to "the general welfare of the people of Palestine judged on the basis of the economic requirements of agriculture, commerce, and industry for immigrants."[20]

Additional memoranda dealt with economic development and land transfers. The authors recommended "large-scale development projects" designed to avert competition between Arabs and Jews, while promoting production in a zone that they foresaw as unappealing to private capital. As to land, they identified the conflict between the demands of Jews for unrestricted access to land purchase and the resistance to the same by Palestinian Arabs concerned with "the menace to the Arab peasantry of further alienation of agricultural land."[21] The authors recommended that both Jewish and Palestinian Arab communities exercise some control over land transfers, prohibiting them in "Haifa, Jerusalem, Safad, and Tiberias," as well as in the "Jordan Valley and the Negeb," where some provisions for such transfers were nonetheless to be made.[22]

Merriam, Wilson, and others who had been involved in formulating these proposals were not invited to meet with Jewish Agency representatives in Washington, D.C., in the winter of 1945. They did meet with Nahum Goldmann several months later. In the interim, the acting secretary of state, Joseph Grew, met with Jewish Agency officials and learned that they had requested increased immigration to Palestine. The British response to similar pressure led to the British recommendation that Libya be a possible homeland for the Jews, which elicited little support in the Arab world. In this troubled period, the Merriam-Wilson proposals were not entirely discarded, and the recommendation that Palestine be an "international territory sacred to all three religions—Moslem, Christian and Jew" was viewed by the U.S. president as an idea that could be brought to the attention of the United Nations.[23]

The White House acknowledged receipt of these proposals, recommendations, warnings, and appeals and simultaneously reaffirmed some of its predecessor's most public positions on Palestine. Hence Truman's statement to Emir Abdullah on May 17, 1945: "As regards the question of Palestine, I am glad to renew to you the assurances which you have previously received, to the effect that in the view of this Government, no decision should be taken respecting the basic situation in that country without full consultation with both Arabs and Jews."[24]

The same theme was reiterated by the acting secretary of state in a pointed reminder to Truman at the end of June, in anticipation of the Potsdam meeting. Full consultation with Arabs and Jews, Grew repeated, was fundamental to the U.S. position. Zionist emissaries to Washington did not object to consultation with Arabs provided that they were free to determine their own future. The head of the Jewish Agency, David Ben-Gurion, chairman of the executive of the Jewish Agency, along with Nahum Goldmann and Eliezer Kaplan of the Jewish Agency made this clear in late June 1945 in their communication with key figures of the State Department's Division of Near Eastern Affairs, including Loy Henderson, Gordon Merriam, and Evan Wilson.

On June 27, 1945, Ben-Gurion declared that the Jews of Palestine wanted to be free to determine their own course, without outside interference, referring to Arab political figures across the region. However, he also insisted on the legitimate interests of the Palestinians. "The Arabs of Palestine were, of course, legitimately interested in that country, and there was no intention of disturbing them or calling their rights into question. Jews and Arabs had lived there in amity for many years, and there was no reason why they should not continue to do so, provided the Arabs elsewhere left them alone."[25]

Ben-Gurion's statement with respect to Palestinian Arabs was belied by the practice of Jewish forces in Palestine. His statement, however, underscored the Zionist movement's position, which was that the Jews of Palestine "had come to the point where they could no longer accept anything less than the granting of all their demands, including the immediate establishment of a Jewish State."[26] As for Loy Henderson's observation that the Arabs would likely cause difficulties if the British supported Zionist goals in Palestine,

Mr. Ben-Gurion and his compatriots expressed complete confidence in their ability to deal with the Arabs. Mr. Ben-Gurion said that he knew the Arabs well and that they would not really put up any kind of fight. The Bedouins of the desert were, of course, good neighbors but it was well known that they had no interest in the Palestine problem and so the leaders of the Arab states would not be successful in rallying their people to support of the Arab position on Palestine.[27]

As pressure on the administration to define its position intensified, Truman asked the British prime minister to consider allowing Jewish immigration to Palestine given the circumstances facing European Jewry. Throughout this period, U.S. officials across the Arab world were sending negative reports of reactions to such a prospect. As he prepared for the meetings at Potsdam, Truman was urged by the team of Near East hands of the State Department to inquire as to Britain's position with respect to placing Palestine under a UN trusteeship. It was an option the Near East team favored although it was by no means their only suggestion.

On August 24, 1945, Loy Henderson sent the secretary of state the plans composed by the Division of Near Eastern Affairs with respect to Palestine. Henderson indicated that "the Division has been studying and living with the difficult Palestine problem for many years" and was prepared to make its experience and knowledge available to those interested.[28] Henderson and his colleagues were sober in their estimate of what proposals might be acceptable to Jews and Arabs in Palestine, concluding that "no solution of the Palestine problem can be found which would be completely satisfactory to both the Arabs and the Jews."[29] Nonetheless, they proposed four options, of which one had their support. The four were summarized by Henderson and then offered in detail in an adjoining Annex. Henderson's list included the following:

1. Palestine: Status as a Jewish Commonwealth
2. Palestine: An Independent Arab State
3. Proposed Plan for the Partition of Palestine under the Trusteeship System
4. Proposed Trusteeship Agreement for Palestine[30]

Henderson made it clear that he viewed the first option as disastrous for U.S. interests in the Middle East. Among his reasons was that it would violate the U.S. policy of "respecting the wishes of a large majority of the local inhabitants with respect to their form of government."[31] In the context of U.S. intervention in Greece in 1946 and the U.S. decision to ignore plans for a Palestinian state in 1948, Henderson's remark may be read as a polite preface to the real problem, which was his fear that support for a Jewish state "would have a strongly adverse effect upon American interests throughout the Near and Middle East."[32] Multiple examples followed, sufficient to make the case that Washington's standing in the Arab world would all but collapse.

Henderson was by no means supportive of retaining Palestine as an independent state, however: "For the United States to support the recognition of Palestine as an independent Arab State would almost immediately mean that we would be endeavoring to assist in setting up a regime which would fail to give to the large Jewish minority in Palestine the just and equitable treatment to which that minority is entitled."[33] Henderson warned that there was much "Jewish-American capital" invested in Palestine that might be lost.

As to the third option, partition, it had little support when it was initially presented by the British in 1938, which brought Henderson to the last, and potentially the only promising, option, that of trusteeship, which he assumed would appeal to "more moderate Arabs and Jews."[34]

In his observations with respect to partition, Merriam noted that it assumed the irreconcilability of Jewish and Arab aims which would not be altered by the proposal to partition Palestine, and that it would "be likely to arouse widespread discontent in the Arab and Moslem worlds which would be somewhat unfavorable to American interests."[35] It was the last option, in favor of the trusteeship plan, that Merriam supported, as did Henderson. Merriam's reasons were a combination of factors that minimized the risks of violent Arab protest and of anti-U.S. actions while being acceptable to non-Zionist Jewish interests. As Merriam concluded, "this would probably receive considerable support from non-Zionist Jewish groups who may be expected to look upon it as a reasonable compromise solution."[36] Merriam's conclusion assumed the influence of non-Zionist groups, a position he did not elaborate on and that proved to be inaccurate.

A short time later, Merriam submitted a summary of a report on the question of immigration prepared by William Yale of the Near East Division of the State Department. After pointing out that "Zionists demand that one million Jews be admitted to Palestine as rapidly as possible," Merriam added that the number of Jews in Europe desirous of migrating to Palestine was probably half that number.[37] Then, reviewing conditions in Palestine, he concluded that unless adequate assistance and protection were provided, it was inappropriate to endorse a policy of mass migration that would, in addition, be opposed by Arabs. On the other hand, the United States could support a policy of limited immigration, assuming the British would be in a position to implement it.

As Merriam faced the succession of conferences and reports bearing on the situation of European Jewish refugees, he reminded President Truman that Palestine could not be treated exclusively in the context of European developments. And as others recognized, European developments—including the problem of displaced persons—could not be treated exclusively in the context of Palestine. As the conference at Evian in 1938 demonstrated, immigration was an unpopular option in nearly every country, including in the United States and other advanced industrialized states.

THE EARL G. HARRISON REPORT

The situation of European Jewish refugees and their resettlement was considered by Truman on his return from Potsdam, as he recalled in his *Memoirs*.[38] In June 1945, Truman moved to "investigate the conditions of those Displaced Persons called 'non-repatriables'" in Europe, which meant investigating the conditions in which Jewish survivors of the war were kept in the American zone of occupation in Germany. The resulting report (the Harrison Report) led Truman to call for the immigration of 100,000 Jews to Palestine, a response that irritated the British who, incidentally, had not been invited or consulted in the investigation that preceded the report. Palestinians were similarly ignored. Truman's support effectively linked the predicament of survivors of the Holocaust to Palestine, thus underscoring a connection that achieved iconic status in the identification of the Holocaust with the formation of the state of Israel.

Instead of endorsing the report, the British recommended another inquiry by what became the 1946 Anglo-American Committee (AAC), which, in turn, gave way to the Morrison-Grady Plan, and in 1947 the mandatory power decided to bring the Palestine case to the United Nations. Less than a month later, the United Nations created the Special

Committee on Palestine (UNSCOP), which was to set the stage for the UN deliberations on partition. The list of successive developments provides little evidence recognizing the profound human, social, and political difficulties involved in the attempt to resolve the refugee problem at local or international levels.

On August 31, 1945, Truman sent British PM Attlee a message that underscored his conviction of the singular human trauma of the refugee situation for those who had experienced concentration camps. This persuaded him to support immigration into Palestine, which he claimed the American people believed "should not be closed and that a reasonable number of Europe's persecuted Jews should, in accordance with their wishes, be permitted to resettle there."[39] In the interim, Merriam urged that plans be made for the absorption of European Jewish refugees not only in Palestine but in the United States and other nations and that Arabs and Jews be consulted with respect to Palestine.

Meanwhile, the passage of Britain's 1939 White Paper on Palestine ignited a nationwide campaign of pro-Zionist supporters, including congressional figures who opposed British policies and demanded that Washington endorse Jewish statehood in Palestine as being in harmony with the Balfour Declaration of 1917. Yet there was far from a monolithic bloc within the American Jewish community in the early 1940s with respect to how to respond to the situation in Europe, let alone Palestine. There were those, in addition, who feared that the predicament of European Jewry could be worsened by overt agitation.[40] Rabbi Stephen Wise, a prominent spokesman for American Zionists until he was replaced with the more militant Rabbi Abba Hillel Silver, was the force behind the call in 1933 for a New York rally in which church and labor leaders participated that denounced German policy.

With the expansion of the war in Europe, Roosevelt and the State Department pressed Zionist supporters in the United States to modify their antagonism toward Britain, including in Palestine. But FDR and his supporters were also well aware of the domestic opposition to expanding immigration quotas to allow increased admission of European Jews into the United States. In 1936, when FDR was reported to have directed "the State Department to loosen some of its red tape and facilitate the issuance of visas to those people eligible to enter the United States under the quota system," opposition came from those who felt that the president ignored domestic economic conditions.[41] It was in this context that Roosevelt was moved to initiate planning for an international conference at Evian, France, in 1938. Of the thirty-two countries that participated, virtually none were willing to change their immigration laws to accommodate those in desperate plight. The resulting deferral to Palestine was regarded by some as the inevitable and just end.

Why were the doors to the United States closed to European Jewish immigration? The subject has led to numerous inquiries of U.S. immigration practice and restrictions, and parallel studies of State Department positions on Palestine, as well as more general accounts of popular attitudes toward immigration in the late 1930s and 1940s. The role of the Visa Bureau of the State Department in this period was influenced by the racist views of Director Breckinridge Long and his associates. They opposed immigration reform, a position adhered to for a variety of reasons by those aware of the situation of European Jewry, including American Jews who found Palestine a preferable solution.

The combined impact of the failure of Evian and Britain's adoption of the White Paper of 1939 served to intensify Zionist mobilization in the United States as organization of the 1942 Biltmore Conference demonstrated. Among the Biltmore demands was Britain's admission of Displaced Persons to Palestine; the granting of responsibility to the Jewish Agency for immigration to Palestine; and, most important, that "Palestine be established as a Jewish Commonwealth integrated into the structure of the new democratic world."[42] The Biltmore resolutions became an integral part of the Zionist program. Adopted in New York, they were accepted by the Zionist executive in Jerusalem and, in October 1942, by the Zionist Steering Committee, thus becoming part of the World Zionist movement's official program. Within two years, the Palestine question was on the Republican as well as the Democratic Party agendas, and Congress moved to pressure Britain to abandon its immigration policies in favor of Zionist objectives in Palestine.

Before he became president, Harry S. Truman was among those openly critical of the British White Paper, and in 1941 he is reported to have "joined the American Palestine Committee to lend moral support to Zionism. He signed its commemoration of the twenty-fifth anniversary of the Balfour Declaration, and at a Holocaust 'rescue' rally in Chicago in 1943 proposed to create a 'haven' for Jews."[43]

On November 26, 1945, Jacob Blaustein, then chairman of the executive committee of the American Jewish Committee, wrote to Secretary of State Byrnes, requesting his assistance in enabling refugees in the American and British occupation zones of Germany and Austria to immigrate to the United States under existing and unfilled immigration quotas. As Blaustein pointed out, "during the fiscal year 1944 (July 1944–June 1945), not more than six percent of the available immigration quotas for the European area were filled."[44] While he admitted that it was unclear what the figures would be for 1945, he assumed that it would remain low. Blaustein's request was motivated by his desire to relieve those suffering the effects of the war, but as he pointed out, it also would serve to relieve pressure on Palestine and strengthen the U.S. position in the 1946 Anglo-American Inquiry. In response to an earlier claim that the shortage of transportation rendered such a request difficult, Blaustein replied that the mere "insurance of visas" in the interim would sustain those seeking entry to the United States. Blaustein's efforts did not lead to any major revision of U.S. immigration practice, but there was no lessening of attention to the situation of European Jewry.

In 1945, Secretary of the Treasury Henry Morgenthau urged the State Department to investigate the conditions of concentration camp survivors in the American zone of Germany. Earl G. Harrison, dean of the University of Pennsylvania Law School and previously wartime commissioner of immigration and naturalization, was chosen by the State Department to lead the commission investigating Jewish camp survivors in the American zone of Germany. His report, written for the president in 1945, played a major role in shaping the White House position on the destination of Jewish refugees. Peter Grose observed that "certain alert Zionists had spotted the potential of the Harrison mission from the start," citing Chaim Weizmann, the Zionist elder statesman, and Meyer W. Weisgal as among those who believed that "this objective but idealistic law professor could become an instrument for combining the political aspirations of Zionism with the plight of the surviving Jews of Europe."[45] Whether or not Harrison was effectively manipulated from this vantage point, his report accomplished this goal.

Truman approved and appointed Harrison to undertake the investigation, whose results he subsequently sent to General D. D. Eisenhower, then in charge of U.S. forces in Europe, including those managing the camps investigated by Harrison. Eisenhower was unprepared for its charge, which was that "we appear to be treating the Jews as the Nazis treated them except that we do not exterminate them. They are in concentration camps in large numbers under our military guard instead of SS troops."[46]

Harrison's report maintained that several distinct needs had to be addressed in investigating camp conditions, given that they housed approximately 100,000 Jewish refugees coming from Poland, Hungary, Romania, Germany, and Austria. In the first place, he counseled that the Jewish refugees be recognized as Jews and not as members of any particular national group; and second, that their living conditions be urgently improved, along with assistance in obtaining information about family survivors. Third was the critical question of repatriation or emigration to a destination of their choice. As the Harrison Report emphasized, above all refugees had to be assisted in finding places of emigration. Palestine was described as "the choice of most," but with the qualification that it "is not the only named place of possible emigration."[47] The question was where to go, and what country would admit them, other than Palestine.

The authors of the report then proposed that the British White Paper of 1939 be amended and that 100,000 of the displaced Jews be admitted into Palestine. This proposal was rejected by the British, but some members of the British Labor Party supported the American position. They insisted, however, as did the Arabs, that the problem was an international one. The USSR opposed the Harrison Report, but they helped Polish Jews emigrate into Palestine, and they eventually endorsed partition.

The key question in Harrison's report concerned the destination of the displaced Jews. The report maintained that

> most Jews want to leave Germany and Austria as soon as possible. That is their first and great expressed wish . . . and many of the people themselves fear other suggestions or plans for their benefit because of the possibility that attention might therefore be diverted from the all-important matter of evacuation from Germany. Their desire to leave Germany is an urgent one. The life which they have led for the past ten years, a life of fear and wandering and physical

torture, has made them impatient of delay. They want to be evacuated to Palestine now, just as other national groups are being repatriated to their homes.[48]

Admitting that some Jews wishing to resettle sought admission to the
United States, England, or South America, the Harrison Report then
affirmed that "with respect to possible places of resettlement for those
who may be stateless or who do not wish to return to their homes, Palestine is definitely and pre-eminently the first choice." Some came to
realize that it might also be their only choice if they were unable to get
into the United States or some country in the Western Hemisphere.[49]

The Harrison Report did recognize that Palestine's appeal was in part
a function of restrictive immigration policies that effectively barred
other options. But it did not call for the amendment of existing U.S.
immigration laws or review the history of the 1938 Evian Conference
and its failure to generate international support for European refugees.
The authors of the report recommended that the United States "should
under existing immigration laws, permit reasonable numbers of such
persons to come here, again particularly those who have family ties in
this country."[50]

The worsening of conditions in Europe had earlier led to proposals
for refugee colonization efforts in parts of Africa and the Dominican
Republic in Latin America. Even the attempt to allow liberalization of
the U.S. Immigration Act of 1924 to permit entry of 20,000 German
refugee children failed. Despite this, the U.S. record was considered
superior to that of other countries. "From 1933 through 1945, something like 250,000 refugees from Nazism reached safety in the United
States. This excludes the underground collaboration for emigration of
German Jews, arranged between Gestapo and the Sicherheitsdienst, in
1938–39."[51] Only Palestine, which received approximately 150,000 refugees, approached the American record. In the period to 1938, Arno
Mayer points out that "fewer than 150,000, or 30 percent, of Germany's
Jews had either emigrated or gone into exile. Over 20 percent of these
went to Palestine, but fully half of the German-Jewish émigrés preferred
to seek asylum in western Europe."[52] Between 1933 and 1938 some 42,000
Jewish and non-Jewish refugees had gone to Palestine, while a smaller
number, 30,000–35,000, had emigrated to the United States.[53]

In December 1945, Truman urged various government agencies to enable displaced persons to enter the United States. At the time, Truman knew that existing immigration quotas had not been filled. As David McBride has argued, however, "following the Second World War, there remained strong nativist sentiments in America by which the majority of the public and government officials opposed easing America's restrictive immigration quotas that would have allowed the resettlement of a large number of Displaced Persons."[54] In the spring of 1946, Congressman William Stratton did initiate legislation to bring some 400,000 refugees to the United States. The legislation failed to pass, but it brought about immigration reform at a later date.

Opposition to immigration was evident in the Immigration Subcommittee of the Senate Judiciary Committee, where Senator Chapman Revercomb of West Virginia strongly opposed such action, claiming that it entailed risks of communist infiltration. The visit by House and Senate members, including Revercomb, to Displaced Persons (DP) camps in Europe converted some congressional leaders, however, with the result that in the second session of the 80th Congress some measures approving immigration were passed.

Roosevelt's emissary Ernest L. Morris, who visited Germany, insisted that had there been adequate options only a minority of Jews in the camps would have elected to go to Palestine. American Zionists, including Stephen Wise, insisted on Britain's openness to Jews in Palestine and "opposed a congressional effort in 1943 to set up a commission 'to effectuate the rescue of the Jewish people of Europe,'" a conclusion conceded by others in later inquiries.[55]

In practice, Zionist leaders encouraged the admission of Jewish refugees into U.S. controlled camps and found U.S. military leaders such as Eisenhower helpful in facilitating training programs in agriculture, vocational, and military training. The camps proved to be the site of Zionist mobilization in this period as well. In addition to other paramilitary groups, the "Haganah, also came to the camps, initially to help the DPs train for self-defense in the camps, and later to prepare combat reserves [for] an army of a state just about to be born."[56]

Records of the U.S. Office of Military Government for Germany (OMGUS) indicate that in early 1948 the Revisionist party, the Irgun, was among those seeking to "recruit" in the camps and, as did Haganah, at times used coercive methods.[57] Prof. William Haber, adviser on Jewish Affairs to the American Supreme Commander, was in touch with Jewish organizations in New York and informed them of the pressure being exerted on refugees in the DP camps. The response at the level of the U.S. secretary of state appears to have been to withhold approving requests by the U.S. military to permit the exit of men of military age.

At the end of June 1948, Secretary of State Marshall disclosed that the "U.S. Army AmZone Germany has requested State-Army for directions re movement DPs to Palestine. Depts Army-State cabling U.S. mil authorities Germany Austria text para VI containing immigration provisions truce and simultaneously authorizing exit AmZones Germany and Austria of Palestine certificate holders specifically excepting fighting personnel."[58] Marshall, who was secretary of state from 1947 to 1949, deferred approval to allow "men mil age" to exit until he had heard from the UN mediator, Count Bernadotte, who clearly indicated that he had neither the intention nor the time to visit the AmZone in Germany and Austria.

In 1946–47, an estimated "50,000 Jews (mostly Eastern European) immigrated to countries other than Palestine."[59] But "the vast majority of the population of the Jewish DP camps (more than 90 percent) strongly supported the establishment of a Jewish state in Palestine."[60] Yet "(more than 60 percent) did not emigrate to Palestine/Israel and chose other destinations, despite the fact that at any given point in time during the relevant years (1945–1951), Palestine/Israel was the least difficult target location to which to obtain passage."[61] Shortly before passage of the UN Partition Plan on November 29, 1947, the CIA reported on the existence of a secret transport system for Jewish DPs organized by the Haganah that crossed from Eastern Europe to Palestine.[62] In the summer of 1947 a special committee of UNSCOP reported on its own visit to DP camps in Germany and Austria. Its findings and conclusions confirmed the combination of factors identified earlier, in which emigration was the primary wish among survivors who confronted the limited options, some of whom were committed Zionists, and others who acknowledged the activity of Zionist organizers in their midst.

Independently, Arab intellectuals had expressed their own views of the manner in which the Jewish refugee question was dealt with in the

United States and in Europe. Lebanese, Egyptian, Syrian, and Palestinian voices were raised against Nazism and fascism and in solidarity with those who were its victims.[63] Mohamed Hassanein Heikal, then a journalist at *Akhbar al Yawm*, recalled that Egyptian Jews "were advertising the establishment of camps to accommodate those Jews who had been persecuted by the Nazis. These were staging camps in which these Jews would stay temporarily before going on to Palestine."[64] Eric Rouleau, the French correspondent who would later become *Le Monde*'s chief Middle East correspondent and French Ambassador to Tunis and Turkey, recalled the presence of European refugees in Egypt, some of whom had come from Turkey.[65]

Heykal reported that Hashomer Hatzair was among the Zionist organizations active in Egypt, but both he and Rouleau observed that such activities failed to attract any sizeable element of Egyptian Jewish support. According to Heykal, it wasn't until 1946 at the Bludan Conference of the Arab League in Syria that Egyptians began to become aware of what was taking place in Palestine. After meeting with Ben-Gurion in Palestine, Heykal reported his astonishment that the Jewish leader and Jewish Agency were "talking openly about a Jewish state."[66]

Egyptian feminists at their inaugural meeting in October 1938 addressed the significance of the failures of the Evian conference in a manner that placed them unconditionally in solidarity with opponents of Nazism and fascism. Huda Shaarawi, an internationally recognized symbol of Egyptian feminism, spoke directly to the issue when she declared that

> not a single representative of one of the participating states, not even the representative of Great Britain or the United States, has dared declare that his government was prepared to provide a haven to these rejected, shelterless people, while Palestine, to which they have no familial or national ties, has taken in four hundred thousand of them down to the present day.[67]

Palestinians who responded in opposition to European fascism and Nazism found themselves in the position of supporting "the oppressor of their own nation in its war against the sworn enemy of those who were trying to conquer their land."[68] According to Orayb Aref Najjar's analysis of *Filastin* (Palestine), one week after the outbreak of the Second World War, its leading editorial declared that

> war has placed us in a new situation with regard to our relations with Britain. We are connected to it today in a matter that is more universal than our private cause. We are not calling on Arabs to sacrifice their cause, but we are asserting that the present conflict between the democratic forces and dictatorial forces has dictated that we take sides with one or the other.[69]

By no means does this describe the totality of Palestinian Arab reaction to Nazism and the outbreak of war, which remained little known among U.S. officials, save for the pro-Nazi position of Haj Amin al-Husseini.

In Washington and London, however, the focus was on the need to determine how to confront the Harrison Report's findings and recommendations, which led to yet another committee of inquiry.

THE REPORT OF THE ANGLO-AMERICAN COMMITTEE OF 1946

The response of British Foreign Secretary Ernest Bevin to the Harrison Report was to call for yet another inquiry with the hope that this one would contribute to reorienting the Truman administration more favorably toward British policy in Palestine. The opposite occurred, and it was not Bevin but Truman who gained the upper hand in the process, even as the United States remained committed to Britain's continuing role in Palestine. The resulting Committee of Inquiry was formally announced in November 1945, and it presented its final report in April of the following year. Far from resolving the differences the Harrison Report had exposed, the Anglo-American Committee hearings further exposed the depth of disagreement between Zionist representatives and Palestinians and their respective U.S. and British supporters.

The committee was made up of representatives of the United States and the UK, with Truman directly involved in selecting the American participants. The exercise generated predictable controversy as Truman "apparently aimed at securing a 'balanced' committee, one that would represent both State Department and Zionist views."[70] David Niles, whom

Loy Henderson described as the president's adviser on Jewish affairs, selected Bartley Crum and James McDonald.[71] Nahum Goldmann regarded both as good friends of the Zionist movement.[72] Cohen maintained that the connection between Crum and Niles proved critical "in securing Truman's goal of a recommended solution to the Jewish DP problem."[73] State Department efforts to turn down clearance for Crum failed, as Truman approved the selection.[74] According to Dean Acheson's account, the U.S. Committee included "Judge Joseph C Hutcheson of the U.S. Fifth Circuit Court of Appeals, a fiery Texan and friend of the President, [who] was American chairman, flanked by Dr Frank Aydelotte, former President of Swarthmore College; Frank W. Buxton, editor of the *Boston Herald*; William Philips, former Under-Secretary of State; James G McDonald, former League of Nations High Commissioner for Refugees; and Bartley C. Crum, a California lawyer."[75]

Earl G. Harrison proved to be an influential member of the American team as well, largely due to his well-known report. British members of the committee included Sir John Singleton; Lord Robert Morrison of the labor party; Sir Frederick Leggett, member of the International Labour office; Wilfred Crick, who focused on the Palestinian economy; Reginald Manningham Buller, a Tory MP described as "'devoted to the Kipling idea of empire' by an American member of the committee";[76] and finally, Richard Crossman, who was a Labour MP at the time as well as serving on the editorial board of the *New Statesman*.

Committee members initially met in Washington, D.C. on January 4, 1946, to hear those invited to testify in the first series of meetings. In the spring they traveled to select countries in Europe, including Germany, Austria, Poland, Czechoslovakia, Italy, and Greece, where they visited DP camps and spoke with Allied military, political, and religious figures before going to the Middle East and visiting Palestine, Transjordan, Syria, Lebanon, Egypt, Iraq, and Saudi Arabia.

Committee members were instructed

1. To examine political, economic and social conditions in Palestine as they bear upon the problem of Jewish immigration and settlement therein and the well-being of the peoples now living therein.

2. To examine the position of the Jews in those countries in Europe where they have been the victims of Nazi and Fascist persecution, and

the practical measures taken or contemplated to be taken in those countries to enable them to live free from discrimination and oppression and to make estimates of those who wish or will be impelled by their conditions to migrate to Palestine or other countries outside of Europe.

3. To hear the views of the competent witnesses and to consult representative Arabs and Jews on the problems of Palestine . . . and to make recommendations to His Majesty's Government and the Government of the United States for *ad interim* handling of these problems as well as for their permanent solution.

4. To make such other recommendations to His Majesty's Government and the Government of the United States as may be necessary to meet the immediate needs arising from conditions subject to examination under paragraph 2 above, by remedial action in the European countries in question or by the provision of facilities for emigration to and settlement in countries outside Europe.[77]

The committee produced both a report and a set of hearings. The former reflected the orientalist outlook of its authors, whose contrasting views of Arabs and Jews had little merit other than to provide a language with which to justify its policy recommendations. Its emphasis was largely, but not entirely, on the postwar situation of European Jewry, the failure of international assistance and immigration reform, and the role of Palestine. Under the headings of the Jewish Attitude and the Arab Attitude, the authors offered their observations on various aspects of contemporary Jewish and Arab reactions related to Palestine.

With respect to Jews in Palestine, the authors described the varieties of political forces at work, but underscored what they understood to be the collective support for the establishment of a Jewish state in Palestine. The report described the Jews in Palestine as being caught between pride in their achievements and frustration at the constraints imposed on them by the continued British presence.

Committee members were not hesitant in describing the extent to which Palestine had become "an armed camp" with "a sinister aspect of recent years" due to the emergence of "large illegal armed forces."[78] These forces were described as the three branches of the Haganah, estimated to include between 58,000 and 62,000 fighters,[79] and "two further illegal armed organizations," the Irgun, composed of an estimated 3,000–5,000 forces, and the Stern Gang with between 200 and 300 fighters.[80]

The authors also noted what they perceived to be the near inability of Jews to consider their impact on Palestinian Arabs. Referring to the Jew in Palestine, the report stated: "passionately loving every foot of Eretz Israel, he finds it almost impossible to look at the issue from the Arab point of view, and to realize the depth of feeling aroused by his 'invasion' of Palestine."[81] Moreover, the authors recognized that "the Jewish community in Palestine has never, as a community, faced the problem of cooperation with the Arabs."[82] They concluded that Jews in Palestine were unaware of the depth of Arab opposition. If there was an exception, it was to be found in the Ihud group that advocated bi-nationalism, and in socialist supporters of Hashomer Hatzair. Committee members were well aware of the views of Magnes, as well as others of similar outlook in the League for Jewish-Arab Rapprochement and Cooperation. They were also aware of right-wing groups who "openly support the present terrorist campaign."[83]

The authors of the report did not mention Fawzi al-Husseini, the Palestinian political figure who prior to his assassination in the fall of 1946 had "signed an agreement in the name of a new organization, Falastin al-Jadida (New Palestine), with the League for Arab-Jewish Rapprochement that had been founded in 1939 and headed by Kalvarisky."[84] But they endorsed the position he advocated, which was the "principle of non-domination of one nation over the other and the establishment of a bi-national state on the basis of political parity and full cooperative effort between the two nations in economic, social and cultural domains."[85]

Despite their criticism of Jewish attitudes and policies toward Palestinian Arabs, committee members were impressed by the achievements of the "pioneers" and claimed that "there had been no expulsion of the indigenous population, exploitation of cheap Arab labour has been vigorously opposed as inconsistent with Zionism."[86] Committee members appear to have known little of the conditions that led to "the expropriation between 1920 and 1947 of about 26 percent of Palestine's cultivated land, and the consequent eviction of a large number of direct producers estimated in 1930 at 48 per cent of the total peasant population, [that] was effected to a great extent by the use of political force. . . ."[87]

Turning to the: "Arab Attitude" the committee recognized the roots of Palestinian opposition to Zionism and British policy: "Palestine is a country which the Arabs have occupied for more than a thousand years," and which is therefore the basis of their opposition to Jewish historical claims.[88] The committee also noted the fact that, unlike its Arab neighbors, Palestinian Arabs had not been granted independence. Palestinian Arabs objected to the failed promises made by the British in 1939 and by the U.S. president in 1945. In addition, they objected to the role assigned to Palestine in solving the European refugee problem.

The Palestinian leadership was described as divided and representative of a fundamentally anti-Western political class fearful of the advances of western civilization. The authors of the report depicted the conservative, traditional, and highly restrictive operations of this political class as brooking neither opposition nor reform, as promoting an inferior educational system, and as stalling economic development. In sum, in the words of the committee, "one witnesses in Palestine not merely the impact of European culture upon the East, but also the impact of Western science and Western technology upon a semi-feudal civilization."[89]

In the report, the authors reverted to a cultural explanation for Arab attitudes claiming that

> the Arab adheres to a strict social code far removed from the customs of the modern world, and he is shocked by innovations of dress and manners which seem completely natural to the Jewish immigrant. Thus, the sight of a Jewish woman in shorts offends the Arab concept of propriety. The freedom of relations between the sexes, and the neglect of food form as he conceives it violate the entire code of life in which the Arab is brought up.[90]

At the first set of meetings in Washington, the committee listened to speakers, the majority of whom were Americans speaking on behalf of Zionist, non-Zionist, or anti-Zionist organizations, although some members of the Arab delegation spoke as well. Arabs did address the committee when members visited the Middle East, as did major Zionist leaders. Included among Jewish political figures who spoke was

Judah Magnes, whose views were debated both by members of the committee, such as Richard Crossman, and by Arab delegates, such as Albert Hourani.

At the preliminary meetings in Washington, committee members were introduced to the findings of an economic study of Palestine whose authors maintained that Palestinian economic development undertaken by Zionist leaders benefited Jews in Palestine as well as Palestinian Arabs, and, more generally, Arabs across the region.

The lead author of *An Economic Study of Palestine* was Robert Nathan, former director of the National Income Division of the Commerce Department and former chair of the Central Planning Division of the War Production Board. With his co-authors Oscar Gass (Eliahu Epstein's "economic adviser"),[91] and Daniel Creamer, Nathan addressed the committee and discussed issues such as Palestine's absorptive capacity and its significance for immigration.[92] The three had spent several months in Palestine between December 1944 and March 1945 studying existing conditions, on the basis of which Nathan concluded that Palestine could absorb large numbers of incoming immigrants in the coming decade. From the perspective of Zionist supporters, the main contribution by these economists was their claim that "the Jews have been a great progressive force in Palestine. . . . They can serve the whole Middle East as a progressive, Westernizing influence in the development of modern industry, scientific agriculture, education, and political democracy. They can be an outpost of Western culture without being an outpost of Western imperialism."[93] The three authors nonetheless conceded that it would be difficult to persuade Palestinian Arabs to leave, or to approve "land transfer," which they regarded as "perhaps the most delicate questions of public policy that a development-minded Government must confront in the next decade."[94]

Committee members were given an abridged history of Arab-Jewish relations as viewed by Arab historians and political figures, as well as introductions to diverse U.S. Zionist and non-Zionist organizations. The committee moved its operations to the Middle East in the spring and met in Jerusalem on March 6, 1946. Among those who testified were Chaim Weizmann, David Ben-Gurion, Moshe Sharett, Golda Meir, Judah Magnes, and two chief rabbis. Palestinians were represented by members of the Arab Higher Committee, Jamal al-Husayni; the Arab

Higher Front, Awni Abd al-Hadi; and the Arab Office, Albert Hourani and Ahmed Shuqayri.

Among Arab delegates, Albert Hourani was generally viewed as the most effective speaker. He was little known in the United States until his academic career assumed importance some years later. Hourani had previously headed the research department of the Arab Office in Jerusalem, moving to Washington where it was established until it was obliged to close under pressure and relocate to London in 1947. Another Palestinian figure of interest was Khulusy Khairy, who traveled from the Arab Office in Washington to Ottawa in 1946 on behalf of the Canadian-Arab Friendship League, an advocate for a unitary democratic state in Palestine.[95]

In their final deliberations in Lausanne, members of the Anglo-American Committee offered a number of recommendations that reflected both their despair of existing conditions and their optimism with respect to the possibility of creating a different order in Palestine. The committee declared it imperative that the national aspirations of Jews and Arabs be recognized and reconciled, while affirming that neither Jew nor Arab should dominate; that Palestine should not become a Jewish or an Arab state; and that the interests of the three major religions were to be protected. This collective effort stands in sharp contrast to the struggle over Palestine that would mark the coming years.

The committee emphatically declared that "Palestine alone cannot meet the emigration needs of the Jewish victims of Nazi and Fascist persecution. The whole world shares responsibility for them and indeed for the resettlement of all 'Displaced Persons.'"[96] To this end, it recommended international cooperation to help in the relocation of those displaced. At the same time, committee members voiced their opposition to the mass emigration of European Jews, a subject raised by various delegates concerned with the implications of Zionism for Jews of the diaspora.

In declaring their opposition to Jewish statehood, committee members rejected the very foundation of Zionism:

Further, while we recognize that any Jew who enters Palestine in accordance with its laws is there of right, we expressly disapprove of the position taken in some Jewish quarters that Palestine has in some way been ceded or granted as their State to the Jews of the world, that every Jew everywhere is, merely because he is a Jew, a citizen of Palestine and therefore can enter Palestine as of right without regard to conditions imposed by the government upon entry, and that therefore there can be no illegal immigration of Jews into Palestine. We declare and affirm that any immigrant Jew who enters Palestine contrary to its laws is an illegal immigrant.[97]

In place of this, they urged that Palestine be recognized as the home of both Jews and Arabs. At the same time, they declared that

we have reached the conclusion that the hostility between Jews and Arabs and, in particular, the determination of each to achieve domination, if necessary by violence, make it almost certain that, now and for some time to come, any attempt to establish either an independent Palestinian state or independent Palestinian states, would result in civil strife such as might threaten the peace of the world. We therefore recommend that, until this hostility disappears, the Government of Palestine be continued as at present under mandate pending the execution of a Trusteeship Agreement under the United Nations.[98]

This in no way eliminated the importance of resolving the situation of the 100,000 would-be immigrants into Palestine. Committee members supported their entry, without committing themselves to the future of immigration.

The Anglo-American Committee Report, predictably, ignited passionate rejoinders, most of them negative, from all interested parties. Evan Wilson, a member of the original committee, was among the few who considered its findings sobering and was in general agreement with them, reflecting in later years that

we in the [State] Department had reason to be aware of the force of the Zionist drive toward a Jewish state, we continued until the end of 1946, at least, to think in terms of a compromise solution in Palestine. We thought there should be a solution under which, in the words of the Anglo-American Committee of Inquiry, Jew would not dominate Arab and Arab would not dominate Jew. In other words, we were thinking of a bi-national state long after the conflict between the parties had become so complete, and their oppositions so intractable, as to put this out of the question. As men who tried to be reasonable, we thought that it should be possible to achieve a compromise, but the hard fact was that neither of the two parties in the dispute wanted a compromise; the depth of the nationalistic feeling on both sides precluded this.[99]

Wilson aside, the response to the Anglo-American Committee Report was overwhelmingly negative. There were exceptions, such as Eleanor Roosevelt, who at the time did not support a Jewish state. Wilson claimed that Truman later said that "the United States was willing to accept the Anglo-American report as a whole—a considerable advance over his earlier response."[100] According to contemporary press coverage, Truman was reported to have told the publisher of the *Philadelphia Record* "that although he favored the creation of a democratic state in Palestine, he did not favor one based on religion, race, or creed. Palestine, he thought, had to be 'thrown open' to Jews, Arabs, and Christians alike. It should aspire to be a pluralistic society like that of the United States."[101] This was not the objective of Zionist officials who were critical of the report for its failure to support a Jewish state. Truman was prepared to follow up the committee's recommendations and established a cabinet-level committee made up of the secretaries of State, War, and Treasury, who, in turn, were assigned to select representatives from their respective departments to work with some of the former members of the Anglo-American Committee in implementing the AAC report.

THE MORRISON-GRADY PLAN

The resulting arrangement, designated the Morrison-Grady Plan, involved Britain as well as the United States in efforts to divide Palestine "into a Jewish province, an Arab province, and the districts of Jerusalem and Negeb. The execution of the plan might lead ultimately either to a unitary, bi-national state or to partition."[102] The formula proposed separate British administration for Jerusalem and the Negev and continued British control over all aspects of domestic and foreign relations. It accepted the U.S.-backed plan to admit 100,000 Jewish DPs and called for U.S. funding for a development project in Palestine.

Averell Harriman, then Ambassador in London, wrote to Acheson on July 24, 1946, with his evaluation of the plan, pointing out how advantageous it would be for Jews in Palestine.

> Proposed provincial boundaries give Jews best land in Palestine, practically all citrus and industry, most of the coast line and Haifa port. Jewish legitimate demands including large measure of control of immigration and opportunity to develop national home, have been met with exception of Jerusalem and Negev. Christian interests must be taken into full account in Jerusalem and Bethlehem, and disposition of Negev is remaining undetermined until its potentialities can be ascertained.[103]

Truman did not endorse the plan, citing the absence of popular as well as political support. Nor did the U.S. president participate in the follow-up conference the British organized, hoping to have both Arab and Jewish support for what was now known as the Morrison Plan. Dean Acheson, in his memoirs, recalled this as a period of "civil war along the Potomac," with members of the Anglo-American Committee attacking those of the cabinet committee responsible for the plan, and more.[104] As Acheson pointed out, recriminations aside, the Morrison-Grady Plan "had in it the makings of a compromise; indeed, later on the Jewish Agency suggested some helpful amendments, and the United Nations Special Committee report of August 31, 1947, shows its influence."[105]

In the interval, London turned to the idea of a conference in which to launch its Morrison Plan, although both the United States and the Jewish Agency refused to attend. The reason given by the latter was the failure of the plan to "give the Jews sufficient assurances regarding immigration and autonomy in economic matters."[106] But under pressure at home from Zionist supporters, Truman concluded that he would do well to issue a statement in support of the emigration of the 100,000 Jewish displaced persons to Palestine, which he did in the context of support for a partitioned Palestine. The statement, issued on October 4, 1946, came to be known as the Yom Kippur statement. Although controversy remains regarding the motives for Truman's pronouncement, it was heard as the president's undisguised support for partition.[107]

According to Evan Wilson, the Yom Kippur statement "was drafted primarily by Eliahu Epstein (later Elath), the Washington representative of the Jewish agency." But according to Michael Cohen, the draft that Epstein had worked on was altered in the State Department.[108] Nonetheless, it did not fail to be interpreted as evidence that the U.S. president supported partition.

How and why Epstein was in a position to draft a statement of such importance remains subject to speculation. The simplest explanation lies in Epstein's connections in White House circles with David Niles, and through him to Clark Clifford, and in his active role in meeting with State Department officials. Thus, when Epstein met with Henderson, Merriam, and Wilson on September 5, he confirmed that the Jewish Agency had come to the conclusion that it was prepared to accept partition. Nahum Goldmann maintains that through the intermediary of the president of the non-Zionist American Jewish Committee, Judge Proskauer, he had earlier persuaded members of the Anglo-American Committee to accept the principle of partition as the only solution to the existing dilemma in Palestine. Goldmann then consulted with David Niles who, with Acheson, conferred with Truman. "On the afternoon of August 9 Niles asked me to come to his hotel and told me with tears in his eyes that the President had accepted the plan without reservation and had instructed Dean Acheson to inform the British government."[109]

GORDON MERRIAM: CENSORED

In the eyes of State Department officials such as Gordon Merriam there was reason for tears, but they were not tears of joy. Merriam wrote a response to Truman's Yom Kippur statement, but when Loy Henderson showed it to Dean Acheson, he apparently called for Merriam's response to be destroyed. Merriam kept a copy, which he gave to Evan Wilson, who discussed its significance in his study on U.S. policy in Israel.[110] On the basis of Wilson's account, we learn that Merriam's daring pronouncements were, first, that the refugee problem required an international solution, and second, that agreement between Jews and Arabs in Palestine was a prerequisite to any policy. Acheson's fear lest

Merriam's statement become public knowledge is revealing, given the nature of what Merriam proposed. Merriam proved to be right insofar as the refugee problem was by its nature an international problem that could not be satisfactorily resolved by any single state. Intervening developments have served to reinforce the verity of Merriam's second proposition as well.

Wilson explained that Merriam agreed with the president's insistence on the admission of the 100,000 refugees to Palestine, but he insisted on the limits of such a policy "so long as there was no worldwide program aimed at solving the refugee problem and so long as there was no progress in the direction of an acceptable solution to the Palestine question as a whole."[111] More fundamental was his insistence on Jewish-Arab consensus as the basis of any policy. Merriam's reasons were straightforward:

> Otherwise we should violate the principle of self-determination which has been written into the Atlantic Charter, the Declaration of the United Nations, and the United Nations Charter—a principle that is deeply embedded in our foreign policy. Even a United Nations determination in favor of partition would be, in the absence of such consent, a stultification and violation of UN's own charter.[112]

Merriam returned to these themes in a critical analysis of U.S. policy in his year-end evaluation, which he submitted to Loy Henderson. In it, he described U.S. policy as one of expediency and claimed that it was unsatisfactory to all parties concerned.

Merriam and others in the State Department considered this U.S. policy to be inimical to U.S. interests because "it already handicaps and may eventually jeopardize our political and other interests in the Arab world."[113] Merriam pointed out that there was no satisfactory solution to the mandatory status of Palestine save independence, an independence that would have to satisfy both Jews and Arabs.

> 1. Palestine is an A Mandate. As such, it was to be prepared for independence. Were it not for the complication of the Jewish National Home, it would be independent today, as all the other A mandates have become. Arabs and Jews live there and must, sooner or later,

come to some sort of a political agreement based on a minimum of mutual confidence and give-and-take, if they are to govern Palestine.

2. The Jewish National Home was and is a new concept, undefined. The British statesmen who worked out the Balfour Declaration thought that the Jewish National Home would probably develop into a Jewish state, but they underestimated or misjudged the Arab reaction (Balfour did not realize that Arabs lived in Palestine).

3. The Jews could run Palestine if it were full of Jews; the Arabs if it were full of Arabs.

4. The Jewish DP problem, as well as the almost universal Jewish feeling of insecurity, presses powerfully and perhaps irresistibly upon Palestine in both the human and political sense.

5. The reception accorded by Arabs, Jews, or both, to the report of the Anglo-American Committee of Inquiry, to the Grady Mission plan—indeed, to all schemes and plans proposed by third parties— strongly indicates that no third-party plan has any chance of success, unless imposed and maintained by force.[114]

Merriam then turned to the principles that he argued "could appropriately constitute our Palestine policy."[115] What emerged from Merriam's recommendations was a Palestinian mandate transformed into a UN trusteeship, with a privileged position reserved for both the Trusteeship Council and the General Assembly, and a continuing role for the British.

Merriam's starting point was that the existing mandate—or trusteeship—was to be converted to independence as soon as possible, with interim arrangements arrived at through Arab-Jewish consensus in accord with UN principles, and authorized by the General Assembly on the Trusteeship Council's recommendation. Further, access to the Holy Places would be in the hands of the Trusteeship Council, working with the British, while issues pertinent to immigration and land would be resolved through the institutions created with Arab-Jewish accord, and once again subject to UNGA approval as recommended by the Trusteeship Council.

Merriam's second principle was the commitment of the United States to "support any political arrangement for Palestine agreed to as the result of the negotiations between Arabs and Jews and approved by the United Nations."[116]

This was followed by the third principle, which confirmed Britain's role as being responsible for the security of Palestine and, through it, the region until such time as the United Nations was in a position to assume such a position.

Finally, the fourth principle repeated the theme introduced earlier, according to which a UN trusteeship under British rule was to replace the mandate, and the recommendations of the international Committee on Refugees was to be taken into consideration.

Here it may be useful to recall that the leadership of the Jewish Agency, and Ben-Gurion in particular, were reported to have considered trusteeship in February 1947, some six months after accepting the idea of partition. Ben-Gurion is reported to have suggested a possible five-year trusteeship arrangement, provided certain conditions were met, including the transfer of 100,000 Jewish refugees to Palestine in an exchange with Lord Jowitt, the Lord Chancellor of Britain. According to Evan Wilson,

> Ben Gurion, in a meeting with the Lord Chancellor, Lord Jowitt, on February 13 agreed to a five year trusteeship during which the Jewish Agency would cease all agitation for a Jewish state, on condition that the one hundred thousand Jews would be admitted at once and that certain other demands would be met. The offer was too late. When it was put to the Cabinet the next day, Bevin announced that the decision had already been reached to place the matter before the United Nations.[117]

With respect to Merriam's position, Henderson wrote to Acheson suggesting that he read Merriam's memorandum, adding, "of course we have practically been forced by political pressure and sentiment in the U.S. in direction of a 'viable Jewish state.' I must confess that when I view our policy in light of principles avowed by U.S. I become uneasy."[118] Merriam's position in 1946 echoed that which he had co-authored in January 1945, when it was permissible to make the same recommendations, although it was to have no influence then or later.

Precisely how uneasy Henderson felt about U.S. policy in Palestine and the Middle East, more generally, was revealed in an undated memorandum he sent to Acheson, which appeared at the very beginning of the Foreign Relations Volume for 1946. Titled "Aspects of Thinking in the Department of State on Political and Economic Policies of the United States in the Near and Middle East," the memorandum offered a bitter criticism of the policies of the major powers, including the United States.[119] Henderson defined U.S. policy at the outset as committed to the survival of the United Nations and the equality of its members. He was critical of Washington for paying inadequate attention to the economic conditions of states in the Near East that had suffered during the war, comparing Washington's largesse toward Britain and the USSR to the little provided to the "small and backward peoples."[120] But it was U.S. policy toward Palestine that Henderson especially decried:

> The special interest of the United States in Palestine has also created the impression that the United States is not only willing to aid people of Jewish blood in a manner in which it would not be ready to assist other peoples of the Near East, but that it is prepared to back a political program in Palestine which is opposed by two-thirds of the people of that country, and by the neighboring countries.[121]

The result was inimical to U.S. policies in the area, Henderson warned in his racist comment. In place of such policies, Henderson recommended holding an international conference with the major powers, including Great Britain, France, and the Soviet Union. Without illusions as to the difficulties involved, Henderson feared that in the absence of such efforts there was a risk of war and the undermining of the United Nations.

What then was to be done? Henderson's pessimism was well placed, unlike his recommendations. The United Nations became deeply involved in the Palestine question, but not in the manner Henderson had suggested.

PART II

The Question of Partition and the Oil Connection, 1947–1948

Part II examines the period between passage of the November 29, 1947, partition resolution and the winter of 1948, when doubts about support for partition became increasingly important in policymaking circles. This led to the initiative taken by the Jewish Agency representative in his historic encounter with the director of the Oil and Gas Division of the Interior Department.

Chapter 3 introduces the key arguments that figured into the divisive debates on the partition of Palestine as viewed from the perspective of officials in the State Department and the Central Intelligence Agency. Chapter 4 provides a key to the turbulent period that followed as the Truman administration confronted the escalating violence that consumed Palestine after passage of UN General Assembly (UNGA) Resolution 181. Amid increasing doubts about the viability of partition, alternative views were aired, including the possibility of replacing partition with a UN trusteeship. The prospect alarmed the Jewish Agency, as chapter 5 indicates. It was in response to this prospect that the encounter between the director of the Oil and Gas Division of the Interior Department and the representative of the Jewish Agency led to talk of the hitherto unlikely possibility of an "oil connection," as this chapter demonstrates.

3

The Critical Year: 1947

WASHINGTON'S VIEW OF PARTITION

Dean Acheson, under secretary of state in 1947, concluded that "1947 is going to be a bad year in Palestine and the Middle East, with increasing violence and grave danger to our interests in that area."[1] Acheson's view reflected Anglo-American deliberations that similarly concluded that postwar economic conditions in the Middle East meant increasing poverty, depression, the intensification of class differences, and the ensuing risks of regional instability and radicalization.[2] The question of Palestine served to deepen existing antagonism in the Middle East toward the United States, and at home it did little to temper the debate on the future of partition.

U.S. interests—that is, continuing U.S. oil company access to Arab oil and defense arrangements—were under threat. Loy Henderson described Washington's predicament in facing the decision over partition in stark terms:

> We are learning that at this stage of industrial development oil, like food, is essential to the operation of our very economic life and to the maintenance of what we consider as civilization.
>
> In view of their economic and strategic importance the Middle East and Southeast Europe are prizes most tempting to an aggressive and ambitious great power. Such a power might well be able, if once in possession of the strategic facilities and economic resources

of this area, to decide the destinies of at least three continents and to cast a dark shadow over the whole world for many years to come.[3]

The *Oil and Gas Journal*, which reviewed Henderson's talk, emphasized that the strategic value of "the Persian Gulf oil area" was a function of its possibly more than 30 billion barrels of oil, which explained why its control by an "unfriendly power" threatened the present and future development of Western Europe, as well as Africa and Southern Asia.[4] In 1947 Henderson found himself among many in the State Department who were fearful of the potential damage partition of Palestine and a Jewish state could do to U.S. interests.

Opposition to partition was the common denominator among the president's top advisers, including "the formidable front of General Marshall, Under-Secretary of State Robert Lovett, Secretary of the Navy James Forrestal, Policy Planning Staff's George Kennan, State Department Counsel Charles Bohlen, and Marshall's successor as secretary, Dean Acheson."[5] Their position was unwavering.

Reflecting the views within the departments of State and Defense and the CIA, David Painter explained that U.S. officials feared

> that U.S. support for the creation of a Jewish state in Palestine could undermine relations with the Arab world, provide an opening for the Soviet Union to extend its power and influence, and lead to loss of access to Middle East oil at a time when the West needed it for European and Japanese reconstruction.[6]

Britain did not dispute this position, but it regarded U.S. diplomacy, notably in Palestine, as inept. They reminded their U.S. allies that for them Palestine represented an area that included some fifty million inhabitants living aside "the only possible communication routes between Europe, Asia, Africa and the Far East."[7]

Matters came to a head when the British brought the Palestine question to the United Nations in the spring of 1947. This led to establishment of the Special Committee on Palestine (UNSCOP), whose members toured Palestine, Lebanon, and Europe's Displaced Persons camps. When committee members returned to the UN, they outlined the position that became the basis for the UN General Assembly's partition resolution.

In mid-January 1947, Fraser Wilkins, who was Palestine desk officer, was among the U.S. officials on record as having supported the Anglo-American Committee Report of 1946. He did so persuaded of the "strategic and economic importance of American oil, aviation and telecommunications facilities in Palestine and neighboring countries."[8]

Wilkins did not overlook the population imbalance between the future Jewish state and its surrounding neighbors, and he recognized Arab opposition to partition. Wilkins nonetheless supported partition, believing that it offered a means of satisfying the "national aspirations" of both peoples, while excluding the Holy Places. Yet he also maintained that "Palestine would enjoy partial self-government under United Nations trusteeship"[9] prior to achieving its independence.

Acheson, on the other hand, frankly supported partition as the least undesirable option. Moshe Shertok, the future Israeli Foreign Minister, courted both Acheson and Henderson. Shertok sought to convince Acheson to endorse the immigration of 100,000 Jews to Palestine. Shertok also tried to convince Henderson of the economic importance of including the northern part of the Negev in a future Jewish state.[10] Henderson and Acheson concluded that partition would be "the solution which it would be easiest for the American government to support," in light of domestic factors and what they regarded as the inherent complexities of the problem.[11] Henderson, however, was not in favor of partition.

Partition was by no means the unanimous choice of Zionists in Palestine and the United States, where Chaim Weizmann and U.S. Rabbi Abba Hillel Silver clashed, the former favoring partition and the latter demanding "a Jewish state in the whole of Palestine."[12] David Ben-Gurion and the Labor Party ultimately emerged as victors in the debate in which the tactical advantages of partition trumped other options. In 1938, Ben-Gurion had "made the stunning acknowledgement that the entire presence of the Zionists in Palestine was 'politically' an aggression. The fighting, he said, 'is only one aspect of the conflict which is in its essence a political one. And politically we are the aggressors and they defend themselves.'"[13] By early September 1946, the Zionist Executive moved to accept partition, the position Eliahu Epstein reflected when he met with Henderson and other officials in the State Department's Near East Division.[14]

At this point in time, President Truman held that any change in Palestine required consultation with both Jews and Arabs. In communicating with the Saudi king, Truman affirmed U.S. respect and friendship for the king and his people and claimed that U.S. support for the Jewish National Home involved nothing inimical to Palestinian interests. Truman maintained that the United States "had no thought of embarking upon a policy which would be prejudicial to the interests of the indigenous population of Palestine."[15] The U.S. president insisted that "we would be firmly opposed to any solution of the Palestine problem which would permit a majority of the population to discriminate against a minority on religious, racial or other grounds."[16] Truman maintained that "responsible Jewish groups and leaders interested in developing the Jewish National Home in Palestine have no intention of expelling now or at a later date the indigenous inhabitants of that country or of using Palestine as a base for aggression against neighboring Arab states."[17]

Such pronouncements were politically tactful but bore little relation to practice as Truman moved to endorse partition. At the same time, Acheson and Henderson were deliberating on the risks that such a move entailed, despite its domestic advantages.

Washington insiders were critical of both Truman's deference to domestic politics and the State Department's narrow outlook. J. C. Hurewitz, who served as an expert on Palestine in the OSS, as an officer in the State Department's intelligence division, and as a political officer in the UN Department of Security Council Affairs, warned that "Jewish terrorism thrived as never before, despite the statutory martial law and the execution of condemned terrorists."[18] Hurewitz believed Truman was moved by election politics to emphasize the advantages of the admission of the 100,000 refugees into Palestine, even as he was inclined to liberalize immigration laws.

As for the State Department, Hurewitz maintained that it "had never developed an integrated American policy toward the Near East, into which Zionism, not in its most extreme form to be sure, could fit."[19] In practice, State Department officials looked to such liberal Zionists as Judah Magnes, recognizing, however, that they had little influence on the views of the Zionist leadership.

In London, the government found the case for partition wanting, preferring instead to support bi-nationalism, as Bevin argued in a parliamentary debate on February 25: "Either the Arabs in the partitioned State must always be an Arab minority, or else they must be driven out—the one thing or the other." Though his critics pointed out that he could just as well have developed the same case for a Jewish minority in an Arab state, Bevin argued that a bi-national state would best secure the "national home" promised by the Balfour Declaration.[20]

It was in April that London took the initiative to bring the Palestine question before the United Nations General Assembly, inaugurating a new phase in its evolution. The UN Special Committee on Palestine (UNSCOP) was established to examine the overall Palestinian situation, and it eventually endorsed the majority plan that favored partition with economic union, the internationalization of Jerusalem, and independence to follow within a two-year period. Those favoring the majority position included Canada, Czechoslovakia, Guatemala, Netherlands, Peru, Sweden, and Uruguay. The minority plan, representing the positions of Iran, India, and Yugoslavia, opposed partition and the accompanying land distribution as depriving the future Arab state of essential resources, pointing out that "the Arabs constitute a majority of the population of the proposed Jewish State, and own the bulk of the land."[21] Its members favored federation. As to the problem of European refugees, they argued that it was "not strictly relevant to the Palestine problem," which it would serve to complicate.[22]

Palestinian Arabs rejected UNSCOP's deliberations and, specifically, partition. UNSCOP then turned to Arab League diplomats. In September, members of the Arab Higher Committee testified before the UN Special Committee, offering a plan akin to the minority plan that they viewed as supporting the integrity of Palestine under a federal state.

The United States chose to ignore the fundamental question raised by the Arab Higher Committee—that is, the legitimacy of considering partition without the consent of the majority. Instead, it supported the majority plan, according to which UNSCOP assigned the proposed Jewish state a population of some 1,008,800, with 509,780 Arabs and 499,020 Jews.[23] Conceived at a time when the Jews of Palestine "owned less than six percent of the total land area of Palestine and constituted no more than one third of the population," the arrangement aroused opposition among Palestinians and other Arabs.[24] And, as the minority report pointed out, of the three areas allocated to the Jewish state, two included regions heavily dominated by Arab populations. In the southern Negev around Beersheba "there are 1,020 Jews as against an Arab population of 103,820," and in eastern Galilee, "the Arab population is three times as great as the Jewish population (86,200 as against 28,750)."[25] The only area where Jews were in a majority was in the center, and well within the cities of Tel Aviv and Petah Tiqva.

The conception of Palestine envisaged in the minority report was of a unitary state with a constitution providing representation at the legislative, executive, and judicial levels in accord with population, the whole designed to protect minorities with their participation and consent. For the UNSCOP members who favored the minority position, there was satisfaction in knowing that populations such as those in urban centers that were totally mixed would continue to live as they had. "Apart from Tel Aviv, which is a totally Jewish town, in practically all the other towns such as Haifa, Tiberias and Safad, the Jewish population is completely intermixed with the Arab population and it would be impossible to draw boundaries separating them from each other."[26]

Other proposals concerning European refugees were put forth by Arab representatives at the United Nations in 1947. Arab ambassadors, along with those representing Afghanistan, Colombia, and Pakistan, joined in a subcommittee to oppose partition and proposed a solution to the situation of European Jewish refugees. "The gist of the resolution, put to the General Assembly for a vote, was that the task of finding a home for the refugees should be equitably shared," which was not the case at the present time, as the subcommittee members pointed to the "disproportionately large number of Jewish immigrants" absorbed by Palestine as compared to other countries.[27]

In Washington, Henderson was frankly opposed to partition and the creation of a Jewish state. He reviewed U.S. arguments in a position paper titled "Certain Considerations Against Advocacy by the U.S. of the Majority Plan," in which he summarized U.S. views, including that partition could endanger U.S. interests in aviation and petroleum. In addition, as Henderson pointed out, the U.S. position was that partition risked promoting the emergence of "fanatical extremists" in the Arab world, simultaneously alienating those who could be useful in curbing nationalist uprisings across North Africa.[28]

The only viable position, according to Henderson, was one based on consensus between Arab and Jewish moderates who might come to agree on a trusteeship arrangement. Several years later "there could be a plebiscite on the question of partition, in the light of which the General Assembly could make its final decision on this fateful question. Any kind of temporary arrangement should probably provide for immediate Jewish immigration of at least 100,000 persons."[29]

Henderson reflected on different facets of partition, its historical, legal, and political dimensions, concluding that it had no backing in international law, the UN Charter, or American domestic law.[30] He identified proposals that ignore "self-determination and majority rule" and that recognize "a theocratic racial state" as inimical to U.S. foreign policy, insisting that "whether persons are Jews or non-Jews is certain to strengthen feelings among both Jews and Gentiles in the United States and elsewhere that Jewish citizens are not the same as other citizens."[31]

Years later, in an interview with Richard McKinzie, Henderson took issue with the claim that there had been anti-Jewish sentiment among his colleagues in the State Department.

> I believe and I am including personnel in offices other than my own office, that thought the establishment of a Jewish State in Palestine by sheer force would cause endless trouble for Arabs, Jews, and the United States and might eventually even lead to wars in which the United States might become involved. The Policy Planning Staff in the Department, according to my recollection, made a study of the Palestine problem which resulted in recommendations similar to those made by us.[32]

Henderson speculated about key figures in the Department such as Dean Rusk, admitting that while he could not speak for him, he "was confident that Dean Rusk also thought that the establishment by force of a Jewish State in Palestine would be a mistake."[33] He also noted that both Dean Acheson and Robert Lovett were "careful never to approve the views expressed by my office, they were continually asking for them and encouraging us to give them voluntarily."[34]

Henderson was present and privy to the conflicts surrounding support for the majority plan, which passed with U.S. backing. He explained his position to Secretary of State Marshall (who had replaced Byrnes in 1947) among others on September 15, 1947, when he argued that without acceptance by the Arab world, violence, suffering, a diminishing status of the United States in the Arab world, and a corresponding increase in Soviet influence were to be expected. Henderson had been consistent in his opposition to partition and statehood and had supported the immigration of Jewish refugees to the United States and other countries.

> Some people may think that I had no sympathy for those poor refugees looking for a place to go. I, in fact, had deep sympathy for them, but it seemed to me at the time that civilized countries throughout the world should lower their immigration barriers and welcome them. The United States, Canada, Australia, a number of Latin-American countries could have made room for them.[35]

Moreover, he predicted that Jews who did get to Palestine would encounter a hostile environment and would displace Palestinians, who would "become refugees, homeless and miserable. I used the word 'displacing' because I could not conceive how there could be a Jewish State in Palestine unless many members of the Arab majority were pushed out."[36] What Henderson was referring to was the policy of "transfer," which had figured in the Peel Commission Report of 1937 and was not foreign to Zionist thought.[37]

THE QUESTION OF "TRANSFER"

Describing the forced displacement of populations as "transfer" made it appear to be a voluntary and pacific undertaking, when in practice it was neither. It was not unique to the Palestinian case, but it played a critical role in the evolution of the Palestinian question as it was an integral part of Zionist planning. In October 1941, Ben-Gurion "formulated a blueprint for future Zionist policy, in which he expatiated at length about the possibilities of transfer."[38] Shertok and Weizmann were advocates of transfer as well.

Observing that "there are 40% non-Jews in the areas allocated to the Jewish state," Ben-Gurion believed that "this composition is not a solid basis for a Jewish state. And we have to face this new reality with all its severity and distinctness. Such a demographic balance questions our ability to maintain Jewish sovereignty. . . . Only a state with at least 80% Jews is a viable and stable state."[39] Palestinians who were within the area of the Jewish state could constitute a risk, and therefore "they can either be mass arrested or expelled; it is better to expel them."[40] Yet the idea of transfer remained "morally problematic" among Zionists, particularly as they recognized that Palestinian Arabs represented a distinct national identity that would interfere with the resettlement of Palestinians elsewhere.[41]

Zionist leaders eventually accepted Ben-Gurion's view of transfer as an indispensable aspect of Zionist policy. What it meant for Palestinians was the creation of conditions leading to flight and expulsion, which was at the root of the Palestinian refugee problem. Josef Weitz, director of the Jewish National Fund in charge of transfer policy, was convinced that there was no room in the future State of Israel for Palestinian Arabs and Jews. As he wrote in 1941, "except perhaps for Bethlehem, Nazareth, and Old Jerusalem we must not leave a single village, not a single tribe. And the transfer must be directed to Iraq, to Syria, and even to Transjordan."[42] Among those who were engaged by Weitz to implement such plans was Moshe Shertok. Two weeks after the declaration of Israeli independence, a committee was established to implement the plan that led to the "actual destruction of Palestinian villages," as Weitz later conceded.[43]

Sixty-six years later, an Israeli journalist recalled the conquest and expulsion of the Palestinian population of Lydda as a necessary part of the Zionist revolution, without which there would have been no state.[44] It was a position to which Benny Morris subscribed as well, then and later.[45]

In 1947, Bevin continued to oppose partition, basing his position on demographic considerations. He regarded U.S. policy in Palestine as an additional burden on Britain's already difficult situation. He did not mute his criticism of U.S. support or tolerance for "the terrorists in Palestine," who "received the bulk of their financial and moral support from the United States."[46] Such support extended to organizations that "carried on extensive publicity campaigns with the purpose of encouraging the Palestinian terrorists and the smugglers of illegal immigrants and of discrediting the attempts of the British

Government to maintain law and order." Bevin conceded that efforts by his government to "prevail upon the American Government to take steps to prevent American encouragement of terrorists and illegal activities in Palestine" had failed.[47]

While U.S. officials continued to deliberate on U.S. policy in Palestine, the Jewish Agency proceeded with plans for a clandestine meeting with the king of Transjordan. Washington was aware of these plans and supported them. On November 17, Jewish Agency officials, including Elihau Sasson, Ezra Danin, and Golda Meyerson, met secretly with King Abdullah of Transjordan on the border between Transjordan and Palestine.

The king agreed to the partition of Palestine as long as it did not discredit him in the eyes of the Arabs. He said that he did not wish to fight the Jews or to cooperate with their adversaries and that he was prepared to help them oust the Mufti, Haj Amin al-Husseini. King Abdullah declared that he was opposed to the establishment of a separate Arab state in Palestine and inquired what the Jewish attitude would be if he attempted to seize the Arab part of the country. The representatives of the Jewish Agency replied that they would welcome such a step if it was explained as a temporary measure. The king added that he would be prepared to sign an agreement with the Jews if they helped him to annex the Arab part of Palestine to his kingdom, in conformity with his plan to establish a Greater Syria. He also suggested that the Jewish state might later join Transjordan in a union, with a common economy, army, and parliament.[48]

Ilan Pappé points out that "the Jews never promised Abdullah the whole area allocated to the Arab state by the UN, but asked him to decide first, as indeed he did, which parts were vital to him."[49] Abdullah, in turn, obtained the agreement of his Jewish interlocutors not to dispute his selection, agreeing not to attack Jewish controlled territory. Such arrangements, some maintained, were known to the British who approved them despite their overt violation of UN Resolution 181.[50]

Washington was aware of and supported these secret arrangements. It recognized the Arab Legion's role in Palestine and eventually supported recognition of Transjordan and its admission to the United Nations.

CRISIS AT THE UN: McCLINTOCK AND THE CIA
CONSIDER PALESTINE

On October 11, 1947, the U.S. representative to the United Nations Special Committee, Warren Austin, announced U.S. support for UNSCOP's majority plan, adding a reservation that came as a shock to the White House. As Austin declared, "we consider that certain amendments and modifications should be made in the plan in order to give effect to the principles on which it is based."[51] Austin reiterated the view that a solution to the Palestinian problem rested with its people, while insisting on the role of the General Assembly in offering a just solution acceptable to international opinion. Predictably, Austin's statement roused a storm in Washington, where Truman interpreted it as damaging the U.S. position and his own credibility.

Henderson's office was directly implicated in the controversy. Henderson insisted on taking responsibility for the position presented, explaining in his 1973 interview that "I contributed to it, and since I approved the final draft, I did not hesitate to take personal responsibility for it when the question of authorship was raised."[52] Henderson also pointed out that the final statement was a collective effort "worked on by members of my office, of the Office of Special Political Affairs, of the Legal Adviser's Office, and by personnel from the economic areas."[53]

Henderson further recalled that with the approval of the secretary and under secretary, who had shown the document to the president, Henderson was informed that "the President had read the document, approved it, and had suggested that it be sent to Ambassador Austin with the suggestion that when he came to the conclusion that the time had come for him to deliver the speech, he was authorized to do so."[54] Austin acted and the president reacted, but not as Henderson and others expected. Truman claimed not to have been consulted.

Toward the end of October, Robert McClintock, then special assistant to Dean Rusk, observed that "if the Partition Plan fails of acceptance at this assembly [General Assembly] we shall be involved in a most unpleasant mess."[55] McClintock thought a compromise based on the minority report of UNSCOP would encounter staunch Jewish opposition, and given both U.S. and Soviet support for partition, it would have little chance of passage. As a result, McClintock counseled support for the majority plan, in short, for partition, with amendments to mollify the Arabs. McClintock indicated that he had discussed another option, the so-called Greater Syria scheme, with U.S. Ambassador George Wadsworth. According to Wadsworth, this plan would allow for the absorption of Palestinian Arabs, leaving a "Jewish State in the Holy Land."[56] If that failed, another option was the Iraq irrigation project, which could similarly be offered to Palestinians. McClintock's cynicism was reflected in his further suggestion regarding immigration:

> As a sop to the Arabs I would propose that there be no Jewish immigration into Palestine in the interim period. After all, the Jews have been waiting 2000 years to get back to Palestine and they certainly can wait eight months before resumption of immigration on a controlled but increased scale.[57]

More than a year before the Defense Department concluded that Jewish military forces represented a promising element, McClintock reported that he had been informed that "the Commandos of the Irgun and Stern organizations are exceedingly tough and well trained and that, in sum, the Jewish military strength is considerable. Opposing this strength it would seem that the Arabs also can muster forces which would make up in fanaticism and courage what they might lack in training in modern warfare."[58]

CIA ASSESSMENTS OF THE PALESTINE QUESTION

At about the same time, the CIA cautioned against the expansion of Soviet influence and the risks to U.S. interests in the Middle East. In its October 1947 report, the agency maintained that

> Arab determination to resist the partition of Palestine is such that any attempt to enforce that solution would lead to armed conflict, presenting an opportunity for the extension of Soviet influence. Any firm establishment of Soviet influence in the Arab states would not only be dangerous in itself, it would also tend to isolate Turkey and Iran. Furthermore, irrespective of the possibility of Soviet penetration of this area, U.S. support of the partition of Palestine might lead the

Arab states, on their own, to take steps which would adversely affect U.S. economic and strategic interests in their territories.[59]

Within a matter of days, the CIA warned that "the seemingly insoluble Palestine problem, because of the ever-present possibility of widespread civil and para-military strife, threatens the stability not only of Palestine but of the entire Arab world as well."[60]

> Rightly or wrongly, the Arabs feel that the establishment of a Zion-ist state endangers their sovereignty and independence, and they are therefore determined to oppose it with all the means at their disposal. Even if this opposition does not result in the immediate can-cellation of U.S. oil concessions in Arab lands, it will almost certainly lead to such unrest and instability that Soviet infiltration will increase and may eventually achieve the same result.[61]

The Joint Chiefs of Staff were of the same opinion, concerned lest U.S. interests in the Middle East and the Gulf be undermined as a result of partition, which would additionally enhance the position of the USSR in the area.[62]

The United Nations General Assembly (UNGA) prepared to vote on the majority plan with the help of high-level U.S. manipulation of votes toward the end of November.[63] Henderson recalled pressure being put on the Firestone Rubber Company and its host country, Liberia; Greeks in New York claimed similar pressure. Henderson also recalled the "great pressure" to which he and Robert Lovett were subject to ensure UN votes; in addition, Henderson pointed out that "Felix Frankfurter and Justice Murphy had both sent messages to the Philippine delegate to the General Assembly strongly urging his vote."[64]

During the same period Warren Austin's assistant, Herschel Johnson, informed Henderson that "the President had instructed him [David Niles] to tell us that, by God, he wanted us to get busy and get all the votes that we possibly could; that there would be hell if the voting went the wrong way."[65]

One day before the passage of the UN partition plan, on November 29, 1947, the CIA issued a comprehensive review of "The Consequences of the Partition of Palestine," which was unequivocally pessimistic in its assessment of the likely outcome of a UN vote in support of partition. The reasons were to be found in the agency's assessment of Zionist objectives and anticipated Palestinian and Arab reactions.

> In the long run no Zionists in Palestine will be satisfied with the territorial arrangements of the partition settlement. Even the more conservative Zionists will hope to obtain the whole of the Nejeb [Negev], Western Galilee, the city of Jerusalem, and eventually all of Palestine. The extremists demand not only all of Palestine but Transjordan as well. They have stated that they will refuse to recognize the validity of any Jewish government which will settle for anything less, and will probably undertake aggressive action to achieve their ends.[66]

The CIA believed this policy would be pursued at an international level with a Zionist propaganda campaign and Arab atrocities in the aftermath of partition.

> The Zionists will continue to wage a strong propaganda campaign in the U.S. and in Europe. The "injustice" of the proposed Jewish boundaries will be exaggerated, and the demand for more territory will be made as Jewish immigration floods the Jewish sector. In the chaos which will follow the implementation of partition, atrocities will undoubtedly be committed by Arab fanatics; such actions will be given wide publicity and will even be exaggerated by Jewish propaganda. The Arabs will be accused of aggression, whatever the actual circumstances may be. This propaganda campaign will doubtless continue to influence the U.S. public, and the U.S. Government may, consequently, be forced into actions which will further complicate and embitter its relations with the entire Arab world.[67]

The CIA described Palestinians and Arabs as supportive of nationalist movements across the Arab world whose "political aims are the independence of all Arab lands and the establishment of some degree of unity among them."[68] This applied to Palestinian nationalists, whose anti-Zionist position was supported across the Arab Middle East. This sentiment was directed at the feared establishment of a Jewish state, which was viewed as the prelude to more extensive Jewish control whose political and cultural aims were at the root of Arab opposition.

The CIA maintained that religious movements, such as the Ikhwan al Muslimin (Muslim Brotherhood), were critical to such forces, pointing out that "the Arabs are capable of a religious fanaticism which when coupled with political aspirations is an extremely powerful force."[69] But it is significant that in the agency's view the problem was political not religious in origin.

> The Arabs violently oppose the establishment of a Jewish state in Palestine because they believe that Palestine is an integral part of the Arab world. In addition, they fear that the Jews will consolidate their position through unlimited immigration and that they will attempt to expand until they become a threat to the newly won independence of each of the other Arab countries. They believe that not only politically but also culturally the Jewish state threatens the continued development of the Islamic-Arab civilization. For these reasons, the Arab governments will not consider any compromise, and they categorically reject any scheme which would set up a Jewish state in Palestine.[70]

The Agency predicted that Arab governments would not openly defy the UN support for partition, although they would support the Arabs who joined militias fighting Zionism. However, the CIA also argued that Jews living in Arab states would be victimized by these developments, citing attacks on Iraqi Jews in Baghdad in 1941. The agency reproduced a Jewish Agency statement "that in the event of partition the 400,000 Jews in the Arab states outside Palestine may have to be sacrificed in the interest of the Jewish community as a whole."[71]

In addition to its political evaluation, the CIA produced a comprehensive analysis of military forces operating in the conflict. They confirmed the superiority of Jewish forces with respect to numbers, organization, and equipment, with an "excellent intelligence system" and "high standard of security," as well as an effective "clandestine radio" service.[72]

Described as being divided in three groups distinguished by "their tactics and in the degree of ruthlessness employed in their operations," the CIA reported favorably on the largest group, the Haganah, as defensive, with "non-extremist intentions," and as numbering some 70,000–90,000, with the capacity to mobilize a total of 200,000.[73] The Irgun was described as "rightist in political sympathy," its followers "well armed and trained in sabotage, particularly in the use of explosives."[74] Its ultimate aim, "an independent state in Palestine and Transjordan."[75] The Stern Gang, in turn, was described as sympathetic to the USSR due to their common anti-British and anti-imperialist positions. They had an estimated "400 to 500 extreme fanatics. They do not hesitate to assassinate government officials and police officers or to obtain funds by acts of violence against Jews as well as others."[76]

The contrast between Jewish and Arab forces, according to CIA assessments, was striking. The agency anticipated that the largest number of Arab forces engaged against the Zionists "will be between 100,000 and 200,000, including Palestine Arab volunteers, Beduin, and quasi-military organizations from the other Arab states."[77] Arabs in Palestine numbered roughly 33,000 men drawn from "quasi-military organizations as the Futuwwa, the Najjada, the Arab Youth Organization, and the Ikwan (Moslem Brotherhood)."[78] The latter, identified as being located in Egypt and Syria, were expected to send volunteers as well, numbering some 15,000 and 10,000, respectively.[79] The cumulative number of Arab forces from neighboring states was estimated at some 223,000 men, in addition to the limited naval and air forces available.

The CIA emphasized the role of guerrilla warfare and assumed Arab superiority, in large part as a function of what the agency perceived to be the more primitive nature of Arab fighting forces and their knowledge of the terrain. Unlike the Jews, the CIA report maintained, the Arab was an experienced guerrilla fighter and "tribesmen will engage in activities not requiring technical training or extensive coordination such as attacks on isolated villages, assassination, continual sniping to prevent cultivation of the fields, and attacks on transportation, communications, and supply lines."[80] The agency maintained that the Arabs had leftover U.S. and UK arms that were adequate and were well equipped for guerrilla warfare.

More recent estimates by scholars such as Avi Shlaim and Walid Khalidi have contributed to our knowledge of the imbalance of forces in this period. Shlaim stated that Jewish forces were "better prepared, better mobilized, and better organized when the struggle for Palestine reached its crucial stage than its local opponents."[81] In compiling data for the period January 15, 1948, to May 15, 1948, Khalidi distinguished between forces trained by the Arab Liberation Army and forces sent by Arab states. The Arab Liberation Army numbered 3,830 volunteers, of which about 1,000 were Palestinians.[82] "These units entered Palestine only gradually and over a period of four months. About 1500 entered in January 1948, 500 in February, 1000 in March and the balance in April and the first half of May."[83] Arab forces sent by Arab states on the day of Israel's declaration of independence, May 15, 1948, "numbered 8 brigades, whose total strength was rather less than 15,000."[84]

In its report, the CIA predicted that the Soviets, who sought the exit of the British and continued instability in the area, would focus on providing arms and assistance primarily but not exclusively to Jewish forces. Instability would discourage investment and commercial activity, and along with partition might undermine U.S. involvement in the economic development of the region. The agency considered it unlikely that Arab regimes would cancel oil contracts, citing the Saudi delegate who, at the Arab League meeting in Alley, Lebanon, announced that "the oil companies were private corporations and did not represent the U.S. Government, [and] opposed the Iraqi delegate's stand that the contracts should be cancelled."[85] The Saudi position was designed to absolve the king from overt complicity with Washington's stance in favor of partition. The CIA report concluded, however, that this did not eliminate the risk of having oil installations and "occasional Americans" attacked by "irresponsible tribesmen and fanatic Moslems," which would discourage Arab regimes from agreeing to further contracts.[86]

In retrospect, the CIA maintained that the political disruption caused by partition would increase poverty and political despair, thus opening the door to communist propaganda. Furthermore, despite its positive evaluation of Jewish military forces, the CIA concluded that they would be unable to survive a "war of attrition," and without external assistance, they would not last longer than two years.[87]

In February 1948, the CIA once again reviewed the situation in Palestine, predicting a permanent conflict resulting from the incompatible aims of Zionists and Palestinian and Arab nationalists. In this scenario, Zionists would fight to expand the territory under their control, and the consequences of the conflict would extend beyond Palestine.

Several days before the UNGA passage of the Partition Resolution on November 29, 1947, Truman "approved a paper stating that the security of the Eastern Mediterranean and of the Middle East was 'vital to the security of the United States.'"[88] The formula was to become standard fare in official references to U.S. policy in the Middle East, a reminder of priorities.

The UNGA voted in favor of Resolution 181 for partition of Palestine into a Jewish and Arab state by a vote of 33 in favor, 13 against, and 10 abstaining.[89] The nonbinding resolution recommended establishment of two states to be bound by an economic union. The future Jewish state was allotted 56 percent of Palestine, and the future Palestinian Arab state received 44 percent of Palestine. The discrepancy with respect to the population–land ratio was stark as Jews constituted less than one third of the population and owned only 7 percent of the land, whereas Palestinian Arabs made up an estimated 95 percent of the population and owned up to 93 percent of Palestinian land. The United States voted in favor of the UNGA resolution as did the USSR, which caused consternation and confusion among communist parties in the Arab world, who followed suit, including the Palestinian Communist Party.[90]

In Palestine, the partition proposal was met with adamant opposition by the Arab Higher Committee, and across the Arab world representatives of Egypt, Iraq, Lebanon, Saudi Arabia, Syria, Transjordan, and Yemen condemned the UN resolution as null and void. They vowed to adopt measures to "defeat the unjust partition plan and give support to the right of the Arabs."[91] Transjordan's exceptional situation did not prevent it from taking a public stance in common with other Arab states.

Strikes, demonstrations, and attacks on Jewish commercial centers and other areas accelerated with the entry of Arab volunteers. At a meeting of the Arab League held in Lebanon, plans were made for the Palestinians to be responsible for their own defense, and "the Arab governments would furnish their share of military financing (Egypt, 42 per cent; Iraq, 7 percent; Lebanon, 11 per cent; Saudi Arabia, 20 percent; Syria, 12 percent; Iraq, 7 percent; and Yemen, 3 per cent)" in addition to promising to station their armies on the Palestinian frontier.[92]

Pablo de Azcarate, who was to become the UN's deputy principal secretary of the Palestine Commission, concluded shortly after passage of the UNGA resolution that with this event partition and establishment of a Jewish state were all but assured.[93]

Assessments by U.S. intelligence as well as State Department officials recognized that despite vehement expressions of opposition, neither Egypt nor Saudi Arabia was prepared to take decisive action against U.S. or British interests. Egypt was simultaneously seeking to curtail Britain's demands for continuing access to Suez-Cairo and Dhahran airfields, while dealing with domestic opposition in the form of labor strikes. In Riyadh, the Saudi monarch was keen to maintain a relationship of friendship with the British, as well as the United States, hoping thereby to prevent the emergence of a rival Hashemite order.

Insofar as Zionist objectives were concerned, the leader of the Labor Party, Ben-Gurion, had made his position clear months earlier. In a speech delivered before the People's Council on May 22, 1947, he asked—albeit in a rhetorical manner—whether anyone doubted that the meaning of the Balfour Declaration, the mandate, as well as the millenarian yearning of the Jewish people was to establish "a Jewish state in the whole of Eretz-Israel."[94] Insofar as borders were concerned, they were not final. Acceptance of UN Res. 181 was a tactical move that left the question of how to deal with problematic conditions, such as those involving population, to be resolved by force. Nearly a month prior to the UNGA vote on partition, Ben-Gurion had "addressed the question of how most effectively to assure the demographic basis of a future Jewish state. The Palestinians inside the Jewish state could become a fifth column, he claimed and so to avoid this, 'they can either be mass arrested or expelled; it is better to expel them.' "[95]

In the month following the partition resolution, Ben-Gurion advocated "aggressive defense; with every Arab attack we must respond with a decisive blow; the destruction of the place or the expulsion of the residents along with the seizure of the place."[96] The consequences, Ben-Gurion observed, would "increase the Arabs' fear and external help for the Arabs will be ineffective."[97] The means used included the destruction of urban infrastructure and the accompanying demoralization of the population, and the "outright intimidation and exploitation of panic caused by dissident underground terrorism; and finally, and most decisively, the destruction of whole villages and the eviction of their inhabitants by the army."[98]

Ben-Gurion's diary for December 11, 1947, reported that

> Arabs are fleeing from Jaffa and Haifa. Bedouin are fleeing from the Sharon. Most are seeking refuge with members of their family. Villagers are returning to their villages. Leaders are also in flight, most of them are taking their families to Nablus, Nazareth. The Bedouin are moving to Arab areas.
>
> According to our "friends" [advisers], every response to our dealing a hard blow at the Arabs with many casualties is a blessing. This will increase the Arabs' fear and external help for the Arabs will be ineffective. To what extent will stopping transportation cramp the Arabs? The fellahin [peasants] won't suffer, but city dwellers will. The country dwellers don't want to join the disturbances, unless dragged in by force. A vigorous response will strengthen the refusal of the peasants to participate in the battle. Josh Palmon [an adviser to Ben-Gurion on Arab affairs] thinks that Haifa and Jaffa will be evacuated [by the Arabs] because of hunger.[99]

Ben-Gurion's entry coincided with resolve on the part of U.S. officials in the National Security Council to clarify U.S. policy in Palestine.

From Jerusalem, U.S. Consul Robert B. Macatee (1946–1948) offered his assessment of conditions at the end of 1947, followed by a description of the Jewish, Arab, and British situations. As Macatee wrote to Marshall,

> terror is prevalent and normal, life (i.e. normal for Palestine) is disappearing. It is, however, compared with what may be expected in future, a period of relative quiet and restraint. This phase may continue until the withdrawal of the British is more imminent and until the Arabs have made more definite plans to give effect to their determination to prevent partition. Present outbursts are, it is felt, comparatively unimportant and disorganized and are merely the inevitable concomitants of a situation that is tense and waiting. They are prompted by hatred of the Jews mixed with feelings of intense patriotism, and may be expected to increase.[100]

Describing the situation of Jews in Palestine, Macatee wrote of random attacks in which "they are picked off while riding in buses, walking along the streets and stray shots even find them while asleep in their beds. A Jewish woman, mother of five children, was shot in Jerusalem while hanging out clothes on the roof. The ambulance rushing her to the hospital was machine-gunned, and finally the mourners following her to the funeral were attacked and one of them stabbed to death."[101] He cited attacks on trains, the theft of food, the existence of an arms market, the desertion from British mandatory service, and the evidence of coordination between Palestinian and Arab Legion members. In a telling aside, Macatee suggested that while the Jewish Agency had not called for "organized defense," the recent attacks that involved Mrs. Golda Myerson, a prominent Labor Zionist, "may give the JA an excuse for setting up an active defense against the Arabs."[102]

Uri Bialer observes that the situation in which the Jewish Agency found itself worsened as a result of the UN partition resolution. The leadership turned to arms acquisition, which led to Czechoslovakia. Ben-Gurion had foreseen the need for arms a year earlier in a statement he made before the Judicial Committee of the Zionist Congress. In December 1946, Ben-Gurion had observed that

> the major problem is defense. Until recently it was only a question of defending ourselves against the Palestinian Arabs who occasionally attacked Jewish settlements. But now we confront a totally new situation. Israel is surrounded by independent Arab states . . . which have . . . the capacity to acquire arms. . . . While the . . . Palestinian Arabs do not endanger the Jewish community, we now face the prospect of the Arab states sending their armies to attack us. . . . We are facing a threat to our very existence.[103]

Within a matter of months following the passage of UNGA Res. 181, U.S. officials conceded that outside intervention would probably be necessary for its implementation, and short of such action a radical reconsideration of U.S. policy might be necessary. In response to news of Washington's growing doubts about partition, the American Zionist Emergency Council mobilized supporters to flood the White House with mail in support of partition and arranged for state legislatures to pass "resolutions favoring a Jewish state in Palestine. Forty governors and more than half the Congress signed petitions to the President."[104]

In early January 1948, Fraser Wilkins hosted an exchange between two representatives from the Jewish Agency, Abba Eban and Eliahu Epstein, and three key figures responsible for Near Eastern affairs, Gordon Merriam (chief of the Division of Near Eastern Affairs), Dean Rusk (director of the Office of Special Political Affairs), and Loy Henderson (director of the Near Eastern Affairs Division). According to Wilkins's memo, Epstein and Eban visited the U.S. officials separately "for the purpose of reporting current developments with regard to Palestine and eliciting the further support of the United States Government in implementation of the recent UN recommendation to partition Palestine."[105]

Henderson was concerned about the outbreak of violence at the Haifa refinery, a matter of concern to the British and the Americans because of the IPC oil company connection. Eban and Epstein urged the United States to issue a public statement denouncing such violence. Eban emphasized the urgency of arming the Haganah, which would stabilize the area. U.S. officials may have been unaware of Jewish–Arab relations in the Haifa refinery, which "had a history of close cooperation between Arab and Jewish unionists" before the outbreak of violence.[106] Furthermore, did U.S. officials know about the attacks carried out by Jewish military forces that led to "the collapse and surrender of Haifa, Jaffa, Tiberias, Safed, Acred, Beit-Shan, Lydda, Ramleh, Majdal, and Beersheba"?[107]

4

The Winter of Discontent: 1948

RECONSIDERING PARTITION AND ADMITTING FAILURE

It was in this context that in the winter of 1948, U.S. officials decided to reconsider partition, emphasizing that the UN partition resolution was but a recommendation. Its implementation, as Robert McClintock recognized, would satisfy neither Jews nor Arabs. But turning the Palestine question over to the United Nations was no simple matter. The risk was that the Palestine case might then be brought before the International Court, which the State Department's legal adviser feared. Ernest Gross counseled Dean Rusk "not to support a motion in Security Council to refer any question on Palestine to the International Court."[1] At stake in any such action was the very question of the legitimacy of United Nations General Assembly (UNGA) Resolution 181.

Yet there was no disputing the cascade of negative reports coming from U.S. officials, such that by February 1948 there was broad consensus that the existing situation was untenable. In sum, McClintock and others had now arrived at the position advocated by Loy Henderson and Gordon Merriam in 1946—according to which a trusteeship arrangement was preferable to violent stalemate.

Among the most consistent critics of partition was George Kennan, who issued a number of reports on U.S. policy as director of the Policy Planning Staff (PPS).[2] PPS/19 of January 19, 1948, composed with the assistance of Loy Henderson and Ambassador Henry Grady, underlined the fact that Resolution 181 "left unanswered certain questions regarding the legality of the plan as well as the means for its implementation."[3] Kennan's position reflected his fear that support for partition in the absence of an Arab–Jewish consensus would endanger U.S. interests.

> Palestine occupies a geographic position of great strategic significance to the U.S. It is important for the control of the eastern end of the Mediterranean and the Suez Canal. It is an outlet for the oil of the Middle East which, in turn, is important to U.S. security. Finally, it is the center of a number of major political cross-currents; and events in Palestine cannot help being reflected in a number of directions.[4]

Samuel K. C. Kopper was among those preoccupied with the evident difficulties facing partition. In his capacity as specialist on the Arab world, Kopper was a member of Philip Jessup's team of advisers at the United Nations. At the end of January he wrote a memorandum arguing that "there is no clear cut solution to the Palestine problem which would be completely acceptable to all parties."[5] Kopper advocated for a trusteeship, emphasizing that the original UNGA Resolution 181 was a recommendation. Under existing circumstances in Palestine, he maintained, "there are serious doubts as to whether the Arabs of Palestine are under any obligations whatsoever, legal or moral, to be bound by the General Assembly recommendations."[6] In place of the existing resolution, Kopper suggested that the U.S. endorse "a new solution in the form of (1) a transitional trusteeship or (2) a Federal State with liberal immigration provisions."[7] Short of this, Kopper urged the U.S. to assume a "passive role until our policy can be altered or until the situation makes or breaks partition as a solution."[8] Kopper's recommendations appear to have had no influence on U.S. policy.

In Palestine, members of the Arab Liberation Army carried out attacks against Jewish settlements and the convoys sent to assist them. By February, the number of volunteers arriving had reached some three thousand, when the "Irgun used a car bomb to blow up a government center in Jaffa," and later placed explosives at the Jaffa Gate. Arab civilians were killed in each instance.[9]

Confronting these developments, U.S. Consul in Jerusalem Robert Macatee declared that "any hopes we may have held that the disturbances immediately following the UN decision represented a passing phase, and that more tranquil times would soon return, have now been dispelled."¹⁰ He reported that there were more than a thousand casualties, with twice that number wounded. Palestinian government was "in a state of disintegration," with disruption of services attributable in part to the absence of Arab–Jewish cooperation.¹¹ In the midst of this, Macatee reported that "Jewish officials say they have no doubts about their ability to set up their state," or to defend the line between Haifa and Tel Aviv, unlike the Eastern Galilee and the Negev, and the future of the 100,000 Jews in Jerusalem about which they were concerned.¹² He later added that neither U.S. nor UN doubts with respect to partition, or Arab attacks, would fundamentally alter the Jewish Agency's objectives.

Macatee also reported on the "influx of uniformed and trained Arabs, principally from Iraq and Syria," joined with others operating in "Ramleh-Lydda-Tulkarm, Jerusalem and Hebron districts."¹³ Those in command were experienced guerrilla fighters, Fawzi Kawukji and Abdul Kader Husseini. However, as Macatee reported, the Mufti was "the central figure on the Arab stage, his organization shows itself to be ruthless in the pursuit of its aims."¹⁴ The Arab front would likely be weakened by internal divisions, Macatee indicated, pointing out that Arab meetings at Aley, in Lebanon, confirmed the lack of unity among Arab leaders.

Macatee was critical of British policies toward the Jewish Agency with respect to increasing its immigration quotas, gaining access to its capital, or toward its militias. Macatee claimed that the British refused to implement the recommendations for partition; that the British police "have no sympathy for the Jews, and state freely their opinion that the latter will 'collect a packet'" from the Arabs once the British leave; and many added "that in their opinion the Jews have 'asked for it.'"¹⁵

Reporting on the Jewish situation, Macatee indicated that

In the field of offense, which the Jewish Agency prefers to term "preventive defense" we have seen all three Jewish armed groups in action, Haganah, Irgun and the Stern Gang. Their offensives generally consist of demolitions of Arab strong points, and forays into Arab villages which they believe to have been used as bases for

Arab guerillas. The blowing up of the Old Serail in Jaffa (by the Stern Gang), the same type of action against the Semiramis Hotel in Jerusalem (by the Haganah), and the shooting of Arabs in Tireh Village (by the Irgun) are all examples of Jewish offensives. Such activities are designed, according to the Jews, to force the Arabs into a passive state.[16]

As an example of armed action, Simha Flapan reported that

the Irgun used a car bomb to blow up the government center in Jaffa, killing twenty-six Arab civilians. Three days later, they planted explosives at Jaffa Gate in Jerusalem, and another twenty-five Arab civilians were killed. A pattern became clear, for in each case the Arabs retaliated, then the Haganah—while always condemning the actions of the Irgun and LEHI—joined in with an inflaming counterretaliation.[17]

The day after Macatee's report was sent to the U.S. secretary of state, an unproductive exchange took place between Loy Henderson of the Office of Near Eastern and African Affairs and Fraser Wilkins of the Near East Division and the representative of the Arab Higher Committee for Palestine, Isa Nakhleh. The latter wanted to know if the United States planned to pressure members of the Security Council to support implementation of the partition resolution with force, and what the U.S. position would be if the Security Council called for a review of the Palestine question. Henderson denied the first point and claimed to draw a blank on the second.

The president and those involved in the Palestine question appeared to be at a turning point, privately convinced of the inevitable failure of partition and the need for Arab–Jewish consensus in forging a new direction, yet reluctant to take a public stand against UNGA Resolution 181. Overcome with a sense of urgency, meetings were held to define the U.S. position, and participants sought to avoid leaks of these internal deliberations. The secretary of state refused to be drawn out on his views, deferring to Warren Austin, head of the U.S. delegation at the United Nations. Robert Lovett, under secretary of state, counseled his colleagues to refrain from talking shop with outsiders.

THE BUTLER MEMORANDUM

On February 11, 1948, George Butler of the Policy Planning Staff issued a memorandum for Lovett designed to clarify the U.S. position on the Palestine problem and to offer possible alternatives to existing policy. Butler singled out long-term support for what became "the trend of U.S. public opinion and U.S. policy based thereon [that] practically forced official U.S. support of partition."[18] He remarked that "public opinion in the United States was stirred by mistreatment of Jews in Europe and by the intense desire of surviving Jews to go to Palestine."[19] And he recalled that the United States voted in favor of partition despite Arab opposition, claiming that partition would lead to security and prosperity.

Arab leaders consulted by Butler included the kings of Egypt and Saudi Arabia, and General Jinnah of Pakistan. No Palestinian leaders were consulted, a decision that reflected the indifference with which Palestinian political opinion was held.

Against this background, three options were considered: (1) support for the UN partition resolution; (2) adoption of a "neutral" position that Butler thought difficult for the United States to do and that meant detachment from UN activities in Palestine: or (3) armed intervention in support of partition. If the U.S. did not support partition, it had to find an alternative, which meant returning to the UN General Assembly and calling either for an international trusteeship or a federal state, with arrangements for Jewish immigration in either case. Butler concluded that Zionists would strongly disapprove of this but that Arab states and the rest of the world would strongly approve, and the United States would secure its interests and regain its prestige.

Struggling with the Implications of the Memorandum

What became of this memorandum? According to U.S. sources, Marshall planned to present it before the National Security Council (NSC) as a "working paper but not as representing State's position."[20]

Robert McClintock is on record as having admitted at this point that "it would be a drastic step to admit that our advocacy on Palestine for years past and our recent championing of partition, was a mistake."[21] But his handwritten notes reveal his thinking that an "alternative plan [is] imperative if [a] new situation arises, *including readiness [to] use U.S. forces.* Trusteeship."[22] This, however, was not the official U.S. position. That position remained conveniently ambiguous, as instructions given to the U.S. delegate in advance of the UN Security Council meeting on Palestine revealed. In short, the U.S. position was to maintain its support for UNGA Resolution 181 without exercising pressure. As a result, "there would not be sufficient affirmative votes in the Security Council for its implementation. The U.S. Delegation would be instructed not to exert any such pressure."[23]

In the days and weeks that followed, the same questions concerning U.S. and UN policies were repeatedly reviewed. The draft report prepared by the National Security Council on February 17, 1948, was only to be "circulated to the Departments of State, Army, Navy, and Air Force for comment on the consultant ('Kennan-Sherman-Wedemeyer-Weyland') level, (attached memorandum of February 18 by Mr Kennan to Under-Secretary Lovett)." Further exchanges with George Butler disclosed that Lovett did not want the draft to be circulated to the State Department and that it was under consideration by high-level officials in that department.

The FRUS volume which contained the draft offered only its conclusions. This was sufficient to indicate continuing U.S. support for the UN partition plan barring external armed intervention. However, the abridged draft also contained the following notice: "The military members of the Staff do not concur in the above conclusion and offer the following as a substitute."[24] The military members of the Staff opposed partition and supported a special UNGA session to reconsider the Palestine question. They urged the British government to extend its mandate, and, more pointedly, they indicated that if the UNGA did reconsider Palestine, "the United States should propose the creation of a trusteeship in Palestine with the UN Trusteeship Council as the administering authority. If necessary, this proposal should include provision for an international force to maintain internal order during a transitional period."[25] They distinguished between this kind of force and one designed to enforce partition, which they opposed.

An editorial note revealed that Major General Alfred Gruenther of the Joint Chiefs of Staff met with Truman and indicated his concern at the number of troops, estimated to be between 80,000 and 100,000, that would be required to implement partition. Should the United States undertake such action, Gruenther pointed out, it would undermine other military action in the region. In addition, he noted that U.S. support for partition had "pretty well disposed of the idea that the United States would continue to have access to the Middle East Oil."[26]

On February 19, Marshall informed Lovett that "the President assured me whatever course we considered the right one we could disregard all political factors."[27] Truman was on vacation, and arrangements were made to send him the draft of the statement Austin was to make at the United Nations once the secretaries of state and defense had reviewed it. Meanwhile, arrangements were made to bring Austin to the State Department to meet with Lovett, Rusk, Henderson, Gross (the State Department's legal adviser), and Butler.

The message with its enclosed "Working Draft" was labeled "Top Secret," but evidently it was leaked. It was subsequently found in the papers of George M. Elsey, then special assistant to Clark Clifford, the president's legal counsel. Neither Clifford nor Elsey had been invited to the inner circle of policymakers to discuss the predicament that the United States faced.

THE ELSEY-CLIFFORD MYSTERY

So how did this "urgent and top secret" material end up in Elsey's papers, and of what importance was this? The "Working Draft" was meant to be "Top Secret" because it raised the forbidden question regarding partition in a manner that indicated that opposition to UNGA Res. 181, the Partition Resolution, had reached a turning point. If Elsey had this draft, it was accessible to Clark Clifford, who was known to have contacts in the Jewish Agency.

The U.S. policymaking establishment was steadily moving away from partition and toward a policy of trusteeship. Major policymaking officials were in agreement that the United States could no longer ignore the evidence of the failure of partition and the accompanying violence that appeared to justify Security Council action in accord with the United Nations Charter. Yet, in keeping with its past position, the State Department draft urgently counseled that the Security Council attempt to persuade the parties to carry out UNGA Resolution 181.

Absolute clarity with respect to the view of the president was urgent. In its lengthy "Message to the President," the State Department asked Truman to pay particular attention to paragraph 8, which outlined the conditions in Palestine that constituted a threat to international peace.

> The Security Council is required by the Charter to take the necessary action to maintain international peace if it finds that a threat to the peace, breach of the peace or act of aggression exists with respect to Palestine. This might arise either in connection with incursions into Palestine from the outside or from such internal disorder as would itself constitute a threat to international peace. Although the Security Council is empowered to use, and would normally attempt to use, measures short of armed force to maintain the peace, it is authorized under the Charter to use armed forces if necessary for that purpose.
>
> A finding by the Security Council that a danger to peace exists places all Members of the United Nations, regardless of their attitudes on specific political questions, under obligation to assist the Council in maintaining peace. If the Security Council should decide that it is necessary to use armed forces to maintain international peace in connection with Palestine, the United States will be ready to consult under Article 106 of the Charter with a view to such joint action on behalf of the Organization as may be necessary for the purpose of maintaining international peace and security. Such consultation would be required in view of the fact that armed forces have not as yet been made available to the Security Council under Article 43.[28]

The president was also asked to comment on three final paragraphs of the draft that were not meant for Warren Austin, but for internal deliberation on what was to be done in Palestine. The first paragraph spelled out the conditions under which the Palestine case would be brought to the UNGA, and the implications of such actions for U.S. policy. In the absence of

> acquiescence on the part of the people of Palestine to permit its implementation without enforcement measures, and If the Security

Council is unable to develop an alternative solution, to the Jews and Arabs of Palestine, the matter should be referred back to a special session of the General Assembly. The Department of State considers that it would then be clear that Palestine is not yet ready for self-government and that some form of United Nations trusteeship for an additional period of time will be necessary.[29]

The paragraph that followed indicated that it might prove necessary to ask London to extend its stay in Palestine as a mandatory power, given the difficulty of existing conditions. The third paragraph was merely a statement to the effect that the Department of State planned to take strong diplomatic action vis-à-vis all parties concerned in an effort to obtain "an immediate cessation of violence and illegal acts of all kinds."[30]

There is some confusion regarding the precise date the text was sent to the president. The State Department message contained a footnote indicating that the text was dated February 23, yet the draft was transmitted on February 21. "The latter point is definitely established by the copy of the message, identified as White 4 and marked 'urgent and top secret' in the George M. Elsey Papers in the Harry S. Truman Library at Independence Missouri. Mr Elsey was Assistant to Clark M. Clifford; Mr. Clifford was Special Counsel to President Truman."[31] The document in question can also be found in the papers of Clark Clifford.[32]

For Epstein and the Jewish Agency, signs that Washington was turning away from partition were cause for alarm. Without knowing the details of the State Department's "Message to the President," Ben-Gurion and other Jewish Agency officials warned of the need to take urgent action.

In a biography of Secretary of State Marshall, Forest C. Pogue indicated that "despite the extreme care exercised to keep these discussions quiet, rumors reached the Jewish Agency, which brought them at once to Lovett."[33] The position outlined in the draft may also have inspired the rebuttal prepared by the Jewish Agency in its "Notes on Palestine," which became the basis for discussion with U.S. officials. The same themes figured prominently in Clark Clifford's exchange with Secretary of State Marshall in the famous May 12, 1948, White House debate on U.S. policy.

AT THE UNITED NATIONS AND IN WASHINGTON

On February 24, Warren Austin called on the Security Council to form a five-member committee to investigate "possible threats to international peace arising in connection with the Palestine situation" and to consult with the various parties, including those in Palestine, concerning UNGA Resolution 181 and its implementation. Henderson and McClintock counseled U.S. diplomats on how to handle the U.S. position, while Lovett dealt with U.S. allies at the UN.

Kennan continued to warn against the United States assuming "major responsibility for the maintenance, and even the expansion of a Jewish state in Palestine," which, in his view, was inimical to U.S. interests.[34] He feared that Washington would agree to send troops to Palestine along with those from Soviet controlled areas, a move he believed would undermine U.S. strategic planning for the Mediterranean and the Middle East.

On February 28, 1948, the CIA issued its report on "Possible Developments in Palestine," which had been "concurred in by the Intelligence Agencies of the Department of State, Army, Navy, and Air Force on 19 February."[35] As the agency declared in its opening lines, "it is apparent that the partition of Palestine into separate Arab and Jewish states (and an intermediary zone), with economic union between the two states, as recommended by the United Nations General Assembly (UNGA) on 29 November 1947, cannot be implemented."[36]

Predicting what would happen after Britain's anticipated departure, the agency warned that Arabs would use force to prevent the establishment of a Jewish state, and the Jewish Agency would rely on the Haganah as well as the "extremist groups" (the Irgun and the Stern Gang) to respond. The agency described the arming of Palestinian partisans and the mobilization of Arab forces entering Palestine, which were estimated at some 8,000 men. Jewish forces were described as conducting "terrorist raids against the Arabs similar in tactics to those of the Irgun Zvai Leumi and the Stern Gang against the British"; both the Irgun and Stern Gang rejected partition in favor of "all of Palestine (and even Transjordan) for the Jewish state."[37]

The CIA report concluded that the United States faced three alternatives: reliance on force to implement partition, which would in all probability include the USSR; inaction by the United Nations; or recognition of the failure of partition and its reconsideration before the UNGA. The agency selected the last of the three options as the most likely and necessary. It maintained that

> to comprehend the overriding necessity for such a step, two factors must be understood; (1) that Arab opposition automatically invalidates the UNGA partition recommendations, whose basic assumption is Arab-Jewish cooperation; (2) that even if a Jewish state could be established and defended by force of arms, it would have to defend itself continuously not only against its hostile neighbors but against the resistance of 450,000 Arabs within its own borders until such time as Arab nationalism no longer existed; and (3) that full recourse to all judicial procedures before action is taken would help to establish world confidence in the fairness and justice of the UN as an instrument for world peace.[38]

The agency report suggested that the Security Council could ask the International Court of Justice for advice on the UNGA partition resolution, and proceed with a truce. If the Security Council failed to act, the secretary general would be informed and the case brought before the so-called Little Assembly, or a special session of the UNGA.

In London, British Foreign Minister Ernest Bevin declared that in current circumstances "either the Arabs in the partitioned State must always be an Arab minority, or else they must be driven out—the one thing or the other."[39] Bevin viewed bi-nationalism as a solution, whereas some in Washington supported federalism, if not trusteeship. Henderson warned against the consequences of Jewish expansion beyond the UNGA Resolution 181 boundaries, predicting that if it occurred it would lead to thousands of Palestinian refugees and a Jewish State dependent on U.S. financial, political, and military aid.

Reflecting on the mood in the State Department many years later, Loy Henderson recalled that by the end of February 1948 U.S. officials had become convinced that Britain's exit from Palestine in May would result in chaos and "the likelihood that some of the Arab States might send in their armed forces to help their fellow Arabs. If such forces should enter Palestine in large numbers, the United States might feel compelled to send in its forces to prevent the extermination of the Jews, many of whom were survivors of Hitler's atrocities."[40]

Others who have written about this period, such as Michael J. Cohen, point out that by the end of February Truman was persuaded that partition would put U.S. interests at risk and, as a result of the chaos following British withdrawal, would open Palestine to Soviet intervention.[41]

5

The Oil Connection

Signs of a shift in the U.S. government's support for partition had a severe impact on Zionist sentiment in the United States and in Palestine. Despite the effective mobilization of support for partition under the umbrella of the Zionist Emergency Council in the past, Zionist leaders in Palestine rapidly concluded that additional action was required. The results surpassed expectations: Washington did not abandon partition in favor of trusteeship. Jewish Agency representatives established relations with one of the leading figures in the vast oil bureaucracy, the director of the Oil and Gas Division of the Interior Department, thereby challenging a long-standing taboo.

In the winter of 1948, the Jewish Agency mobilized its efforts to assess how to respond most effectively to the crisis in U.S. policy. Jacob Robinson, the legal adviser and counselor to the Israeli Delegation at the UN, warned that there was a related risk that could affect the future of American Zionists in the United States. Those identified with a cause viewed as inimical to U.S. interests, such as the feared loss of U.S. oil in the Middle East and its implications with regard to the European Recovery Plan, risked being labeled un-American, with the attendant stigma.[1]

This proved to be a secondary consideration in light of the effort mobilized to contain Washington's increasing opposition to partition.

REASSESSING THE APPROACH TO U.S. POLICYMAKERS

The American Zionist Emergency Council (AMZEC) response to the fear that Washington was abandoning partition was impressive, but in Tel Aviv, David Ben-Gurion decided to appoint Eliahu Epstein to continue the task of organizing support for partition in the United States.[2] Epstein and Moshe Shertok contributed to a major reevaluation of Jewish Agency policy toward the United States, and meetings with State Department officials soon followed.

The new look offered in "The Note on Palestine Policy" targeted key aspects of U.S. interests in the Middle East and focused on persuading Washington that it misunderstood Arab dependency and Jewish promise. Arab oil producers were dependent on U.S. oil companies and the government that backed them in Washington. In the Jewish Agency's new approach, it was important to demonstrate to Washington policymakers that U.S. oil company interests were not in jeopardy because Arab regimes were vulnerable. The fear that U.S. companies risked losing their contracts was mistaken.

As to the promise of partition and a Jewish state, the Jewish Agency's revised strategy emphasized that U.S. relations with the future Jewish state held the possibility of cooperation with a community of common cultural and political values that was far from being a liability. The Jewish state, in sum, could become an asset in U.S. Middle East policy.

On February 21, 1948, Moshe Shertok and Eliahu Epstein met with Under Secretary of State Robert Lovett and Fraser Wilkins of the Near East Division of the State Department to discuss clarification of the U.S. position. Perhaps the timing of their meeting was a product of the Elsey scoop, which had provided evidence of the direction of official U.S. thinking on partition. In addition to obtaining clarification on U.S. policy, the meeting provided the Jewish Agency representatives with an opportunity to delineate their own position and demonstrate how it was compatible with long-term U.S. values and interests.

Shertok wanted to know if the United States would permit arming Jewish forces and whether it planned to provide an international force to endorse the UNGA partition resolution. Lovett's reply was that the United States operated within the framework of the United Nations.

He, in turn, asked for clarification as to who the Jewish Agency represented, as well as who the Arab Higher Committee represented.

Shertok stated that the Jewish Agency had been established under the mandate as a "quasi-official body" that represented Jews in Palestine and around the world through a democratic system of elections.[3] Shertok portrayed the Arab Higher Committee as representing only Palestinian Arabs, those under the leadership of the Mufti in Jerusalem. Asked by Lovett whether the Jewish Agency had met with members of the Arab Higher Committee, Shertok replied that it was pointless to do so given their response to UNGA Resolution 181.

Shertok explained that the UN partition resolution represented a major compromise for the Jewish Agency. "After the cutting away of Transjordan from the area of the Jewish National Home in 1922, the present scheme has reduced the remainder of that area by nearly one-half."[4] From the Agency's perspective, the UNGA resolution deprived the Jewish state of its "historic heritage" by creating "a second independent Arab state."[5] If Jews accepted these "painful and far-reaching sacrifices," it was on the assumption that "their political independence would be recognized, and that they would be able to work out their salvation as a free nation in that territory, which represented the final compromise beyond which they would not go."[6] Shertok concluded by urging the United States to recognize the provisional government and its militia.

THE QUARTET

In addition to contacts with Lovett, long-range Jewish Agency strategy included contacting influential figures in and around the policy-making circles. Among those active in this campaign was a quartet of key players: Eliahu Epstein, Max Ball, James Terry Duce, and Ray Kosloff, who later became Israel's oil adviser and the director of its oil company Delek.

Eliahu Epstein was one of the small group of Jewish Arabists in the Jewish Agency hierarchy.[7] Epstein later became Israel's first ambassador to the United States. He was director of the Jewish Agency's Political Office in Washington between 1945 and 1948 and, with Moshe Shertok, often met with administration officials. In November 1947 Epstein accompanied Dr. Chaim Weizmann to Washington to meet Truman before the UN vote on partition, and he described his duties as including "regular contact with the State Department and our friends at the White House."[8] Clark Clifford was among them, as was David Niles, who had introduced Epstein to Clifford.[9]

Epstein was also in touch with Freda Kirchwey, editor of *The Nation*, who was a critic of State Department oil policies and became a strong supporter of Israel. Kirchwey was instrumental in introducing Epstein to Gael Sullivan of the Democratic National Committee.[10] Epstein was also in touch with sympathetic figures in the U.S. labor movement, as Peter Hahn has shown.[11]

Max W. Ball was the director of the Oil and Gas Division (OGD) of the U.S. Department of the Interior, a geologist with long experience in and exemplary knowledge of domestic and foreign U.S. oil interests. His encounter with Eliahu Epstein and his offers of support established a relationship between the two men that transcended their personal rapport.

The Oil and Gas Division served as "the central oil agency of the Federal Government" and provided "advice and recommendations to other agencies of the Federal Government, to the States and to the petroleum industry, relating to petroleum policy."[12] According to the J. E. Jones oil newsletter, Ball was "Truman's Petroleum Consultant."[13] In a May 1948 article, Ball described the function of the OGD as "to keep the President informed of significant developments in petroleum matters, and to advise him of any steps necessary to safeguard the nation's petroleum future. (4) To coordinate, and so far as possible to unify, the administrative practices and policies of the various Government agencies with respect to oil and gas."[14]

Ball's responsibilities as director of the Oil and Gas Division of the Interior Department included acting "as the government's channel of communication with the petroleum industry."[15] At the annual meeting of the American Petroleum Institute in the fall of 1948, Ball explained that since establishment of the Oil and Gas Division in 1946 it had "advised 80 executive agencies on oil and gas matters, not counting UNRRA. Its men have testified 36 times before 16 Congressional committees. No count has been kept of the many senators, representatives, and their committees it has advised by letter or telephone."[16] Ball remarked that the OGD "alone is charged with responsibility for an overall knowledge of petroleum affairs, and of the effect of any particular action on the country's petroleum economy."[17]

Ball emphasized that his role was only advisory, but the president's oil consultant was unduly modest given his connections in government and the petroleum sector. A broad array of agencies were concerned with oil and gas issues, including "consuming and procurement agencies such as the Armed Services" and "policy-making agencies such as the State Department and the National Security Resources Board."[18] In light of his experience, Ball was recognized by Dewey Short, chair of the Special Subcommittee investigating the role of petroleum in relation to national defense as "a man who perhaps knows as much about oil and gas, the whole petroleum industry, and the world petroleum situation, from the statistical standpoint, as any individual alive."[19] After he retired, Ball became the main author of Israel's and Turkey's petroleum laws.[20]

James Terry Duce was the director of the Petroleum Administration for War prior to becoming the vice president of ARAMCO, the preeminent U.S. oil giant operating in Saudi Arabia. Before he became "that private commercial company's" man in Washington, Duce had had a long history in U.S. oil politics, including as the Petroleum Administration for War's head of foreign operations in the 1940s under Harold Ickes. As vice president of ARAMCO, Duce was the liaison for the Saudi monarchy, the company, and the CIA.[21]

Ray (Israel) Kosloff, the youngest of the four, had a personal relationship with Max Ball and professional experience working in U.S. oil companies that would serve him well when he became Israel's "influential Oil Adviser."[22] Kosloff was born into a prominent Zionist family in Jerusalem in 1921. He studied economics at the University of Chicago where he met Max Ball's daughter Jean, whom he married. He later worked at Standard Oil of Indiana and eventually returned to Israel where he became "Petroleum Director and Oil Adviser to the Ministry of Finance—served on the Executive Committee of the Company [the Israeli Delek Oil Company] and was in charge of its external contracts on behalf of the Israeli Government."[23]

Ray Kosloff and Jean spent a year in Jerusalem, and Ball described his Palestinian son-in-law to a colleague as a "red-haired economist."[24] Ball recalled discussing "Jean's article on Palestine" in late November

1947, albeit without disclosing its contents. And on November 29, 1947, Ball made note of developments at the UN: "Got the news on the radio that the UN Assembly had voted 33 to 13 for the partition of Palestine."[25] Nothing more was said on the subject in this source.

Ray Kosloff was denied a permanent U.S. visa despite his father-in-law's efforts. Under the circumstances, he was advised to accept nonpaying positions, as he did with the Richfield Oil Company in California, although he had other options, including from Continental and Cal-Tex. Eventually, Kosloff and his wife decided to return to Israel on the advice of Kosloff's father who held "a responsible position in the Israeli Treasury," as Eliahu Epstein, who knew the family, explained to Ball.[26]

The encounters that brought the representatives of the Jewish Agency together with Max Ball occurred against the background of worsening conditions in Palestine and the agency's growing concern that Truman would abandon partition. These were not the principal themes discussed in the House hearings on petroleum in the winter of 1948, but they were inevitably part of the discussion and exposed the kinds of issues Jewish Agency representatives addressed in their revised strategy toward the United States.

HOUSE HEARINGS ON PETROLEUM
AND THE NATIONAL DEFENSE

The hearings of the House of Representatives Special Subcommittee on Petroleum in Relation to the National Defense of the United States involved thirty sessions, forty-nine witnesses, and five hearings held in closed session.[27] The list of witnesses included key military, legal, administrative, and political appointees as well as representatives of major U.S. oil companies. Secretary of Defense James Forrestal opened the hearings on January 19, 1948. He was followed by Max Ball on January 20, and several days later by James Terry Duce of ARAMCO. Those who testified included the deputy chief of naval operations; chief, plans and operations, Navy Department; deputy chief of staff for materiel, Air Force; director, Naval Petroleum Reserves, Navy Department; executive officer, Armed Services Petroleum; former secretary of the Interior Harold L. Ickes; assistant secretary of Commerce; assistant secretary of state for Economic Affairs; petroleum adviser to Secretary of State Marshall; and a broad array of representatives of U.S. oil companies.

Discussion of U.S. oil policy and its bearing on U.S. policy in the region—including the construction of Tapline, which was to bring oil from Saudi Arabia to Sidon, Lebanon—was held in closed, executive session. Overall, the inescapable conclusion of speakers such as James Forrestal, Ball, the military and naval cadres, and representatives of U.S. oil interests such as Duce was that access to the Middle East was to be maintained at any cost, given the importance of oil to U.S. policy. The risks of instability and war in the Middle East endangered the peace essential to the operation of U.S. business.

ARAMCO Vice President James Terry Duce offered committee members a global inventory of oil. As Duce explained, "strategically, from a world viewpoint, there are only four areas outside Russia and eastern Europe which are of global importance. They are in order of their importance, the Middle East, the United States, South America, and the Far East, particularly this area in here—my lawyer would remind me that I should say 'in the Dutch East Indies.'"[28] Duce also informed committee members of recent discoveries in Iran by the Anglo-Iranian Oil Company, as well as in Kuwait, with the "immense field of Burgan in Kuwait—probably the largest field in the world."[29] As to ARAMCO, it had "extended its Abqaiq field some 15 miles to the north and discovered a new producing sand."[30] In addition, the fields of Dukan in Qatar were being developed by an Iraq Petroleum Company affiliate in Qatar.

Underlying the importance of such discoveries was the vital role fuel plays in military operations. As Duce explained, "petroleum is a munition of war, probably one of the most important and that should always be remembered when talking about these fields in the Middle East."[31] Duce did not cite the following figures on this occasion, but it is useful to recall that "between 1945–1947 the U.S. Navy bought $68 million worth of oil products from ARAMCO."[32] At the time, the defense secretary pointed out that it was "the cheapest oil delivered, that the Navy ever bought," which contributed to its appeal.[33]

In his testimony before the House Special Subcommittee on Petroleum and Defense, Duce offered a map of Anglo-American oil companies in the Middle East, akin to a global inventory of petroleum operations in the hands of the dominant western companies. It is worth considering the scope of such concessions and the economic power they represented.

> You will note first the Anglo-Iranian concession in Iran owned by the Anglo-Iranian Oil Co., a British corporation. Second, there is the Iraq Petroleum Co. a group of concessions which include all of Iraq, part of Syria, Lebanon, Palestine, Cyprus, Oman, Qatar, Trucial Coast, Trans-Jordan and the Hadramount. There used to be a concession to an Iraq Petroleum Co. affiliate in Saudi Arabia, but this has been surrendered. The concession on the Shekhdom of Kuwait is held jointly by the Anglo-Iranian and the Gulf, an American company. The Saudi Arabian concession is held by the Arabian-American Oil Co., whose stock is owned by the Texas Co. and the Standard Oil Co. of California, and will, as and when certain conditions are satisfied, also be owned by the Standard Oil Co. of New Jersey and Socony-Vacuum Oil Co. The division of ownership will then be 30 percent to the first three and 10 percent to the last. In the case of the Iraq Petroleum Co., this stock is owned 23 3/4 percent by Shell, a British and Dutch corporation, 23 3/4 percent by the Anglo-Iranian Co., an English corporation, 23 3/4 percent by the Near East Development Co., which in turn is owned 50 percent by Standard Oil of New Jersey and 50 percent by the Socony-Vacuum Oil Co. In addition, a gentleman by the name of Gulbenkian, who I believe is a British citizen, owns a 5 percent interest in the corporation.[34]

Duce then turned to the need for pipeline construction to facilitate the transportation of oil across the vast distances separating Saudi Arabia and the Mediterranean coast, explaining the rationale for preferring pipelines to tankers, while recognizing the existing opposition to steel exports in the United States.

Dewey Short, chair of the subcommittee, commented on the exclusion of Palestine from the proposed pipeline routes—"and we all know why."[35] More generally Short emphasized the necessity of consulting with "the military" with respect to locations for pipeline routes. Duce mentioned Max Ball as being among those with whom he planned to consult in addition to the military. He conceded that "the construction of the Trans-Arabian pipe line and to a certain extent the Iraq

Petroleum Co.'s line has been affected by the riots and civil disturbances consequent upon the United Nations' decision for the partition
of Palestine."[36] The major themes in Duce's testimony with respect to oil
transportation were the urgency of steel for pipeline construction; the
transnational role of pipelines; and the implications of these developments for U.S. policy in the Eastern Mediterranean, the Middle East,
Europe, and Central America.

Duce was asked to comment on the political risks facing U.S. companies, to which he replied with reference to the Saudi king's statement
"in which he said he did not intend to do anything about the oil concessions in Saudi Arabia, that we were his friends, and he expected to have
us continue his production."[37] The committee chair was not reassured,
citing Palestine and India, even as he commended Duce and his company. Duce responded by affirming that, indeed, "peace in the Middle
East is an essential to the development of the Middle East."[38]

THE "NOTE ON PALESTINE POLICY"

On the day following Duce's testimony, influential American Zionists
and their supporters held an informal gathering in Washington. Its
purpose was to determine how to persuade Washington policymakers not to abandon partition. Eliahu Epstein and Moshe Shertok were
present, as were two of the three coauthors of the 1946 study on the
economic dimension of Zionist development, Robert R. Nathan and
Oscar Gass.[39]

In the course of this discussion, those identified as significant targets of Zionist efforts included retired Gen. William Donovan, Eleanor Roosevelt, Bernard Baruch, Sumner Welles, John Foster Dulles,
and Henry Stimson, as well as Arthur Vandenberg, Thomas Dewey,
Robert Taft, Paul Douglas, Adlai Stevenson, and Averell Harriman.[40]
Complementing this list were two oil men, Ralph Davies and Max Ball.
Davies, of the American Independent Oil Company, was described as
"one of the few oil executives who gave the Zionists a hearing." He
was to "be encouraged to press for Cabinet-level attention to the matter."[41] Ball, whose professional identity and political influence were well
known, was additionally recognized as having "a nagging admiration
for Zionist spunk."[42]

Shortly before this meeting occurred, Moshe Shertok sent Gen. Donovan, in response to his request, an elaborate statement of the Jewish Agency position. It was the redesigned strategy mentioned earlier, "The Note on Palestine Policy." Shertok indicated that Gen. Donovan was to use this document "in any way he deemed fit with regard to General Eisenhower or Mr. Forrestal."[43]

The "Note on Palestine Policy" systematically addressed arguments for and against partition in a manner that evoked the arguments of the leaked "Top Secret" draft proposal discussed previously. It argued that if the United States decided against partition, its reputation, as well as that of the UN, would suffer; the conflict would be extended; and Britain's exit would create a vacuum that the USSR would exploit. If the United States maintained its support for partition, on the other hand, its commercial and economic interests would not be damaged but, on the contrary, would be enhanced.

> Even today the 700,000 Jews of Palestine import from the United States nearly one-half of the total imported by seventeen million Egyptians. With the establishment of the Jewish State and the initiation of large-scale development projects, all requiring vast quantities of capital goods, American exports to Palestine are bound to increase enormously.[44]

On the crucial question of U.S. oil interests, the "Note" aimed to overturn the commonly held view that partition endangered U.S. interests by exposing Arab dependency on the United States.

> The paramount character of the American oil interest in the Near East is undeniable, but it is a patent fact that the Arab States have a greater interest in yielding their oil to the United States than the United States has in exploiting it. The cow is more anxious to be milked than anybody to milk it. By breaking their contracts with American oil companies, the Arab States would incur such suicidal sacrifices that any such apprehension may be safely dismissed as groundless. Saudi Arabia derives the bulk of its revenues from oil royalties. Iraq would certainly be unable to balance her budget without them. Syria and Lebanon, both in acute financial straits, have

scarcely any prospect of solvency except through the proceeds of pipeline concessions. No Arab country has any means of obtaining revenue from oil resources except through its existing or prospective contracts with the United States.[45]

This assessment aimed to expose the political impotence of oil-rich Arab regimes that had nowhere to turn other than to U.S. oil companies. It explained why oil contracts had not been cancelled, as "King Ibn Saud stated explicitly some time ago that he would in all circumstances fulfill his commitment towards the American oil companies."[46]

As to the USSR, some in the Jewish Agency were persuaded that fear of its exploitation of Arab opposition to U.S. partition policies explained Washington's willingness to reconsider its position. Yet they insisted that the USSR posed no serious threat, it could not compete with the United States in the area, and its ideological orientation threatened the power of the oil-rich states.

It was not the USSR but the risk of Arab League action on pipelines in early 1948 that alarmed Washington and Tel Aviv. According to Peter Grose, "early in 1948 the Arab League had decided to deny pipeline rights to American companies unless Washington's support for partition were withdrawn. The message had its impact."[47] Eliahu Epstein responded by arranging to meet with the director of the Oil and Gas Division of the Interior Department, Max Ball.

MAX BALL AND ELIAHU EPSTEIN: HISTORIC ENCOUNTERS

Accounts of the precise occasion on which Eliahu Epstein met with Max Ball differ. Ball's diaries reveal that he was introduced to Epstein in mid-February 1948 by Ray (Israel) Kosloff and Jean, his son-in-law and daughter. Ball reported receiving a call from Kosloff in New York on February 13 "to ask whether I would see some representatives of The Jewish Agency for Palestine tomorrow or Sunday. I said yes."[48]

On February 14 Ball recorded the encounter in his diary:

At 1:15 Ray and Jean brought in Eliahu Epstein, Washington representative of The Jewish Agency for Palestine, and Mr. Ruffer, who was also of The Jewish Agency, and we discussed the Middle Eastern situation, and what should be the attitude of the United States and American oil companies toward partition and the Jewish State, until 2:45 when we continued the discussion through lunch at the Statler Coffee Shop. Agreed to try to get Mr. Epstein acquainted with some of the proper officials of American companies. He impresses me as much as anyone I have met for some time.[49]

According to Central Zionist records, those participating in this meeting included "Mr Eliahu Epstein, Mr and Mrs Koslov [Kosloff], Mr. Ball, his assistant in charge of Middle Eastern Affairs, Gideon Ruffer."[50] Israel archives identified Israel Koslov as assistant to the president of Richfield Oil Company and Gideon Ruffer as Ball's "assistant for Middle Eastern affairs." Gideon Ruffer, who later changed his name to Gideon Rafael, was a major figure in the Israeli Foreign Ministry and was an adviser to the Jewish Agency delegation at the United Nations in the winter of 1948. That he was also Max Ball's assistant is unlikely, but he may have worked with Eliahu Epstein.

As to Ray Kosloff, Ball reported that on the same day that Eliahu Epstein called to arrange for meetings with officials of U.S. oil companies, Kosloff had come over to meet Charlie Jones, the president of Richfield Oil Company, at his request.[51] Kosloff was offered a job as assistant to the president of Richfield, which Ball described as an "active producing, refining, and marketing Pacific Coast company which also markets on East Coast, and is controlled by Sinclair and Cities Service."[52]

Kosloff also had offers from Continental and Caltex, which suggests that major U.S. oil companies were interested in hiring someone of Palestinian Jewish origin when the course of developments in Palestine was a major preoccupation of U.S. policymakers. Kosloff was unable to obtain a visa that would allow him to accept these offers, or indeed any salaried position. The origin of the problem, as Ball discovered, was that "the Selective Service Board considered Palestine neutral in 1942." Ball sought out officials he thought could be helpful, but to no avail. Kosloff eventually gave up and returned to Palestine with his wife and newborn son.

A summary of the February 14 meeting between Ball, Epstein, the Kosloffs, and Ruffer was conveyed to Moshe Shertok on February 18. Although the author of this report was not identified in official Israeli sources, it appears to have been Epstein, given the context. "I opened by saying that we are fighting on three fronts now: the Arab, the British and the oil front. All these three are unnecessarily opposed to us and not [in] the best of their interests. This applies particularly to the oil front."[53]

Epstein recalled telling the U.S. official, who was in all likelihood Ball:

> We would like to discuss with him [Ball] the ways and means for an approach to the oil companies. Mr. Epstein continued by explaining the necessity of stability and social progress in the Middle East and the fact that the Yishuv belongs to this Middle Eastern pattern, and we would like to talk things over with oil interests, since we are convinced that their opposition is not basic towards us, but more a matter of a short term expediency.[54]

Epstein's message did not convey the brief history of the Jewish Agency's experience with obtaining oil during the mandatory period, when it relied on the then British-owned Haifa refinery that carried oil from the Iraq Petroleum Company (IPC).[55]

Several weeks before Epstein's encounter with Ball, there had been a massacre of Jewish workers at the Haifa refinery, leading to its takeover by Jewish forces. The subsequent crisis in the refinery's production and transport affected states across North Africa, the Eastern Mediterranean, and the Middle East in addition to Palestine.

Ball's response to Epstein's statement, according to Israeli sources, was to explain U.S. oil policy by emphasizing the U.S. reliance on Middle East oil as a tool of foreign policy designed to assist Europe in averting a collapse of its industry and the feared radicalization of its war weary and impoverished populations. The accessibility of Middle East oil, Ball explained, would free the United States to use Caribbean oil for domestic purposes. Ball cited Forrestal as declaring that in the event of war the United States could not guarantee its investments in the Middle East, but "as long as peace exists, Middle East resources must be drained."[56]

Ball did not find "draining" Middle East resources incompatible with his vaunted description of U.S. oil as a progressive factor in the development of the region. Nor did he explain the reasoning behind the reliance on Middle Eastern oil as opposed to oil from the Caribbean, which involved the more lucrative character of the U.S. oil operation in the Middle East. Ball also chose to say nothing, if indeed he was aware, of the nature of U.S. oil company operations in Saudi Arabia with its overtly racist character and its stark prohibition against any contact with Jews or blacks.[57]

Instead, Ball offered Epstein the ARAMCO view "that basically oil is progressive and is interested to raise the standards of living, to bring education, and is interested in dealing with enlightened democratic governments. Social progress, raising of living standards, increases oil consumption."[58] The State Department perpetuated the view that ARAMCO provided the "local populations with a livelihood [and] programs for health, education [and] sanitation," and that Saudi Arabia had "fewer Communists than any strategically located country in the world."[59] There was no mention of repression.

Ball and the authors of the Department of State paper did not refer to the discriminatory practices established by ARAMCO among its Saudi and South Asian workers. The overt racism led to strikes between 1945 and 1949 that were attributed to the communist leanings of Pakistani workers. James Terry Duce, when asked by the State Department to explain the company's deportation of Pakistani workers in 1949, explained that "they were followers of 'the Communist line, particularly as regards evils of capitalism *and racial discrimination.'* "[60]

When Ball offered Eliahu Epstein his glowing image of the achievements of U.S. oil, it was as a preface to his explanation of why the United States needed stability in the Middle East, which meant that "the oil companies must avoid under all circumstances antagonizing the Arabs with regard to Palestine."[61] It also meant having to deal with feudal regimes without complaint. As Ball emphasized, the United States faced an oil shortage that would increase, making it all the more important to develop oil from the Middle East, which would be used to "prevent European industry from collapsing and falling to Communism or the dogs."[62] Under the circumstances, partition was not in U.S. interests, the conclusion to which Ball pointed indirectly, citing "an important personality" who remained anonymous.

In response to such arguments, Epstein moved on another front, trying to persuade Ball that the U.S. withdrawal of support for partition would be interpreted by Arabs as a sign of weakness that would be intoxicating.

> An Arab triumph over the U.N. by defeating the Jews in Palestine and subjugating them would be detrimental to the Western influence in the Middle East because it would increase Arab self-reliance, demands and bargaining power, whereas the imposition of the will of the U.N. by the loyal implementation of the partition scheme would have a soothing effect on the Arabs and make them regain their right sense of proportion. Palestine serves as a unifying factor and as such increases the powers of the Arabs, which are split over all other issues. Western appeasement policy has made the Arabs believe that they constitute a big power, whereas in effect they are weak due to their backward state of social, economic and political development. Firmness, coupled with fairness will make more of an impression upon the Arabs than weakness coupled with reason.[63]

As an example, Epstein offered the case of Syrian opposition to ratifying an agreement that would allow the construction of Tapline, attributing this to the absence of a government majority in Parliament. Epstein's purpose was to emphasize the advantages that would accrue to the United States should partition and statehood be implemented.

> The Yishuv is a Western progressive factor, which will be a great stimulant to any social progress in the Middle East, which will open new commercial markets. The fact of the presence of skilled labour in Palestine brought us an offer to work for British oil companies in Abadan, Persia, during the war. Thus we did not only participate in the construction of new refineries, with some 500 Palestinian technicians, but also cooperated in the supervision of local labour to prevent sabotage.[64]

The exchange then turned to the Negev and its oil potential. Ball observed that there had been exploratory drilling in Gaza and Kurnub, but its commercial possibilities were not yet clear and prospecting for oil was difficult. Nonetheless, Ball indicated that if oil were to be found it would be significant as the "exploitation of oil so near to the shores of the Mediterranean would change the whole oil position in the Middle East, which is not only a question of resources, but also of transport facilities."[65] Epstein added that Ball was under the impression that "people have begun to think of exploitation of Negev oil, more particularly of the Sinai oil."[66] In April 1949, Ball noted in his diary that Epstein had informed him that "a man is here from Israel who wants to talk to me [Ball] about a highly important new mineral development in the Negev."[67]

Returning to the earlier period, Israeli sources claim that Max Ball recommended that "we [Jewish Agency representatives] should have frank talks with the leading oil people, the man at the top and not the field workers."[68]

> These top men are people of vision who know and understand very well the social and economic aspect of the problem, and know that the raising of living standards is beneficial to their interests. These people are not guided by any kind of anti-semitism, but they know that at present the tense situation in the Middle East necessitates their being very careful with regard to Arab sensitivity.
>
> Ball suggests meetings between our people and the following three: Terry Duce (ARAMCO), Charlie Harding (Director of Socony Vacuum, in charge of Middle Eastern operations), Sumer (Vice-President of Standard Oil in New Jersey). Ball expressed his willingness to advise us and extend any help to us wherever he can. He is very anxious to have an opportunity to meet Mr. Shertok.[69]

Shertok recognized the importance of these exchanges but remained persuaded that oil still operated against Zionist interests. As Uri Bialer points out, "not only were the Yishuv leaders inexperienced on oil matters: they considered it as axiomatic that British and American oil interests would generate anti-Zionist policies."[70] What led Shertok to have a measure of hope was his conviction that those in charge of decision making in Washington intended to stand by the UN resolution.

In Washington Epstein continued to turn to Ball for assistance. Ball noted that "Mr Epstein called up as agreed about arrangements for meeting officials of American oil companies operating in Middle East. Told Terry Duce out of town and Charlie Harding out of country."[71]

It is not clear whether the vice president of ARAMCO was avoiding such a meeting or agreeable to it in principle. Ball's relations with Duce were friendly and professional. In late January 1948, Ball recalled that he had "got some dope from Terry Duce on Middle East situation. He predicts all-out war as soon as British withdraw in May."[72] The prediction was made at about the same time as the House hearings on petroleum and the national defense previously discussed.

Faced with what he considered a campaign against ARAMCO, Duce did not hesitate to warn the State Department that "Left Wing and Zionist American Press is preparing a smear campaign against him and his company."[73] Freda Kirchwey, editor of the liberal journal *The Nation*, was identified as being critical of Duce's activities.[74] Such incidents did not discourage Duce from agreeing to meet with Epstein, although the meeting took place after Israel declared its independence.

In the intervening period, Ball made note of the request by Eliahu Epstein for an appointment. On March 11, Ball's record of his exchange with Charlie Harding of Socony-Vacuum indicated that they discussed a projected pipeline in Iran that required licenses for steel export. With regard to "the desire of Mr. Epstein to discuss the Middle Eastern situa-tion[,] Charlie will be glad to have lunch with Mr. Epstein but not until after the present situation has quieted down a bit."[75]

Epstein did, indeed, come to Ball's office, although not to meet with Harding. The two men discussed the "situation," a reference to events in Palestine, as well as the "Kosloff case." What Ball and Epstein said with respect to developments in Palestine or other matters related to Epstein's interest in having access to U.S. oil companies was not recorded in Ball's diaries or Israeli sources that have been made public. There is a record of the two talking of more personal matters, namely, Ray Kosloff's visa problem. However, Israeli sources indicate that Epstein and Ball's discus-sion of oil and Palestine was conveyed to the Jewish Agency executive in a summary of the "Position of the Oil Companies in the Palestine Ques-tion."[76] The review of that exchange was sent on March 17, 1948, more than two months before Israel's independence, in a period of height-ened tension over the continued criticism of Jewish military activity in Palestine by U.S. officials and Washington's tendency to lean toward trusteeship. Epstein reported that he had talked "with a high official of the American Government who is closely connected with the American

Oil Companies in this country and abroad, and who has intimate personal contacts with most of the high-ranking executives in oil circles. He is well disposed towards us, and his views can be considered as fully reliable and authoritative." The unnamed official, whom we can safely assume was Max Ball, was unequivocal about what to expect:

> [T]here is not the slightest chance for us to come to an understanding with ARAMCO and other Oil Companies operating in the Middle East until the Jewish State is established both de facto and de jure. The Oil Companies' policies are based on practical advantages, thus when the Jewish State becomes a reality, they will be the first to approach us for the benefit of their present and prospective operations in the area of the Jewish State.[77]

Epstein then reported on what may be considered his peak achievement. Two months before Israel's independence, Truman's recognition of the new state, and the State Department's reevaluation of its prior position, Epstein (who would become Israel's first U.S. ambassador) wrote to the executive of the Jewish Agency to inform him that his "informant" thought the new state would fit in the plans being projected for the Middle East.

> My Informant told me that he gathered from some of his recent conversations with a policy-making member of the ARAMCO Board of Directors that they are seriously thinking about extensive schemes of economic and social development in the Middle East. These plans are hardly philanthropic pursuits, but are considered as a safeguard against Communism, which has good prospects of gaining ground in the backward Arab countries if social and economic progress are artificially repressed by the present ruling classes in those countries. A special Committee was set up recently by ARAMCO to study this question and to present their observations to the Board of Directors of the Company and to the State Department for consideration.
>
> My informant believes that the Jewish State will fit very well into such a scheme of development, and our contributions will be of great value to the Company and will raise our prestige in their own circles and the State Department.[78]

To judge by Epstein's report to the Jewish Agency executive, he had learned from his "informant" that the above contributions of the future Jewish state would raise its prestige in oil company circles and in the State Department. Max Ball, who can be assumed to have been the informant, had significant contacts in both spheres, but particularly among those with an interest in oil. His reassurance suggested a future role for the Jewish state that was sufficient to alter its perception as fundamentally inimical to U.S. interests in the Middle East.

Epstein added that Ernest Bevin was interested in similar development projects and had instructed British experts to pursue these matters with their American colleagues, with the idea of joint development in the Middle East. Ball had further informed Epstein that "the Oil Companies would be ready to spend large funds to subsidize these schemes, as a matter of insurance for their huge investments in that part of the world."[79]

In short, the oil companies anticipated that development projects could function as an effective means of containing opposition movements and movements for change across the oil producing states and, more generally, the Middle East. Ball envisioned the future Jewish state as playing a useful role in this context, for which he offered his assistance, suggesting "that soon after the establishment of a Jewish Provisional Government, an attempt be made to meet, at least informally, some of the top-ranking executives of ARAMCO and to frankly review with them the situation, as we did in our conversation."[80] The "informant" indicated that "he would be glad to be of any assistance to us in this matter."[81]

After May 1948, James Terry Duce "agreed to have Ball set up a meeting with Israeli ambassador Eliahu Elath [formerly Epstein], though he told Ball that ARAMCO's Saudi Arabian concession was conditioned on not doing business with the Israelis."[82] According to Citino's informative essay on "Postwar American Oil Policies and the Modernization of the Middle East," "Duce hoped that regional development would help to address Arab-Israeli tensions, and he gave advice to Ball about the development of natural gas resources in Israel."[83]

In the intervening months, the U.S. Ambassador to Saudi Arabia had conveyed significant information regarding the positions of the monarchs of Transjordan and Saudi Arabia in relation to the question of

Palestine. Their outlook was a source of comfort to U.S. oil companies as well as to the State Department and to the future Jewish state.

In early March, J. Rives Childs, the U.S. Ambassador to Saudi Arabia, informed Secretary of State Marshall that he had learned something of King Abdullah's view of the Palestine conflict from Azzam Pasha, the head of the Arab League. The king reportedly viewed the Palestine struggle as a civil conflict and urged fellow Arab regimes to avoid exacerbating it.

> Azzam Pasha informed me today that after conferring with King Abdullah it had been agreed that he, Azzam, should send a circular telegram to Arab states cautioning them against making any statements or committing any acts which might be interpreted by SC as threat international peace. He had pointed out Palestinian conflict was civil one and it was most important from Arab states' own interest not do anything which would give SC occasion use force in Palestine. Azzam indicated he understood and was in thorough accord viewpoint expressed by Department.[84]

The CIA had previously reported on the Arab League political committee meeting in Alley, Lebanon, in October 1947, at which "the Saudi Arabian, stating that the oil companies were private corporations and did not represent the U.S. Government, opposed the Iraqi delegate's stand that the contracts should be cancelled."[85] The reference was to the feared cancellation of oil contracts with U.S. companies. The formula proposed by Saudi Arabia was clearly a means of distinguishing commercial from political relations, thus justifying the retention of the latter and profiting from the former.

Duce as well as Childs had a clear understanding of the underlying interests of the parties involved, those of Saudi Arabia as well as the United States and ARAMCO. For Saudi Arabia, significant long-term profits were at stake; for the United States, and more particularly for the Joint Chiefs of Staff, Dhahran in Saudi Arabia was the location of a military base that was considered important to U.S. strategic planning for the region. As for ARAMCO, it fueled U.S. policy in Europe and Japan, as in the Marshall Plan, which in no way eliminated the risks posed by the Palestine problem. But as the exchange between Ball and

Epstein revealed, ARAMCO's vice president was prepared to meet with the representative of the future Jewish state when he judged the time to be suitable.

From this vantage point, the future of the Jewish state appeared more promising than expected. As Epstein discovered, through the invaluable assistance of Max Ball, major U.S. oil companies operating in the Middle East were not categorically set against them, which was interpreted as an indication of future interest. Whether Epstein was privy to U.S. diplomacy in Saudi Arabia is another matter. In retrospect, however, the political implications of these factors for U.S. policy and for Arab politics is difficult to exaggerate.

Epstein's laborious and successful lobbying through the winter of 1948 coincided with a period of skepticism, if not outright pessimism, among policymakers concerning the viability of partition. Indeed, Epstein's exchanges with Ball were frankly incompatible with the outlook of policymakers that increasingly pressed the UN for clarity on whether the Palestinian situation constituted a risk to international peace. In this environment, trusteeship emerged as a possible alternative, but it served to deepen the antagonism between advocates and critics of partition in political circles in Washington.

Epstein's experience and his connections with Max Ball and Clark Clifford were not irrelevant to these developments. They would ultimately weigh in on the side of the advocates of partition. Clifford's ability to exercise influence in White House circles, where he disseminated the Jewish Agency strategy developed in the "Notes," appeared to be effective in addressing the fear of partition endangering U.S. oil interests common to U.S. policymakers involved in Palestine and the Middle East. But it was Epstein's relationship with Max Ball that was critical in the light of Ball's vast network of responsibilities and connections across the oil and gas sectors that were essential to domestic production and national defense. Ball's view of Epstein and the extent to which he believed that the Jewish Agency and its successor would be a good "fit" with U.S. policy in the Middle East, notably that related to its regional oil policy, contradicted the perception of the Jewish Agency as endangering U.S. oil interests. Ball's attempt to open the door to contacts with major U.S. oil executives defied such perceptions, a matter of no small importance in the period leading up to Israel's unilateral declaration of independence and—as later chapters indicate—the reassessment of U.S. policy towards Israel later undertaken by the State Department, the Joint Chiefs of Staff, and the Defense Department.

In 1951, after Ball had retired and become a private consultant, he and his son were engaged by the Israeli government to write a special report on Israel's oil and gas prospects and the possibility of attracting U.S. oil companies to investigate them.

PART III

Beware "Anomalous Situation," 1948

Part III continues the analysis of U.S. policy in response to the struggle over Palestine that was intensified in the period between the passage of UNGA Resolution 181 of November 29, 1947, and U.S. recognition of Israel's unilateral declaration of independence on May 14, 1948. Chapter 6 reveals the deepening apprehension among State Department and Intelligence officials about the prospects of implementing the UNGA recommendation for partition. The chapter also includes evidence of what Washington knew regarding the flight and expulsion of Palestinian refugees in the period preceding Israel's independence.

Chapter 7 indicates the extent to which there was ever-broadening agreement among policymakers, including the president, that the implementation of partition was unlikely in the absence of a credible Arab–Jewish consensus. This gave rise to the movement for a truce and for the replacement of the existing partition resolution with a UN-backed trusteeship program, which was conceived as an interim measure pending resolution of major differences between the parties to the conflict.

Chapter 8 describes the historic debate organized in the White House between a select group of advisers and officials on U.S. policy in Palestine, which was rendered irrelevant by Israel's declaration of independence on May 14, 1948. President Truman's decision to recognize Israel, in turn, stunned U.S. officials at the United Nations who were preparing to offer the

U.S.-backed trusteeship proposal for consideration. The resulting disarray is familiar to historians of this period, but far less attention has been paid to the evidence that the United States understood the disparity of forces on the ground and the likely human toll of war.

6

The Transformation of Palestine

From Partition to Expulsion

ISRAEL'S NEW HISTORIANS AND PLAN DALET

Describing the activity surrounding the Palestine question at the UN in this period, Pablo de Azcarate, secretary of the Palestine Conciliation Commission, woefully observed that the cascade of proposals, counterproposals, and amendments voiced in the General Assembly and related committees and subcommittees had lost "all contact with the palpitating and painful reality in Palestine."[1] That reality contributed to the weakness of a Palestinian political class previously undermined by the impact of the British repression of the 1936–1939 rebellion, as a result of which Palestinian leadership was subordinated to the Arab League, itself divided and militarily unprepared to act in Palestine.

The "palpitating and painful reality in Palestine" to which Pablo de Azcarate referred included not only the massacre at Deir Yassin but the expulsion of Palestinian refugees from Haifa and Jaffa and surrounding villages. The cumulative impact of these developments reinforced Washington's commitment to a truce and the introduction of trusteeship arrangements in Palestine in an effort to contain the violence.

The United Nations may have lost contact with reality in Palestine, but that was not the case with Robert McClintock or the U.S. consuls who provided U.S. officials with evidence of developments on the ground. The U.S. source in which McClintock's memorandum to Lovett appears indicates that it was not sent. Was it considered too strong an assessment of Jewish Agency policies and intentions?

Certainly, there was no attempt to mask what U.S. officials knew of the balance of forces in Palestine in 1948. McClintock opened with a sharp reminder that the Jewish Agency had refused to accept the U.S. proposal for truce negotiations in Palestine. He interpreted this as a sign that it is

> the intention of the Jews to go steadily ahead with the Jewish separate state by force of arms. While it is possible that Arab acceptance of our proposal might place the Jewish Agency in such a position vis-a-vis public opinion that it would have to go through the motions of looking for a truce, it seems clear that in light of the Jewish military superiority which now obtains in Palestine, the Jewish Agency will prefer to round out its State after May 15 and rely on its armed strength to defend that state from Arab counterattack.[2]

McClintock believed this would lead the Security Council to look into the legitimacy of Jewish attacks. In the scenario that would result, "the Jews will be the actual aggressors against the Arabs. However, the Jews will claim that they are merely defending the boundaries of a state which were traced by the UN and approved, at least in principle, by two-thirds of the UN membership."[3] Hence, the United States would face the "anomalous" situation in which it would be faced with domestic pressure to support the claims of the Jewish Agency against the Arabs—a position that was "morally indefensible."[4]

The pattern of attacks was not anomalous, however, as some of Israel's New Historians have pointed out in their studies of Israel's state formation. The so-called Plan Dalet was an inseparable part of the extension of Jewish control over Palestine, where "from 1 April 1948 to the end of the war, Jewish operations were guided by the desire to occupy the greatest possible portion of Palestine," as Ilan Pappé has written.[5] Others, such as Simha Flapan and Avi Shlaim, have confirmed that the plan in question was designed to ensure the expulsion of Palestinians and achieve a homogeneous Jewish state. The ensuing developments, in retrospect, were of major importance in shaping the fate of Palestinian Arabs and the Israeli state.

Avi Shlaim observed that

the novelty and audacity of the plan lay in the orders to capture Arab villages and cities, something the Haganah had never attempted before. Although the wording of Plan D was vague, its objective was to clear the interior of the country of hostile and potentially hostile Arab elements, and in this sense it provided a warrant for expelling civilians.[6]

Simha Flapan, who exposed the foundational myths of Israel's origins, described Plan Dalet as including "the destruction of villages, the destruction of armed enemy, and, in case of opposition during searches, the expulsion of the population to points outside of the borders of the state."[7]

Benny Morris, on the other hand, has argued that there was nothing systematic about the expulsion of Israel's Palestinian inhabitants in this period. Their situation, he has argued, was a product of war. Between April and June 1948, when Plan D was in operation, some 200,000–300,000 Palestinian refugees fled or were expelled from Palestine. But according to Morris, "Plan D was not a blueprint for the expulsion of Palestine's Arabs. It was governed by military considerations and geared to achieving military ends."[8] Yet, as Morris points out in the same passage, "given the nature of the war and the admixture of populations, securing the interior of the Jewish State and its borders in practice meant the depopulation and destruction of the villages that hosted the hostile militias and irregulars."[9] Morris's argument suggests that the process of "securing the interior" was a military operation, whereas his own research and that of others has demonstrated the extent to which such an operation was the expression of a political objective, as Zionist leaders recognized.[10]

In 1988 Palestinian historian Walid Khalidi based his analysis of Plan Dalet on the official history of the Haganah and reported the following guidelines and intended targets.

Enemy Cities Will be Besieged According to the Following Guidelines: 1. By isolating them from transportation arteries by laying mines, blowing up bridges, and a system of fixed ambushes. . . .

3. By disrupting vital services, such as electricity, water, and fuel, or by using economic resources available to us or by sabotage.[11]

Khalidi identified the succession of Zionist military plans drawn up by the Haganah for the period 1945 to 1948 as including "Plan B (September, 1945). The 'May, 1946, Plan' and its two appendices of October and December, 1946, respectively, the 'Yehoshua (Joshua Glauberman) Plan' [early 1948], and 'Plan Dalet' [Plan D], finalized on March 13, 1948."[12] As Khalidi concluded, it was "not easy to visualize, after reading the last two, how the Palestinian state under the partition plan could have survived their implementation."[13]

Plan Dalet was built on the practice of population transfer, which had its roots in European policy in the interwar period and was regarded as "an expedient (albeit extreme) method for resolving ethnic conflicts."[14] Israel Shahak maintains that "although isolated, early expressions of support for the idea of 'transfer' among Zionists were made in 1937, at a time when the Zionist movement in Palestine was gaining strength."[15] The idea of transfer was implicit in British plans for Palestine before the British Labor Party recommended the transfer of Palestinian Arabs out of Palestine in 1944.

Zionist leaders, with David Ben-Gurion chief among them, supported the transfer of Arabs out of Palestine in the 1930s, initially maintaining that this was to come about as a result of agreement with the Arabs, only to admit that "few, if any, of the Arabs would uproot themselves voluntarily; the compulsory provision would have to be put into effect."[16]

It appears that the Peel Commission's (1937) proposal regarding transfer "originated from, and had been secretly conveyed by, top Jewish Agency leaders, including Ben-Gurion, Moshe Shertok (later Sharett), and Weizmann."[17] The U.S. consul in Jerusalem in this period, George Wadsworth, is reported to have been aware of this plan and its place in British thinking.[18] It remained an objective of the Zionist movement in the years preceding the UNGA partition resolution in 1947, before being implemented in the course of the 1948 struggle for Palestine.

In an interview he gave to Ari Shavit in the mainstream Israeli daily *Ha'aretz* in 2004, Benny Morris confirmed Ben-Gurion's support for transfer.

From April 1948, Ben-Gurion is projecting a message of transfer. There is no explicit order of this in writing, there is no orderly comprehensive policy, but there is an atmosphere of [population] transfer. The transfer idea is in the air. The entire leadership understands that this is the idea. The officer corps understands what is required of them. Under Ben-Gurion, a consensus of transfer is created.[19]

To the question as to whether "Ben-Gurion was a 'transferist'," Morris replied, "of course. Ben-Gurion was a transferist. He understood that there could be no Jewish state with a large and hostile Arab minority in its midst. There would be no such state. It would not be able to exist."[20]

The Soviet Union was reported to have been sympathetic to the idea of transfer in the early 1940s as well. Chaim Weizmann, president of the World Zionist Organization, met with Soviet Ambassador Ivan Maiskii in London in 1941. According to Maiskii, Weizmann "had proposed 'to move a million Arabs . . . to Iraq, and to settle four or five million Jews from Poland and other countries on the land where these Arabs were."[21] If the Soviet ambassador expressed surprise, it was not to the principle of transferring Arabs out of Palestine but to the sheer number of those whom Weizmann proposed to move.

In retrospect, Plan Dalet built on the foundations of the transfer policy and the rejection of repatriation. The connection between transfer and the rejection of refugee return was clarified in June 1948 when Morris reports that three major figures of the Yishuv—Yosef Weitz of the Jewish National Fund, Elias Sasson of the Foreign Ministry's Middle East Affairs Department, and Ezra Danin in the Intelligence Service of the Haganah—submitted a comprehensive proposal to Ben-Gurion pressing the government to resolve against allowing a return of the Arab refugees to their homes. The three executives, who the previous month had set themselves up as the unofficial "Transfer Committee," outlined a whole range of steps to ensure there would be no return of the Palestine Arabs (about 300,000 to 400,000 thus far) who had fled or been expelled from Israeli-held territory. The committee's second proposal (coming after one calling for the destruction of abandoned Arab villages) was "to prevent all cultivation of land by [Arabs], including harvesting, collection [of crops], olive-picking . . . also during days of 'ceasefire.' "[22]

Morris observes that the "growing pressure by local military commanders for a clear-cut policy" resulted in General Y. Yadin issuing orders prohibiting the return of refugees to harvest their crops.[23] Again, Morris points out that foreign observers criticized such developments, and then in a telling phrase he states the following: "But—unlike Ben-Gurion's internal Yishuv critics, from MAPAM [the semi-Marxist United Workers Party]—these observers *failed to grasp that these 'local' incidents were part of a national policy and design with a clear strategic-political goal.*"[24]

THOMAS WASSON ON DEIR YASSIN

U.S. officials may not have known the origins of Plan Dalet, but they received news of attacks designed to empty villages, such as those carried out on Deir Yassin. It was the U.S. consul in Jerusalem, Thomas C. Wasson, who cabled the secretary of state with news of the Irgun and Stern Gang attack on the village of Deir Yassin that took place on April 9. Wasson sent Secretary of State Marshall a confidential report on what had transpired. He observed that the attack was preceded by a bitter struggle over the village of Castel, where Palestinians fought under Abd al-Qadir al Husseini, who was killed on April 9, the day of the attack on Deir Yassin by the Irgun and Stern Gang. The latter was "located in a largely Jewish area in the vicinity of Jerusalem and had signed a nonaggression pact with its Jewish neighbors as early as 1942. As a result, its inhabitants had not asked the Arab Higher Committee for protection when the fighting broke out."[25] According to Israeli sources, the villagers of Deir Yassin had turned down the offer of having Arab fighters present in order not to disturb their relationship with their Jewish neighbors.[26]

Wasson reported the following:

> Early morning April 9 combined force Irgun and Stern Gang number over 100 attacked Arab village, Deir Yasin, several miles west Jerusalem. Attackers killed 250 persons of whom half, by their own admission to American correspondents, were women and children. Attack carried out in connection battle now still in progress between Arabs Jews on roads leading to Jerusalem from Tel Aviv.

Arab reaction to attack has been violent and emotions, already at high pitch following death April 8 of Abdul Kader Husseini [Abd al-Qadir al Husseini] (Arab Jerusalem commander) during Arab attempt retake village captured by Haganah, now at bursting point. Officer ConGen visiting Hussein Khalidi, secretary Arab Higher Executive, April 11, found him still trembling with rage and emotion and referring to attack as "worst Nazi tactic."

As indignation, resentment and determination to avenge Deir Yasin spread among Arabs, we believe, chance for cease-fire and truce increasingly remote. With growing criticism in Irgun and Stern Gang circles over Haganah leadership further attacks this nature can be expected and Arabs will react violently.[27]

The head of the International Red Cross in Palestine, Jacques de Reynier, reported that "there had been 400 people in this village; about fifty of them had escaped, and were still alive. All the rest had been deliberately massacred in cold blood."[28] Arab scholars maintain that the event of Deir Yasin "became the single most important contributory factor to the 1948 exodus."[29] The reports of the Haganah Intelligence Service confirmed its impact as well.[30] Ben-Gurion himself noted that Deir Yasin had propelled flight from Haifa.[31] Morris reports that retaliation followed several days later in an ambush of "a ten-vehicle Haganah convoy" on its way to the Hadassah Hospital on the campus of Hebrew University.[32]

When he became Washington's first ambassador to Israel, James McDonald was an unconditional supporter of Israeli policies and an apologist for its expulsion of Palestinians, whom he viewed along with other Arabs as inferior. The case of Deir Yasin, in McDonald's view, was an exception. Relying on the Israeli justification for Palestinian flight, McDonald explained it as a panic response induced by the departure of well-to-do Palestinians, as well as "provoked by lurid tales of Jewish sadism issued by the Mufti and his followers, who presumably intended to whip the Arab population up to resisting the Jews."[33] The approach failed, McDonald wrote, citing the case of Deir Yasin as "the only Jewish-executed massacre of the war (the Irgun raid on Deir Yasin on April 9, 1948, in which the Arab village was destroyed together with its inhabitants, women and children included), were sufficient to set off the flight. Superstitious and uneducated, the Arab masses succumbed to the panic and fled."[34]

Deir Yassin was not an exception, as Israelis recognized. Among other cases was that of Duweima, near Hebron, carried out some six months later by members of the Stern Gang.[35]

In 1949 in a heated discussion between various members of the Israeli parliament on whether Israel should permit 100,000 Palestinian refugees to return, the example of Deir Yassin was brought up. Among those present was a member of the right-wing Herut party who, on being criticized for his proposed way of dealing with the prospective returning refugees, was asked if he was planning another Deir Yassin, to which he replied "Thanks to Deir Yassin we won the war, sir!"[36]

On April 9, Henderson and Lovett did not yet know what had occurred in Deir Yassin, but they were concerned about "the extreme public positions taken by the Jewish Agency and the Arab Higher Committee," making a truce unlikely after May 15. They agreed to contact Judah Magnes, of the Hebrew University in Jerusalem, and Azzam Pasha, the head of the Arab League, for assistance in dealing with the deteriorating situation.[37] Magnes was a U.S.-born reform Rabbi in Jerusalem who supported a bi-national-state along with others such as Martin Buber. Magnes had little influence in the executive of the Jewish Agency but was welcomed in U.S. policymaking circles, although he does not appear to have had any influence on U.S. policy either.

On April 10, Henderson contacted Wasson in Jerusalem, asking him to contact Judah Magnes for help in influencing the outlook of Jews and Arabs in accord with a "conciliatory attitude such as yours."[38]

Gravest danger exists that unless success is achieved in UN efforts to bring about truce and an arrangement whereby interim governmental machinery will be provided for Palestine after May 15 chaotic conditions involving great loss of life and property will prevail in Palestine. At no time has there been a greater need for courageously conciliatory attitude such as yours on part of both Arabs and Jews. If such attitude is to prevail cooperation on part of moderate and conciliatory Arabs and Jews is essential. It is therefore hoped that you either alone or accompanied by such other Jewish leaders as you may consider appropriate will come to U.S. at earliest possible moment.[39]

Henderson informed Magnes of the advisability of his coming as a free agent, and not under U.S. auspices so that "everyone understand[s] that you have a free hand."[40]

At the same time Truman received a letter from Weizmann warning of the risks to the Jewish people if they failed to be given the right to obtain arms.[41] Henderson, in the interim, contacted the U.S. Embassy in Cairo, soliciting assistance from Azzam Pasha of the Arab League:

If this disastrous situation is to be avoided counsels of moderate Arabs and Jews must prevail. We therefore feel it is important that there should be wider representation of wise and temperate Arab leadership in U.S. at present time. I urge therefore that you plan to come to U.S. at earliest possible moment either alone or accompanied by other Arab leaders whom you consider might be helpful in this emergency.[42]

The U.S. ambassador sent Henderson a sobering statement, warning him that Egyptian officials did not have much faith in U.S. policy. As he pointed out, the Egyptian prime minister was skeptical of American policy and doubtful that trusteeship, should it pass, would do away with partition plans. Under the circumstances, the Arab League was reported to be prepared to call for an extension of the British presence. Azzam Pasha declared himself to be in favor of the U.S. position but was uncertain about visiting the United States, which the Saudi foreign minister urged him to do.

In Palestine, the Haganah leadership condemned Deir Yassin, but Menachem Begin, whose party was responsible, pointed to the collusion of the Haganah Regional Command. Begin emphasized that "Deir Yassin was captured with the knowledge of the Haganah and with the approval of its Commander."[43] It was not the only such attack, according to a Haganah historian who claimed that it "was in line with dozens of attacks carried out at that time by the Haganah and Palmach, in the course of which houses full of elderly people, women, and children were blown up."[44]

Three days after the Deir Yassin massacre, the General Zionist Council issued a declaration the State Department subsequently requested that Wasson send to Washington. It read as follows:

> We have decided, relying on the authority of the Zionist movement and the support of the entire Jewish people, that upon the termination of the mandatory regime there shall be an end of foreign rule in Palestine, and that the governing body of the Jewish state shall come into being.
>
> The state which the Jewish people will set up in its own country will guarantee justice, freedom and equality for all its inhabitants regardless of religion, race, sex, or land of origin. It is our aim to make it a state in which the exiles of our people are gathered together, in which happiness and knowledge shall prevail and the vision of the prophets of Israel shall illumine our path.
>
> At this hour, when bloodshed and strife have been forced upon us, we turn to the Arabs in the Jewish state and to our neighbours in adjacent territories with an appeal for brotherhood, cooperation and peace. We are a peaceful people, and we are here to build in peace. Let us then build our state together, as equal citizens with equal rights and obligations, with mutual trust and respect, each with a true understanding of the others needs.
>
> Our lives are dedicated to defending the liberty of our people. If further trials and battles are in store for us, we shall defend with all our might the achievement upon which we place our hopes.
>
> Right is on our side. With us are the hopes of the past generations of our people. With us is the conscience of the world. With us are deposited the testament of the millions of our martyred dead and the resolute will to live of the millions who have survived. The sanctity of our martyrs and heroes rests upon us, and the God of our Fathers will help us.[45]

At about the same time U.S. officials were learning of the Zionist pronouncements regarding the future state, they heard about a number of alarming developments affecting Haifa and surrounding areas. It is difficult to exaggerate the impact the struggle over the city had on Palestinians as their flight and their inability to return to their homes became known beyond the city's limits.

British authorities had indicated their intentions to withdraw from the port city, as well as its airport and main roads, irrespective of conflict breaking out between Arabs and Jews. Their only concern was to safeguard their troops in the process of withdrawing. Palestinian historian Walid Khalidi later revealed that there had been an Anglo-Zionist agreement concerning Haifa, according to which the British agreed to cede control of the city to the Haganah in exchange for Britain's secure exit. The results proved devastating to Arab inhabitants who were "entirely cut off from the outside world. British road blocks on the roads to Jaffa, Nazareth, Acre, and Jenin stopped and pushed back Arab reinforcements from the neighboring villages."[46]

Then, between "April 12 and 17 Haganah forces attacked villages in the neighborhood of Tiberias, and on April 18 Tiberias itself fell."[47] Its 5,300 residents fled as a result, which Donald Neff maintains began "the Palestinian refugee problem."[48] What followed was the desperate call to Abdullah from General Ismail Safwat and Shukry Kuwatly to intervene and send its Legionnaires to halt the massacres.

AUBREY LIPPINCOTT AND HAIFA

U.S. sources claimed that Arabs had been urged to flee Haifa. This information later turned out to be false, but it continued to circulate.[49] As Joel Beinin pointed out, "for decades, the state of Israel, and traditional Zionist historians, argued that the Palestinian Arabs fled on orders from Arab military commanders and governments intending to return behind the guns of victorious Arab armies which would drive the Jews into the sea."[50] The claim that Haifa's Arab population was ordered to leave by Arab leaders has been challenged as propaganda by Palestinian and Israeli sources.[51]

As the study by Walid Khalidi demonstrates, the leaders of the Arab Higher Committee (AHC) had no intention of asking Arab leaders to evacuate their populations. In mid-April 1948, Walid Khalidi, acting as private secretary to Dr. H. F. Khalidi, then secretary-general of the AHC, visited Cairo after the massacre at Deir Yassin. His instructions to the Arab Higher Committee expressed its views with respect to the security of major Palestinian towns. The memorandum stated that Arab defense in Palestine should be based primarily on the three mixed towns of

Jerusalem, Jaffa, and Haifa, which were under imminent threat of Zionist takeover. In the secretary-general's view, their fall would result *not only in the expulsion of their inhabitants but also in the collapse of Arab resistance in all the neighboring rural areas.* He strongly recommended that a force of 1,500 trained men (soldiers in civilian garb), suitably equipped, immediately be dispatched to each of these cities. This, he warned, was the minimum force necessary to protect these cities and their inhabitants in the face of Zionist attack.[52]

Israeli sources have confirmed the efforts of the Arab Higher Committee to prevent Arab flight. According to Simha Flapan, "recent publication of thousands of documents in the Israeli state and Zionist archives, as well as Ben-Gurion's war diaries, expose the 'order' theory" as false. They indicate, instead, "the considerable efforts of the AHC and the Arab states to constrain the flight."[53] "[H]undreds of thousands of others, intimidated and terrorized, fled in panic, and still others were driven out by the Jewish army, which, under the leadership of Ben-Gurion, planned and executed the expulsion in the wake of the UN Partition Resolution."[54]

In Washington, the secretary of state received cables from Haifa sent by U.S. Consul Aubrey Lippincott, who described the fighting in the city:

1. The local Arabs are not 100% behind their present effort. Those who are fighting are in a small minority.

2. A large number of Arabs in this country are entirely depending on outside forces to settle this dispute.

3. Such forces as the Arabs have are quite amateur. Although they have some organization, the essential discipline for such an organization is lacking. Their sense of organizational supply and tactics is almost nil.

4. For the time being we shall probably see large Jewish successes in the field. Unless the Arabs get some organization and training, they will be a very minor obstacle to the Jews on the battlefield. If outside forces come in, the whole matter is a different story. Here again, however, there are signs of disorganization, and there have been as yet no signs of discipline and training comparable to that of the Jews.[55]

In his second cable, Lippincott provided additional information:

Jew attack on Arab Haifa night of April 21–22 complete success.

All Haifa outside British control being rapidly consolidated Jew hands.

British now control small section east Haifa, port area, airport, main road to Mt. Carmel and military zone east and Carmel ridge. Arab areas now being evacuated after Arabs refuse meet Haganah truce team which reportedly call for complete surrender arms, equipment, all food supplies, deportation "foreign" Arabs, and surrender to Jews of all former Nazis. Arab families now leaving entire city and refugeeing to villages west of Haifa with two thousand women and children reported fled to Acre by sea.

Haifa now undoubtedly completely Jew controlled. British say cannot interfere Jew occupation all areas if Jews do not impede British movements on roads and in areas necessary for evacuation.

Arab leaders and men proved poor and totally inadequate deal with Jew forces. Survivors claim British prevented seven hundred reinforcements from entering city during battle also claim Abdullah promised help which British also stopped. Arab forces entirely dispersed. Leaders reportedly left before battle occurred.

Most appreciations situation express general feeling Jews will keep Haifa under full control some months. Haganah bringing slightly disrupted public utilities in control with Jewish staffs ordered run post office telephone and electricity.[56]

Haifa's impact transcended the devastated city limits. It was immediately felt in surrounding areas attacked by Haganah forces such as Balad al Sheikh, Hawassa, Tira, and Acre, where "of the city's some 13,400 Arab residents, only about 3,000 remained, including the refugees from the surrounding villages."[57] Jewish forces proceeded to reorder the city, concentrating the remaining Arab residents in specified areas and razing their houses in a demolition project designed to pave the way for settling Jewish refugees. As to Haifa's Arab population, "there were only 8–10,000 Arabs left in Haifa out of a normal population of some 50,000 and later that number was further reduced."[58]

On June 23, Lippincott's third cable concerning Haifa reached Washington. The Honorary Spanish Vice Consul Victor Khayyat, who was also a U.S. citizen, told the U.S. consul that there were only 1,500 Arabs remaining in Haifa. On June 23, Lippincott sent Khayyat's account to the secretary of state.

> 1. All Arabs who remained Haifa being thoroughly screened by Jewish authorities, required obtain identity cards and must swear allegiance to Israel state.
> 2. Arabs who return Haifa are considered illegals. These also required take oath allegiance Jewish state. Result is remaining Arabs determined leave. Khayyat informed that he had recently arranged for departure seven sailing vessels for Lebanon each carrying average 120 persons passage free. One additional vessel scheduled leave twenty-second ending operation. Khayyat said departures were arranged with assistance British commandos now controlling port. Approximately 1500 Arabs now Haifa. Of these some expected infiltrate Nazareth and other towns in nearby Arab controlled areas.[59]

In addition, the Spanish consul confided to Lippincott that he was "issuing 'emergency certificates' for all Arabs applying" for entry into Syria or Lebanon. Lippincott, in turn, wanted to know what orders had been given by Jewish authorities "with regard [to] refusing Arabs return Haifa Khayyat said 'word was just passed around.'"[60]

Golda Myerson (Meir), then a high official in the Jewish Agency's Political Department, visited Haifa "after its conquest" and reported that

> it is a dreadful thing to see the dead city. Next to the port I found children, women, the old, waiting for a way to leave. I entered the houses, there were houses where the coffee and pita bread were left on the table, and I could not avoid [thinking] that this, indeed, had been the picture in many Jewish towns [i.e., in Europe during World War II].[61]

Reflecting on permitting Palestinian Arabs to return to their villages, Myerson remarked that she was not among those favoring such an outcome. She described those who advocated for the Palestinians' return as "extremists." She agreed with Ben-Gurion that the Arabs who had chosen to remain were to be treated "with civil and human equality, 'but it is not our job to worry about the return of [those who had fled].'"[62]

U.S. and British officials were alarmed that Haifa, with the second most important oil refinery in the Middle East after Abadan (Iran), should be the scene of unprecedented political turmoil. They were concerned with the future of the Iraq Petroleum Company (IPC) refinery that had employed "some 1,700 Arab and 270 Jewish manual workers, in addition to 190 Jewish, 110 Arab, and 60 British clerical workers" in late 1947.[63] The employees had participated in struggles that brought Arab and Jewish unions together and were reported to have signed an agreement to maintain peaceful relations within the refinery. Such relations were maintained until several months before Deir Yassin, when an attack by the Etzel (Irgun) on Palestinian workers outside of the Haifa refinery sparked retaliation against Jewish workers inside the refinery. This, in turn, was followed by a Haganah/Palmach attack on the Arab village near Haifa at Balad al-Shaykh as well as Hawasa, where Palestinians known to work in the refinery lived.

In mid-June, the defense minister of Iraq informed the British in Baghdad that "Haifa is most important Palestine problem." He expressed the view that if Haifa cannot be an Arab state it must be a free port; otherwise the pipeline would have to be relaid through Syria and Lebanon because, although the Iraqi economy is dependent on oil royalties, Iraq "could not tolerate outlet for its oil being in Jewish state."[64]

Several days later, in a very different environment, Secretary of State Marshall lost no time in speculating on the potential benefits of the takeover of the refinery in Haifa, fantasying that it provided reason for reconciliation and "mutual accommodation which may serve as a constructive example of how Jews and Arabs can manage to get along peaceably throughout all of Palestine and the Near East."[65] But that was not the principal lesson to be learned. Marshall calculated, as did Bevin, that above all the refinery had to be put back into operation, and UN Mediator Bernadotte should be so informed. Marshall discovered that the Provisional Government of Israel (PGI) had been engaged in discussions with the British Foreign Office regarding the refinery and that

"PGI would not object if representative of Mediator controlled production in Haifa refinery, Arabs receiving a fair share of output."[66] As Marshall reminded the U.S. ambassador to the UK, it was important for the mediator to "keep in mind importance of Haifa production going to ERP and to legitimate civilian requirements of Near East, including Israel."[67] Marshall arranged for the same message to be conveyed to Jerusalem, Cairo, and to the French, who were urged to convey it to the UN mediator.

In early September, the assistant chief of the Petroleum Division of the State Department described the U.S. position as supporting the reopening of the Haifa refinery with Iraqi crude oil. Washington argued that "the gain in terms of world oil supplies would be substantial. The cooperation of Arabs and Jews, which would be necessary to the operation of the refinery, would provide an important precedent for cooperation in other matters."[68] But as the same source indicated, there was little to warrant such hope. Apparently, the United States had been in touch with the mediator, British officials, Israelis representing the Provisional Government, as well as oil companies, but U.S. efforts to reopen the refinery were not successful. Iraqis opposed the passage of oil to Haifa while the refinery remained under Jewish control. Jews, in turn, appeared reluctant "to permit the degree of international control of the refinery and its operation which will satisfy the Iraqi wishes."[69]

The experience of the closure of the Haifa refinery led the Jewish Agency to investigate other possible sources of fuel purchase, including from the Soviet Union. Uri Bialer points out that the Jewish Agency conducted negotiations with the Soviets in the spring of 1948. "Israel's overture to Moscow and its readiness at that time, whatever the consequences, to facilitate Soviet infiltration of the oil business in the Middle East, thereby breaking the West's monopoly remained unparalleled until 1954."[70] But matters did not end well as difficulties emerged in arranging for a tanker to carry the oil, which effectively undermined the contract that was then cancelled.

In the interim, in late December 1948, after IPC failed to convince the Iraqi regime to permit it to carry oil through Haifa to some of the neighboring states, Western officials whose companies were represented in IPC interceded to ensure there was oil for the Marshall Plan. As of December 29, U.S. sources reported that "no decision has been taken, and none can be favorably decided upon until the Government is fully satisfied that the Zionists at Haifa, shall not derive any benefit whatsoever from Iraqi oil."[71]

U.S. as well as Israeli interest in the Iraqi oil connection has persisted into the present day. In the summer of 2003, several months after the U.S. invasion of Iraq, *Ha'aretz* reported that the Pentagon asked Israel "to check on the possibility of pumping oil from Iraq to the oil refineries in Haifa."[72] In April 2003, the *Guardian* reported on plans designed to reconstruct the 1948 pipeline. At that time, Bechtel was to build the pipeline. The project was not only to safeguard Israel's oil supply but to ensure a supply of U.S. oil outside of Saudi Arabia.[73]

Within several days of the 1948 upheaval in Haifa, Arab leaders planned to meet in Cairo to discuss the implications of what had occurred. The U.S. ambassador made it clear to Washington that Egyptian forces were in no condition to fight, but they were worried about the domestic impact of defeat at the hands of Jewish forces. The regime itself was concerned not to antagonize Britain, yet it was in need of troops to deal with strikes and nationalist actions, above all fearful "that Arab forces might prove ineffective in protecting Palestinians, therefore permanently damaging Arab cause in Palestine."[74]

Those considered most likely to provide the core elements of an Arab military force were Transjordan, Iraq, and Syria, with token forces from Lebanon. Egypt would limit itself to providing financial assistance until Britain's departure from Palestine. The Palestinians, on the other hand, were believed to be unarmed, politically divided, and lacking in leadership capable of assessing the force they faced.[75]

LOWELL PINKERTON AND JAFFA

Jaffa, "the Arab enclave" embedded in the area allotted to the Jewish state in the 1947 UN partition agreement, had been under attack by the Irgun since the end of April 1948 although fighting in the city had begun earlier. The Irgun attack against the Manshiya neighborhood led to the flight of its population in the direction of Jaffa. The Haganah attacked villages surrounding Jaffa, expelling their inhabitants. Sir Henry Gurney, chief secretary of the Palestine Government, described Irgun attacks as "indiscriminately aimed at civilian targets" and as being "designed to create panic among the population."[76] The British remained in control of Jaffa and demanded a cease-fire, threatening to counterattack. Reporting on this period, the British commander in Jaffa, General Murray, described "a scene which I never thought to see in my life. It was the sight of the whole population of Jaffa pouring out on to the road carrying in their hands whatever they could pick up."[77] According to Murray, "[i]t was a case of sheer terror." Rejecting claims that residents fled on instructions from Arab leaders, Murray wrote that "[t]hese people had terror written on their faces and they couldn't get on the road to Gaza quick enough."[78]

In April 1949, the U.S. minister to Lebanon, Lowell C. Pinkerton, submitted documents he had received from the Executive Committee of the Jaffa and District Inhabitants Council to Secretary of State Dean Acheson, which he copied to the American member of the Palestine Conciliation Commission (PCC), Mark Ethridge. "Jaffa and District" included the three towns of Jaffa, Ramleh, and Lydda, as well as adjoining villages. As Pinkerton wrote, the members of the council were "men who were responsible for much of the former commercial activity of Jaffa."[79] Their purpose was to mobilize efforts for assistance and to inform the United States of the desperate conditions of refugees who had "lost almost all understanding from the world." They sought to remind the United States of the injustice of displacing a people from its homeland in an effort to find a home for "the wandering and displaced Jew."[80]

Pinkerton's submission of the enclosed documents to Mark Ethridge and the PCC resulted in their becoming part of that commission's record. In presenting the same material to Acheson, Pinkerton had also placed them in the State Department record. The documents described events that occurred in April 1948. Pinkerton submitted them to Ethridge and Acheson in April 1949.

First, we would draw the attention of the Government of the United States to the following important fact: namely, that the conflict did not originally include or involve such a question as the return of refugees; the population itself never envisaged such a possibility. On the one hand a large number of people did not leave their homes voluntarily, but were expelled by order of the Jewish commanders when they entered their towns and villages (Ramleh and Lydda), and were prevented from taking any of their belongings with them. On the other hand, the conditions which prevailed shortly before the termination of the Mandate rendered it impossible for a large section of the people to remain in homes and lands. For, that would have meant the destruction of a large number of them, since they did not possess arms with which to defend themselves.[81]

The Jaffa and District Council representatives asked that the United States support the desire of the refugees to return home immediately, underlining the appalling conditions in which such refugees lived and their desire to save their property and ensure the survival of their crops. The Jews, they argued, under the guise of "innocent regulations," were in effect "bent on destroying Arab property and blocking the right of return."

[I]t is now known that the Jews have destroyed houses, and in some cases whole quarters, under the misleading and apparently innocent pretenses of making public gardens and other improvements; they have occupied Arab homes and used up everything that was left in them; they have deliberately destroyed water pumps in Arab orange plantations, so that the trees would go without irrigation and therefore die, thereby reducing the value of these plantations.[82]

From Beirut, the Jaffa Emergency Committee pressed the United States to "use its influence with the Jewish authorities concerned" to allow those citrus plantation owners who remained in Jaffa, as well as those who left to return, to salvage their fragile crops as "the orange tree is a very delicate tree" and it had been neglected for the past year.[83]

As they reminded U.S. officials, "the citrus industry represents the greatest single item of Palestine's wealth," adding that about 54 percent of the plantations were Arab owned. Yet, as the committee members pointed out, "almost all the citrus belt was included in the Jewish Part," referring to the area allotted under the 1947 partition plan. Reviewing that plan, they recalled its highly uneven allotment of land: the Jewish community, which had then constituted roughly 30 percent of the population, obtained over 70 percent of Palestine, which included roughly

95 percent of irrigable land, "leaving only about 5% to the Arabs" who were given "the arid mountains which do not have enough drinking water for the people in the summer, not to speak of agriculture."[84]

With evident bitterness, the Jaffa delegation questioned whether international law existed. If so, they asked, what was its meaning in terms of the 1947 partition plan that they believed to be "an international law" calling for human rights in addition to partition? The Jaffa and District Council representatives repeatedly expressed the hope that the United States would act in accord with the ideal expected of it.

Members of the Jaffa Emergency Committee signed what, in effect, was a surrender agreement with the Haganah that was labeled "Instructions to the Arab Population by the Commander of the Haganah, Tel Aviv District," dated May 13.[85] Palumbo claims that the committee consulted with Abdullah and the secretary general of the Arab League,[86] but Morris alleges that several of its members had gone to Tel Aviv to "smooth the way for the Jewish takeover and discuss terms."[87]

The signatories included Ahmad Effendi Abu Laban, Salah Effendi El Nazer, Amin Effendi Andraus, and Ahmad Effendi Abdul Rahim. They declared Jaffa "an undefended area," and in their capacity as representatives of "all Arabs in the area," they agreed to carry out all instructions given now and in future by the commander of the Haganah, Tel-Aviv District, or any officer he designated; and they accepted responsibility for the same. This was followed by the declaration "IT IS UNDERSTOOD [caps in original] that the Haganah always does respect and will respect the Geneva Convention and all International Laws and Usages of War."[88]

The agreement opened with the warning that "any shot fired at a Jewish area or at a Jew or at any member of the Haganah, or any resistance to them, will be sufficient reason for the Haganah to open fire at the Offender."[89] Arms, munitions, and other such equipment were to be turned over to the Haganah, as well as information concerning "mines or booby traps or any similar devices," with severe punishment threatened in the event of violation.

All males in the area defined in the Agreement will concentrate in the area between Feisal Street, Al Mukhtar Street, Al Hulwa Street and the Sea until every body has identified himself under arrangements, the particulars of which will be notified later.

During this time, any male found outside this area will be severely punished, unless in possession of a special permit.[90]

With the exception of those identified as "dangerous to the peace and security of the area," who risked internment, those seeking to return to their homes would be free to do so provided they carried the proper identification and their homes were not "in an area which will be declared as a military enclosure."[91] There was to be no seizure of property, and any removal of property had to have official approval by Haganah forces.

In reality, "it is now known that the Jews have destroyed houses, and in some cases whole quarters," the elected Executive Committee reported.[92] They had more to say in a sober warning: unless action is taken immediately, "many of the refugees will be driven to espouse ideas and principles totally inimical to good order and social stability, and that unless they are effectively resettled in their own homes and lands, the peace sought for in this part of the world will never reign, even though it might appear on the surface that the trouble had subsided."[93]

Shortly after the collapse of Jaffa, the "Chief of the Jewish Agency's Department of Immigrant Absorption, went to see how many new immigrants could be settled in the town."[94]

In late May, an Israeli officer testified, "I saw soldiers, civilians, military police, battalion police, looting, robbing, while breaking through doors and walls."[95] Two months later, "Jaffa's military commander repeatedly complained that navy soldiers had broken into several homes, beaten the owners and robbed them. A few days later, a catholic church was broken into and silver chalices and crucifixes were stolen."[96] In the same period, Red Cross officials demanded a meeting with the military governor after they "discovered a pile of dead bodies" that, according to the military governor, "had probably been shot by Israeli soldiers for not complying with their orders."[97]

In June, the Haganah's High Command sent an official to look into reports of violence and vandalism. Abraham Margalit reported that "there are many violations of discipline, especially in the attitude to the Arabs (beating and torture) and looting which emanate more from ignorance than malice."[98]

In July, the military governor of Jaffa, Yitzak Chizik, resigned in the face of "the uncontrollable ongoing crusade of pillage and robbery."[99] When the city fell, "its entire population of 50,000 was expelled with the 'help' of British mediation, meaning that their flight was less chaotic than in Haifa."[100]

7

Truce and Trusteeship

WORKING TOWARD A TRUCE AND TRUSTEESHIP

In the atmosphere of heightened tension generated by the Deir Yassin massacre, U.S. officials were increasingly moved to act against partition and in favor of trusteeship. Within a matter of months, the U.S. administration was prepared to join with others in an effort to promote both a truce and a trusteeship arrangement under UN auspices. Evidence of Truman's support for such a move is on the record, as are his parallel promises to Chaim Weizmann of U.S. support for partition and a Jewish state. By the end of February, Truman had become convinced that partition would not be implemented without force, which he was unwilling to approve. On this, the president and State Department officials were in accord.

The problem became more acute as Secretary of State Marshall and U.S. officials prepared for Britain's departure. Marshall increasingly used the language of trusteeship in rehearsing what Austin might say at the UN in the wake of Britain's exit from Palestine. Marshall proposed drafts of statements that took as their starting point the Security Council's admission of the inability to implement partition without the use of force. Under such circumstances, Marshall instructed Austin to recommend that a special UNGA session be held to consider "that until the people of Palestine are ready for self-government they should be placed under the trusteeship system of the United Nations."[1]

Examining Marshall's statements to U.S. officials on the subject of partition and its alternatives, Robert McClintock was convinced, as he told Lovett, that the United States would soon be facing a special UNGA session with trusteeship the probable outcome. Under those circumstances, "a new threat of Jewish attempts by violence to establish a de facto State in Palestine" would replace the previous threat of Arab aggression.[2]

Sensing the accelerating change in the direction of U.S. policy, Clark Clifford reminded the president of his long-standing U.S. commitments to partition and statehood, and the extent to which these protected U.S. interests. Some have argued that the timing of Clifford's remarks to the president was a function of his response to rumors of heightening tension between the USSR and the United States, and even the possibility of war.[3] Others disputed the veracity of the claim. Clifford, however, maintained that supporting partition was the best way of excluding the USSR from Palestine.

In preparing his presentation to the president, Clifford had the assistance of Max Lowenthal, attorney and Zionist supporter, and Eliahu Epstein. Epstein had previously confronted Lovett with Israel's response to U.S. fears of partition. As discussed earlier in connection with the Elsey scoop, Epstein may well have been informed of the extent of internal discontent in policymaking circles. Clifford, in turn, was joining the argument in support of partition and evoking some of the themes that had appeared in the "Note on Palestine Policy." He described the United States as being "in the ridiculous role of trembling before threats of a few nomadic desert tribes. This has done us irreparable damage. Why should Russia or Yugoslavia, or any other nation treat us with anything but contempt in light of our shilly-shallying appeasement of the Arabs."[4] Clifford insisted that "not only is partition in conformity with established American policy, not only is partition the only hope of avoiding military involvement of the United States in the Near East, but, in addition, partition is the only course of action with respect to Palestine that will strengthen our position vis-à-vis Russia."[5]

In the very different political environment of the UN, Warren Austin attempted to establish contact with Arab leaders who were calling for a clarification of Washington's position. Austin's exchanges with Faris Bey el-Khouri of Syria, Camille Chamoun and Charles Malik of Lebanon, and Mahmoud Fawzi Bey of Egypt revealed that "insofar as the Arab states are concerned they would be willing to suggest possible solutions to the Palestine Question which in the judgment of Mr. Wilkins and myself go further than any previous position taken by the Arab states."[6] Arab states were willing to consider three options, in two of which "a democratic constitution and government" was the first condition cited (unitary state and federal or cantonized state). The third option was trusteeship. All three options involved "constitutional organization; b. immigration, and c. guarantees for minorities."[7]

In addition, Austin reported learning that "moderate elements in the Arab states such as King Ibn Saud, Azzam Pasha, Secretary-General of the Arab League, Nokrashi Pasha, Prime Minister of Egypt and others" were eager to eliminate "the Mufti and the extremist Arab elements in Palestine" and to move toward a "moderate solution of the Palestine Question."[8] These delegates also recommended that the European refugee problem be turned over to the United Nations.

Austin gave no indication of the covert arrangements between Abdullah and the Jewish Agency leadership. He may not have known that Abdullah's prime minister, along with Sir John Bagot Glubb, commander of the Arab Legion, had met with Bevin in London on February 7, 1948, and had arrived at a plan that was subsequently implemented. According to Abu al-Huda, the Transjordanian prime minister, it consisted of a proposal "to send the Arab Legion across the Jordan when the mandate ended and to occupy that part of Palestine awarded by the UN to the Arabs that was continuous with the frontier of Transjordan."[9] Bevin found the arrangement entirely satisfactory. Washington would endorse it as well, preferring it to the UNGA partition resolution's recommendation for a Palestinian state linked in economic union with a Jewish state.

Another dimension to developments in Palestine was addressed by Ernest A. Gross, U.S. legal adviser to the director of the Office of United Nations Affairs. In the vacuum that would be left with Britain's departure, Gross reminded U.S. officials that "local agencies of administration" might arise that would "assume a governmental character and secure international recognition, thus achieving status as members of the family of nations, with corresponding rights and duties."[10] This was an unmistakable reference to the political and administrative infrastructure organized by the Yishuv in Palestine.

Such considerations may well have sharpened Marshall's desire to clarify President Truman's position. On March 20, Marshall addressed the Palestine question at a press conference on the west coast. He referred to the policy proposed on the previous day by Warren Austin, which Marshall supported.

> I recommended it to the President, and he approved my recommen-
> dation. . . . The United States suggestion is that a temporary trust-
> eeship should be established in order to maintain the peace and
> to open up the way to an agreed settlement. This trusteeship itself
> would be established without prejudice in any way to the eventual
> political settlement which might be reached for Palestine.[11]

However, as the State Department learned, Truman had met with Dr. Chaim Weizmann the evening prior to Austin's UN speech and "assured him [Dr. Weizmann] that we were not changing our policy with respect to Palestine. Then within less than twenty-four hours, Ambassador Austin had made the speech that represented a complete reversal of our attitude."[12]

Where, then, did Truman stand? In the course of an exchange at the UN, Lovett attempted to clarify the president's position. He recalled that if the U.S. failed to get support for partition, Truman had indicated that "we could take the alternative step. That was perfectly clear. He said it to General Marshall and to me."[13] As Lovett told McClintock, "there is absolutely no question but what the President approved it. There was a definite clearance there. I stress it because Clifford told me the President said he did not know anything about it."[14]

In this unsettled atmosphere, Clifford called for lifting the arms embargo to Palestine at the very time that Marshall and the State Department were working toward "the laying down of arms, the cessa-tion of the illegal entry of either Arabs or Jews and of the cessation of all smuggling of arms into Palestine."[15]

In an effort to arrange for a truce, U.S. officials consulted with the Jewish Agency about meeting with members of the Arab Higher Com-mittee, but had no success. Moshe Shertok denounced both truce and trusteeship, insisting that the United States failed to understand the responsibility of the Arab states for the violence the truce was allegedly designed to contain. As to trusteeship, Shertok pointed out that it was inappropriate given that preparations were under way for establishment of the Provisional Council.

Nonetheless, in early April, weeks prior to Britain's departure from Palestine, the State Department produced a "Draft Trusteeship Agreement for Palestine" that assumed the form of a constitutional document for a unitary state.[16] What is striking about this document is the extent to which it echoed the "[p]rinciples underlying the constitution of a unitary State in Palestine," recommended in the 1947 minority report of subcommittee 2 of the UN Ad Hoc Committee on Palestine. However, the later draft went further in its coverage.[17] Secretary of Defense Forrestal was asked for his assessment of the forces that would be needed to implement such an agreement, and he provided this assessment on several occasions.

Several weeks later, Austin was authorized to present the draft proposal before the first subcommittee of the United Nations, which had initially supported partition. The proposal envisioned an egalitarian society organized under bi-national auspices and operating under UN authority. As stated in article 4 of the 1948 U.S. draft, "The administration will be conducted in such a manner as to encourage the maximum cooperation between Jews and Arabs in Palestine leading to a form of self-government which will be acceptable to both communities."[18] Provisions for a bicameral legislature reflected the same intention.

The draft also defined conditions determining eligibility for citizenship.[19] There was to be no discrimination on the basis of "race, religion, language or sex," and no restriction would be placed on the "free use by any person of any language in private intercourse, in religious matters, in commerce, in the press or in publications of any kind, or at public meetings."[20] On the controversial question of immigration, the U.S. draft proposed the admission of Jewish Displaced Persons (DPs), their number to be determined by the International Refugee Organization for the first two years of the trusteeship's operation. Following that period, immigration was to be open to all, but the number admitted was left blank, apparently a concession to Zionist positions.

On the question of land policy, article 31 prohibited discriminatory practices with respect to land purchase or use, additionally underlining the importance of protecting "the interests of small owners or tenants in cases of transfer of arable or grazing lands."[21] The reference applied to Bedouins, among others, deemed vulnerable under existing partition plans. Finally, the assurance of equality, as opposed to privileged access, in "economic, industrial and commercial" undertakings in Palestine addressed ongoing concerns articulated in the report of UN subcommittee 2.

The U.S. consul in Jerusalem reported that "the Jewish Agency does not find in the draft agreement even a basis for discussion, since it does not provide for establishment of Jewish state."[22] Shertok, speaking before the Security Council on April 1, suggested conditional acceptance of the truce insofar as it assumed implementation of the partition resolution, and total rejection of the trusteeship proposal as inappropriate for "a country ripe for independence."[23] As for Arab delegates, U.S. sources cited Mahmoud Fawzi Bey of Egypt as rejecting a truce if it was linked to partition, but otherwise supporting it.

The Joint Chiefs of Staff had consulted with Admiral Sidney W. Souers, executive secretary of the National Security Council; W. Stuart Symington, secretary of the Air Force; and Major General Lauris Norstad, deputy chief for operations of the U.S. Air Force. Forrestal met with William Leahy, fleet admiral of the U.S. Navy and chief of staff to the commander in chief of the Armed Forces, to determine the army, naval, and air requirements "to be supplied from outside of Palestine in order to maintain law and order under a temporary trusteeship, including any necessary action to control borders to prevent the illegal entry of persons, either Jewish or Arab, from other countries."[24] Leahy urged that Britain participate and, in addition, he recommended that France join. Indifferent to France's colonial role in Syria, Lebanon, and the Maghreb, U.S. officials subsequently turned to Egypt, requesting its participation in the same joint effort.

Two weeks later, the secretary of defense renewed his concern with the limits of American military capacity and the risks of a U.S. "commitment to undertake a proportionate share of the burden of providing the police forces required during a truce and temporary trusteeship in Palestine."[25] The Joint Chiefs of Staff estimated that the United States would have to provide some 50,000 troops, which Forrestal argued "represents substantially our entire present ground reserve, both Marine and Army."[26] The defense secretary suggested that such a commitment involved a reassessment of U.S. plans for such diverse areas as Italy, Greece, Turkey, Iran, and China.

THE "CANCEROUS PALESTINIAN SITUATION"

According to Abba Eban, "the President had given Weizmann a specific commitment that he would work for the establishment and recognition of a Jewish state of which the Negev would be a part."[27] When he met with Ambassador Austin and Philip Jessup, who was U.S. representative to the Special Session of the General Assembly, Weizmann asked for an explanation of U.S. policy. "Was it fear of the Arabs? Was it oil? Or was it fear of Russia? He said there was no reason whatever to fear the Arabs. They were woefully weak. The Arabs could do nothing with their oil except sell it to the U.S."[28]

Further, as Austin pointed out, if the General Assembly failed to obtain the necessary two-thirds majority to alter existing UN policies—that is, partition—then "the Jews would have the legal, and if not the legal certainly the moral right to go ahead with their plans to establish the Jewish state."[29] Weizmann, however, appeared to be more open to trusteeship than expected. He indicated "that trusteeship might be beneficial to the Jews, and also provide an opportunity for cooperation of the closest kind between Jews and Arabs, ending in due course to an agreed political settlement."[30] This was not the position generally conveyed by Israeli officials to Washington.

On April 17, the UN Security Council passed Resolution 46 by a vote of 9 to 0, with the USSR and Ukraine abstaining, in support of a truce in Palestine that urged the cessation of violence while condemning the entry of illegal arms and fighters.

In Washington, preparations were being made for Austin to address the UN in which he would relay the U.S. agreement to contribute a part of the forces (some 45,000 troops) necessary to implement truce and trusteeship. At the same time the U.S. ambassador in Cairo sent news of the Arab League's positive though conditional response to an armistice or truce. It was not to be used as a cover to allow the armament of the Jews and was interpreted as a step toward a final settlement.[31] But Arab officials understood that the arrangements for trusteeship were designed to be temporary, leading them to fear that Washington continued to support a Jewish state. In Jerusalem, Consul General Wasson reported that "the Jewish Agency does not find in the draft agreement even a basis for discussion, since it does not provide for establishment of a Jewish state."[32]

In the midst of these developments, Henderson sent Lovett a memorandum in which he referred to the "cancerous Palestine situation" as a threat to U.S. security and global peace, urging Washington to deal with it "as one of our most vital and urgent international problems."[33] Current U.S. policy, he pointed out, assumed that Washington would only act within UN parameters, endorsing the UNSC call for a truce and backing the idea of General Assembly support of temporary trusteeship. Elaborating on what the UN faced, Henderson addressed the national and international dimensions of the Palestine problem and called for the United States to remove this issue from domestic politics. He urged the U.S. president and secretary of state to act on Congress and American Jewish opinion to hasten a resolution of the conflict lest it imperil peace in the Middle East and U.S. security. Henderson urged Britain and U.S. allies to assist in this goal in no less stringent terms.

Fearing that the UN might not agree to the U.S. proposal and assuming that the situation in Palestine would only worsen in the absence of a truce, Henderson submitted another proposal, this one for a trusteeship plan covering Jerusalem. The proposal defined the Jerusalem area as inclusive of Jerusalem and its surrounding towns and villages. It went on to add that it "should also include the area of Palestine between Jerusalem and the Mediterranean and should include the ports of Tel Aviv and Jaffa and the airport at Lydda in order to prevent the inland isolation of Jerusalem and its environs and to provide access to the sea and the outside world."[34] Washington agreed to aid in providing police support and, "as a last resort," to act alone, albeit with UN authorization. When Secretary of State Marshall sent Rusk a draft of the proposed trusteeship arrangements for Jerusalem, the identification of the area of Jerusalem was left blank, with reference to an attached map.[35]

While U.S. proposals for Jerusalem were being drafted, Warren Austin was sending "Top Secret" messages from the UN of possible breakthroughs on the aggravated question of a truce. At the end of April, Austin was engaged in personal diplomacy and made it clear to all concerned that his were not official exchanges, but he clearly felt encouraged by his encounters on April 25 with Joseph Proskauer, president of the American Jewish Committee (AJC), and Mahmoud Fawzi Bey of the Egyptian delegation, who was also described as "spokesman for the Arab League."[36] Proskauer was not a representative of the Jewish

Agency in Palestine, but he was a highly respected figure in the AJC, which was among the more moderate American Jewish organizations in its positions on Palestine.[37]

Austin assured Marshall that "both Proskauer and Fawzi Bey have been sufficiently receptive to encourage a further effort along these lines. For example, Fawzi Bey now has permission from Cairo (which he says must mean the Arab League as well) to sit down with a go-between and Jewish representatives for an informal talk not involving a commitment on his part."[38] Even if such efforts failed, Austin remarked, they merited recognition, much as did the intransigence of those who opposed them. Austin went so far as to speculate that Marshall might one day take the initiative and expose such opposition to encourage and mobilize public opinion in favor of a truce. Marshall, in fact, made reference to the informal efforts involved in a subsequent press conference.

Austin also reported on his success in promoting the idea of trusteeship among members of the Saudi delegation who were prepared to consider it, provided that "articles on immigration, land policy, and termination can be drafted more specifically."[39] If Arab fears were recognized, Prince Feisal of the Saudi delegation maintained, "there was a good chance that, with United States and Arab influence and support, trusteeship would get a two-thirds vote in the General Assembly."[40] Henderson reminded Feisal that "Arab and Jewish positions were still far apart" before asking him whether "the Arabs had been in touch with any moderate Jews such as Dr. Magnes. The Minister indicated that they had not."[41]

On April 22, Henderson, in his capacity as director of the Office of Near Eastern and African Affairs, sent Lovett a lengthy message laden with ominous warnings and urgent recommendations for the days remaining before Britain's departure from Palestine. As Henderson soberly stated, "any kind of an international arrangement which we may effect for preserving world peace on a basis which would be compatible with the security of the United States is lacking in substance so long as the cancerous Palestine situation continues to develop unchecked."[42]

Henderson warned that Washington would not act alone. It was

supporting the Security Council's call for a truce in Palestine and believes that a temporary trusteeship for Palestine should be established by the General Assembly which would provide interim governmental machinery in Palestine following the termination of the British Mandate on May 15 and which would be without prejudice to the rights, claims and position of the Jews and Arabs of Palestine and without prejudice to the eventual political settlement for Palestine.[43]

There was another aspect of Henderson's review of U.S. policy in Palestine—namely, his insistence that it be withdrawn from domestic politics, which he believed were being influenced by extremist Zionist positions. On April 22, 1948, Henderson called on those he described as

the more moderate Jews in this country to break the hold which a minority of extreme American Zionists now has on American Jewry so that Jewish leaders in this country, instead of continuing to push Palestine Jews into an extremely nationalistic position, will endeavor to impress upon them the importance of assuming a reasonable and moderate attitude of cooperation with the Arabs.[44]

To this Henderson added the warning to Arab leaders, including those in the Arab League, "that unless they on their part are willing to adopt a conciliatory and reasonable attitude of cooperation with the Jews, the security and prosperity of the whole Middle East will be gravely threatened."[45]

MARSHALL, McCLINTOCK, AND RUSK AND PROPOSALS FOR A TRUCE

At the end of April, Marshall sent Austin a proposal whereby Jerusalem would be placed under a UN trusteeship accord. McClintock, on behalf of the State Department, submitted a "Text of Informal Truce Proposals for Palestine" to Lovett. At the UN, McClintock reported to Lovett that with the exception of the article that dealt with immigration, all others "have been provisionally agreed upon, subject to approval by their principals, by representatives of the Jewish Agency and the Arab League in New York City."[46] But it quickly became clear that article 10, which dealt with the proposed immigration of 4,000 Jewish Displaced Persons into Palestine every month, elicited strong objections on the part of the Jewish Agency.

Moreover, Shertok objected to a truce as blocking statehood and extending Britain's presence in Palestine. Eliahu Epstein, in turn, stated, "the Jewish State already exists and the Jews have no use for trusteeship," and further, "no foreign troops are necessary. The Jews need arms and diplomatic action to prevent the invasion of outside countries."[47]

Meetings with Saudi, Syrian, Iraqi, Egyptian, and Lebanese delegates proved no less sobering as they vowed permanent opposition to Jewish immigration unless certain conditions were met. These included the request that immigration cease after the truce; that the number of immigrants remain 1,500 per month and not more; and that young males be excluded from the lot of immigrants. In exchange for the above conditions, Prince Feisal maintained that "the Arabs would promise to curb the Arab people and to acquiesce although they could not sign any documents. This according to Prince Faisal was frankly all that could be done at this time."[48]

In an attempt to salvage the truce and prior to learning of Shertok's response, Dean Rusk proposed to Lovett that temporary arrangements under the Security Council Truce Commission be pursued. These would allow both parties flexibility while committing them to a truce. Rusk was persuaded that Nahum Goldmann and Moshe Shertok would be amenable to such proposals, unlike more militant American Zionists.[49] But Rusk underestimated Shertok's objections, which were made to both Marshall and Rusk in April and May. As Shertok explained,

the main objections as I saw them were: first, that the proposed truce entails the deferment of statehood and renders its attainment in the future most uncertain, thereby gravely prejudicing our rights and position; second, that as the effective operation of the truce obviously involves the presence and the use in Palestine of a considerable force, we cannot but assume that the intention is to keep the British forces in occupation and control of Palestine. I was also greatly concerned about the gross inequality under which we would be placed as regards arms and military training: the Arab states would be entirely free to acquire arms and stock-pile them for eventual use in Palestine against us; Palestinian and other Arabs would be free to train en masse in any of the neighboring countries; we would be precluded from either acquiring arms abroad or from any large scale training—training which we could only organize in Palestine.

We are most vitally interested in a truce, but, with every desire to be helpful, I am sure you will appreciate our anxiety to protect ourselves from the grave dangers with which it may confront us.[50]

Rusk was nonetheless persuaded that the only stumbling block was immigration, for which he had a solution. Rusk's solution entirely ignored the Arab position by proposing the figure of 4,000 Displaced Persons per month, the Jewish Agency figure. Under the circumstances, his proposal that the Security Council Truce Commission arbitrate the matter was not promising. Rusk reported that he had warned Truman that it was possible "that the Arabs would accept the truce and that Jews would not, and that they might create difficult problems for him." Apparently the president replied to this, stating that "if the Jews refuse to accept a truce on reasonable grounds they need not expect anything else from us."[51]

Truman was adamant about wanting a truce and as he responded in the same passage, "tell the Arabs that our policy is firm and that we are trying to head off fighting in Palestine. Remind them that we have a difficult political situation within this country. Our main purpose in this present situation is to prevent a war." What Truman did not make public, or indeed convey to his advisers, save for one, was that in addition to committing himself to preventing war, the U.S. president had committed himself to supporting and recognizing a Jewish state. This, at the end of April, was what Truman communicated to Chaim Weizmann through Samuel Rosenman. "On the 23rd April Weizmann was told that the President would do all in his power promptly to recognize the Jewish state, if the United Nations would continue to support partition."[52] Apparently, this exchange remained unknown, or largely unknown, to the Jewish Agency, the Foreign Office, and the State Department.[53]

From Cairo came news that the Arab League was prepared to accept a truce in Jerusalem to protect holy sites. But the Palestine Truce Commission sent a very different message regarding the situation in Palestine, which it described as deteriorating, with government offices closing, communications systems collapsing, and the airport in Lydda out of commission. "JA [Jewish Agency] acting as a general organizing body for Jewish areas and attempting to replace suspended governmental activities," and by contrast "Arab areas are depending on municipal authorities within the townships and villages without any central authority."[54] The commission expected worse to come, warning that "operations on larger and more important scale than Haifa expected shortly."[55] Its prediction proved to be accurate.

In Cairo, the U.S. ambassador, citing the prime minister, reported that Egyptian troops were needed to counter what it viewed as a possible coup coming from nationalist forces. There was a general sense of the inadequacy of Egyptian forces and fear of their defeat if sent to Palestine, with resulting harm to the Palestinian cause. Iraq attempted to bolster support for Transjordan, but Baghdad as well as Beirut turned to the United States for assistance, the latter for economic development programs.

In meetings with members of the Saudi delegation that included Prince Feisal, Sheikh Hafiz Wehba, and Sheikh Alireza, the objectives of the U.S. trusteeship agreement as well as the questions of immigration and land policy were raised. Feisal questioned the lack of U.S. recognition, as evident in the trusteeship agreement, of the Palestinian capacity for self-government. Feisal subsequently requested a meeting with Henderson to discuss these questions.

Marshall, in turn, was preoccupied with the possibility of Arab intervention in Palestine. If this occurred, he reflected, "we do not see how U.S. Govt could avoid taking energetic position in UN pointing out that invasion is violation of Charter and insisting that appropriate steps including if necessary dispatch of forces under auspices UN be taken to eject invaders."[56] But it was also becoming clear that the structure of the future Jewish state was virtually in operation, and some UN officials believed that Britain favored the better organized Jewish forces at this stage. In the opinion of Pablo de Azcarate, by the beginning of March 1948, the experienced hands of the Jewish Agency were running a "state in embryo, capable of undertaking the administration of the most technically complicated public services (including, naturally, the police and the maintenance of public order) with as much, if not more efficiency than the same organs of the Mandatory Power."[57]

On May 1, two weeks before the assigned date of the British with-drawal, the Jewish Agency cabled the Security Council with claims of an Arab invasion of Palestine, prompting Marshall to request verifi-cation from U.S. officers in the field. From Jerusalem, Wasson cabled back on May 3, reporting the British disclaimer of such a charge as "complete moonshine," as they pointed to Arab military "dribbling in" whose strength was variously estimated to be from 7,000 to 10,000 men who had been trained in neighboring countries but who did not make up a coherent force.[58] Little more was expected, according to the Brit-ish, until their departure. In the interim, the United States confirmed that Arab forces had been put on alert and that "about 650 Egyptian and North African volunteers had crossed into Palestine within the last ten days."[59]

On April 30, Austin sent Marshall a telegram from the "Palestine Truce Commission to SC President" without identifying its author.[60] It may have been written by Wasson, who in the interim had been named by Truman as U.S. Representative to the Truce Commission. Although awaiting Senate approval, on May 3 Wasson sent Marshall a report on conditions leading to the collapse of the Palestinian government.

Palestine Government has generally ceased to function and central public services no longer exist. In Jewish areas Jews have taken effective control and are maintaining public services within those areas. Preparations for establishment Jewish state after termination mandate are well advanced. Confidence in future at high peak and Jewish public support for leaders overwhelming. In Arab areas only municipal administration continues without any central author-ity. In Samaria food and gasoline are in very short supply. Morale following Jewish military successes low with thousands Arabs flee-ing country. Last remaining hope is in entry Arab regular armies spearheaded by Arab Legion. . . . Unless strong Arab reinforce-ments arrive, we expect Jews overrun most of city upon withdrawal British force.[61]

Wasson described Jewish forces as adopting a "defensive offensive" role whose main purpose was improvement of their positions and the liquidation of "Arab interference."[62] The Haganah and Irgun persisted in "aggressive and irresponsible operations such as Deir Yassin massacre and Jaffa," Wasson reported, observing that they were repudiated by the Haganah only if they failed.[63]

Wasson predicted an "all-out offensive" by the Haganah after May 15. The British and others, he informed the secretary of state, "believe Jews will be able sweep all before them unless regular Arab armies come to rescue. With Haifa as example of Haganah military occupation, possible their operations will restore order."[64] In the period that followed, the liquidation of Arab villages involved as many as 100 massacres in 1948–49 alone.[65]

FACING AN "ANOMALOUS SITUATION"

On the same day that Wasson sent out his assessment of the situation, Lovett informed the U.S. Embassy in London of steps the U.S. delegation was planning to take at Lake Success. There was to be an immediate ten-day cease-fire as of May 5; a ten-day delay in Britain's departure; a ten-day break in the UNGA Special Session; and the transportation of selected representatives of the Arab Higher Committee, Arab states, the Jewish Agency, and members of the SC Truce Commission from France, Belgium, and the United States to facilitate action on the truce.[66]

Shertok rejected what he described as the "somewhat spectacular proceedings," insisting that "peace can in present circumstances best be achieved by an unconditional agreement for an immediate 'cease fire.' "[67] If the Arabs agreed to such, Shertok indicated the Jewish authorities would do the same. In the midst of these exchanges, the UN General Assembly's First Committee proceeded to approve a proposal dealing with the establishment of a provisional regime in Palestine.

The response to Shertok's rejection of the U.S. initiative led U.S. officials to conclude that the Jewish Agency would proceed with its intention "to go steadily ahead with the Jewish separate state by force of arms."[68] McClintock reasoned that "in light of the Jewish military superiority which now obtains in Palestine, the Jewish Agency will prefer to round out its State after May 15 and rely on its armed strength to defend that state from Arab counterattack."[69] His views were reflected in the unsent memorandum, written in the name of Dean Rusk, whose special assistant McClintock was at the time.

If these predictions come true we shall find ourselves in the UN confronted by a very anomalous situation. The Jews will be the actual aggressors against the Arabs. However, the Jews will claim that they are merely defending the boundaries of a state which were traced by the UN and approved, at least in principle, by two thirds of the UN membership. The question which will confront the SC in scarcely ten days' time will be whether Jewish armed attack on Arab communities in Palestine is legitimate or whether it constitutes such a threat to international peace and security as to call for coercive measures by the Security Council.[70]

The above predicament would be intensified, McClintock suggested, if Arab armies entered Palestine, leading Jewish forces to claim "that their state is the object of armed aggression and will use every means to obscure the fact that it is their own armed aggression against the Arabs inside Palestine which is the cause of Arab counter-attack."[71] What would the U.S. position be, McClintock asked rhetorically?

There will be a decided effort, given this eventuality, that the United States will be called upon by elements inside this country to support Security Council action against the Arab states. To take such action would seem to me to be morally indefensible while, from the aspect of our relations with the Middle East and of our broad security aspects in that region, it would be almost fatal to pit forces of the United Sates and possibly Russia against the governments of the Arab world.[72]

The position attributed to the Jewish Agency was, in fact, that adopted at the UN by Moshe Shertok.

Faced with what he termed "this almost intolerable situation," McClintock's response was telling. His criticisms aside, he urged the United States, with the British and French, to intervene by promoting an accord between Abdullah and the Jewish Agency. The plan McClintock envisioned was designed to assuage Washington's Arab allies. According to his account, Abdullah would grant Aqaba to King Ibn Saud, the Syrians would be mollified by "some territorial adjustment in the northern part, leaving the Jews a coastal state running from Tel Aviv to Haifa."[73] Abdullah, however, was not mollified after learning of Deir Yassin, which inspired him to think less of partition than of granting Jews a place in a unitary state where they could have "full Arab nationality in a unitary state sharing all that we share while yet enjoying a special administration in particular areas."[74] To this Abdullah added the hopeful message, "Thus will end the slaughter and the people will live in peace and security forever."

In the midst of these developments, Judah Magnes arrived in Washington to meet with Secretary of State Marshall, as foreseen in the invitation that had been issued in early April.[75] Magnes, a U.S.-born rabbi living in Jerusalem, was welcomed as a moderate, though he was understood to have little influence among Zionist leaders, whether in the United States or in Palestine. U.S. officials were also partial toward Nahum Goldmann, viewing him as another moderate Zionist who was closer to the Zionist establishment but did not wield significant influence.

Marshall was nonetheless interested in Magnes's assessment of the situation in Palestine and eager for him to meet the president. Magnes was blunt about the prospects of implementing either trusteeship or a truce, although he believed the former offered the only way out of the existing quagmire, whether it assumed the form of individual states, cantons, or provinces in a federal arrangement. What mattered was forging an agreement between the parties, without which, Magnes insisted, no settlement would work. An attempt at working out a federal arrangement had, in fact, been tried and failed, as the U.S. effort revealed. Further, both the Jewish Agency and the Arab Higher Committee rejected trusteeship, although both accepted a truce in Jerusalem as of May 2, 1948.

When he arrived in Washington, Magnes had little hope short of Washington cutting off funding to the Jewish Agency. He depicted the Jewish community in Palestine as "an artificial development" and argued that "the Haganah costs $4 million a month to run. He was certain that, if contributions from the United States were cut off, the Jewish war machine in Palestine would come to a halt for lack of financial fuel."[76] He recommended cutting off financial contributions to Palestine and Arab states, but recognized the precarious financial condition of Syria and Iraq.

As McClintock recalled, Magnes reported that "he had lived in Jerusalem for 25 years. He knew its people, both Arabs and Jews, perhaps as well as any living man. He assured me with great conviction and intensity that the populace of Jerusalem—Arab and Jew alike—is heartily sick of the situation in which they find themselves and that their burning desire is peace."[77] Magnes pointed out that there were Arab and Jewish police and municipal councils, but some other public services were in need of restoration, such as the water supply. He appeared confident that a UN officer would succeed in carrying out such responsibilities, assuming that he was protected by a bodyguard, and that he was "preferably a man from a religious call of life."[78] The reason for protection was that "there was always the danger of physical violence, since the young Jewish zealots believed fanatically in their cause and were truly idealistic in the thought they had a mission to restore the land of the Jews to its people."[79] Among those Magnes suggested were Dr. Bromley Oxnam, the former president of the Council of Churches, and Charles Taft, the current holder of that position.

Magnes endorsed trusteeship proposals that the United States had proposed, but he was critical of what he viewed as Washington's excessively apologetic approach toward Jewish forces. He viewed trusteeship as the only available option, noting that "it could be made up of states, as in the federal union, or it could consist of cantons or provinces inhabited by Jews and Arabs separately."[80] He urged the United States to indicate that the resulting settlement was to be worked out by Arabs and Jews, otherwise there would be no solution.

Before leaving, Magnes requested permission to pose a blunt question: "Do you think there is any chance to impose a solution on Palestine?" "I [Marshall] replied that imposition of a regime implied the use of force. It was clear as daylight that other governments were eager to sidestep and leave Uncle Sam in the middle. I did not think it was wise for the United States alone to take the responsibility for military commitments in Palestine but I would be glad to give this matter further thought."[81] The secretary of state commended Magnes for "the most straightforward account on Palestine I had heard," on the basis of which he asked Magnes if he had plans to see Truman and thereupon urged McClintock to arrange such a meeting.

THE LINES ARE DRAWN

Magnes's visit coincided with a period in which the lines were increasingly sharply drawn between critics and supporters of partition. Among the critics were figures such as Warren Austin and his more cautious colleagues—Acting Secretary Lovett, McClintock, and Rusk. Partisans of partition included Clifford and John Horner, adviser to the UN delegation at the Second Special Session of the General Assembly.

On May 4, Warren Austin submitted the statement he wanted to make before the UN to Dean Rusk for approval. It opened with the observation that existing conditions in Palestine made it impossible to implement partition on May 15, hence the need to "suspend November 29 resolution and to support SC truce terms."[82] Lovett objected and, as McClintock reported, contacted Dean Rusk and John C. Ross, the deputy to Austin at the United Nations, to emphasize that "our principal effort at the moment should be on the truce and cease-fire," although as McClintock added, "one of the articles of the proposed truce did, in fact, include provision for suspending the effect of the resolution of November 29, 1947, for the duration of the truce."[83] Rusk agreed with the urgency of a truce, persuaded that in its absence Britain's withdrawal would be followed by the mobilization of each community, the concentration of Islamic and Arab support for the Palestinians, and a long attrition war between Jewish and Arab states in which control in the Jewish sector would pass to Jewish extremists. Rusk predicted that there would be an increase of anti-Semitism in the West.

Within a week, the State Department urged the president to support the Security Council's truce efforts as well as the UN General Assembly's appointment of a UN Commissioner for Palestine. U.S. supporters had few illusions as to the feasibility of implementing the truce. As Rusk argued,

It seems if we go back to what we are after, it has been all along a peaceful settlement of this thing in Palestine. As late as March 17 we were trying to find some inkling of some sort of agreement between the Jews and the Arabs with the help of the Security Council, with some effort to adjust the partition plan in what they would accept, but we went black-out because the Arabs would not talk about it.

So we shifted on March 19, the whole emphasis, to a straight truce. That truce would have taken us beyond May 15 and beyond the period when there was no government in Palestine. If we had gotten a truce we were prepared to go in on a trusteeship to formalize the truce arrangement and for that we made suggestions to various governments about going in with us to establish this trusteeship.[84]

Rusk's concern, shared by others, was the future of Palestine in the aftermath of Britain's exit. But something had changed: "there is a community in existence over there, running its own affairs."[85] Rusk understood that "the boss" would never oppose a request for assistance if it made a difference. As he phrased it, "I don't think the boss will ever put himself in a position of opposing that effort when it might be that the U.S. opposition would be the only thing that would prevent it from succeeding."[86] By comparison, Rusk envisioned the situation on the Arab side as equivalent to the status quo, indicating that he was uncertain in what direction Arabs would go, and whether or not they would "invite Abdullah in."[87] In any case, as Rusk concluded, the United States faced Arabs and Jews, "each fairly responsible for its own community but with a political settlement which has to be negotiated because you have these succeeding claims."[88] In this situation, Rusk recommended that the United States focus on obtaining an international trusteeship arrangement for Jerusalem.

In the course of his review, Rusk described Lovett as eager for a "clean break of all these negotiations," adding that a statement on U.S. efforts since mid-March would be useful.

In other words, we have literally done our damndest on this thing. Now if it doesn't work, we certainly aren't going to take this thing on our own backs singlehanded and it is not up to us to continue to bat our brains out on the theory we are solely responsible for what the General Assembly does on this situation and what action the Assembly takes has got to be something which is either a provisional or final solution of this thing.[89]

Clark Clifford agreed that things had changed in Palestine, but he remained steadfast in support of recognizing the Jewish state, which he regarded as "consistent with U.S. policy from the beginning."[90] He had an ally in John Horner, adviser to the U.S delegation at the UN. In a memorandum on the "Future of Palestine," Horner warned that many at the United Nations were skeptical about the consistency of U.S. policy, advocating that it support partition and focus on keeping the USSR out of the Middle East and mending its relations with the U.S. Jewish community.

Horner also called "for the annexation by the Kingdom of Trans-Jordan of that part of Palestine which the November 29 scheme had intended to be a separate Arab state."[91] His reasoning was,

> (1) that it would be acceptable to the Jews, (2) that it probably would be acceptable to King Abdullah, (3) that it is not basically incompatible with the November 29 recommendation, (4) that it offers a relatively permanent solution, (5) that it would create a viable Arab state in the enlarged Trans-Jordan thereby achieving the objectives of the economic union proposal of November 29, (6) that it would effectively eliminate the Grand Mufti of Jerusalem and his followers, and, most important, it would face up to the inescapable fact that a Zionist State already is in being in Palestine.[92]

Horner recommended that a plebiscite be held among Palestinian Arabs on the question of "union with Trans-Jordan."[93] No such plebiscite was held, nor was there any evidence to demonstrate that, if held, it would prove Palestinian support for absorption into Transjordan. Horner seemed oblivious of the differences between Jordanian and Palestinian politics and society. He proposed that the "exchange of populations between Trans-Jordan and the Zionist state" take place, referring to past precedents, as in the case of Greece and Turkey after the First World War.[94] With the provision of generous UN and U.S. aid and development projects, Horner foresaw the establishment of "two ethnically separate states which would have their origin in agreement between the two groups."[95]

Clifford, unlike Horner, focused on the existence of a Jewish state in Palestine. In Clifford's private papers is a statement by Truman "of his intention to recognize the new Jewish State in Palestine as soon as it comes into existence."[96] In Clifford's view, developments in Palestine were irreversible insofar as the Jewish state was concerned. Moreover, the United States could use them to its advantage by "an immediate statement by the President that he intends to recognize the Jewish state when it is proclaimed."[97]

While U.S. officials were debating what to do at the UN, Thomas Wasson, the U.S. member of the Truce Commission, reported from Jerusalem that both Jews and Arabs were making it difficult to implement the cease-fire, but that the Truce Commission would continue to seek terms for a truce.

8

Recognition and Response

THE MAY 12 DEBATE

On May 12, 1948, Truman invited a number of key State Department officials, as well as those who were identified only as "White House," to discuss U.S. policy in Palestine and assist him in making a decision on the issues. At this historic debate, George Marshall, Robert Lovett, Fraser Wilkins, and Robert McClintock faced off against Clark Clifford, David Niles, and Matthew Connelly.[1] Truman was initially moved to support Marshall, but his response to Israel's unilateral declaration of statehood on May 14 did not reflect Marshall's position.

The events of May 14 altered the geographical and political map of Palestine and the Middle East, and with it the balance of military power in the region. Washington was unprepared, and the British looked on their American colleagues as woefully inept in their contradictory policies. Working through a highly charged and unforgiving political atmosphere in Washington, Truman's decision to recognize Israel undercut the position of the U.S. delegate to the UN, Warren Austin, who had been operating on the assumption that the United States supported a cease-fire and truce in Palestine.

On May 11, Clark Clifford advised the Jewish Agency representative Moshe Shertok to go ahead with plans for independence. According to Israeli sources, Shertok was told that "Clifford advised we go firmly forward with planned announcement of State," and that "President considering recognition," even though, as the same sources stated, Lovett and Dean Rusk were reported to be hostile.[2] That hostility did not prove to be permanent.

David Ben-Gurion's reflections of this period were revealing of the Zionist leader's understanding of U.S. policy:

> At the beginning of May, some of the great world figures, including General Marshall, warned us not to establish the State of Israel. And there were good friends who told us that we had no alternative but to accept Marshall's views. It seems, superficially, that these advisors were right. Marshall was backed by a gigantic force, which no Jewish force in Israel or elsewhere in the world could withstand. We would not have had the least chance if we had gone to fight the American Army. When we failed to accept Marshall's views, it was not because we thought our forces were stronger; we could not have been so foolish. We acted as we did because we doubted whether Marshall was willing to utilize the forces he represented to prevent the establishment of the State of Israel. The State was set up in opposition to Marshall, and the American Army was not used against us. Had it been, the State would have been destroyed at once. However, the very opposite happened: the United States immediately accorded de facto recognition to the State of Israel, although it had not yet recognized Israel de jure.[3]

The Zionist leader concluded that "those who advised us not to establish the state did not err in their evaluation of the forces that stood behind Marshall; they did not exaggerate it [in] the least; they erred in that they could not differentiate between what the American representative said and what the American Government would do."[4]

In preparing for the May 12 debate, Clifford offered a view of U.S. policy that echoed the arguments the Jewish Agency representatives had circulated earlier. Clifford had the assistance of Max Lowenthal, former counsel to the Interstate Commerce Committee, who prepared a top secret file for Clifford dated May 11 marked with this warning: "Clark: Please do not let anyone else read this dynamite," signed Lowenthal.[5] The "dynamite" consisted of evidence that Marshall, reputed to be hostile to recognition of the Jewish state, had met with Shertok and indicated interest in the possibility of an accord between the future Jewish state and Abdullah of Transjordan.

On the basis of this disclosure, it appeared that the secretary of state was prepared to support the future recognition of the Jewish state. Hence, the principal figure in the policymaking circle alleged to be hostile to the recognition of Israel was exposed as sympathetic—provided certain conditions were met. Those conditions were, in fact, identified in the covert report that Clifford received. "Mr. Shertok's Washington representative privately reports that Secretary Marshall twice said: there is nothing I would like more than such an agreement between Abdullah and the Jews."[6]

Lowenthal's secret data included other information, such as the extent of Jewish military preparedness, arms, and the mobilization of Jewish youth. It disclosed "that the Jews have youths of military age in Italy, North Africa, Germany, Yemen, France, Cyprus, all picked for prior immigration."[7] The number of volunteers and their means of reaching Palestine was unclear: "despite a naval blockade that may be set by American ships of war?"[8] This led Lowenthal to question what U.S. policy should be.

Lowenthal's secret file also contained information about the British Foreign Office. According to this source, the British were prepared to recognize the Jewish state, which it regarded as a bulwark against the USSR. In addition, a prominent Labor Party figure was cited speaking of "the heavy financial investments in Jewish Palestine now being negotiated by big British concerns, and the doubled and tripled current credits now being granted by such concerns as Hambros Bank of London to business in Jewish Palestine," with the Foreign Office's approval.[9] Accompanying this report was a letter from the head of the Palestine Economic Corporation, Julius Simon, indicating that "this corporation is one of several which supply millions of dollars of capital on loan or as investment for the up-building of Palestine."[10]

On the day of the historic debate, Lovett opened with his own revelations concerning the prospective Jewish Agency–Transjordan accord. He reported on a visit by Moshe Shertok, who informed him and Secretary of State Marshall of the momentous developments regarding Abdullah's plans with respect to Palestine. Lovett maintained that the impact of this development, in conjunction with the evidence of Jewish military successes in the field, convinced the Jewish Agency that a truce was unnecessary.[11] To this Marshall added that he had warned Shertok of the dangers in basing "long-range policy on temporary military success."[12] Further, he warned Shertok not to request U.S. help if things did not work out, given Washington's advance warning.

When Clifford was invited to present his case, he began by objecting to U.S. support for a truce in Palestine, arguing that it had been superseded by "the actual partition of Palestine" that had taken place "without the use of outside force."[13] He recommended that the president recognize the Jewish state and instruct U.S. representatives at the United Nations to do the same once the mandate was terminated.

Lovett reminded the White House Counsel that the United States was currently a member of the UN Truce Commission, and he decried support for a state whose borders had not been internationally recognized. He also criticized Clifford for exploiting the Palestinian question in domestic politics, remarking that the question of recognition of the Jewish state "was a very transparent attempt to win the Jewish vote," though he claimed that it would backfire.[14]

On May 13, Marshall sent a report on Palestine and the Arab region to U.S. diplomatic offices in London, Jerusalem, and across the Arab world, commenting on the comparative weakness of Arab regimes, which impaired their ability to act in Palestine. However, Marshall also observed the limits of Jewish impunity toward Arabs. In the long run, he argued, "if Jews follow counsel of their extremists who favor contemptuous policy toward Arabs, any Jewish State to be set up will be able survive only with continuous assistance from abroad."[15]

From Jerusalem Thomas Wasson reported on the jubilation of the Jewish population in anticipation of Britain's exit and the imminent declaration of independence. He described Jewish authorities as staying within the boundaries defined by the November 29, 1947, UNGA Resolution 181. But Wasson also took note of the response of a Jewish official to an AP correspondent who inquired about the fate of Resolution 181 if Arab states invaded Palestine. The Jewish official's response was that "Ben-Gurion had always said that main aim of Jews was to get all of Palestine."[16] Wasson insisted, however, that to date he had no evidence of Jewish forces abandoning the UN partition resolution boundaries, even though "most observers believe that Jews are winning first round at least of their battle and will desire consolidate positions."[17]

Wasson sent the following assessment of Arab resistance in Palestine, the anticipated response of neighboring Arab states, as well as Abdullah's informal accord with the Jews.

> Arab opposition to Jews in towns has completely disintegrated. Haifa is under Jewish domination; Jaffa is a deserted city and has been declared "open city"; and the Arabs have been given much needed breather by cease-fire. It is not believed Jerusalem Arabs would be able to prevent much opposition to Jews if latter decided to occupy city. Most representative Arabs have fled to neighboring countries and Arabs of authority are found only after most diligent searching. Consequently truce and cease-fire talks are greatly hampered and slowed down. It is possible Arabs do not wish to be placed in difficult position of having to make definite decisions which would be public admission of fact that Jews have upper hand. Perhaps they hope events will decide future course of policy. We believe Arab Legion and possibly other Arab armies will march into Arab areas of Palestine after termination of January date but will not risk major operation with Jews. Evidence of informal arrangements between Jews and Abdullah should not be overlooked. Abdullah's desire for additional territory and lucrative neighbor as well as his present strong position with fellow rulers may make such agreement possible of execution.[18]

Lovett met with Clifford after May 12 to express uneasiness about the outcome of the debate. According to Jonathan Daniel's study of the president, Clifford succeeded in convincing Truman to insist on immediate recognition to preempt recognition by Poland and the USSR.[19] Lovett's account of his conversation with Clifford differed. He emphasized that he repeatedly asked for a delay in recognition for several important reasons. The first was to allow the Jewish Agency Executive to submit its appeal for recognition to Washington; the second was to have the time to inform U.S. allies; and the third was to give the president and policymakers time to inform U.S. officials, including those at the United Nations, where havoc would ensue on the announcement of U.S. recognition of Israel. Unable to influence the course of events, Lovett added sardonically, "I can only conclude that the President's political advisers, having failed last Wednesday afternoon to make the President a father of the new state, have determined at least to make him the midwife."[20]

THE IMPACT OF TRUMAN'S RECOGNITION OF ISRAEL

On May 14, Eliahu Epstein, acting as agent of the Provisional Government of Israel, sent Truman a letter announcing the proclamation of the new state. Epstein had acted on the instructions given by Clark Clifford concerning how to request U.S. recognition. The new state, Clifford had pointed out, was to "claim nothing beyond the boundaries outlined in the UN resolution of November 29, 1947, because those boundaries were the only ones which had been agreed to by everyone, including the Arabs, in any international forum."[21]

On May 14, 1948, Epstein delivered the following letter to President Truman:

My dear Mr. President:

I have the honor to notify you that the state of Israel has been proclaimed as an independent republic within frontiers approved by the General Assembly of the United Nations in its Resolution of November 29, 1947, and that a provisional government has been charged to assume the rights and duties of government for preserving law and order within the boundaries of Israel, for defending the state against external aggression, and for discharging the obligations of Israel to the other nations of the world in accordance with international law. The Act of Independence will become effective at one minute after six o'clock on the evening of 14 May 1948, Washington time.[22]

The declaration concluded with the statement that Epstein had been "authorized by the provisional government of the new state to tender this message and to express the hope that your government will recognize and will welcome Israel into the community of nations."[23]

Epstein's statement, however, did not correspond to the position of the "Provisional Administration" on the key issue of defining boundaries. On May 12, in accord with Ben-Gurion, the Provisional

Government voted that "the boundaries of the state should not be mentioned in the Declaration of Independence."[24] In a departure from Epstein's declaration, Ben-Gurion eliminated any reference to the UN partition plan in the statement read on May 14 declaring Israel's independence at midnight.

Simha Flapan reports that "Epstein was probably aware of the discrepancy between his statement to Truman and the decision of the People's Administration not to mention borders, because he cabled Sharett the same day to explain that he had been advised by friends in the White House to mention the November borders."[25] Other representatives of the Jewish Agency in London and the United Nations were reported to have called for a correction favoring mention of the November borders, as Epstein had done.

Other developments in Palestine appear to have escaped notice in Washington. A "state of emergency" was announced in Palestine on May 14, and "all combatant units received orders to execute Plan D [Plan Dalet]," which succeeded in the conquest of "about 20,000 square kilometers of territory (compared with the 14,000 square kilometers granted them by the UN Partition Resolution) and cleansed them almost completely of their Arab inhabitants."[26] There was no indication that Marshall was aware of any of this when he informed Mr. Epstein of the U.S. president's recognition of the Provisional Government of Israel.

On May 15, Secretary of State Marshall duly responded to Mr. Epstein:

Dear Mr Epstein: I have the honor to acknowledge the receipt of your letter of May 14, 1948 and to inform you that on May 14, 1948 at 6:11pm, Washington time, the President of the United States issued the following statement:

"This Government has been informed that a Jewish state has been proclaimed in Palestine, and recognition has been requested by the provisional government thereof.

"The United States recognizes the provisional government as the de facto authority of the new State of Israel."

Sincerely yours,
G.C. Marshall[27]

On May 16, Loy Henderson proposed that the United States reply to Eliahu Epstein's letter to Truman notifying him of the proclamation of the State of Israel with a series of questions, one of which dealt with borders. Henderson suggested that "at the appropriate time" the United States might take the position that its "de facto recognition does not necessarily mean that we recognize that the frontiers of the new Jewish state are the same as those outlined in the recommendation of the General Assembly of November 29, 1947, that those boundaries had been determined upon the understanding that there would be an economic union of all Palestine and a special international regime for Jerusalem."[28] Henderson penned his memorandum after Truman's statement of recognition. Its tone was one of deference and understanding that boundaries were, in effect, susceptible to change in accord with altered conditions. Was this a cover for Ben-Gurion's position, which was that the boundary was where people determined it to be?

The Minister of Justice in the new state, Pinhas Rosen, asked for a clarification of borders in the Declaration of Independence, to which Ben-Gurion replied that "if we decide here that there's to be no mention of borders, then we won't mention them. Nothing is a priori [imperative]."[29] Rosen's response was that the question at hand was a legal issue, to which Ben-Gurion replied that "the law is whatever people determine it to be."[30] Ben-Gurion made it clear that he agreed with Haganah Chief of Staff Israel Galili who, on April 8, 1948, declared that "the borders of our state will be defined by the limits of our force. . . . The political borders will be those of the territories that we shall be able to liberate from the enemy; the borders will be the fruit of our conquests."[31]

Dean Rusk later recalled the sequence of events on May 14 at the United Nations. He received a call from Clark Clifford informing him of the precise time the State of Israel would be declared; the United States would then recognize the new state. Rusk added that Clifford also told him that "the President wished me to inform our Delegation at the United Nations," to which Rusk replied that "this cuts across what our Delegation has been trying to accomplish in the General Assembly under instructions and we already have a large majority for that approach."[32] Rusk then called Warren Austin, who was in the General Assembly. On learning the news, Austin left and did not return, which Rusk interpreted as Austin's way of informing the UN Assembly that "this was the act of the President in Washington and that the United States Delegation had not been playing a double game with other Delegations."[33] When Philip Jessup took the podium at the General Assembly to confirm what had occurred, Rusk said the Assembly "was then in pandemonium."[34] Rusk was instructed by Marshall to go to the UN to "prevent the U.S. Delegation from resigning en masse."[35]

The damage was not easily contained. As Austin wrote to Marshall several days later, U.S. recognition of Israel "has deeply undermined the confidence of other delegations in our integrity and [that] this is a factor which the Department will want to keep in mind in the immediate future and for some time to come."[36] Moreover, for many delegations, Washington's act of recognition "constituted reversal of U.S. policy for truce plus trusteeship as urged in special session of G.A. and, in later stages, U.S. compromise resolution laying stress on truce plus mediation," to which Austin added further implications of this U.S. action.[37]

Within a matter of hours after Washington's recognition of Israel, U.S. officials in Cairo and Jidda cabled ominous warnings of the Arab response. British officials questioned the legitimacy of the Israeli action in light of the 1947 UN resolution: "Foreign Office view is that it is not correct to consider that the 29 November resolution establishes a legal basis for creation of a Jewish state."[38] UN Secretary General Trygvie Lie, apprehensive about the future of the UN, informed Marshall and other Security Council members of the Egyptian government's announcement of its planned intervention in Palestine. The Arab League issued a parallel declaration, endorsing a unitary, democratic state in Palestine for all of its inhabitants.

Why did Truman recognize Israel, and why did he do it so precipitously? It is easier to answer the second question, with its suggestion of competition with the USSR, than the first, whose explanation covers a range of possibilities. For some, the domestic political environment was key, meaning that electoral politics played a role in Truman's decision to act. But domestic politics were not entirely separated from international affairs. The impact of the Second World War, the Holocaust, and the activity of Zionist forces in Europe, the United States, and Palestine provide a potent example. But there was also the question of the role of the Cold War, particularly the concern with whether or not a pro-American Jewish state would be an asset in postwar planning.

Writing in 1994, Douglas Little pointed out that "America's role in the creation of the Jewish state has received more scholarly attention than almost any other diplomatic issue in the immediate postwar period."[39] In his analysis of the question, Little emphasized domestic factors, suggesting, in addition, that Truman believed recognition would put an end to the conflict and would arrest Soviet entry and communist influence in the region.[40] Many accounts emphasize a combination of domestic politics; the president's religious, moral, and humanitarian sentiments; his close personal ties with Jewish friends and colleagues who were Zionist supporters; and, finally, the commitment to recognize the Jewish state before the expected Soviet move to do the same.[41]

Michael J. Cohen argues that Truman was moved by the situation of the Jewish Displaced Persons (DP) in the camps described by Earl Harrison.[42] In combination with other factors, such as domestic politics, Truman moved to support "refugee Zionism," approving Jewish DP immigration to Palestine. But Cohen points out that "this never led him to support the Zionist goal of a Jewish state. His aides in the White House and the march of events in Israel itself, not conviction, influenced his decisions on Palestine."[43]

William Roger Louis maintains, in keeping with a Truman biographer, that the impact of the Holocaust and domestic pressure proved irresistible.[44] Others, such as Peter Hahn, have underscored the importance of public support in the United States for partition and the role of effective lobbying.[45]

Omitted in existing explanations and speculation regarding Truman's decision is any reference to the interaction between Max Ball and Eliahu Epstein. Ball was not part of the policymaking establishment, but his prestige among those concerned with petroleum and national defense suggests the need for further investigation. Ball's encounters with Epstein gave him a view of the Jewish Agency's objectives, including its desire to be regarded as an asset rather than a liability in U.S. regional policy, which Ball appeared to promote.

Given the pervasive concern with U.S. policy toward Palestine and the fear that U.S. support for partition would endanger U.S. oil interests, Ball's meetings with Epstein seemed to open unforeseen possibilities. At least, they invited the U.S. oil company executives, who were discreetly responsive to Ball's invitations to meet with the Jewish

Agency representative, to think pragmatically about future possibilities after independence.

In addition, given Epstein's relations with Clark Clifford, it is possible that the president's legal counsel was aware of these exchanges, and that they figured in his calculations, much as did the "top secret" information regarding Secretary of State George Marshall that Max Lowenthal provided. The combination covered many critical areas relevant to U.S. policy.

THE CONTINUATION OF WAR

For Truman and his advisers, the question of what would happen in Palestine after Britain's departure was a major preoccupation. It was used to rationalize immediate recognition of the Jewish state by White House advisers and to justify urgent support for truce and trusteeship by the majority of the policymaking elite. Before Britain's exit, however, as U.S. officials in Palestine recognized, the framework of a Jewish state was in operation, whereas Palestinian forces were in disarray.

With Israel's declaration of independence on May 14 and Britain's departure on May 15, the second part of the war, which had begun with the passage of UNGA Resolution 181, was under way. It would end with the inauguration of armistice agreements designed to prepare for the final settlement of the conflict, but no such finale occurred. Failure to come to a final settlement reflected conditions on the ground: the comparative military strength of Jewish, Palestinian, and Arab forces; the effect of the destruction of Palestinian urban centers; the accompanying flight and expulsion of Palestinian refugees; and Israel's expansion of territorial control.

Avi Shlaim described the war of 1948 as "long, bitter, and very costly in human lives. It claimed the lives of 6,000 soldiers and civilians, or 1 percent of the entire Jewish population of around 650,000."[46] Ze'ev Maoz, by contrast, argued that Jewish forces were inadequately equipped, lacked training, and that their leading commanders predicted "the chance of survival of the Jewish state as even at best."[47] Avi Shlaim provides a different view:

[I]n mid-May 1948 the total number of Arab troops, both regular and irregular, operating in the Palestine theater was under 25,000, whereas the IDF [Israel Defense Forces] fielded over 35,000 troops. By mid-July the IDF mobilized 65,000 men under arms, and by December its numbers had reached a peak of 96,441. The Arab states also reinforced their armies, but they could not match this rate of increase. Thus, at each stage of the war, the IDF significantly outnumbered all the Arab forces arrayed against it, and by the final stage of the war its superiority ratio was nearly two to one.[48]

Simha Flapan described the situation facing Jewish forces in the first month following the Arab invasion as "largely defensive."[49] Ten days after Israel's declaration of independence, the first Messerschmitts arrived from Czechoslovakia and were assembled by Czech technicians. A shipload of rifles and cannons was almost at hand. Ben-Gurion called this "the beginning of the turning point." On May 24, he told the general staff, "We should [now] prepare to go over to the offensive." By July 8, Yadin reported "at the termination of the first truce, we took the initiative into our own hands; and after that we never allowed it to return to the Arab forces."[50]

Flapan estimates that a total of 5,708 Jewish forces were killed between November 29, 1947, and March 10, 1949. Of this number, "more Israeli soldiers died while attacking than while defending against attacks by Palestinians and Arab armies"; 1,581 Israelis were killed fighting within the UNGA partition resolution's borders, as opposed to 2,759 killed outside of these lines.[51]

According to Ilan Pappé, within days of Britain's withdrawal, Arab forces

entered Palestine and attacked Jewish settlements in the north and south. At the same time an Egyptian contingent began a long journey along the coast and into the Negev capturing areas which in the partition resolution had been designated to the Jewish state. Another Egyptian contingent was stationed in the Bethlehem area and captured Kibbutz Ramat Rahel. Tel Aviv was bombarded from the air by Egyptian aircraft and Jerusalem remained cut off from the coast by Palestinian and Legion forces. The Syrians meanwhile succeeded in establishing a bridgehead in the Jordan Valley, whereas the Iraqis, who had failed to do so, entered Samaria thereby facilitating the annexation of that area to Transjordan. Only Abdullah frustrated the general Arab war plan by concentrating most of his troops in the vicinity of Jerusalem, rather than having them join forces with the Arab armies in the north.[52]

One day after Britain's withdrawal, U.S. Minister Lowell Pinkerton in Lebanon sent Washington a statement from the Arab League Political Committee describing the situation:

[M]ore than quarter million Arabs have been compelled by Jewish aggression [to] seek refuge in other Arab countries, and Palestine has been left with no administrative authority "entitled to maintain and capable of maintaining a machinery of administration of the country adequate for the purpose of ensuring due protection of life and property."[53]

Members of the Muslim Brotherhood and Egyptian volunteers had gone to Palestine before the government officially declared its determination to enter the war on the eve of Britain's departure. Mohamed Hassanein Heikal, who was to become a renowned political journalist, described what he found.

The Egyptian army had entered Palestine. But no one seemed to realize that they were entering a war, nor were there enough maps of Palestine for the troops. Worse, the troops were transported in old and broken tourist cars provided by a travel agency. They did not know the directions, so they were forced to follow the railroad track.

The Egyptian army entered the war without really knowing what it was facing.[54]

In his notes to "Nasser's Memoirs of the First Palestine War," Walid Khalidi observed that

the bulk of the Egyptian army was held back in Egypt for a variety of reasons: indecision about intervention, local security considerations and utter organizational unpreparedness. The Secret Report on Military Operations . . . estimates, for example, that 60 percent of transport available was unoperational, and that the lack of equipment for the reserves reached 90 percent in certain instances.[55]

Gamal Abdel Nasser, sent to Palestine as a staff officer, recalled the woeful lack of preparation and the utter confusion of orders that contributed to the feeling that this was a "political" war. His fellow officers were convinced that

> this could not be a serious war. There was no concentration of forces, no accumulation of ammunition and equipment. There was no reconnaissance, no intelligence, no plans. Yet they were actually on the battlefield. The only conclusion that could be drawn was that this was a political war, or rather a state of war and no-war.[56]

On May 14, Nasser received orders from Cairo to move against Dangour. He recalled that

> there was no time to carry out a reconnaissance of the objective, nor was any information available about this objective. There was one Arab guide whose task was to lead the battalion to the site of the settlement. The guide had no information about the fortifications of the settlement or its system of defences. Such information as he did possess was vague and unspecific.[57]

An Israeli member of the Israeli Palmach later recalled the entry of the Egyptian army in a landscape of utter impoverishment and military unpreparedness.

> When the Egyptian army arrived, it was a completely different situation. The Egyptian army arrived when we had wiped out all Arab resistance which wasn't that strong, it would be an exaggeration to say we fought against the Palestinians . . . in fact there were no battles, almost no battles. In Burayr there was a battle, there were battles here and there, further up north. But there were no big battles; why? Because they had no military capabilities, there [they?]weren't organized. . . .[58]

In the north they fought. In the south they didn't, they didn't have anything. They were miserable, they didn't have anywhere to go, or anyone to ask. . . .[59]

The first time I entered Kawkaba and Burayr I was amazed by their poverty. There was nothing there. No furniture and no nothing, there were shelves made of straw and mud, the houses were made of mud and straw. They lived there for thousands of years without any changes, and the only thing that happened to them was the disaster of the Nakba in "Tashah" [1948].[60]

In the period leading up to and after May 15, Jewish forces attacked major urban as well as rural areas. Arab populations were either expelled or fled in Jaffa, Haifa, Lydda, Ramla, Acre, Safad, Tiberias, Bayson, and Bir Sabi', which collectively represented "those Palestinians with the highest levels of literacy, skills, wealth and education."[61] An estimated sixty-four villages between Tel Aviv and Haifa were either destroyed or occupied in this period. Two villages were spared to provide workers for neighboring Jewish settlements.[62] By 1949 and the conclusion of armistice agreements between Israel and its neighbors, "more than 400 of the over 500 Arab villages in Palestine had been taken over by the Israeli victors."[63] According to Walid Khalidi's study, *All That Remains*, 418 villages were destroyed in the course of the war in 1948.[64]

Safad and the surrounding villages in Galilee had a population of 10,000 to 12,000 Arabs and approximately 1,500 Jews. This area was assigned to the Yishuv in the UN partition plan, and fighting there led to massive destruction and demoralization, and with it flight or surrender.[65] According to Yigal Allon, the Palmach officer assigned to the Eastern Galilee, the object was to rid the area of Arabs before the anticipated Arab invasion that was assumed to follow on Britain's departure. On an earlier reconnaissance trip, "Allon concluded that clearing the area completely of all Arab forces and inhabitants was the simplest and best way of securing the [Syrian] frontier."[66] In Allon's words, "the echo of the fall of Arab Safad carried far. . . . The confidence of thousands of Arabs of the Hula [Valley] was shaken. . . . We had only five days left . . . until 15 May. We regarded it as imperative to cleanse [of Arabs] the interior of the Galilee and create Jewish territorial continuity in the whole of Upper Galilee."[67]

Acre, in the western Galilee, fell to Haganah forces between May 13 and May 18. After Jaffa, Acre was "the first major town outside the territory allotted to the Jewish state to fall to the Haganah forces," as Mustafa Abbasi reminds us.[68] It had previously been the destination for refugees fleeing Haifa and surrounding villages, which aggravated conditions when Acre was attacked by Haganah forces in late April. According to a Palestinian resident of Acre, the population had increased from approximately 12,000 to some 50,000 people. Under siege, Acre was further devastated by "fear, dirt and hunger and disease and epidemic," in the words of Moshe Carmel, commander of the Carmeli brigade.[69] The final siege of the city, undertaken by the same brigade, reported that "the objective is to attack the city with the aim of killing the men and destroying property by burning and to subdue the city."[70]

On May 17, Warren Austin, the U.S. delegate at the United Nations, argued that the Security Council should declare the situation in Palestine a threat to peace under article 39, and under article 40 should call for cessation of all military activities in Palestine in advance of establishing a truce. Austin followed this with a list of questions for Arab and Israeli forces, asking the former whether "armed elements of your armed forces, or irregular forces sponsored by your Governments, [were] now operating in Palestine?"[71] The Provisional Government of Israel was asked what area it actually controlled and whether it had "armed forces operating outside areas claimed by your Jewish State."[72]

APPOINTING A MEDIATOR

On May 20, Count Folke Bernadotte was appointed the UNSC mediator, and he proceeded to work toward a cease-fire and truce, aiming for a comprehensive solution. He envisioned a settlement that corresponded in some respects to that outlined in UNGA Resolution 181, with its two states collaborating in a union that went beyond economic considerations to deal with issues such as immigration and refugees and matters related to foreign policy. He proposed "that recognition be accorded to the right of residents of Palestine who, because of conditions created by the conflict there have left their normal places of abode, to return to their homes without restriction and to regain possession of their property."[73] This was the prelude to what became the reference to the "Palestinian right of return," as expressed in UNGA Resolution 194 on December 11, 1948.

Bernadotte's proposals included the following:

1. Inclusion of the whole or part of the Negeb in Arab territory.
2. Inclusion of the whole or part of Western Galilee in Jewish territory.
3. Inclusion of the City of Jerusalem in Arab territory, with municipal autonomy for the Jewish community and special arrangements for the protection of the Holy Places.
4. Consideration of the status of Jaffa.
5. Establishment of a free port at Haifa, the area of the free port to include the refineries and terminals.
6. Establishment of a free airport at Lydda.[74]

The territorial changes Bernadotte proposed, which would have altered previous arrangements stated in UNGA Resolution 181, were rejected by Arabs as well as Israelis. The latter were persuaded that they undermined its sovereignty; and the former were unprepared to accede to arrangements they viewed as enforcing partition and enhancing Abdullah's power. The UN mediator responded to Israeli charges by offering "an explicit recognition of the right of Israel to exist" in his second, revised proposal.[75] As for Jerusalem, Ben-Gurion declared that it "was no longer a political question but essentially one of military capability and that, like any area that was under the control of the IDF, it formed part of the state of Israel."[76]

The Israeli response to the mediator's proposals was influenced by developments on the ground as was the response of the Arab states. At the beginning of June, Israelis were "in control of the mixed Arab-Jewish towns in Palestine that they had captured in April; they had driven back the invading Arab armies from the north of Palestine; and also caused an Egyptian debacle in the south."[77]

Toward the end of May, the UN mediator's plans were disrupted by another development—namely, the attack, occupation, and massacre of the villagers of Tantoura on May 22–23, 1948. At about the same time, U.S. Consul Wasson in Jerusalem sent a message to the secretary of state, indicating that it had become "extremely difficult [to] get in touch with prominent and representative Arabs but such Arab reaction to

American de facto recognition of Israel as has become available to us is that [the] United States has betrayed Arab states."[78] Arab sentiment toward the United States was described as being of extreme bitterness, reinforced by the anticipation of military defeat and political collapse leading to radical disorder. As far as the Jews were concerned, Wasson reported that those in Jerusalem faced the "immediate and grim task of warfare."[79] What they expected from the United States was support.

THOMAS C. WASSON: U.S. CONSUL ASSASSINATED

Wasson did not live to see the results of U.S. policy. He was assassinated on May 22, 1948. The truce he had worked for was finally accepted by Israelis and Arabs on June 11. The United Nations was apprised of the shooting of the U.S. consul in Jerusalem, who was also a member of the UNSC Truce Commission. "Following for your information is the report just received from the American Consul in Jerusalem Regarding the shooting of Thomas C Wasson U.S. Consul General and U.S. Representative on the Security Council Truce Commission."[80] Details of Wasson's assassination reported in the United States were few and contradictory.[81] Either Washington did not investigate the assassination, or its findings were and remain classified. The Security Council was informed of the attack, but Pablo de Azcarate, chairman of the Palestine Commission, reported that he

> never found out whether the Security Council adopted a special resolution or expressed their feelings in any other way about the tragic death of the American member of the Truce Commission. In any case, the Commission never received any communication from the Security Council about the melancholy incident and this silence made a deplorable and painful impression on us all.[82]

Because Wasson was killed while a member of the Truce Commission, Azcarate added that "he had therefore, the tragic privilege of being the first victim sacrificed to the cause of peace in Palestine."[83]

In an oral history interview with Stuart W. Rockwell, officer in charge, Palestine-Israel-Jordan Affairs, 1948–1950, Richard D. McKinzie questioned the U.S. officer about conditions in Jerusalem at the time of his appointment. Rockwell had come from Ankara and described the atmosphere in Jerusalem as politically and physically tense, recalling that "we lost the Consul General, who was killed by a sniper and we lost two other members of the staff by shrapnel and various other accidents of war."[84]

Well, we resided in the YMCA and worked in the Consulate, which was right on the front lines between Jewish New City and the Old City. I recall that one day, when I was going for lunch at the YMCA from the Consulate, I crossed a small street that borders the rear end of the Consulate, and I encountered Mr. Wasson coming from a meeting of the Truce Commission at the French Consulate General. And just as I crossed the road, I was fired on by a sniper, and I said to Mr. Wasson, "Watch out; this area" (which was within site of the Old City wall) "is covered by snipers."

He [a reference to Wasson] said, "Thank you for the warning; I have my bullet proof vest on."

So, I went on my way to lunch, and I subsequently learned that when he crossed that street he was fired on by the sniper, and the bullet struck him in the top of the shoulder where there was no plating. It went into him diagonally, and then hit the bullet proof vest on the inside and ricocheted back into him. And he died in about three hours. But it was obviously the same man, and, judging from the angle of the bullet, it seemed to me he must have been in one of the abandoned buildings on the Israeli side, on the Jewish side, of the front line. He must have gotten in there, somehow.[85]

The State Department acknowledged Wasson's death by paying tribute to his "great ability, judgment, and courage' and pointed out that although in carrying out his duties he had had to pass constantly through 'bullet swept streets and battle lines,' he had never once mentioned in his reports the physical dangers to which he was exposed."[86]

The overall mood of U.S. diplomats at this juncture was grim. The news conveyed to Washington gave little reason for hope. In Jerusalem at the end of May, U.S. Vice Consul Burdett was reporting on unconditional surrender of Jews in the Old City, where some "2000 women, children, old and religious people to be evacuated to Jewish quarters new Jerusalem under supervision International Red Cross," while 300 men considered of military age were sent to Amman as prisoners of war, and those seriously wounded were taken over by the International Red Cross.[87] Writing from Saudi Arabia, the vice president of ARAMCO sent news that King Ibn Saud "indicated that he may be compelled, in certain circumstances, to apply sanctions against the American oil concessions."[88] The Saudi regime was prepared to accept any Arab League move on sanctions against U.S. interests. Four months later, members of the Saudi delegation at the UN were described by U.S. officials as opposed to the Bernadotte plan and expecting a similar response from other Arab states.

Late in June, the Saudi king was reported to have warned the U.S. ambassador that "if hostilities renewed and U.S. pursues policy susceptible interpretation as substantial departure from one neutrality as between Israel and Arabs vigorous counteraction may be anticipated by Arab League with which SAG [Saudi Arabian Government] will conform."[89] There could well be sanctions in addition to "(a) transfer Dhahran air base to British; (b) cancellation ARAMCO concession; (c) break in diplomatic relations."[90] None of these threats was carried out, and U.S.–Saudi relations improved after the Arab defeat.[91]

Reporting from Cairo at the end of June, the U.S. consul informed the secretary of state that Amir Faisal of Saudi Arabia and Mardam Bey of Syria were adamantly opposed to Bernadotte's territorial plans. Mardam Bey feared that the arrangements "would make Transjordan a Jewish colony through joint economic functions and constitute even greater menace to Arab world. Both clearly indicated opposition to aggrandizement of Abdullah."[92] As for the Emir, he reminded the U.S. charge that "Arabs could impose sanctions, including cancellation oil concessions," that could subsequently be offered to other states, citing as examples "Belgium, Italy or even Russia."[93] This was accompanied by threats of war, which materialized in July when Egypt took the lead in the campaign against Israel that succeeded in exposing the weaknesses of the Arab military.

Similar warnings had been received from the U.S. minister in Saudi Arabia only days earlier, when J. Rives Childs reported that the king could not accept a Palestine settlement that involved Israel, and that he would align Saudi policy with that of the Arab League, which might involve the imposition of sanctions against the United States should it fail to maintain a position of neutrality between Arabs and Israelis. In addition to a break in U.S.–Saudi relations at the diplomatic level, sanctions might include Dhahran becoming a British (not American) base and the ARAMCO concession being cancelled. Childs must have known that however dramatic these threats were, there was little likelihood that they would be carried out given the Saudi regime's eagerness for U.S. aid and support.

This was not the only warning the secretary of state received. On June 25, Vice Consul Burdett in Jerusalem sent the secretary of state a copy of a "Memorandum of the Cease-Fire" from the Stern Gang, which had been left at the U.S. Consulate.[94] Accusing states that "party to intrigues of British policy," which was designed to "whittle down already shrunken Jewish state," the Stern Gang claimed that "Americans, French, Belgians, Swedes, are all in effect acting as British agents to fulfill a British mission."[95] The only states excluded from this list of guilty parties were the Soviet Union and states of Eastern Europe. In Washington, such news worried officials concerned with Israeli–Soviet ties, as well as those afraid that the Israeli Provisional Government was unable to control the Irgun and the Stern Gang.

These fears were superseded by the practical necessity of reconsidering U.S. policy toward Israel and Palestine in light of the momentous developments of the previous months. How much changed and with what effect?

PART IV

Rethinking U.S. Policy in Palestine/Israel, 1948

Chapter 9 considers Washington's reaction to the momentous events in the region, a reaction that involved the reassessment of U.S. policy toward Israel and Palestine as a result of the struggle over Palestine in 1948. It provides a new look at some major figures who had been severely critical of partition but emerged as stalwart defendants of the new state. Among them were those who calculated that the new state's military strength could prove useful to the United States. The CIA, while recognizing Israel's military, predicted that Tel Aviv would continue to expand its military and violate truce efforts.

Chapter 10 examines the U.S. and the UN record of, and response to, Israeli expansion and the expulsion of Palestinians, who increasingly swelled the ranks of refugees. U.S. sources also provide evidence of the Israeli denial of responsibility for the creation of the problem, which led to Israel's categorical rejection of repatriation. This chapter contributes significantly to our understanding of Washington's response to the Palestinian refugee problem and the role it played in relations between Israel and the United States.

Chapter 11 sets the record straight with regard to the refugee problem and the views of State Department officials and the CIA. However, this chapter also exposes the manner in which Washington deferred to Israeli policies, adopting a more "realistic" view of Israel's situation with respect to territory and, eventually, to refugees.

9

Reconsidering U.S. Policy in Palestine

DEFINING U.S. POLICY

U.S. officials dealing with Palestine clearly understood that the United States was facing a new order in the Middle East. Hence the urgency of defining U.S. policy in the aftermath of Britain's exit and Israel's declaration of independence. Declaring their recognition of the new state's sovereignty, the heirs of Wilsonian diplomacy were less concerned with affirming support for the principle of self-determination than they were with drafting maps for territorial expansion and population to ensure a homogeneous Jewish state. In the process, they confronted major political and legal questions, such as the continued validity of UNGA Resolution 181, which they reconsidered in a manner favorable to Israel. Their rationale was that developments on the ground had so profoundly altered the political reality facing the region that the UNGA resolution of November 1947 was very nearly irrelevant. In practice, however, the same UNGA resolution continued to figure in Anglo-American, U.S.–Israeli, and U.S.–Arab deliberations.

Among the dramatic characteristics of Washington politics in this period was the evident shift in outlook of officials who had previously been ardent opponents of partition and statehood but who now emerged as its equally ardent defenders. Unlike Gordon Merriam, who questioned why Palestine was not granted independence, most State Department officials involved in the Palestine question accepted Israel's goal of a homogeneous Jewish state with a minimum of Palestinian

Arabs. Loy Henderson, George Marshall, and Robert McClintock were among those who now supported population "transfer," as did Philip Jessup, whose analyses outlined the logic of the U.S. policy.

Within two weeks of Israel's declaration of independence, the Policy Planning Staff signaled the importance of developing a policy on Palestine for submission to the secretary and under secretary of state, as well as to the National Security Council. In mid-July, Merriam, who was a member of the Policy Planning Staff, reminded his colleagues that the United States did not have a Palestine policy, but "we do have a short-term, open-ended policy which is set from time to time by White House directions."[1] Merriam opposed this policy as his views made clear.

U.S. officials faced the need to redefine its policy toward Israel, Arab Palestine, and London, where long-standing differences compelled attention. Henderson was among those persuaded that the British could be useful in persuading Arab states to accept the existence of the Jewish state. Jessup, on the other hand, was skeptical of the British role, convinced that British influence in Palestine was limited, even though the British had a "better 'feel' for the Palestine problem" than did the United States.[2]

One of the more dramatic shifts in outlook following Israel's emergence was that of Loy Henderson, for many the symbol of U.S. State Department opposition to partition and Jewish statehood. Henderson, in fact, was exiled as a result of his views and appointed ambassador to India in August 1948. As he explained in his interview with Richard D. McKinzie in 1973, he had been identified with "the nefarious 'pro-Arab' group in the State Department who had opposed the establishment of such a State," referring to Israel.[3] Henderson admitted that he had been warned that he was "making powerful enemies" as a result of the views he expressed between 1945 and 1948.[4] In "the latter part of 1947 and the first six months of 1948, thousands of letters came into the State Department demanding my immediate dismissal."[5] By mid-1948, his presence in the State Department had come to be seen as a liability, both for the department and for the administration. Yet he and others dealing with Palestine and the Near and Middle East in the summer of 1948 argued that "the Jews had, in fact, a state, and we had recognized it. We would probably follow a policy of continuing to recognize it unless the Zionists of their own accord merged it into some other entity."[6] Insofar as territory was concerned, Henderson believed that "if there were boundary modifications in the Negev" that recognized the validity of the Palestinian position, "we might find it necessary to ask for a *quid pro quo* such as the cession of Western Galilee to the Jewish State."[7]

On June 19, Lewis Douglas, the U.S. ambassador to the United Kingdom, sent the U.S. secretary of state notice that the British had given up their support for a federal state in Palestine. The British had come to appreciate "the contrast between the efficiency displayed by Jews in setting up Israel and in defending it, and the Arab counter-performance."[8] Secretary Marshall was impressed and wrote a letter of appreciation to the British Foreign Office.

Following U.S. recognition of Israel, the secretary of state emerged as an advocate for Israel and the "enlarged Transjordan" with which it might enter into a customs union.[9] This was the "top secret" message Clifford had discovered when preparing for the May 12 debate with Marshall. King Abdullah had, in fact, informed the U.S. vice consul in Jerusalem of his support for an "end to present hostilities." Burdett reported to Marshall that Abdullah "indicated it would still be possible for Arabs Jews [to] live together [in] Palestine. Said he did not hate Jews did not wish make war on them and stated that war had been forced on him by Arab League which had placed entire responsibility on him."[10]

Reflecting on the evolution of his views, Marshall described U.S. policy, as of June 19, in the following terms:

> Dept is rapidly evolving its line of policy re future settlement of Palestine problem. For your own info and not for use as yet with UK officials, our thinking—conditioned by fact of recognition of State of Israel—is that best solution for a sensible adjustment of Palestine problem would be to re-draw frontiers of Israel so as to make a compact and homogeneous state; remainder of Palestine to go largely to Transjordan with appropriate transfer of populations where necessary; Jerusalem to remain an international entity with free access to outside world; boundaries of Israel and enlarged Transjordan to be guaranteed mutually between themselves and UN; and economic prosperity of region to be enhanced by a customs union between Israel and Transjordan.[11]

As did other U.S. officials, with the exception of Henderson, who was concerned with the consequences of transferring Palestinians, Marshall does not appear to have entertained doubts on this subject. He continued to support the UN truce and endorsed Count Folke Bernadotte's efforts to organize a conference at Rhodes. As he wrote to Ernest Bevin, he hoped that "a final settlement [could] be evolved without recourse to sanctions."[12]

On June 23, 1948, Robert McClintock submitted his proposal for a revised U.S. policy under the title "Peaceful Adjustment of the Future Situation of Palestine" to the associate chief of the Division of International Security Affairs, Harding Bancroft, as well as to Loy Henderson, Robert Lovett, and the secretary of state. McClintock, who had been critical about partition, as Rusk had been, now emerged as a frontline defender of Israeli sovereignty. McClintock was prepared to defer to the new state with respect to territorial and other changes and to endorse the transfer of Palestinians to ensure a homogeneous state.

> The policy of the American Government in this regard has been conditioned since May 14 by the recognition that day of the Provisional Government of the State of Israel as the *de facto* authority in that new republic. Because of the act of recognition, United States policy with relation to the Palestine settlement is postulated upon the continuing existence of the State of Israel. The sovereignty of Israel is a fact so far as the United States is concerned and this government could not agree to any diminution of its sovereignty except with the consent of the Government of Israel.[13]

McClintock did not question the extension of Israeli sovereignty as he had endorsed the need to redraw Israel's borders as a necessary revision of the 1947 UNGA partition resolution. Nor does he appear to have questioned the incorporation of Haifa, Jaffa, Lydda, and Ramle into the Jewish state, overlooking the bitter fighting and expulsions of Palestinians that had taken place in these areas. As to the future of Haifa, McClintock stressed that "Haifa is an integral part of the state of Israel" and that it offered "a unique opportunity for practical cooperation between the Arabs and Jews, since one side controls the crude oil, and the other the refining capacity, while both sides need the final product."[14]

McClintock apparently had no knowledge of prior Arab–Jewish labor relations in the refinery that had demonstrated cooperation in different political circumstances. McClintock concluded, however, with the thought that "the habit might spread to other areas."[15]

In turning to the partition resolution's reference to a Palestinian state, McClintock adopted the position that "it is now clear in the light of facts and events which have supervened that there will be no separate Arab State and no economic union as envisaged in the General Assembly resolution."[16] In this, McClintock made no attempt to argue that the UNGA partition resolution retained any validity under current circumstances. The operating assumption, in his view, was that the time had come for a "new drawing of the frontier which circumscribes the State of Israel."[17] McClintock then proposed a return to the boundaries proposed in the Peel Commission Report (1936), following which a transfer or exchange of populations would take place "so that the State of Israel would contain most of the Jews of Palestine and the Arabs would reside in purely Arab areas."[18] Such arrangements, according to McClintock, would result in a state "possessing an improved economic patrimony,"[19] and it offered "a sensible territorial solution for the Palestine problem."[20]

What Palestinians thought of such solutions did not figure in McClintock's calculations. On his map, Arab Palestine disappeared under Transjordan's control. Syria was granted Safed in the north, Saudi Arabia had the port of Aqaba in the south, and Egypt and Transjordan were granted "territorial adjustments" in the Negev.[21] Jerusalem was to be "administered by the United Nations as a separate international entity," and, assuming agreement by Israel and Transjordan, Haifa and Jaffa were to become "free port facilities."[22]

McClintock concluded that a sensible territorial solution for the Palestine problem would be to redraw the frontiers of Israel to make a compact and homogeneous state. The remainder of Palestine was to go largely to Transjordan with appropriate transfers of populations where necessary. The formula relevant to the transfer of populations echoed Marshall's statement of June 22. Jerusalem was to remain an international entity with free access to the outside world. The boundaries of the two new states were to be guaranteed mutually between themselves and the United Nations, and the economic prosperity of the region was to be enhanced by a customs union between Israel and Transjordan.[23]

The advantages of such arrangements in McClintock's view were that they would contain "the wider pretensions of the Jewish revisionists and such fanatics as those of the Irgun who have pretensions to the conquest of Transjordan."[24] As for Rabbi Judah Magnes and his idea of a "United States of Palestine" with joint Arab and Jewish jurisdiction, McClintock concluded that the Jewish state would not be sympathetic.[25]

Operating in the radically changed environment following the events of May 1948, the UN mediator, Count Folke Bernadotte, produced his own assessment of what was to be done to ensure a resolution of the conflict. In practice, the mediator's proposals pleased neither Arabs nor Israelis, although Marshall declared them to be fair even as his deputy, John Foster Dulles, effectively blocked their acceptance. After initially finding the mediator's position worthy of support, Truman turned against it during the election campaign, only to return to it at a later stage.

JESSUP'S ANALYSIS OF THE UNITED STATES, ISRAEL, AND THE ARABS

Philip Jessup's analysis of developments in Palestine/Israel and the region as a whole did not differ radically from that of his colleagues or superiors in the State Department. Generally, they exhibited limited knowledge of the Arab world beyond the prized oil-rich regimes of Saudi Arabia and the Gulf. For the rest, they seemed to know little of the intense extent of politicization across the Arab world or the role of radical political movements in the region. Jessup's starting point, as that of most U.S. officials, was Palestine in the years from 1945 through 1947 and the upheaval of 1948. The U.S. president and his advisers were sensitive to the domestic political impact of Zionist activity, whereas many State Department officials dealing with Palestine, Israel, and the Arab world were primarily consumed with the impact of instability on U.S. economic interests and the attendant risks of Soviet inroads, but they had abundant evidence of the impact of Zionist developments on Palestinian Arabs.

In the heady atmosphere of Israel after May 1948, compliant regimes such as that of King Abdullah were regarded favorably in Washington, while other Arab states were judged in terms of their response to Israel's emergence. Israel was newly appreciated as a state with an experienced and disciplined political class, an impressive military, and a worrisome tendency to turn toward the USSR.

On June 30 and July 1, 1948, Jessup introduced a two-part analysis designed to assist in the formulation of U.S. policy "with regard to the 'peaceful adjustment of the future situation of Palestine.'"[26] What emerged from his evaluation was the sense that the new state could be a positive factor in U.S. regional planning.

Jessup declared that the state of Israel was "no longer a speculative proposition but a hard political reality that neither we, nor the British, nor the Arabs, nor anyone else could escape even if they wanted to."[27] He viewed Israel as politically strong and capable of controlling its dissidents. Jessup concluded that in comparison with its Arab neighbors, Israel was "more than a match for most of Arab states put together." King Abdullah was the only possible exception as "none of the other Arab states have armed forces available which can even begin to compare in organization, efficiency, and numbers with the Haganah."[28]

Turning to the Palestinians, Jessup suggested that "we should make up our mind whether we favor establishment of a Palestinian Arab state or extension of the boundaries of Transjordan to take in the Arab areas of Palestine as those areas may be determined."[29] He favored the latter course because Arabs lacked leadership and were "poorly organized and equipped from [a] military viewpoint."[30] Jessup gave no indication that he or anyone else in Washington had consulted with Palestinian Arabs to determine their views on being placed under Abdullah's control. As Avi Shlaim pointed out,

> the most sophisticated among them saw little attraction in the political despotism of Transjordan, dependent as it was on the volatile temper of the king. They were also aware of the economic non-viability of Transjordan and realized that Arab Palestine and Transjordan together would be even less of a going concern. Hence their opposition to Transjordanian rule and insistence on a unitary state.[31]

The same view was expressed by Palestinians to Elias Sasson, who offered David Ben-Gurion and Moshe Sharett his proposals for negotiations with Palestinians in place of the deal with Abdullah in the spring of 1949, but to no avail.

The absence of adequate leadership was routinely repeated by U.S. officials in their depiction of Palestinians and Arabs as a whole, thereby justifying their view of Abdullah's takeover of Arab Palestine. No attention was paid to the role of past British policies that decimated the Palestinian leadership in response to its opposition to the Peel Commission's recommendation of partition in 1936. The ensuing revolt between 1936 and 1939 was harshly repressed by mandatory authorities. The resulting struggle led to the destruction of the Palestinian political class as well as to the isolation of Palestinian villages and towns, which were left without arms or leaders and were practically devoid of Arab support later in the 1940s.[32] Britain's attempt to assuage Palestinian Arab hostility through its subsequent passage of the White Paper with its limitation on Zionist immigration to Palestine only served to expose the deep roots of conflict in Palestine.

From 1947 to 1949, Palestinians were confronted by a "divided leadership, exceedingly limited finances, no centrally organized military forces, and no reliable allies."[33] This contrasted sharply with the situation of the Jewish community in Palestine, which was bolstered by the Zionist movement that was further mobilized as a result of the revelations of the Holocaust. In retrospect, the events of May 1948 gave rise to a gradual awakening and sense of identity among Palestinians, despite their separation across states that offered them neither citizenship nor equal rights.

In his assessment of the conditions in post-1948 Palestine, Jessup described the "vacuum" left by Britain's withdrawal as filled, in part, by "proclamation of Israel, which might be described as an extra-legal act, and by outbreak of violence and hostilities on a serious scale."[34] Nonetheless, Jessup maintained the new state was a "responsible member of the international community" and would eventually make the concessions necessary for a peaceful resolution of the situation in Palestine.

There was little evidence of this in the summer of 1948 when Jessup discussed Israel's situation with Abba Eban, who informed Jessup of Israel's view that the territory it held was based

on the November 29 resolution and on *de facto* military control. We have expressed the personal view to Eban here that Israel's legal case under the November 29 resolution with respect to boundaries is relatively weak. Also personally, Eban has in effect admitted this and indicated they consider their *de facto* position resulting from military operations much stronger. On the latter point, Eban claims that Israel is in de facto control not only of the November 29 territory but also of western Galilee.[35]

Jessup did not question Eban's wish that the United States "support the 'territorial integrity' of Israel," but then Jessup and the Provisional Government of Israel were not entirely in accord on territorial matters. Jessup believed that the Negev should go to Transjordan, and the western Galilee to Israel, even though he conceded that if the Negev turned out to be rich in resources, arrangements for joint development could be made. In short, Jessup was prepared to envisage modifying his position in Israel's favor.

Overall, Jessup viewed Israel's "superior organizing ability; efficiency and resources, both human and financial" as factors that would enhance its economic development as opposed to that of the Arab states.[36] He recognized the possibility of Israeli expansion and the further enmity it would arouse among Arab regimes. His response was to emphasize the importance of promoting economic development and Arab–Jewish cooperation similar to what he believed would take place between Israel and Transjordan.

Jessup was also interested in the possibility of encouraging regional political cooperation between Israel and its neighbors. Such arrangements would address Arab fears of Israeli expansion, although Jessup was persuaded that Israel's neighbors (citing Syria in particular) were primarily concerned with Transjordan's potential expansion. In that vein, Jessup thought the idea of "nonaggression and mutual defense pacts" between Israel and her neighbors could transform Arab policies. Jessup specifically pointed to the Arab League, speculating that it might be moved to change from an organization "based on racial, religious and nationalist lines, into a politically mature organization along the lines of the Western European Union and our own arrangements in the Western Hemisphere."[37]

Jessup apparently had little knowledge, let alone understanding, of European imperialism and its effect on the Middle East. Instead, identifying U.S. interests in the evolving situation, Jessup stressed the importance of peace and stability, as well as the exclusion of the USSR. Unlike the State Department Middle East specialists who were far more anti-Soviet in outlook, Jessup did not believe that the USSR represented an imminent threat to U.S. interests in the region. He nonetheless subscribed to the view of a dangerous Soviet influence in Greece, Turkey, and Iran. He remained convinced, however, that "although there are some individuals in the Arab countries inclined towards communism, for religious reasons, as well as because of the low economic and cultural level of the masses of the population of the Arab countries, it is not apparent that communism has any substantial following among the masses."[38]

On the other hand, Jessup was preoccupied, as were other State Department and Intelligence officials, with the risks of Soviet inroads in Israel. The ideological orientation of the Stern Gang worried them, as did what they perceived to be the risks of neutralist tendencies in the Israeli Provisional Government (PGI). Jessup argued against subjecting Israel to excessive pressure because he feared that it risked turning Israel against the United States and the West. He argued that Israel was a responsible member of the international community, unlike Arab states who had evidence of its violations of international law, claiming that the PGI "have shown dignity and strength in UN. There is no reason to believe they will not be willing to make concessions, even substantial ones, in interest of a peaceful adjustment of future situation of Palestine."[39]

Jessup either discounted or was unaware of what was happening in Palestine. He seemingly ignored U.S. consular reports in promoting his view that the government in Tel Aviv should not be subjected to undue pressure.

If in process of negotiation PGI is pushed too hard to accept arrangements intolerable from their point of view, [it] seems clear that this will increase its difficulties in dealing with Communist-inspired dissident elements and will also force it to rely more extensively on Russian support.[40]

The PGI, according to Jessup, recognized that it was to its advantage to be associated with the United States rather than the USSR. As Jessup argued, "if in effect Israel is thrown into arms of Soviet Union it could become a force operating to very great disadvantage to U.S., UK and other western powers, and to Arabs."[41] On the other hand, "if fairly treated, [Israel] could become a force operating to our own advantage and to advantage of Arab countries."[42] "Fairly treated," in Jessup's interpretation, as in that of other State Department officials, meant that Washington should cease pressuring Israel on issues such as the Palestinian refugee problem, or the illegal acquisition of land. The same position was later taken up by the Joint Chiefs of Staff.

Jessup envisioned the advantage of Israel being associated with the United States in terms of its potential contribution to U.S. strategy.

> Israel is also in strong military position, perhaps stronger than they thought they might be. From point of view of numbers, organization, discipline and efficiency they are more than a match for most of Arab states put together. Abdullah has only very effective force on Arab side and effectiveness of this force is almost undoubtedly due to British elements. Israel has been successful in holding its own positions and beyond this has established effective control of western Galilee.[43]

On the basis of these considerations, Jessup concluded that Israel could be an asset in U.S. regional planning.

> From the strategic viewpoint we assume that Palestine, together with the neighboring countries is a major factor presumably in any future major conflict this region would be of vital importance to U.S. as a potential base area and with respect to our lines of communication. Presumably also the oil resources of the area are considered vital. It is our feeling that this last point may not perhaps have been dealt with adequately and frankly enough in official and public discussion of the Palestine question.
>
> From the economic viewpoint it is probable that with the exception of oil our trade and other economic relations with Palestine and the other Near East countries are not directly of any substantial importance. Indirectly, however, the economic stability and developing prosperity of Palestine and the Middle East area under peaceful

conditions could make a very substantial contribution to the economic recovery of the world generally and thus contribute to the economic welfare of the U.S. With respect to oil, we recognize that the oil supply from the area is of great importance in the European recovery program. Were it not for this factor, however, and the strategic importance of oil, we should probably not allow the economic importance of this commodity to condition our judgment substantially with regard to Palestine.[44]

Where did the Arab states fit in this order? Their location and resources accounted for their importance in Jessup's analysis, but their inability to accept the Jewish state accounted for their incompatibility with U.S. policy. That incompatibility was explained in terms of Arab political immaturity and economic underdevelopment.

Arab countries are also relatively new states participating in international affairs on their own responsibility for a very short period. From a political viewpoint, both domestic and international, they are relatively immature. From economic and cultural viewpoints, they are relatively underdeveloped.[45]

Jessup concluded that in the light of their inability to accept the Jewish state, the Arabs were responsible for perpetuating regional instability and increased Soviet and communist influence in the region. Hence the comparative value of Israel in U.S. strategy and the importance of pursuing policies that would ensure its pro-Western orientation.

Although written in a period of continued Israeli expansion during which the White House and U.S. officials expressed frustration with Israel's repeated rejection of Palestinian refugee repatriation, Jessup maintained that the Provisional Government of Israel "fully recognizes responsibility which go along with statehood. It is our impression that they desire to live as a good neighbor with surrounding Arab states."[46]

Unable or unwilling to comprehend the Palestinian and Arab opposition to Israel, Jessup relied on mythical claims that served his purpose. He stated that Arabs have been "accustomed for so long to look upon Jews as root of all evil that it is difficult for them to see contributions for good that Jews might make politically, economically, and culturally to welfare of Arabs."[47] Correcting this outlook was a prerequisite of peace in Jessup's view. "[I]f even a small number of Arab leaders would be convinced of desirability from their own viewpoint of adopting a positive rather than a negative attitude towards Israel," there would be hope for a settlement.[48] Others had claimed that Zionism and Israel could contribute to Arab welfare, as in the study of Palestine by Nathan, Gass, and Creamer, cited earlier.[49] Jessup went further and suggested that the Arab inability to deal with Israel was "a complex psychological problem," turning to psycho-cultural apologetics as a way of deflecting attention from the roots of the problem.

The Zionist leader who became prime minister was less inclined to blame psychology than political conditions for the Israeli victory and Arab defeat in 1948. As David Ben-Gurion declared, "let U.S. recognize the truth: we won not because our army is a performer of miracles but because the Arab army is rotten. Is this rot bound to persist? Is an Arab Mustafa Kemal not possible?"[50]

For Jessup, the problem remained Arab blindness, or what he termed the Arab "blindspot."

The immaturity of Arabs is revealed in blindspot which prevents even more moderate Arabs from recognizing existence of Israel as a political fact. Because of this blindspot the more extreme Arabs seem determined to continue their efforts to eliminate the Jewish state. While admitting that Arabs might continue a form of guerrilla warfare for many years against the Jews, it seems axiomatic to U.S. that Arabs could never eliminate Jewish state which, failing support from U.S. and other western countries, could get support from Soviet Union, and the eastern European countries. Moreover, even more moderate Arabs who consider themselves "realistic" and are therefore prepared to recognize existence of Israel are nevertheless apparently holding to line that Jews might be brought to agree (if there were sufficient pressure by U.S.) to a drastically reduced territory and impaired sovereignty. We consider that even this moderate Arab viewpoint is unrealistic because we do not feel that Jews will accept any substantial reduction of territory without compensation, nor any impairment of their sovereignty. Furthermore, we doubt whether U.S. would be likely to bring any pressure at all to bear upon them to these ends.[51]

McCLINTOCK'S INTERPRETATION
OF THE NEW SITUATION

As Jessup completed his second comprehensive analysis and recommendations for U.S. policy, Robert McClintock submitted his own lengthy "Check List on Palestine" to Dean Rusk. It included McClintock's exchanges with George Kennan of the Policy Planning Staff and McClintock's personal assessment of the possibilities of achieving a settlement. McClintock noted that Kennan submitted his report to Lovett who, in turn, sent it to Marshall. The report did not reach the National Security Council, but McClintock's view of the situation was circulated among policymakers.

Without compunction, McClintock argued in favor of redrawing the frontiers "to make a compact and homogeneous state, the remainder of Palestine to go largely to Transjordan with appropriate transfers of population where necessary." Jerusalem was to remain "an international entity" with open access, and the Jewish and Transjordan states along with the UN would guarantee their boundaries.[52] Finally, a customs union would be established between the states. This echoed Marshall's position, and was the position to which McClintock had earlier subscribed.

McClintock was concerned that the United States might become the scapegoat for Arab hostility in the wake of the Arab defeat in Palestine. To this he responded with overt contempt.

> As for the emotion of the Arabs, I do not care a dried camel's hump. It is, however, important to the interests of this country that these fanatical and over-wrought people do not injure our strategic interests through reprisals against our oil investments and through the recision of our air base rights in that area.[53]

Some years later, George Kennan gave vent to similar sentiments, albeit otherwise clothed, lamenting the State Department's failure to come to grips with what he described as "the depth of irrationality and erraticism of that region's inhabitants—particularly evident among its intellectuals—in responding to Western ideas and political purposes."[54] Kennan's reduction of political opposition to deviant psychology was designed to mask the popular expression of anti-Americanism that in Kennan's terms was a symptom of "psychological reactions and the origins of various forms of neurosis."[55]

THE VIEW FROM THE CIA

In July, the Central Intelligence Agency offered its evaluations of the evolving situation in Palestine. It was similar, in some respects, to the view from the State Department, particularly in its concern with Israel's future isolation and dependence on external support as a result of the continued conflict.[56]

Asked by the Office of the Defense Secretary to estimate the durability of the July 18 truce in Palestine, the CIA responded pessimistically. It confirmed that Israel's violations of the preceding truce had allowed it to improve its military situation and anticipated that the current truce would be similarly violated in the absence of enforcement measures. The agency assumed that "the Jews will, as before, bring in men, aircraft, and heavy military equipment; present Arab opposition to the truce will then become intensified, and the Arabs will probably reopen hostilities."[57]

As a result, the CIA report continued, the Israeli state would be further consolidated and the Arab governments that did not recognize it would be further weakened. Should the existing truce be enforced, some movement on this score might be possible if moderate Arab governments survived. But the agency noted that even such governments hoped for a revision of the partition resolution, whereas the Irgun and the Stern Gang would not tolerate any compromise, whether by Bernadotte or as agreed to by the Provisional Government of Israel.

Within two months of Israel's declaration of independence, the disparity between Israel's military capacity and that of Palestinian and Arab forces had become stark. According to the Agency, Israel had approximately 97,800 military forces, consisting of Haganah, Irgun, and the Stern Gang. The total for all the Arab states—including Transjordan, Iraq, Egypt, Syria, Lebanon, Saudi Arabia, and "Irregulars"—was believed to be 46,800.[58] Egypt had the highest number of forces with 13,000; Iraq and Transjordan each had 10,000; Syria had 2,500; Lebanon had 1,800; Saudi Arabia had 3,000; and the "irregulars" were estimated to be 6,500. All of the Arab forces were described as being "in" or "near" Palestine.[59]

The CIA concluded that "the truce resulted in so great an improvement in the Jewish capabilities that the Jews may now be strong enough to launch a full-scale offensive and drive the Arab forces out of Palestine."[60] The cumulative effect of these developments, in the CIA's estimate, was that Arab forces "could not continue to fight, even on the previous moderate scale, for more than two to three months."[61]

At the end of July, the CIA estimated that

the military situation on 18 July, the beginning of the second truce in Palestine, shows that the Jews have made substantial gains during the nine-day period of fighting between 9 July and 18 July. (See map)[62] During that period the Jews captured Lydda, Ramle and Ras el Zin, thereby removing the danger of an Arab thrust on Tel-Aviv. In the north they took the strategic Arab-Christian town of Nazareth and consolidated their positions along the roads between Jerusalem and Tel-Aviv. The only successful Arab action during that period, the Iraqi advance north from Jenin toward Afule, was halted by the truce before any significant gain was made.[63]

The CIA said nothing about the nature of the fighting in Lydda and Ramle, nor about the expulsion of Palestinians that followed. How could it not have known what had occurred? The CIA observed Israel consolidating its positions both along the Lebanese border, where its forces had moved, and "throughout southeast into the Egyptian-occupied area near Isdud and widened and strengthened the strip of Jewish-controlled territory along the roads between Jerusalem and Tel-Aviv."[64] Arab action in this period was limited to an "Iraqi advance north from Jenin towards Afule," which was effectively stopped.[65]

Avi Shlaim stated that Israeli forces "captured parts of Western Galilee and Lower Galilee. In the south they captured a number of villages and widened their hold on the northern Negev approaches."[66] In addition to the 250,000 to 300,000 Palestinian refugees who, in the time between April and mid-June, had fled or had been expelled, continued Israeli operations resulted in the expulsion of an additional 100,000 refugees. Israeli action was not limited in this period, as Israeli sources revealed.

On July 12, 1948 Israeli soldiers battling the Arab Legion and local irregulars in the towns of Lydda and Ramle, just south of Tel Aviv, were ordered to empty the two towns of their Arab residents. Over two days, between 50,000 and 60,000 inhabitants were driven from their homes. Many were forced to walk eastward to the Arab Legion lines; others were carried in trucks or buses. Clogging the roads, tens of thousands of refugees marched, shedding their possessions along the way.

The expulsions, conducted under orders from then-Lt Col. Yitzhak Rabin, were an element of the partial ethnic cleansing that rid Israel of the majority of its Arab inhabitants at the very moment of its birth.[67]

By July 13, Lydda was the scene of "a continuous curfew with house-to-house searches, a round-up of able-bodied males and the separation of families, lack of food and medical attention, the flight of relatives, continuous isolation in their houses and general dread of the future."[68]

According to Israeli historian Benny Morris, "the bulk and end of the exodus from Ramle and Lydda took place on 13 July. Many of the inhabitants of Ramle were trucked and bussed out by Kiryati troops to Al Qubab, from where they made their way on foot to Arab Legion lines in Latrun and Salbit. Others walked all the way. All Lydda's inhabitants walked, making way to Birt Nabala and Barfiliya."[69]

The CIA may not have been privy to Israeli military planning, but what explains its silence in the face of the evidence of Israel's expulsions of Palestinians? The CIA concluded that the truce benefited "Jewish capabilities" to such an extent that it altered the "previously held estimate of the probable course of the war in Palestine."[70]

As to the "Reaction of Arab Peoples," the agency suggested that "serious Jewish violations of the truce (particularly the bombing of Arab cities) would further inflame Arab public opinion and make it more difficult for the Arab governments to continue the truce."[71] Inadequate enforcement of the truce would not only fail to bring about a compromise but would enable Israel to enhance its military power while Arab weaknesses grew. If the truce was implemented, the agency maintained that moderate governments would survive, although it predicted that

Arab regimes might well be overthrown, turning against the United States and toward the USSR.

The agency predicted a shift in Soviet strategy following Britain's weakened influence in Arab states. Rather than continuing to support "Jewish independence," the USSR would begin to attack "U.S. imperialism in Israel" and promise military assistance to the Arab states.[72]

10

The Palestine Refugee Problem

THE ORIGIN OF THE PALESTINIAN REFUGEE PROBLEM

No single issue in the evolving relationship with Israel was more trou-
bling to U.S. officials than Israel's rejection of responsibility for creating
the Palestinian refugee problem and its accompanying rejection of the
prospect for refugee repatriation.[1] Even as the United States increasingly deferred to Israeli policies, such as the transfer of Palestinians out
of Jewish controlled areas to satisfy the objective of creating a homogeneous Jewish state, U.S. officials insisted that the increasing refugee
problem was one of the principal causes of the continued conflict in
Palestine. Washington remained adamant and, at the same time, chose
to remain impotent in responding to Israel's repeated denial of responsibility and rejection of repatriation.

From the president to the secretary of state and his subordinates,
there was no disputing this position. It applied as well to the U.S. ambassador to Israel, James McDonald, otherwise supportive of Israeli policies. At the end of June, McDonald sent George Marshall an account of
Israel's position on the possibility of refugee repatriation.

> Foreign Minister Shertok in speech in Tel Aviv on June 15 formally
> stated position of PGI that there can be no mass return of Palestin-
> ian Arabs to Israel until general political settlement and end of war.
> Shertok speech also stated that Arabs could not return except as full
> citizens Jewish state acknowledging its authority and sovereignty.

Reference was also made to screening. Israeli Foreign Office representing Jerusalem indicated this speech does represent stated policy of PGI and as such is shift from previous policy.

Consulate General believes that majority of Arabs now refugees from areas within Israel will never return under conditions and that their bitterness, already deep rooted, will only be increased by PGI statement. So far, however, Palestinian Arabs with whom Consulate General officials have talked have not commented on Shertok's statement.[2]

The CIA reported that between July 9 and July 18 the "Jews captured Lydda, Ramle, and Ras el Zin" in operations that "were designed to induce civilian panic and flight—as a means of precipitating military collapse and possibl[y] also as an end itself."[3] Benny Morris goes on to say that the attacks on Lydda and Ramle "result[ed] in the almost complete exodus of their inhabitants to Arab-held territory."[4]

In mid-July, Shertok sent explicit instructions telling Israeli diplomats how to respond to questions about refugees. In part, the necessity for such a response was a product of the UN mediator's pronouncements on the subject. On June 27, Count Folke Bernadotte "demanded that Israel recognize the 'right of the residents of Palestine who, because of conditions created by the conflict there, have left their normal places of abode, to return to their homes without restriction and to regain possession of their property.'"[5] Bernadotte subsequently acknowledged that this objective might well be undermined by the destruction of the very homes to which the refugees aspired to return, and by the more general changes that had occurred in Israel and among the Palestinian refugees themselves.

Moshe Sharett (formerly Shertok),[6] Israel's first foreign minister, wrote to Nahum Goldmann describing the desperate flight of Palestinians as constituting

the most spectacular event in the contemporary history of Palestine—more spectacular in a sense than the creation of the Jewish state—is the wholesale evacuation of its Arab population which has swept with it also thousands of Arabs from areas threatened and/or occupied by us outside our boundaries. I doubt whether there are

100,000 Arabs in Israel today. The reversion to *status quo ante* is unthinkable. The opportunities which the present position opens up for a lasting and radical solution of the most vexing problem of the Jewish State are so far-reaching as to take one's breath away. Even if a certain backlash is unavoidable, we must make the most of the momentous chance with which history has presented us so swiftly and so unexpectedly.[7]

But as other Israeli officials, including Yosef Sprinzak, secretary general of the Histadrut, understood, the key question was, "Who made this history?"

The question is whether the Arabs are [being or have been] expelled or not. . . . This is important to our moral future. . . . I want to know who is creating the facts [of expulsion]? And the facts are being created on orders. Who was responsible for ordering the expulsions?[8]

Spiro Munayyer, who was a Palestinian paramedic in Lydda at this time, confirmed that "of the 50,000 people in our city a few days before, including both regular inhabitants and refugees, only about 500 remained."[9] It turned out "that another 500 people or so were still living near the railroad station. The occupation authorities had kept them there to run the station and operate the trains so as to transport food and munitions for the Israeli army."[10]

On the same day that the CIA sent its report to Washington describing Israel's capture of Lydda, Ramle, and Ras el Zin, Philip Jessup sent the secretary of state a letter he had received from the Israelis (Comay) stating the official position of the Provisional Government of Israel on the refugee question. The claim was that Palestinian flight was a response to Arab orders and the product of war, in this instance the Arab invasion of Israel on May 15.

The Government of Israel must disclaim any responsibility for the creation of this problem. The charge that these Arabs were forcibly driven out by Israel authorities is wholly false; on the contrary, everything possible was done to prevent an exodus which was a direct result of the folly of the Arab states in organizing and launching

a war of aggression against Israel. The impulse of the Arab civilian population to migrate from war areas, in order to avoid being
involved in the hostilities, was deliberately fostered by Arab leaders
for political motives. They did not wish the Arab population to continue to lead a peaceful existence in Jewish areas, and they wished
to exploit the exodus as a propaganda weapon in surrounding Arab
countries and in the outside world. This inhuman policy has now
faced the governments concerned with practical problems for which
they must assume full responsibility.[11]

Amnon Kapeliuk described a very different account drawn from Israeli
sources.

A twenty-four page report from the military intelligence SHAI (information service) of the Haganah dated 30 June 1948, affirms that
"70 percent of the refugees had abandoned their homes at the
time of the first wave (up until 1 June 1948) because of hostile acts
committed by the Haganah, Irgun, and the Stern group." This first
wave involved some 400,000 people. The second wave, of some
300,000, set out for exile between June and December of 1948.
It was thus that a number of cities and about 250 villages were
emptied of their inhabitants. The two main reasons for the Palestinian exodus of 1948 were expulsion by the Israeli army and fear of
massacre.[12]

Israel's response to the U.S. and UN demand for repatriation was accompanied by confirmation that the land and property to which Palestinian
refugees aspired to return was no longer available, having been assigned
to incoming Jewish refugees.

Fearful of the consequences and persuaded that Israel's position
blocked any resolution of the conflict, U.S. officials urged the PGI to
accept repatriation or at least to make a symbolic gesture toward its
acceptance. Washington's ambassador to Israel, James McDonald, on
the other hand, justified Israeli actions except for Deir Yassin, which he
saw as an exception.[13]

McDonald reported that Israelis insisted that the refugee problem
would have to await the more comprehensive settlement, although they

were prepared, in accord with UNGA Resolution 194, to provide compensation for abandoned land "only if its counterclaims were taken into account, and only if there were real peace."[14] McDonald recognized, however, that Jewish immigrants had already settled in formerly Palestinian homes, making repatriation problematic.

Despite McDonald's sympathetic view of Israel's position, he decried "a certain lack of imagination and humanity. What was wanted was a more humane, a more creative approach—one that would have preserved security but still allowed for positive action. Such an approach was lacking."[15] He maintained that "no one of the big three—Weizmann, Ben-Gurion or Sharett—seemed to have thought through the implications of the tragedy or of Israel's lack of concrete helpfulness."[16] McDonald claimed that Sharett thought the problem a matter of Arab responsibility, whereas Ben-Gurion "held out some hope for large-scale repatriation once there was formal peace."[17] Chaim Weizmann, in turn, was described as "speaking to me emotionally of the 'miraculous oversimplification of Israel's tasks,' and cited the vaster tragedy of six million Jews murdered during World War II." He wondered "what did the world do to prevent this genocide? Why now should there be such excitement in the UN and the Western capitals about the plight of the Arab refugees?"[18]

In Washington, Truman himself was moved by the situation of the Palestinian refugees and eager for some indication of Israeli flexibility, as were Marshall and the high-ranking officials of the State Department responsible for the Middle East, as well as those in the Defense Department and the CIA. They understood that Arab regimes would face substantial difficulties in dealing with the vast scope of their unexpected influx, recognizing that it was tangible proof of Arab military defeat.

On August 31, 1948, the CIA issued its assessment of "Possible Developments From the Palestine Truce" in response to the request of the secretary of defense. Among its conclusions was a dire statement concerning Palestinian refugees.

The most serious population upheaval since the termination of World War II, has been the exodus of Palestinian Arabs from Israeli-held areas. The Arab refugees, conservatively estimated at 330,000, exceed in number the Jewish DP's in Europe. The Arab countries have neither the economic resources nor the political stability to absorb such large numbers of destitute refugees. Israel's decision not to allow the refugees to return to their homes has greatly exacerbated Arab bitterness against the Jews.[19]

The contrast between the Palestinian exodus and the influx of Jews into Israel was recognized by virtually all officials, including Bernadotte. For the CIA, the admission of some 125,000 Jews into Israel by the end of 1948 explained "in large part Israel's refusal to readmit Arab refugees," as well as its desire for more land.[20] Dean Rusk, director of the Office of UN Affairs, suggested it appropriate to remind Israeli representatives at the UN of the striking disparity between Israel's capacity to integrate new immigrants and its refusal to consider the repatriation of Palestinian refugees. Rusk added, as did other U.S. officials, that contrary to Israeli claims the refugees constituted no risk to Israel's security.

The same argument was offered by UN mediator Count Bernadotte who, in early August, reported through the U.S. Charge in Egypt (Patterson) "that he was making progress in obtaining acquiescence existence Israeli state if not its formal acceptance by Arab states."[21] According to Bernadotte, both the prime ministers of Transjordan and Lebanon "sought speedy decision. Azzam Pasha also apparently convinced necessity to admit existence Jewish state although not ready to make statements now since he believed time should be given for preparation public opinion."[22] Bernadotte conceded that there would be greater resistance from Syrian and Iraqi officials. The mediator nonetheless considered his efforts promising in this regard, unlike his attempt to persuade Israel to act on the question of repatriation.

Bernadotte declared that the "condition [of] 300,000 to 400,000 Arab refugees without food, clothing and shelter was appalling."[23] He expressed the hope that private welfare organizations would assist, but the basic problem was their eventual return to their home. In this connection, Bernadotte said PGI was "showing signs of swelled head." When Bernadotte confronted the Israeli foreign minister with the need to allow Palestinian refugees to return home, he responded that "politically PGI could not admit Arab refugees as they would constitute fifth column. Economically PGI had no room for Arabs since their space was needed for Jewish immigrants."[24]

Bernadotte added that Palestinian homes in Ramle had their belongings removed and redistributed to Jewish immigrants. In confronting Sharett with some of these problems, the UN mediator indicated that Sharett replied that his government maintained the right to replace Palestinian refugees with Jews coming from Arab countries.[25] To this Bernadotte replied that "it seemed anomaly for Jews to base demand for Jewish state on need to find home Jewish refugees and that they should demand migration to Palestine of Jewish DP's when they refused to recognize problems of Arab refugees which they had created."[26]

The U.S. Charge in Egypt (Patterson), who conveyed the UN mediator's views to Marshall, described Bernadotte's proposals to the Arabs. In addition to acknowledging the existence of the Jewish state, they included the possibility of resuming war; accepting UNGA Resolution 181; or having Arab states partition Arab Palestine among themselves. Bernadotte was in favor of the last option, while recognizing continued Israeli expansion as "it demanded all Galilee by right of conquest, corridor from Jerusalem to Tel Aviv, and the return of Negeb as an area promised Israel in partition scheme."[27]

MARSHALL, RUSK, LOVETT, AND THE UN MEDIATOR

Bernadotte's views impressed Secretary of State Marshall, as well as Dean Rusk and Robert Lovett, all of whom were in accord with the mediator's position on Jerusalem, the fate of the refugees, and the general contours of a settlement. Marshall also supported Bernadotte's goal of having foreign observers "in strategic positions evacuated by Jews and Arabs by mutual agreement, such as Mt Scopus, Victoria Augusta Hospital, and water pumping station at Latrun."[28] He saw no reason for the United States to object to participating in such a program, although the Joint Chiefs of Staff disagreed.

Where Marshall was at odds with Bernadotte was on the latter's wish to bring the Palestine question to the UNGA. Marshall preferred that Israel and Transjordan reach an accord through diplomatic means, and then bring that accord before Arab states for their approval. With regard to the refugee problem, Marshall identified private, nongovernmental organizations who could assist in these matters, pointing out that U.S. funds were currently unavailable for Palestinian refugees. The State

Department subsequently adopted a plan to raise contributions from the UNGA through the mediator and the International Refugee Organization (IRO), with Washington playing an increasingly important role in attracting nongovernmental sources of assistance.

Among the agencies that responded to the refugee crisis was the War Relief Services of National Catholic Welfare Conference; the Near East Foundation working in Syria and Lebanon; the International Children's Emergency Fund; and Amcross, the American Red Cross. The latter had committed to provide "14,000 dollars to cover 20 tons DDT specifically requested by Bernadotte, and has now authorized additional 200,000 dollars medical supplies for immediate shipment Near East."[29] The Federal Council of Churches, the Christian Rural Overseas Program, American Middle East Relief Incorporated, Lutheran World Relief Incorporated, and the U.S. oil giants ARAMCO and Bechtel contributed to the general effort to assist refugees as well.

It was in August 1948 that "serious American pressure" on Israeli policies toward the Palestinian refugees led to what Eliahu Elath (formerly Epstein), who was now Israeli ambassador to the United States, described as undermining U.S. public opinion. Elath claimed to be puzzled by the U.S. response, as "all hostile forces unite in publicizing and shedding crocodile tears regarding plight Arab refugees."[30] It was not hostile forces alone, however, that pressed for action on this score, as Ambassador McDonald's efforts to obtain agreement from Ben-Gurion indicated.

Only a week earlier, on August 14, Marshall sent the U.S. Embassy in London his impressions of Bernadotte's views on Israeli policies on land and refugees. His position was similar to what he and Ernest Bevin had discussed earlier. With respect to land, Marshall indicated "Bernadotte thinks that Jews should be given valuable lands in western Galilee which they now hold by virtue of military conquest but in return for this acquisition should permit Arabs to take over most of Negev."[31] Marshall agreed with Bernadotte that the refugee question was basic to a settlement of the conflict. He repeated his position in a communiqué to the U.S. Embassy in London.

> With ref to economic, political military factors in connection with return Arab refugees to Israel, we appreciate security considerations

governing PGI attitude but believe that under supervision Mediator substantial number refugees so desiring could be permitted gradually return their homes and resume occupations without prejudicing maintenance internal security Israel. From economic viewpoint, Israel now demonstrating ability absorb large numbers European DPs monthly. It would therefore be unfortunate for PGI, by continuing refuse permit Arab repatriation, to create impression that assimilation Jewish immigrants was taking place at expense former Arab inhabitants Israel. From political standpoint, PGI action to permit gradual return Arab refugees would provide Arabs with tangible assurance of PGI desire establish cooperative relations with Arab states on long range basis.

We consider overall solution Arab refugee problem intrinsic to final settlement Palestine problem, but believe increasingly critical nature refugee problem makes it essential that at least partial return of refugees should be permitted for those so desiring prior to achievement final settlement. Moreover, we believe PGI assistance in alleviating situation would substantially improve chances securing early peaceful settlement Palestine problem. Conversely, PGI failure to cooperate by partial repatriation refugees might create difficulties for 265,000 Jews permanently residing Arab states.[32]

Marshall recommended that the Security Council ask Bernadotte to provide an assessment of the total number of refugees, their location, as well as an assessment of what their return would entail. His own view was that the major problem was material, assuming that Israel was prepared to allow repatriation. By 1948–49, "the best estimates arrive at between 750,000–800,000 refugees. Or about 85% of the Palestinian population from what became the state of Israel."[33]

In mid-August, Marshall wrote directly to Truman to express the State Department's concern about Israel's assumption of "a more aggressive attitude in Palestine."[34]

The Department has noted evidence of hostility of Israelis in Palestine towards the military observers serving under Count Bernadotte; the inflammatory speeches of the Israeli Foreign Minister, Mr. Shertok, with regard to alleged "rights" of Israel in Jerusalem; the military occupation by Israel of much of the Jerusalem area; and the refusal of the Israeli military governor in Jerusalem to cooperate with Count Bernadotte in discussions regarding the demilitarization of Jerusalem. The Department has likewise noted increasing evidence of systematic violations of the United Nations truce by the forces of Israel, including forward movement of Israeli forces from agreed truce positions, continued sniping and firing against Arab positions; and conclusive evidence of the organized transport of arms shipments to Palestine from France, Italy and Czechoslovakia. Furthermore, the Israeli Foreign Minister has officially proclaimed that Israel will not accept, pending negotiation of a final peace settlement, the return of the approximately 300,000 Arab inhabitants of that part of Palestine now comprising the Jewish State who fled from their homes and are now destitute in nearby Arab areas.[35]

Marshall suggested that Truman discuss U.S. concerns with the Israeli representative of the PGI, while emphasizing that "the United States is the best friend of Israel."[36] Marshall was concerned that Israel would "resume hostilities" just as Washington was considering its request, favored by the president, for a loan from the Export-Import Bank.[37]

On August 20, 1948, Dean Rusk, the director of the Office of UN Affairs, sent Lovett an elaborate statement on the subject of refugees in which he included three recommendations that had been approved by Truman, the third of which was:

That, as part of this government's diplomatic participation in securing a peaceful settlement of the Palestine problem, it urges upon the Provisional Government of Israel and other governments concerned the need for repatriating Arab and Jewish refugees under conditions which will not imperil the internal security of the receiving states.[38]

Rusk informed Truman about exchanges that had taken place on the question of Palestinian refugees, including Bernadotte's view that "a very large proportion of the 330,000 Arabs who fled from their homes in Jewish Palestine to other areas should return to those homes. A very large percentage of these refugees consist of children, women and aged who under no stretch of the imagination could be regarded as a security threat against Israel."[39] The UN mediator described their situation as one of utter desperation. "They exist in terms of utmost destitution and if adequate relief is not forthcoming or they are not returned to their homes a large proportion will die before the end of winter."[40] Rusk repeated Bernadotte's statement that many Palestinian homes seized had been turned over to Jewish immigrants. Rusk suggested that Israel might be using the refugee problem as leverage in the context of a future settlement.

In response to the Israeli claim that political and economic factors precluded repatriation outside the framework of a settlement, Rusk insisted that Truman convince Eliahu Epstein that "if the Provisional Government continues to prevent the repatriation of Arab refugees, it will strengthen the already prevalent impression that the entry of European displaced persons is being accomplished at the expense of the former inhabitants of Israeli territory."[41] Rusk advised Truman to remind Epstein that repatriation under Bernadotte's supervision would not constitute a risk. Repeating what had become the American formula, Rusk emphasized that repatriation would serve as evidence of Israel's willingness to cooperate with the Arabs, and thereby improve the chances of arriving at a settlement. The Israeli government was already moving to settle Jewish immigrants on Palestinian land at this time, however.

> In August 1948, the Ministerial Committee discussed creation of sixty-one new settlements. The settling authorities recommended that only thirty-two of them, on some 30,000 acres, be built for the time being. Of those lands, some 14,500 acres belonged to Arabs, 5,000 acres to the government, and 5,000 acres to other owners, chiefly German and in one case the Waqf. Only about 5,000 acres belonged to Jews. The ministers considered the future of the Arab inhabitants and made suggestions for transferring them legally. The minister of Agriculture described the legal arrangements as "a fiction."[42]

In Washington, far from such scenes, Marshall and Rusk continued to support Bernadotte's position and to urge the president to confront the Israelis on key issues as Marshall had previously done. Working through separate channels, U.S. Ambassador James McDonald returned to Washington for a visit and checked in with the president, State Department colleagues, and Clark Clifford, among others.

He informed Clifford of Israel's frustration with U.S. support for the truce and its skepticism with regard to the UN mediator, whom McDonald depicted as lacking credibility. On meeting with Truman, McDonald intervened on behalf of Eliahu Epstein who had complained to him about the United States having decided to withhold the loan to Israel from the Export-Import Bank. It was reinstated in short order. The $100 million loan had been requested by Shertok in early June.

Referring to difficulties and differences between U.S. officials and Israel on questions of refugees and more, McDonald was clearly frustrated with his visit. He had hoped to obtain greater clarity with respect to U.S. policy, but he failed to do so. Perhaps, he wrote, he had found "the key to the whole problem in a chance comment which Louis Johnson, then Secretary of Defense, had made to me in a talk about our military representation. 'Israel is important strategically and we must support her. But they ought to try to take some more refugees in.' "[43] Johnson's phrase pointed to a dimension of U.S. policy toward Israel that was seldom openly discussed. The encounter exposed U.S. priorities and the secondary importance of the Palestinian refugee problem. However, there was no lessening of its importance in the exchanges of State Department officials from the secretary of state to his subordinates.

At the end of August, Marshall was in contact with McDonald about the truce. As Marshall stated,

the truce is a necessity to any hope for a peaceful settlement and the present evident aggressive tendencies of the Israeli Government to capitalize to the limit on military advantages, real and anticipated, is bound to have unfortunate results where a more conservative course can well lead to a settlement advantageous to that Government.[44]

Marshall contacted McDonald again on September 1, at which time McDonald referred to the Israeli advocacy of direct negotiations while steering clear of what Marshall regarded as essential steps, including those related to the truce, the demilitarization of Jerusalem, the refugee problem, and the problem of borders.

Marshall could not avoid the refugee question, particularly as he attributed responsibility for it to Israeli actions, as in the occupation of Haifa and the invasion of Jaffa.

Arab refugee problem is one which, as you quote PGI as saying, did develop from recent war in Palestine but which also began before outbreak of Arab-Israeli hostilities. A significant portion of Arab refugees fled from their homes owing to Jewish occupation of Haifa on April 21–22 and to Jewish armed attack against Jaffa April 25. You will recall statements made by Jewish authorities in Palestine promising safeguards for Arab minority in areas under Jewish control. Arab refugee problem is one involving life or death of some 300,000 people. The leaders of Israel would make a grave miscalculation if they thought callous treatment of this tragic issue could pass unnoticed by world opinion. Furthermore, hatred of Arabs for Israel engendered by refugee problem would be a great obstacle to those peace negotiations you say PGI immediately desires.

In the light of the foregoing I do not concur in your conclusion that "Jewish emphasis on peace negotiations now is sounder than present U.S. and UN emphasis on truce and demilitarization and refugees."[45]

Marshall reminded McDonald of U.S. efforts to forge a settlement, adding that Washington had the impression that the Provisional Government was not only bent on obtaining what UNGA Resolution 181 had decreed but "such additional territory as is now under military occupation by Israeli forces, including the rich area of western Galilee and a portion of Jerusalem."[46] Marshall acknowledged that the United States was aware of the difficulties posed by "extremists," but it wanted to have "some indication of the true intentions of PGI in respect to their territorial claims."[47] At the same time, the secretary of state conceded that the new state "should have boundaries which will make it more homogeneous and well integrated than the hourglass frontiers drawn on the map of the November 29 Resolution."[48] Marshall was in favor of Israeli expansion into the Galilee, which he conceded Israel held in occupation, but only insofar as it was prepared to return "a large portion of the Negev to Transjordan."[49]

The question of territorial expansion was directly related to the issue of boundaries, or "permanent frontiers," which Marshall and Bevin had discussed. The two disagreed on the contentious issue of bringing the Palestinian case before the United Nations. Marshall questioned whether the UN Security Council had the power to determine boundaries and to apply sanctions. But the underlying fear among U.S. officials was that bringing the Palestine case back to the United Nations risked opening the Pandora's box of questions concerning the very legitimacy of the partition resolution.

As Marshall told McDonald, given U.S. skepticism about the possibility of bringing Jews and Arabs together for direct negotiations, Washington "would be content with acquiescence of the parties to an equitable settlement."[50] McDonald duly conveyed Marshall's questions to the Israeli government, on whose behalf Sharett responded. He recounted his trip to Paris and meetings with Syrian and Lebanese ministers as well as the minister to Great Britain from Transjordan. He described how Abdullah had indirectly let him know "that he was most anxious for peace with the Jews."[51] Nothing came of this at the time, which Sharett attributed to probable British pressure on Abdullah.

There may have been other factors, as revealed by Azmi Nashashibi, brigadier in the Arab Legion, who outlined conditions permitting direct talks in what the U.S. consul in Jerusalem described as "Transjordan controlled Ramallah radio."[52] Nashashibi was reported to have said that "Arabs might consider direct talks with Jews under following 'conditions': Jews return to areas held before November 29, return of all Arab refugees, payment by Jews for damages. Jews not attempt to dictate to Arabs."[53]

The U.S. consul general remarked that although the above conditions were "inacceptable, [the] speech [was] significant as further indication [of] possible Arab willingness [to] negotiate directly with Jews."[54] The Israeli government found the conditions unacceptable, whether in relation to refugees, boundaries, or compensation.

It was also clear to the Americans, the British, and the Israelis that King Abdullah was in a position so vulnerable in relation to other Arab regimes as to undermine the impact of whatever he might do in relation to Israel. The U.S. ambassador to London sent Marshall a report of Britain's position, in which he explained that the perception of "'Rabbi' Abdullah" had to be seen as independent of foreign support, as well as in solidarity with Arab leaders if Transjordan was to be useful in reaching a settlement.[55]

Insofar as the Palestinian refugees were concerned, David Ben-Gurion, the Israeli prime minister, made it clear that "he saw no possibility mass return refugees until peace settlement effected and that comprehensive solution must wait on peace."[56] Sharett, in turn, distinguished between an interim as opposed to a permanent settlement of the refugee problem, the latter to be in Arab areas, in which Israel was willing to assist. In addition, Sharett indicated that the Israeli government would consider "individual family hardship cases," although he was vague on the subject, as McDonald pointed out.[57] Ben-Gurion also challenged what he viewed as unwarranted U.S. contestations of Israeli controlled territory.

Marshall had evidence of different Arab responses, including from the Egyptian representative to the UN Fawzi Bey, who had earlier suggested that the principle of self-determination, if applied to the Jewish and Arab populations of Palestine, might be promising. Neither Israeli nor U.S. officials shared Fawzi Bey's optimism about alternative possibilities; none ventured to speculate on what self-determination for Arabs and Jews might look like.

In 1982 Seth Tillman, a member of the Senate Foreign Relations Committee's professional staff and its Subcommittee on Near Eastern and South Asian Affairs, briefly discussed the applicability of the principle of self-determination to Palestine. He concluded that the United States was necessarily ambivalent toward its application, "there being no way to reconcile Zionism with the self-determination of an established population."[58] Yet, as Tillman pointed out, successive administrations reiterated support for it, in principle. Tillman's account also included a grim portrait of a Palestinian refugee camp he visited in Beirut in 1970.[59]

BERNADOTTE'S "SEVEN BASIC PREMISES"

The "Progress Report of the United Nations Mediator in Palestine" was presented to the UN on September 16, 1948, in the form of "Seven Basic Premises." The following day, McDonald, U.S. consul general in Jerusalem, sent a report to the U.S. secretary of state announcing "Count Folke Bernadotte, United Nations Mediator on Palestine, brutally assassinated by Jewish assailants of unknown identity, in planned, cold blooded attack in the new city of Jerusalem at 1404 GMT today, Friday, 17 September."[60] On September 18, the consul general informed the department that the "general assumption of UN observer group, this office and Jewish military authorities, [is] that assassins were of terrorist group, LHY, commonly known as Stern Gang."[61]

In addition to the predictable shock, the response in Washington and London to Bernadotte's assassination was to reaffirm the value of the UN mediator's efforts, as exemplified by his report on the Palestine problem. Secretary of State Marshall declared it a "generally fair basis for settlement of the Palestine question," urging the parties concerned to accept it.[62] Marshall pointed out that no plan would satisfy all parties, and, indeed, none of the parties found it satisfactory. Abdullah, who had been favorably inclined, decided against it in response to the negative Arab consensus.

In Washington, however, the Joint Chiefs of Staff reproduced the mediator's "basic premises," with the secretary of state's supportive statement. But as McClintock indicated, tremendous pressure was being applied by the American Zionist Emergency Council against Bernadotte's proposals. The result, McClintock warned Rusk, who was then in Paris, was that the United States would probably have to

adjust our sights at least to the point of agreeing that the territorial recommendations of the Mediator be modified in favor of Israel to the extent of giving the Jewish State a salient into the Negev which would include most, if not all of the Jewish settlements in that area. Such a salient would not extend further than the Gaza-Beersheba Road and would in fact put U.S. in precise accord with the proposed territorial settlement which was approved by the President on September 1.[63]

This position had previously been rejected by Bernadotte and the British, with the UN mediator insisting that "the responsibility was to propose terms founded on strict justice."[64] McClintock indicated that he was privately in accord, but he rationalized supporting Israel's desire to control the Negev, which would give Israel "a token holding in that area," as a politically sound decision.[65]

What of the UN mediator's report and its "Seven Basic Premises"? Criticized by Israel for an inadequate recognition of Israeli sovereignty, Bernadotte had reaffirmed recognition of Israel. In addition, he had stated his support for "the principle of geographical homogeneity and integration, which would be the major objective of the boundary arrangements" to be implemented.[66] These, the UN mediator had added, "should apply equally to Arab and Jewish territories, whose frontiers should not, therefore, be rigidly controlled by the territorial arrangements envisaged in the resolution of 29 November."[67]

Bernadotte had indicated that in the absence of Arab and Jewish approval, the UN would proceed with a "technical boundaries commission appointed by and responsible to the United Nations."[68] The resulting boundaries, as Bernadotte had indicated, were designed to make them "more equitable, workable and consistent with existent realities in Palestine."[69]

> (i) The area known as the Negeb, south of a line running from the sea near Majdal east-southeast to Faluja (both of which places would be in Arab territory), should be defined as Arab territory;
>
> (ii) This frontier should run from Falujah north northeast to Ramleh and Lydda (both of which places would be in Arab territory), the frontier at Lydda then following the line established in the General Assembly resolution of 29 November;
>
> (iii) Galilee should be defined as Jewish territory.[70]

The UN mediator also supported Abdullah's takeover of Palestinian Arab territory outside of Israeli control, while claiming the importance of consultation with Palestinians. Bernadotte's justification for such a policy was that there existed a "historical connexion and common interests of Transjordan and Palestine," which made it preferable to other arrangements with Arab states.[71]

Bernadotte affirmed that his position involved no denial of the existence of Palestinian Arabs as a separate people. On the contrary, he affirmed that the "Arab inhabitants of Palestine are not citizens or subjects of Egypt, Iraq, Lebanon, Syria and Transjordan, the States which are at present providing them with a refuge and the basic necessities of life."[72] But he also recognized the transformation of Palestine that had occurred since his June 27 report. There was no longer talk of two states; instead, there was an urgency focused on the humanitarian crisis of Palestinian refugees. He repeatedly emphasized that "the choice is between saving the lives of many thousands of people now or permitting them to die," a choice in which the UN and its specialized agencies, Arab states, the Provisional Government of Israel, and voluntary agencies would have to play a decisive role.[73]

Among U.S. journalists covering the refugee problem, Dana Adams Schmidt, writing at this time from Damascus, offered an account that corresponded to Bernadotte's description of the impoverished state of Palestinian refugees: "most of them [are] huddled under trees in tents, shanty towns and slums of Arab lands, surrounding Israeli-held parts of Palestine."[74]

Anticipating what would become of UNGA Resolution 194, passed by the UN General Assembly on December 11, 1948, Bernadotte's "Seven Premises" included the "Right of repatriation," which affirmed "the right of innocent people, uprooted from their homes by the present terror and ravages of war, to return to their homes," a position that he urged be implemented with guarantees of compensation for those choosing not to return.[75]

Among Bernadotte's "premises," Jerusalem was to be "accorded special and separate treatment."[76]

The UN mediator may not have had a full account of the number of Palestinian villages destroyed and urban centers fallen and largely emptied of their Palestinian inhabitants by 1948. Palestinian historian Walid Khalidi stated that "418 Palestinian villages [were] destroyed and depopulated in the 1948 war."[77] In addition, there "was the fall of more than a dozen of the major urban centers of the Palestinian people— towns exclusively populated by them (Acre, Beersheva, Baysan, Lydda, Majdal, Nazareth, al-Ramla), others where they were either the vast majority (Safad) or had substantial pluralities (Tiberias, Haifa, and West Jerusalem), and their ancient seaport Jaffa."[78] Khalidi adds that with the exception of Nazareth, "these urban centers were also emptied of their Palestinian residents."[79] The 418 villages destroyed "constituted almost half of the total number of Palestinian villages that existed within the borders of Mandatory Palestine on the eve of the UN General Assembly partition resolution in November 1947."[80]

Of the Palestinian villages that remained within Israel, "over 80 percent of the lands of these Palestinian/Israeli citizens who never left their homes have been confiscated since 1948 and put at the exclusive disposal of the Jewish citizens of the state."[81] Recent efforts to reframe the "Roots of Palestine and Israel," which attest to the history documented by Palestinian historians, may be found in the project Towards a Common Archive, organized by the Israeli nongovernmental organization Zochrot.[82]

11

The State Department on the Record

REFUGEES, BOUNDARIES, AND JERUSALEM

In the fall of 1948, following Count Folke Bernadotte's assassination, George Marshall, Robert Lovett, and the State Department came out strongly in support of the former UN mediator's proposals, paying special attention to the key issues he had addressed: boundaries, refugees, and Jerusalem. Differences aside, U.S. Ambassador to Israel James McDonald joined his voice to those decrying the condition of the Palestinian refugees. U.S. consul in Jerusalem William Burdett, who had previously reported sympathetically on the situation of Jewish settlers facing Palestinian attacks, was now sending evidence of Israeli territorial expansion and the continued attacks and expulsions of Palestinians.

The fall of 1948 was a period of intense activity on the political, diplomatic, and military levels. In Washington at the end of October, the U.S. president made it clear that he wanted minimal action during the election period and shortly after that was on record as being prepared to approve a truce in Palestine. Truman's position reflected his deference to domestic political pressures, to which the secretary and under secretary of state and others engaged in Israeli–Palestinian issues were obliged to abide. Once election fever passed, U.S. policy continued to be constrained by factors that were not immediately apparent.

At the United Nations, the mood was very different. The UN mediator "had visited refugee camps in Palestine and had seen for himself the appalling conditions there" before he presented his progress report on the Palestinian situation to the General Assembly in September.[1] The UN subsequently adopted Bernadotte's recommendations with respect to the right of refugees to repatriation and compensation, as UNGA Resolution 194 confirmed.

On October 15, Secretary of State Marshall wrote to Acting Secretary Robert Lovett, asking for his and the department's comments on a resolution that he, Harold Beeley, and Ralph Bunche had worked on together.[2] Marshall explained that he was planning to present it to the U.S. delegation at the UN. The composite draft was a restatement of the UN Security Council resolution of July 15, 1948 (Document /S902), which called for an end to military action and the maintenance of the truce, with the objective of promoting a resolution of the conflict. It was the same resolution that called for the creation of the Palestine Conciliation Commission. The importance of Marshall's statement rested in its identification of U.S. policy with the UN resolution.

Among the initiatives offered under the General Assembly resolution following Israel's independence on May 14, 1948, was Resolution 186 (S-2), according to which the UN mediator was given the power to "exercise certain functions including the use of his good offices to promote a peaceful adjustment of the future situation of Palestine."[3]

On October 16, 1948, Secretary of State Marshall informed Lovett from Paris that the General Assembly acknowledged having received the late Count Bernadotte's progress report (Document A/648). In addition, the Assembly acknowledged the UNSC Resolution of July 15, 1948 (Document S/902), which ordered the governments concerned to cease military action and to abide by the truce. Marshall's statement indicated that the United States had accepted the UNSC resolution of July 15, 1948, whose contents were then reviewed. It included reference to the establishment of a "conciliation commission" that was "to make arrangements for the transition from the existing truce to a formal peace or armistice in Palestine," and until that time to support the existing truce.[4]

The conciliation commission was to "appoint a technical boundaries commission to assist in delimiting the frontiers in Palestine based on the specific conclusions of the UN Mediator," to which the authors of the draft resolution added the phrase "subject to such adjustments as may promote agreement between the Arabs and the Jews (without altering the general equilibrium of the Mediator's conclusions), and taking into account the nature of the terrain and the unity of village areas."[5] Some viewed it as among the most important attempts to achieve a peace settlement.[6]

Without mentioning Transjordan or King Abdullah by name, the UN resolution described the future of Arab Palestine, recommending consultation with Arabs, including Palestinians, as well as plans for the protection of Holy Places, with Jerusalem "placed under effective UN control with maximum feasible local autonomy for the Arab and Jewish communities," and with proposals for more permanent arrangements to be brought to the forthcoming session of the General Assembly.[7]

Among its most contested recommendations was item 12 concerning repatriation:

> Recognizes the right of the Arab refugees to return to their homes in Jewish controlled territory at the earliest possible date; and the right of adequate compensation for the property of those choosing not to return and for property which has been lost as a result of pillage or confiscation or of destruction not resulting from military necessity; and instructs the conciliation commission to facilitate the repatriation, resettlement, and economic and social rehabilitation of the Arab refugees and the payment of compensation.[8]

The day after Marshall wrote to Lovett, James McDonald was moved to write directly to Truman expressing his fear lest the existing situation of Palestinian refugees fail to be properly addressed. McDonald warned of a "tragedy reaching catastrophic proportions."[9] He condemned existing relief efforts and resources as wasteful and inadequate, adding that UN officers involved were not to blame; "it is the system which is at fault."[10] He reminded the president that he spoke on the basis of fifteen years of experience in work with refugees, warning that of 400,000 refugees, one fourth of the elderly and the children would die in the approaching winter as they were without food or shelter. "Situation requires some comprehensive program and immediate action that dramatic and overwhelming calamities such as vast flood or earthquake would invoke. Nothing less will avert horrifying losses."[11]

McDonald recommended that the International Red Cross take over responsibility for the refugees, and he urged that Stanton Griffis, then U.S. ambassador to Egypt, be appointed its director. Griffis was duly named director and turned to the League of Red Cross Societies as well as the American Friends Service Committee for assistance.

Throughout this period, Washington remained sensitive to the changing balance of power in the region. Israel's military superiority was enhanced by the covert entry of Czech arms, and the parallel embargo on Arab arms that left even the vaunted Arab Legion in "a position of relative impotence," as British and U.S. officials recognized.[12] With tensions constantly rising and Britain fearful lest its position in Transjordan and Egypt be fatally undermined by the failure to arrive at a settlement in Palestine, U.S. officials attempted to persuade Israel to accept territorial compromise. The process failed, leaving State Department officials as well as consuls and ministers across the Middle East and at the United Nations increasingly bitter at the routine manner in which their recommendations were ignored.

By mid- to late December, there was ample evidence of Israeli violations of the UN truce and an escalation of the Palestinian refugee problem that left the prospect of a settlement null and void. From London, U.S. Ambassador Lewis Douglas sent an extensive report of British views, including those concerning the Palestinian situation, as well as their impact on Anglo-Arab and Soviet relations.

In the eyes of Lt. General Templer, vice chief of the Imperial General Staff, the Soviets "managed to transfer Palestine into the spearhead of its attempt to disrupt ME and make it untenable for U.S.-UK defense purposes."[13] In Templer's view, they did not have far to go given the existing disruption caused by the failure to resolve the Palestinian crisis. Aside from establishing a large Soviet mission in Tel Aviv, in addition to one in Lebanon, Templer believed that "Communist headquarters" would eventually be in Israel, and Arab–Jewish cooperation would be furthered through communists. Further, Templer was persuaded that the Soviet Union was effectively promoting revolutionary fervor among disillusioned Arabs, convinced that "even if present Arab Governments survive their disillusion with West (ie. U.S. and UK), vapid UN handling Palestine problem may cause them to look for more purposeful world power and decide this is U.S.S.R."[14]

Templer also took note of Israeli relations with the Eastern bloc. In addition to arms from Czechoslovakia, "Palestine turmoil has stopped Haifa oil dock and refinery to cost ERP and to possible benefit Rumania with which PGI is discussing oil supplies."[15] To make matters worse, Templer pointed out that the "Jewish thrust into Negev has for first time in history split Arab world; there is now no practicable land communication between Egypt and other Arab states—a feat never achieved even by Crusaders."[16]

WARNINGS FROM LONDON

When sending his report to Washington, U.S. Ambassador Douglas concluded with a message he had previously sent, recommending that it be shown to Senator Arthur H. Vandenberg of Michigan, chair of the Senate Foreign Relations Committee. The message was brief and pointed: the United States was ignoring the danger represented by the Palestine situation.

> Palestine situation is probably as dangerous to our national interests as is Berlin. The danger of the latter has been played up in the headlines. The danger (not the situation) of the former has been ignored in the headlines. I have sometimes thought that this concealment of the danger in Palestine has permitted the Soviet to play her game in the Middle East without attracting attention.[17]

The very next day Lovett underscored Douglas's concern in a message to Marshall in which he pointed to the "increasingly belligerent attitude [of] Israelis" and, on the home front, the dangers stemming from the fact that both major U.S. political parties avowed their support for Israeli claims.[18] Lovett made it clear that from Douglas's perspective "matters of greatest urgency requiring full agreement appear from this distance to be action to be taken in event continue truce violations, position on frontiers—especially Negeb, status Jerusalem, Arab refugee problem, provision of UN supervisory force and makeup any UN police force."[19] He did not hesitate to add that he regarded the practice whereby agreed-upon positions were "suddenly altered or revoked" as intolerable—a reference to the White House and its advisers—and he was candid about the environment in Washington, as he declared, "it has been absolute hell here."[20]

On the same day that Lovett wrote to Marshall, Eliahu Epstein (Elath) sent Moshe Sharett, Israel's foreign minister, then in Paris, a list of issues on which "influential friends" in Washington were at work. The resulting situation may have contributed to the hell that Lovett described, but he was among those who succumbed to some of the pressure that Epstein outlined.

According to Epstein's letter:

Renewed efforts influential friends obtain Truman's support for: (1) no changes Israeli frontiers without our consent; (2) de jure recognition; (3) immediate granting loan; (4) active support our admission UN again produced immediate results. Strong pressure exercised on Dewey for statement which in spite of counter-pressure by State Department may force Truman act before he launches his campaign New York State this week.[21]

Defense Secretary Forrestal was increasingly concerned with the domestic uses of the Palestine question, as was his friend and colleague Robert Lovett. It was Lovett who gave Marshall an indication of how domestic politics, specifically the upcoming national elections, affected Palestine policy, sending him Truman's "personal and top secret" message.

(1) President again directs every effort be made to avoid taking position on Palestine prior to Wednesday [Nov 3]. If by any chance it appears certain vote would have to be taken on Monday or Tuesday he directs U.S.Del to abstain. (2) On Wednesday or thereafter proceed on understanding of American position previously taken as regards truce in May and July resolutions.[22]

In the interim, the British expressed hope that the United States would not endorse Israel's request for admission to the United Nations if it violated the truce as well as the hope that the arms embargo be maintained. Israeli truce violations were on the record and continued through the end of the month, when Israeli forces entered southern Lebanon.

Israeli sources reveal that several days after a UN cease-fire was declared (October 23), "truce violations triggered a succession of IDF 'nibbles' at Egyptian-occupied areas, with the IDF occupying additional villages, including Beit Jibrin, al Qubeiba and Dawayuma, in the Hebron foothills, and Isdud and Hamama along the coast."[23] The village of Dawayuma had offered little resistance, according to Israeli sources, but became the site of a massacre.

THE U.S. CONSUL IN JERUSALEM

William Burdett, the U.S. consul in Jerusalem, was reported to have heard of the attempt by UN officials to enter Dawayma. After making inquiries, on 6 November, he reported to Washington, "investigation by UN indicates massacre occurred but observers are unable to determine number of persons involved."[24] Israelis were aware of what had transpired. Aharon Cizling, agriculture minister, is reported to have told the Cabinet, "'I feel that things are going on which are hurting my soul, the soul of my family and all of us here.' Probably referring to Dawayma, he added, 'Jews too have behaved like Nazis and my entire being has been shaken.' "[25]

Benny Morris reported that "the American consul-general in Jerusalem reported that '500 to 1,000 Arabs' had reportedly been 'lined up and killed by machinegun fire' after the capture of the village."[26] The survivors of Dawayma, along with thousands of other Arabs from the Negev, fled to Egyptian controlled Gaza where an estimated 213,000 refugees were held.[27]

According to a study by the American Friends Service Committee, the number of Palestinian refugees entering the area of the Gaza Strip continued to increase from "83,000 (September 1948) and 250,000 (December 1948). By December 1949, a thorough census by village and town of origin had been taken and the number of refugees was established at 202,606."[28] In September 1948, the All-Palestine Government was set up in Gaza, but it did not survive beyond December. It was taken over by Abdullah and then relinquished to Egypt again when it signed the armistice with Israel.[29] Subsequent Israeli plans to take over the Gaza Strip, albeit without any exchange of territory in the Negev for Egypt, were rejected by Israel and Egypt. As a result, the UN Relief and

Works Agency (UNRWA) became responsible for establishing some eight refugee camps in Gaza.

By the end of October 1948, "the entire Galilee fell into Israeli hands."[30] Israeli sources revealed that the so-called Operation Hiram "saw the biggest concentration of atrocities of the 1948 war. Some served to precipitate and enhance flight, some, as in Eliabun, were part and parcel of an expulsion operation; but in other places, the population remained *in situ* and expulsion did not follow atrocities."[31] Altogether, Israeli attacks in Operation Hiram and Yoav resulted in the expulsion and flight of some 200,000 to 230,000 Arabs, including Palestinians and Lebanese.[32]

In Washington, the under secretary of state received requests for assistance. Did he know of the presence of the U.S. Air Force Captain E. J. Zeuty in central Galilee in this period?[33] There were other UN observers in the area as well, but their presence does not appear to have had a restraining effect.

WASHINGTON, BEIRUT, AND TEL AVIV

On October 30, 1948, Eliahu Elath wrote to Moshe Sharett about Israel's efforts to pressure Washington on its behalf. In early November, Lovett confronted Israeli officials Michael Comay, Israeli representative at the United Nations, and Eliahu Epstein (Elath), then head of the UN mission, about Israel's control of territory.

> I said that if the Israelis intended to claim Western Galilee and Jaffa as well as the Negev, their claims to the November 29 territory could not then be justified on the grounds of right and justice. I said that it seemed to me that if Israel desired to retain the Negev she would have to give up Western Galilee.[34]

Lovett made it clear to Comay and Epstein that sanctions were an option as "the United Nations could not continue to be disregarded."[35] Comay was not moved by the acting secretary's observation that "it would make a most unfortunate impression if Israel in the triumph of its military victories, should adopt an uncompromising attitude."[36] He responded that his government considered "the territory allotted to Israel by the

November 29 resolution as belonging to Israel by right, and considered that the territory militarily occupied outside of this area could be a matter for discussion."[37] Lovett's reply was unusually blunt this time, eliciting what appeared to be a conciliatory response from Epstein.

> I said that one could discuss all one wanted to, but the fact was that the retention by Israel of Western Galilee as well as the territory allotted to Israel under the November 29 resolution could not be justified on the grounds of right and justice. Mr Epstein said that the position I had described was entirely correct, and that the Provisional Government of Israel wished to abide by decisions of the United Nations.[38]

But the head of the Israeli mission to the UN went on to claim that the United Nations was to blame for encouraging Arabs to reject direct negotiations with Israel. Epstein's response was part of a more general Israeli rebuttal of charges emanating from the United States and the UN. This attempt to contain what Israeli officials viewed as unacceptable pressures would prove effective.

Comay prepared a list of government officials, labor leaders, and media executives that he and Epstein saw in Washington during their visit between November 6 and November 13.

> Together with Eliahu Epstein, I had talks with various individuals in Washington, such as Lovett, Oscar Ewing, Federal Security Administrator; Charles Brennan, the Secretary for Agriculture; David Niles; Sumner Welles; and Elliston, Editor of the Washington Post. While in New York, I talked to a number of our friends, such as Freda Kerchwey; Thackrey of the New York Post; Herbert Bagard Swope; George Backer; Turner-Catledge, Managing Director of the New York Times; David Dubinsky, the labour leader, and Potofsky, another Jewish labour leader in the top circles of the CIO. In addition, I had Press Conferences in New York and Washington, which were given a fair amount of coverage.[39]

On November 9, Lovett received a secret memo from Wells Stabler, who had temporarily replaced the late Thomas Wasson, informing him that Abdullah had sent the Egyptian king a message indicating that many Palestinian Arabs had approached him about ending the war and arriving at a settlement.

> Numbers of delegations of Palestine Arabs, residents of towns as well as refugees, have approached King in past weeks requesting, and some even demanding, that he undertake negotiations. While probably idle threats, several delegations have said that if King would not negotiate with Jews, they would.[40]

U.S. officials also realized that no other Arab leader had volunteered to support Abdullah lest they be considered traitors for doing so.

On November 10, Truman discussed U.S. policy with respect to territory with Lovett and the U.S. ambassador to London. Truman appeared to accept Israeli pressure to cease and desist making demands on Tel Aviv. Was it the election and the fear of Dewey's stand that moved Truman to defer to Israel? Whatever the case, the president's response became the model for others in the policymaking hierarchy to follow.

In explaining the president's stand, Lovett stated that "in plain language, the President's position is that if Israel wishes to retain that part of Negev granted it under Nov 29 resolution, it will have to take the rest of Nov 29 settlement which means giving up western Galilee and Jaffa."[41] But Truman added the refrain that modifications in the November 29, 1947, resolution "should be made only if fully acceptable to the State of Israel."[42] The president's qualification was straightforward; less clear were the long-range consequences of Truman's deferral.

Truman returned to the formula according to which Israel "might well consider relinquishing part of Negev to Arab States as *quid pro quo* for retaining Jaffa and western Galilee."[43] Not only did Truman repeat the proposition that a more homogeneous arrangement was preferable to that in the November 1947 resolution, but he suggested that Israel's retention of the Galilee in exchange for the Negev would be advantageous given how rich the former territory was in comparison with the latter.[44]

On November 11, the day following Truman's statement of deferral with respect to Israel's demand, Lovett turned to the Israeli occupation of villages in southern Lebanon. In response to the complaint brought by the Lebanese government, Lovett expressed concern but took no action "over reported occupation by Israeli forces area in southern Lebanon."[45]

Lovett's explanation was that the State Department felt it inappropriate to intervene because this issue involved "incursion into its [Lebanese] territory by external forces."[46] Lovett suggested to the U.S. legation in Beirut that "if reports are indeed true that Israeli forces are now on Lebanese territory," the question could be taken to the Security Council. He then indicated to the Lebanese president that there was a draft resolution under consideration in the Security Council that might be applicable. Lebanese President Khoury understood and acted accordingly, downgrading his request for assistance to unofficial because "he did not wish to be placed in a position of entering formal negotiations concerning any phase of the Palestine problem."[47] This exchange reflected the limited leverage exercised by the Lebanese republic.

One month later Lovett raised the question of Lebanon with Eliahu Epstein, who had come to Washington to consult on Israel's application for UN membership.

> I pointed out in this connection that we had recently again been approached with regard to the Israeli troops on Lebanese territory and asked Mr. Epstein if he could tell me anything about it. I said that if Israel troops were in the Lebanon it would undoubtedly serve as a basis for further Arab charges in the Security Council which might, as in the case of El Faluja, have a continuing adverse effect on Israel's application for membership. Mr. Epstein said he had no recent information and was not informed on the subject but understood Israeli troops were on Lebanese territory because Syrian troops were in occupation of Israeli territory. Mr. Epstein said he realized this was not an answer to my question but that it was the best he could give me at this time.[48]

Lovett persisted in his cautious mode, but in London, where Prime Minister Clement Atlee had the same information regarding Israeli occupation of southern Lebanon, the response differed in tone.

Atlee considered Israel's occupation an example of Israel's violation of the existing truce, which he sharply criticized, along with a number of other worrisome developments. In mid-December, Lebanese President Khoury met with Lowell Pinkerton, the U.S. minister in Lebanon, to review the matter. As Pinkerton reported to Lovett, "he [Khoury] is worried. While he favors and will support Arab cooperation with newly created conciliation commission, he said other members Arab League will consider his support as strange so long as Jews continue [to] occupy Lebanon."[49] But the Lebanese president also understood that "any Lebanese attempt [to] forcibly remove Jews would result in reopening of hostilities generally which Lebanon does not desire and is not in position to pursue."[50] What Khoury was asking, as Pinkerton explained, was evidence of U.S. support for Lebanon.

From London, U.S. Ambassador Douglas hastened to inform Lovett of the political urgency of Washington and London standing together on the Bernadotte plan. Anything less would endanger the necessary two thirds vote in the General Assembly. Ambassador Douglas reminded Lovett and Truman that Britain had dramatically altered its policy in Palestine. But the British also reminded Washington that they had commitments to Amman and Cairo. If these states were under threat, Britain would find itself in a very awkward situation in relation to the United States, but it was no less important that its entire Middle East position risked being undermined.

THE UNITED STATES AND THE REFUGEE QUESTION

On November 15, 1948, Marshall proposed a comprehensive statement of U.S. policy that was the product of a joint effort with the president. It addressed the issues regarded by the highest officials of the U.S. policymaking elite as critical to the resolution of the conflict. The response among U.S. officials at the UN and in Washington was one of profound pessimism, if not overt criticism, at a statement that appeared to make a mockery of their efforts, including UN resolutions that Washington had endorsed.

Marshall's statement opened with the pronouncement that

> the U.S. considers that Israel should now be dealt with as a full-fledged member of the community of nations. It follows that Israel should be entitled to the normal attributes of independent states; it should now, for example, have full control over immigration into its territory; its economic arrangements with neighboring areas should be on the basis of treaty or other agreement.[51]

The Palestinian state recommended in the partition resolution was no longer considered viable, hence the plans to incorporate Arab Palestine into Transjordan. Marshall envisaged this process as involving the consensus of Palestinians. In practice, Palestinians were not consulted. As to boundaries, the secretary of state's statement was deliberately vague save that they were to conform to the November 29 partition resolution to the extent possible, and if not, that they be subject to consultation by the Palestinian Conciliation Commission (PCC).

On the day Marshall issued his policy statement, Dean Rusk sent Lovett a secret memo alerting him to the fact that the statement had been agreed to by the entire U.S. delegation, save Warren Austin, who was still hospitalized.[52] Rusk added the revealing message that the purpose of issuing the statement was to contain the opposition of the U.S. delegation at the UN. Within a matter of hours, however, Robert McClintock informed the acting secretary that the statement had been "unanimously adopted by our Delegation in Paris with much misgiving."[53] He described the "working paper" as "the lowest common denominator which would win agreement among the strong personalities composing our Delegation," pointing out that it would not be a useful guide at the UN.[54]

McClintock was persuaded that Marshall's proposals echoed those of the Israeli government. McClintock argued that "our Delegation will find itself as a matter of practice recommending to the Assembly precisely what Mr. Shertok asked for in the conclusion to his speech of November 15. I recall that the President said to you that 'If the Jews hold me to my contract, they will have to keep theirs.' "[55] Moreover, McClintock pointed out that in endorsing Marshall's statement, the United States would be ignoring previous statements of U.S. policy with which this statement was not in accord. At the least, McClintock argued, an effort should be made to incorporate an introductory statement "referring to the November 29th resolution and the Bernadotte Plan, with the operative part of the resolution recommending a territorial settlement to be worked out, invoking the good offices of the Conciliation Commission."[56]

Britain's response to the statement was negative and would remain so in the coming days despite efforts to reformulate the U.S. position. On November 22, Lovett sent a communication to the U.S. delegation in Paris in which he pointed out that in his view the British were rigid and failed to recognize that the conditions that had led the United States to support the Bernadotte plan no longer prevailed "as result of military operations and political conditions in countries concerned."[57]

In short, Lovett accepted Israel's arguments that its control of territory determined its boundaries. He relayed his efforts to convince the British that there were "recent significant indications of Israeli statesmanship and moderation," as in the case of its "deference to Mediator's order for withdrawal from Negev to Oct 14 positions."[58]

Differences between Washington and London as well as among U.S. officials persisted over procedural and substantive matters. For example, there was the question of Israel's request for U.S. support of its application for UN membership. The U.S. minister to Tel Aviv, James McDonald, was discovered to have gone directly to Truman, bypassing the State Department and John Foster Dulles, to urge Truman to rein in the latter and unconditionally affirm U.S. support for Israel's UN admission. The British were opposed to Israel's approach and timing, and Dean Rusk, in whose name Dulles wrote to Marshall from Paris, suggested that Truman remind David Ben-Gurion that Washington believed the time was right to move toward a final resolution of the conflict. Some UN Security Council members were prepared to cooperate along these lines provided Israel planned no further military operations.

John Foster Dulles, acting chair of the U.S. delegation in Paris, observed that Arab delegations were puzzled that a state without internationally recognized borders was eligible to apply for UN membership. On November 29, Dulles reported that "Dean Rusk was convinced that the U.S. must support Israel's membership, as well as persuade Arab states of continuing U.S. interest in other matters."[59]

In Washington, Truman celebrated the first anniversary of UNGA Resolution 181 by sending a letter to Israeli President Chaim Weizmann reaffirming his support of Israeli retention of the Negev. As the U.S. president said, "I agree fully with your estimate of the importance of that area to Israel, and I deplore any attempt to take it away from Israel."[60] Truman's personal letter to Weizmann also reviewed other aspects of U.S. policy, while pointing out that he had a "mandate" to implement the program of the Democratic Party, including its position on Israel.[61] Was this a none-too-subtle reminder of the president's bowing to domestic pressures manipulated by Tel Aviv?

On December 1, Lovett sent a letter to the U.S. Embassy in London reiterating the U.S. position on territory. Israel could not hold both western Galilee and Jaffa and the Negev. If Israel chose to hold on to western Galilee and Jaffa, then "it would be desirable that southern Israeli border be extended to thirty-first parallel within that portion of Negev allotted to Israel under Nov 29 resolution."[62] However, that reminder was preceded by another which virtually nullified it insofar as it described the U.S. attitude as "based on view matter is one for settlement by negotiation, either directly bet parties or through Conciliation Commission, and upon premise that modifications of Nov 29 boundaries of Israel should be made only if fully acceptable to Israel."[63] It was not only with respect to boundaries that Washington was to defer to Israel, as the case for repatriation demonstrated.

On December 4, Washington was informed of the Second Palestine Arab Conference, which was taking place in Jericho with the mayors of Hebron, Bethlehem, and Ramallah, and the military governors of all districts in Palestine, as well as the military governor general of the Arab Legion. Its members agreed to the unity of Arab Palestine and Transjordan and recognized Abdullah as its king. Abdullah was reported to have declared that he would seek the views of Arab states, a mere formality.

In a footnote to the communiqué between Wells Stabler and Lovett on these developments, the king was reported to have indicated that when officially informed of the "Jericho resolutions" he would "'proclaim annexation Arab Palestine to Transjordan.' The King indicated further that 'he would also announce his readiness to negotiate settlement of Palestine question with anyone, even Jews.'"[64]

Writing from London in this period was Lewis Jones Jr., first secretary of the UK embassy. In early December, Jones wrote to the director of the Office of Near Eastern and African Affairs, Joseph C. Satterthwaite. "Dear Joe: I write to you at another one of the periodic low water marks of Palestine. The boys in Paris from Jack Ross down feel completely sunk and I must say I share their feeling because we were on a good bicycle until somebody let the air out of the tires."[65] As Jones explained, he would "blush to report" what his friends in the Foreign Office were saying. Although the British claimed not to wish to take a "further initiative on Palestine," they would find this difficult given their interests in the region. Jones then offered his version of the Foreign Office position.

> UNGA has made hash of our fine theory of acquiescence and the resolution (if we get one) will be only a little better than no resolution at all. A kind of chaos will ensue in Palestine: the Jews will expand their holdings in Palestine in a relatively ordered fashion and the Arabs, without any formal basis, will shape themselves into new lines of occupation. Open negotiations between Arabs and Jews are most unlikely for the next few months, either with or without the Conciliation Commission. Moreover, UK cannot advise the Arabs to negotiate unless UK is convinced that Arabs have a sporting chance of gaining something from such negotiations. Unreserved U.S. support for Israel's territorial claims makes such negotiations difficult.[66]

Jones's fantasy was not far from reality.

On December 7, Lovett informed the U.S. delegation at the United Nations of the White House position on Palestinian refugees. Lovett explained that the United States would announce its continued support of the November 19 General Assembly resolution in support of Palestinian refugees.

In the words of UN Resolution 212 (111) of November 19, 1948, "Assistance to Palestine refugees," the "Acting Mediator, in successive UN reports of September 18, 1948 and October 18, 1948, drew attention to the increasingly dire condition of Palestinian refugees for whom assistance was a matter of life or death."[67] The situation had only worsened in the intervening period, a condition whose consequences were inseparable from the resolution of the conflict. "[T]he alleviation of conditions of starvation and distress among the Palestine refugees is one of the minimum conditions for the success of the efforts of the United Nations to bring peace to that land," a quest that fell short of its objective.[68]

The UN resolution assumed that close to $29.5 million would be necessary to provide for the 500,000 refugees for the period December 1, 1948, to August 31, 1949, excluding moneys for related expenses.[69] Truman recommended that Congress approve 50 percent of the total budget proposed, although no more than its share of $16 million. By the end of 1948, Arab contributions had reached $11 million.

On December 11, 1948, the UNGA passed Resolution 194 (111), the "Progress Report of the United Nations Mediator."[70] As Salim Tamari and Elia Zureik point out in their study of Palestinian refugee archives, the UN Conciliation Commission established by the UN resolution "was instructed by the UN to facilitate the repatriation of the refugees, their resettlement, rehabilitation, and economic compensation. Implicit in this mandate was the need to carry out valuation of refugee property."[71] Among the legacies of UNGA Resolution 194 was the establishment of the United Nations Relief for Palestine Refugees (UNRPR), which was succeeded by the UNRWA, the United Nations Relief and Works Agency, "the longest serving refugee organization dedicated to one specific group," which survived the wars of 1948, 1956, 1967, 1973, and 1982, and those that followed.[72]

At the end of December 1948, Lovett addressed the question of refugee repatriation, pointing out that the United States would attempt to promote "the purposes envisaged in this resolution." However, Lovett felt it was important to consider that Israel would refuse to "accept the return of all those Arabs who fled from territory under Israeli control or that many of those who fled will not wish to return to the Israeli state."[73] Lovett was repeating what he and other U.S. officials had repeatedly been told by Israeli leaders, who rejected responsibility for the refugee problem and viewed repatriation as dangerous to Israel's security. Meanwhile, Eliahu Epstein was in touch with American Zionists in the United States to discuss a projected plan for the "transfer" of Palestinians to Iraq.[74]

Included as a footnote in Lovett's message was a map indicating the numbers and location of refugees:[75]

160,000–220,000 Northern Palestine
200,000–245,000 Southern Palestine
75,000–80,000 Transjordan
100,000–110,000 Syria
90,000 Lebanon
5,000 Iraq
8,000 Egypt
7,000 Israel

Lovett asked U.S. officials in the various capitals with which he was in contact to inform him of the impact of the refugee presence. The news he received was alarming.

In Cairo, the distinction was made between the approximately 8,000 refugees who constituted "a sizable drain on the Egyptian treasury" and the "roughly 250,000 refugees now in the Egyptian occupied area of Palestine."[76] If the latter group entered Egypt, the effect would be near catastrophic.

> There is ample evidence that the Egyptian Government has decided that the refugees are not in Egypt to stay. The refugees have been kept isolated in the desert on the far side of the Suez Canal where a strict guard is maintained over their camp. No new refugees have been allowed to come to Egypt since last May and the Government predicates its whole approach on forcing the refugee problem on the Jews and the United Nations to the greatest extent possible.[77]

The news from Amman was no less sobering.

> Amman informed, on February 3, that the continued presence of 89,000 refugees in Transjordan and 302,000 in Arab Palestine would adversely affect both areas "in serious way through constant drain on almost nonexistent resources" and that the areas under Transjordanian control could only assimilate a "very small number refugees under existing conditions since money, jobs and other opportunities scarce."[78]

In Beirut, the presence of some 90,000 refugees risked the political and economic stability of the country. "The continued presence of some 90,000 Arab refugees . . . would almost undoubtedly be considered unacceptable by the Government and an unbearable burden."[79] Economic conditions were poor and discouraged the prospect of absorbing large numbers of refugees. Further, there was the politically sensitive question of the confessional system and the potential impact of absorbing large numbers of Palestinian Muslims. Israel was well aware of this. In its policies in the south of Lebanon, it had favored Lebanese Christians.

In Damascus, 80,000 to 100,000 refugees were described as living on a "cash dole and foodstuffs supplied to them," as they were in a state of "utter demoralization and impoverishment."[80] The government was unable to sustain its relief measures.

The situation in Baghdad differed in that the total number of refugees was estimated to be 5,000, although they were reported to be living in a state of economic distress, which meant that no additional refugees were conceivable at present.

As to Saudi Arabia, "up to the present, no Arabs from Palestine have sought refuge in Saudi Arabia."[81]

From Washington's perspective, the situation at the end of the year held little encouragement. The process of defining and refining U.S. policy in the wake of Israel's emergence led to the reassessment of U.S. policy in a fundamentally altered environment. This reassessment involved a shift from a critical to a supportive stance vis-à-vis the sovereignty of the new state as well as a reconsideration of U.S. policy toward the key issues Washington recognized as obstacles to the resolution of the Arab–Israeli conflict: refugee repatriation, territorial expansion, and the future of Jerusalem.

It became clear that there were major differences between those at the highest policymaking levels and their subordinates. The widening gap between the secretary and under secretary of state—who were prepared to compromise U.S. and UN positions, as Marshall's draft proposal indicated—and the responses of McClintock, Gordon Merriam, and Mark Ethridge, for example, was instructive. Internal differences were not surprising in and of themselves. The question was what accounted for the shift at the top, whose influential figures accepted the president's deferral policy legitimizing Israel's rule of force with respect to territory, boundaries, and refugees.

The combination of a number of factors deserves attention. First, evidence of external pressure from Tel Aviv directed at arresting the president's critical stance toward Israeli policies; second, the effort from the same source directed at influencing Israel's friends in Washington, along with media and labor, in an effort to influence domestic politics during the campaign season; and third, recognition of the role of the president's legal counsel, a long-standing supporter of Israel and among those actively committed to the president's reelection against the Republican candidate.[82]

Election politics, evidence of Israeli pressure, and the exploitation of differences within the policymaking establishment and those with access to the president undeniably affected the president's pronouncements on Israel and the conflict with Palestine and the Arab world. But they were not the only forces at work; nor were they the decisive forces that shaped U.S. policy at this juncture.

The importance of the changing assessments of Israel and the Middle East by the Joint Chiefs of Staff (JCS) and the secretary of defense following May 14, 1948, cannot be overestimated. For reasons unrelated to domestic politics, the JCS concluded that Israel's military justified U.S. interest, and such interest merited lowering the pressure on Israel to ensure that it turned away from the USSR and toward the West and the United States. The practical effect of such a policy was to reinforce the dynamic of deferral, with implications that transcended domestic politics. This affected U.S. relations with Israel and the Palestinians and with the Arab world as well. It remains to be seen how the Defense Department and the Joint Chiefs of Staff would view this situation.

PART V

The End as the Beginning, 1948–49

The opening chapter of the final part of this study examines the role of the Palestine Conciliation Commission (PCC) in relation to the major issues raised during the armistice negotiations and the Lausanne Conference that followed. Chapter 12 reveals the frustrations of the U.S. delegate to the PCC at the Lausanne Conference and his conclusions with respect to the future of the conflict and Israel's responsibility for the refugee problem.

Chapter 13 describes Washington's reluctance to engage Israel on this and related issues, which was not the result of caution but of priorities that in practice excluded alleviating—let alone resolving—the Palestinian refugee problem. The view from the Pentagon is critical in understanding the logic of this policy, which, in effect, legitimized Israel's use of force, its expulsion of Palestinian refugees, its control over territory held by force, and its stand on Jerusalem.

Chapter 14 demonstrates that U.S. support for Israel did not endanger U.S. oil company operations or, indeed, their capacity to expand in the area. This outcome was contrary to predictions from insiders of policymaking circles and outsiders at the time. The final chapter concludes by examining the extraordinary role Max Ball played on behalf of Israel after his retirement from office.

12

The PCC, Armistice, Lausanne, and Palestinian Refugees

ARMISTICE WITHOUT PEACE

Israel's unilateral declaration of independence on May 14, 1948, was followed by Washington's immediate granting of de facto recognition that was raised to de jure status on January 23, 1949. Israel was accepted as a member of the United Nations on May 11, 1949. Working through the acting mediator appointed by the United Nations, Ralph Bunche, Israel and its neighbors signed a series of armistice agreements between January and July of 1949. The agreements were negotiated between Israel and Egypt, Lebanon, Transjordan, and Syria, The Lausanne Conference overlapped with some of these negotiations, as it sought to move from armistice to permanent settlement, with the Palestine Conciliation Commission playing a leading, if permanently frustrated, role in these efforts.

The Palestine Conciliation Commission (PCC) was formed at the beginning of 1949 with a three-member directorate including Mark Ethridge (United States), Claude de Boisanger (France), and Husayn Jahed Yalcin (Turkey). Ethridge was the publisher of the *Louisville Courier Journal,* and, during the Roosevelt administration as James Forrestal recalled, he had "been in Rumania and Bulgaria under State Department auspices."[1] Ethridge had a liberal reputation on questions of race and class and was outspoken in his views. He was named by President Truman to the PCC, where he fought for recognition of UNGA Resolution 194.

The armistice agreements negotiated by Ralph Bunche, Count Bernadotte's successor, began under United Nations auspices in the winter of 1949. On January 4, 1949, John C. Ross, deputy to Warren Austin at the United Nations, contacted both Dean Rusk, director of the Office of UN Affairs, and Joseph Satterthwaite, director of the Office of Near Eastern and African Affairs in the State Department (replacing Loy Henderson), with promising news. According to Ross, Ralph Bunche's representative in Cairo, Pablo de Azcarate, revealed that Egypt was prepared to engage Israel in direct talks provided Israel complied with the UN cease-fire arrangements. Bunche regarded this as a significant move that should not be missed because it could encourage other Arab states to follow.

Ross reported that Bunch had instructed his representative in Tel Aviv "to sound out Israelis on holding a high level conference on Rhodes with civil and military authorities of both Israel and Egypt under UN chairmanship. He thinks Transjordan could relatively easily be persuaded to join such a conference."[2]

Several weeks later, U.S. officials concluded that "a number of the Arab leaders would like to get out of the Palestine situation as gracefully as possible."[3] U.S. officials believed that "most of the Arab leaders seem to realize that their cause against the establishment of a Jewish state in Palestine is now hopeless."[4] Further, as the U.S. delegate on the PCC knew, Arab states were eager to normalize relations with the United States and to obtain financial aid in the process.

When difficulties threatened talks with Egypt, Philip Jessup urged Secretary of State Dean Acheson to warn the Israeli representative in Washington of their possible collapse "unless there is some modification of the Israeli position."[5] Although insisting on Israeli action, U.S. officials, including Robert Lovett, made it clear to Mark Ethridge—then on his way to the Middle East to take up his role in the PCC—that major moves involving Israel would have to be cleared with the Israeli government. Such clearance was not official policy, but it became an unofficial practice that meant a deferral to Israeli positions.

Agreement was reached between Israel and Egypt, and the first in a series of armistice accords was signed on February 24, 1949. Two issues dominated the agreement: Egyptian military control of Gaza and the presence of Egyptian troops in the Negev. Gaza held some 300,000

Palestinians and remained under Egyptian control, but it was not officially annexed. Israel, in turn, retained military outposts surrounding Gaza. According to Israeli sources,

> the armistice agreement with Egypt was based primarily on the existing military situation. Israel had to agree to an Egyptian military presence in the Gaza Strip, and to withdraw her own forces from the area of Beit Hanoon and the sector near the Rafah cemetery. However, she was allowed to keep seven outposts along the Strip.[6]

Ilan Pappé has pointed out that the armistice revealed a change in Egypt's previous position in support of Palestinian nationalism during the period of the all-Palestine government in Gaza, and its position on the Negev. By signing the armistice accord with Israel, Cairo indicated that it favored a separate agreement with Israel.[7] Prime Minister Ben-Gurion wrote in his diary, "after the creation of the state and our victories in battle—this is the great event of a great and marvelous year."[8]

Throughout this period, Washington insisted on the importance of maintaining close relations with London. In early January, the British wanted clarification of the U.S. position on territorial questions affecting Egypt as well as Transjordan. Acting Secretary of State Robert Lovett insisted that Washington's policy had been clarified in 1947 when it acceded to UNGA Resolution 181. In compliance with UNGA Resolution 194, if Israel retained areas assigned to the Arab state, it would be expected to offer proper compensation. London was not reassured. Washington, in turn, claimed that British officials failed to grasp the importance of not keeping Israel in "a straitjacket" insofar as territory was concerned.

Lovett responded by emphasizing the importance of promoting Israel's western orientation, a theme that assumed importance in State Department arguments and was appreciated by Pentagon sources as well. Lovett reminded the British that

> real strategic security lay in encouraging development in Israel of a westward outlook. Confining Israel in a straitjacket and surrounding this new nation with a circle of a weak Arab enemies kept in a ring only by Brit armed assistance, would inevitably result in creation

of a hostile state which would turn almost automatically toward USSR. . . . Real security therefore lay not in any particular road in Negev but in attitude of Israel, which would be conditioned by attitude of Great powers.[9]

Cultivating that "attitude" in a manner conducive to U.S. interests was implied by Lovett's statement.

With respect to Israel–Transjordan relations, Washington received what appears to have been a steady stream of information from Eliahu Sasson, the chief Israeli figure involved in those negotiations. As reported by U.S. Ambassador James McDonald and the U.S. consul in Jerusalem, Sasson's information revealed virtually no areas of disagreement between the two parties. Abdullah was a self-confident monarch eager for U.S. support to supplant that of the British. Persuaded that Arab regimes including Syria, Egypt, Iraq, Saudi Arabia, and Yemen were approving of, or at least prepared to follow, him, Abdullah was confident that the Palestinian refugees constituted no problem at present and would "solve itself" after peace. As to his own rule, Abdullah apparently believed that elections were unnecessary in his country because "he rules and Parliament carries out his will."[10]

This was the King who was "anxious speedy peace negotiations which should follow immediately after arrangement armistice which in his opinion should involve slight difficulty."[11] His view of Britain's role was that it interfered in order to pressure neighboring countries such as Syria. As for Jerusalem, Abdullah was prepared to partition the city with the Israelis rather than to consider the idea of internationalization, which was supported by the United States and the UN.

In offering this account, U.S. Ambassador McDonald made no reference to the fact that Israel's move to incorporate part of Jerusalem was in opposition to UN policy (UNGA Resolution 194), which supported internationalization, a position Washington endorsed. Israel did not, as U.S. Consul Burdett reported to Acheson.

[U]nder Israeli theory all territory allotted by Nov 29 U.N. Resolution to Israel is Israeli territory regardless whether occupied by Israel or Arab forces at time truce went into effect. Therefore presence Arab force on such territory is "invasion." At same time Israel maintains right of conquest to territory allotted Arabs by November 29 GA resolution and now held by its forces. ConGen unable reconcile claim Arab occupation is "invasion" while Israel occupation is not.[12]

Israel's foreign minister Moshe Shertok explained his government's position to the members of the PCC as a function of Israeli experience, which taught Israelis that they could only rely on themselves for protection. Further he stated that "Jerusalem to all practical intent and purpose is now part of Israel. PGI does not deny its intent to keep it."[13]

Shertok offered Israel's understanding of the refugee problem as well, emphasizing that in its view Palestinian refugees had fled voluntarily, albeit encouraged by the British.

> If refugees had stayed in Israel, PGI policy would have developed differently. Since they fled voluntarily and at British instigation PGI policy has been based on *status quo*. Exodus was primarily caused by aggression of Arab states. Return now would undermine security of Israel and would impose impossible economic burden on Israel to integrate refugees in Israeli economy. Arab refugees are essentially unassimilable in Jewish Israel. Efforts can now be made in direction radical sound solution, namely integration in neighboring Arab states, especially Iraq, Syria and Transjordan which Shertok claims are under-populated and require more people and development to fill dangerous vacuum.[14]

Ethridge described Israel's intentions as "unyielding." He considered Shertok's statement as offensive insofar as the PCC was concerned, admitting that he hoped that Israel would "adopt more humanitarian measures" that would serve its own interests as well as those of the Arab states.[15]

In March 1949, Burdett reported to Washington that the Israeli prime minister had declared that "Jerusalem was part of Jewish state, and there was no difference between Jerusalem and other part of Israel. World recognition would be sought for this."[16] Within a day of Burdett's message, Wells Stabler wrote that Transjordan, "facing realistically its present position vis-a-vis Israel, would be willing [to] conclude peace with that country notwithstanding developments in Negev, there is considerable question as to whether Israel will cease its aggression at this point."[17]

On March 11, 1949, Israel and Transjordan signed a general cease-fire agreement. On March 30, "in the presence of the Israeli and Transjordanian delegations in Rhodes and the entire Transjordanian cabinet, but with no Israeli ministers present, the formal armistice between Israel and Transjordan was signed."[18] The armistice signified official Israeli approval for Transjordan's annexation of the West Bank, in exchange for which Israel obtained the area known as the "Little Triangle."[19] In addition, a special committee was created to carry out the partition of Jerusalem, which was crucial to Israeli–Jordanian deliberations.

From Jerusalem on April 8, U.S. Consul Burdett reported on the "extreme bitterness and resentment among Palestine Arabs over signature Israel Transjordan armistice. Particularly angered over provisions in Article 6 for turning over to Jews area in triangle containing 16 villages and reportedly 35,000 inhabitants."[20] However, as Avi Shlaim has pointed out, from the distinct perspectives of Transjordan and Israel, the armistice agreement represented "a major victory for Israeli diplomacy" and "a major diplomatic triumph" for King Abdullah.[21]

The Israeli–Lebanese armistice followed, marked by Lebanon's bitterness about Washington's refusal to pressure Israel to withdraw from its occupation of some fourteen villages in the south of Lebanon. Warren Austin warned Israel to change its position or he would bring the situation to the attention of the Security Council.

Lebanese agreement held up solely by Israeli intransigeance on question of removing Israeli forces from Lebanon territory even after the armistice agreement would be signed in which Lebanon would give solemn pledge that its territory would not be used by any party for any warlike acts against Israel. Israelis wish Lebanese to sign agreement sanctioning Israeli forces in Lebanon until Syria negotiates an agreement, that is, for an indeterminate period.

I have informed Shiloah yesterday in most emphatic terms that Israeli position in this regard is utterly unreasonable and that if it is not changed before end of this week, I must report to SC that Israelis are deliberately blocking Lebanese agreement in apparent attempt to bring pressure on Syria.[22]

Austin was prepared to withdraw from both the negotiations involving Israel and Lebanon barring a change in Israel's position. Apparently, Austin was unaware that Israel was conducting its own negotiations with the Lebanese, who informed their Israeli counterparts "that they were not really Arabs and that they had been dragged into the Palestine adventure against their will."[23] This confession could not have come as a surprise to Israelis, who had long contemplated an accord with Lebanese Maronites, and even the prospects of a Maronite state in Lebanon with which they could be allied. Israel and Lebanon signed an armistice accord on March 23.

Two months later, Sasson and Zalman Liff, who worked in David Ben-Gurion's office as "Adviser on territorial and development matters," met with members of the Lebanese delegation at Lausanne to review issues related to refugees, territory, and other elements affecting relations of Arab states and Israel. According to the Israeli summary of this exchange, the Lebanese delegates "admitted that the refugee problem was of secondary importance and that many of the refugees would be absorbed in the Arab countries. Exploitation of this issue was of a tactical nature, the Arabs' main concern being the size of Israel's territory."[24]

Dean Acheson met with Lebanese Minister Charles Malik, who was understood to be pro-Western, eager to strengthen Lebanese–U.S. relations, and eager to obtain funding from the International Bank. Malik did not hesitate to tell Acheson that the Lebanese feared Israel. Malik was straightforward in telling the U.S. secretary of state that, although Lebanon was "an oriental country which identified itself with Western Christian civilization," Lebanon not only feared the Islamic world but Israel as well. Acheson asked whether this was the result of "the pressure of continued Jewish immigration into Palestine," to which Malik replied in the affirmative, indicating that continued immigration would increase Israel's strength in the region.[25] Given Israel's powerful friends in the world, its influence would be enhanced because "Zionism was a dynamic force and the people of Israel were energetic and possessed industrial and other potentials to a far greater degree than the Arabs now have."[26] Malik requested a commitment from the United States to prohibit further Jewish immigration into Israel and to maintain the status quo in the Middle East, which required western support for economic and cultural development of the region. Acheson's reply was a polite rejection of a commitment that the secretary claimed the United States was not yet ready to make. Nonetheless, he promised to look into Lebanon's fears.

Several days later, Acheson received a communiqué from Ethridge that echoed Malik's request, confirming that "we are not in possession of any assurance that could be given Arabs that any settlement on any question will be respected. As previously reported, this was a major theme of Arabs during our tour of capitals."[27]

Syria underwent a coup while the armistice was being negotiated. The Syrian president and prime minister were arrested, and the constitution was suspended in a coup closely tied to U.S. intelligence efforts to ensure Syria's acceptance of the pipeline (TAPLINE) deemed essential to ARAMCO's operations in Saudi Arabia. President Quwwatli, who had not acceded to the conditions for TAPLINE, was replaced by Husni Zaim, who did.[28] Zaim did not survive for long, however, nor did talk of Syria's absorption of Palestinian refugees in exchange for financial aid. The success of the coup spurred other negotiations over oil in Abadan, Iran, whose investors included the Anglo-Iranian Oil Company and the Kuwait Oil Company. The latter was preparing to be purchased by Standard Oil Company of New Jersey and the Socony-Vacuum Oil Company.

David Ben-Gurion's distaste for the Syrian leader impeded Israeli–Syrian negotiations, which faced difficulties over issues of land and water. Ben-Gurion reportedly believed "that Za'im had been for months if not years (before 1949), a Yishuv intelligence 'asset' (as he was a CIA 'asset'), and it is probable that Za'im even received Israeli funding."[29] Contrary to this, the U.S. ambassador, who may not have been informed on the subject, maintained that the Syrian regime "now offers best Arab leadership in reaching overall peace settlement."[30] The ambassador's optimism proved misplaced.

Reflecting on the overall significance of the armistice accords, Israel's prime minister and foreign minister both concluded that they held positive advantages for the new state, although they had no illusions about their adequacy in place of a final agreement. However, for the prime minister, they went far enough. More would have involved compromise, which he was unwilling to contemplate.

At the Lausanne Conference that opened in the spring, the Israeli foreign minister instructed the Israeli delegation that "control over

Israeli sovereign territories, hitherto dependent on a shaky balance of armed forces, is now reaffirmed by agreements binding on the other parties and endorsed by the U.N."[31] Sharett declared that the new situation freed Israel from the need for a permanent settlement in that it provided for the "stabilization of the boundaries and a guarantee against renewed aggression."[32] But he conceded that "it would be a delusion to imagine that a state of armistice is in itself sufficient and that the idea of a formal peace treaty may be abandoned as irrelevant and nonessential."[33] The absence of such would leave Israel isolated, "an alien body in the Middle East" whose potential development would be reduced.[34]

In Ben-Gurion's view, the armistice agreements were sufficient, and to go beyond them involved compromises he was unwilling to make.

> Peace with the Arab was certainly something Ben-Gurion desired, but it was not his main priority at this particular time. His top priorities were the building of the state, large-scale immigration, economic development, and the consolidation of Israel's newly won independence. He thought that the armistice agreements met Israel's essential needs for external recognition, security, and stability. He knew that for formal peace agreements Israel would have to pay by yielding territory to its neighbors and by agreeing to the return of a substantial number of Palestinian refugees, and he did not consider this as a price worth paying. Whether Ben-Gurion made the right choice is a matter of opinion. That he had a choice is undeniable.[35]

Ben-Gurion was reported to have been more than satisfied, although he faced a public that accused him of defeatist policies, the expression of a public mood hardened by the toll of war. "Some 6,000 Israelis had died in the war, or 1 per cent of the total population."[36]

J. C. Hurewitz, Palestine expert in the Office of Strategic Services and later in the intelligence division of the Department of State, summed up Israel's position after the armistice agreements as constituting a major achievement, which did not mean peace:

> The armistice lines left in Israel's de facto possession almost all the territory occupied by its troops within the boundaries of the former Palestine Mandate: the entire Galilee, the Negev (including Beersheba

but excluding al-'Awja and the Gaza strip), the Coastal Plain, and a sizable corridor to Jewish Jerusalem.[37]

As Hurewitz pointed out, the efforts of the members of the Palestine Conciliation Commission to move the parties from the armistice agreements to a more comprehensive peace conference failed.

By this time, the United States had effectively replaced Britain, even though U.S. officials repeatedly emphasized the importance of the two powers adopting a common stance. While bilateral negotiations over armistice accords were ongoing, Washington focused its attention on three issues that were key to the resolution of the conflict: the future of Jerusalem, repatriation of the Palestinian refugees, and the question of permanent boundaries.

LAUSANNE AND THE REFUGEE QUESTION

The conference held in Lausanne was technically a continuation of the armistice talks. It was designed to provide the venue for the next stage in Israeli–Arab relations, with the armistice accords forming the basis of a lasting settlement. It offered the opportunity for informal bilateral talks between Israel and various Arab delegates.

Israel's position at Lausanne, including the multiple bilaterial meetings with various groups of Palestinian refugees, held out what Walter Eytan, one of Israel's delegates at Lausanne, regarded as possibly allowing for some accord. But as Avi Shlaim points out, "neither Sharett nor any other prominent Israeli leader genuinely desired the establishment of an independent Palestinian state in the spring of 1949."[38]

For Washington, and more specifically for the U.S. delegate Mark Ethridge and his colleagues Claude de Boisanger and Huseyin Jahid Yalcin from the PCC, the critical problem was the familiar one involving Palestinian refugee repatriation. Ironically, the course of the Lausanne Conference coincided with release of the State Department's most comprehensive report to date on the U.S. position on Palestinian refugees, which reiterated its endorsement of Palestinian refugee repatriation.

Ethridge denounced Israel's denial of responsibility "in face of Jaffa, Deir Yassin, Haifa and all reports that come to us from refugee organizations that new refugees are being created every day by repression and terrorism."[39] But the problem was not only one of acknowledging responsibility, as Lovett discovered from the U.S. consul in Jerusalem. The Israeli defense minister, Moshe Dayan, had made it clear that there was nowhere to which the Palestinian refugees could return. According to U.S. Consul Burdett in Jerusalem, Dayan

> admitted Arab quarters Jerusalem held by Jews completely settled by new immigrants and becoming thoroughly Jewish. Asserted PGI would have great difficulty forcing people move from homes now consider theirs and Army would probably be required use force with adverse political repercussions. Stated if return of certain sections to Arabs contemplated, agreement should be reached immediately.
>
> According Dayan new immigrants now occupying Arab property throughout Israel and homes no longer exist to which Arab refugees could return.[40]

The Provisional Government of Israel had made plans for the possible settlement of the refugees in Arab countries, to which Dayan explained Israel would contribute.

Eliahu Elath (Epstein), who had become the Provisional Government's first minister to Washington, agreed, with the provision that Christian Arabs might constitute an exception because they were unlike Muslim Arabs who "would be an intractable element who could not assimilate in Israel."[41] Israel's view of Lebanon's Christian Maronite minority remained a constant in its policy toward Beirut, whether in the first civil war of 1958, Israel's invasion of Lebanon in 1982, or subsequent Israeli invasions. Maronites were held to be a species apart, susceptible to cooperating with Israel.

In the same month in which negotiations with Egypt began, the Palestine question was raised by U.S. officials. Robert McClintock defined U.S. objectives as designed to obtain a "prompt and lasting cessation of hostilities; the negotiation by means of the Palestine Conciliation Commission of which this Government is a Member, of a permanent political settlement; and the relief and eventually rehabilitation of the Arab refugees, for which purpose the President will ask the Congress for an appropriation of $16 million."[42]

Shortly thereafter, Lovett informed U.S. officers in Latin America that the U.S. military was concerned with the conditions for refugees, "whose fate if not promptly relieved will lead to further deterioration [of] our strategic position in this important area."[43]

THE STATE DEPARTMENT REVIEW ON THE REFUGEE QUESTION: MARCH 15, 1949

Before the Lausanne Conference opened, the decision was made to transfer "all matters related to the refugee question to Washington. Dean Rusk informed Ethridge of the State Department's plan to put George McGhee in charge, under the title 'Special Assistant to Secretary of State.'"[44] McGhee was assigned to implement the refugee resettlement plan devised by the State Department's Arab Refugee Working Panel.[45] He was to be sent to Beirut to become acquainted with the details of the refugee problem through a series of interviews and meetings, after which he would return to Washington. As Rusk described to Ethridge, "upon his return he will deal not only with immed[iate] and interim phases refugee problem but, more particularly, long-range measures designed for final settlement."[46] This was to remain confidential until McGhee returned from Beirut.

The move confirmed Washington's recognition that refugee repatriation, as recommended by UNGA Resolution 194, was unlikely given Israel's position. Hence the decision to appropriate the problem by transforming it from a refugee problem to one of development. The result was not only to increase U.S. responsibility with respect to Palestinian refugees but to deliberately redefine their status. Palestine all but disappeared in political talk in Washington. Palestinian refugees, forcibly exiled from a land that was no longer on the map, were no longer recognized as Palestinian nationals but exclusively as deracinated and depoliticized refugees. This in no way lessened Washington's insistence on the urgency of taking action to improve the refugees' lot. Nor did it diminish Washington's pressure on Israel to at least respond to requests for repatriation with a symbolic gesture of acceptance.

The State Department's major review of U.S. policy issued in mid-March 1949 based on material prepared by the Office of Near Eastern and African Affairs and the Office of UN Affairs, reinforced the U.S.

position in favor of repatriation.[47] It provided a history of the origin of the refugee problem, the positions of various parties, the role of UNGA Resolution 194 in establishing the PCC, and its intended role with respect to refugee repatriation.

Although calling for compliance with UNGA Resolution 194, U.S. officials did not disguise their limited expectations of Israel's response. They did, however, hope for a symbolic gesture to appease Arab regimes and to strengthen Washington's stance in the Middle East. The policy paper offered estimates of the numbers of refugees that ranged in the month of April alone from 700,000 to 800,000 to close to 950,000.[48] It addressed the cause of this forced exodus as a product of "hostilities in Palestine" related to the mandate and the establishment of Israel, as a result of which "almost the entire Arab population of Palestine fled or was expelled from the area under Jewish occupation. These Arabs, now estimated at 725,000, took refuge in Arab-controlled areas of Palestine and in the neighboring Arab states."[49]

Focusing on Israel, the State Department continued, stating that

> if Israel indicates agreement in principle with the December 11 resolution, or expresses its willingness to cooperate in resolving the refugee question, we also contemplate making representation to the Arab states, with a view to their adoption of a more realistic attitude towards the question of accepting a share of the refugees on a permanent basis and with a view to stimulating them to make constructive plans to this end.[50]

The statement recalled past history, when in accord with UNGA Resolution 181 Jews had accepted that the Jewish state would have included some 500,000 Arabs. At present, "it is doubtful that the State of Israel would now permit more than a small number of refugees to return to Israel."[51] As a result, it estimated that that some 600,000 Palestinian refugees would have to be settled in Arab countries, which had neither the means nor the infrastructure to do this. And as its review of Israeli policy emphasized,

> Israeli authorities have followed a systematic program of destroying Arab houses. In such cities as Haifa and in village communities

in order to rebuild modern habitations for the influx of Jewish immigrants from DP camps in Europe. There are, thus, in many instances, literally no houses for the refugees to return to. In other cases incoming Jewish immigrants have occupied Arab dwellings and will most certainly not relinquish them in favor of the refugees. Accordingly, it seems certain that the majority of these unfortunate people will soon be confronted with the fact that they will not be able to return home.[52]

This realization would have immense repercussions, and the paper concluded that the primary fear was that those without hope would prove open to the appeals of communism and revolution.

In addition, State Department officials criticized the extent of public ignorance on the refugee problem due to the inadequacy of media coverage. The problem "has not been hammered away at by the press or radio. Aside from the *New York Times* and the *Herald Tribune*, which have done more faithful reporting than any other papers, there has been very little coverage of the problem."[53] If reports were filed, they were not necessarily used. "Editorial comment is still more sparse. Freda Kirchwey in *Nation*, a few editorials in *America* (Catholic), an editorialized article in the *New Leader* and one editorial each in the *Baltimore Sun* and the *Des Moines Register* nearly exhausts the list. Most of the news articles and editorials have had a friendly slant, except for the *New York Post*, which was violently opposed to helping the Arabs."[54]

In practice, Israel engaged in campaigns to mold public opinion and to lobby members of Congress, as well as those in U.S. labor circles. On the contentious issue of lifting the arms embargo to Arab states, Israeli sources reveal that efforts were made to engage Senators Henry C. Lodge and Herbert Lehman and House Representatives such as Joseph Savitz, A. J. Sabath, and Anthony Tauriello to pressure Acheson to oppose such measures.[55]

Several days after issuance of the State Department policy paper, a review of the U.S. position labeled "top secret" focused on territorial issues, along with Ethridge's response.

The President has defined our attitude regarding the territory of Israel by stating that Israel is entitled to the areas allotted to it under the

General Assembly's Resolution of November 29, 1947, and that no changes should be made in these boundaries without Israel's free consent. However, if Israel seeks to retain territory in Palestine which has been allotted to the Arabs under the General Assembly's resolution, such as Jaffa, Western Galilee, and the corridor leading to Jerusalem, Israel should be expected to make territorial compensation elsewhere, presumably in the Negev. However, the British Foreign Secretary and our own representatives in Jerusalem and Transjordan have expressed the fear that the Israeli Government would seek to take even more Arab territory, specifically in Samaria. Meanwhile, the Israeli authorities evince no intention of relinquishing Western Galilee, Jaffa or the corridor to Jerusalem. Although the General Assembly of the United Nations, in the resolution of December 11, 1948, declared that Jerusalem should be internationalized under effective UN control, the Israeli Prime Minister has publicly declared the intention of his government to regard New Jerusalem as an integral part of Israel.

Confronted with this situation, the United States Member of the Palestine Conciliation Commission, Mr. Mark Ethridge, on March 14, telegraphed the Secretary of State that the Department is faced with a major decision—whether or not to seek to persuade the Israeli Government to make territorial compensations, presumably in the Negev, if it desires to retain Arab areas now held in military occupation, or else to relinquish those areas.

A primary problem with regard to Palestine is the fate of the 700,000 Arab refugees who have fled from areas occupied by Israel. The Israeli Government has shown no intention of permitting the return of the bulk of those refugees, although the General Assembly, in its resolution of December 11, established their right to return if they would live at peace with their neighbors and the right of compensation for the property of those choosing not to return. Eventually, resettlement will have to be provided for perhaps half a million people in contiguous Arab country or in the Arab portion of Palestine. Unless this problem is met with adequate means and with imagination, there is every prospect that the refugees will become the victims of communist agitation and a situation paralleling that in China will threaten the vital strategic and economic interests of the United States in the Near East.[56]

Coinciding with the issuance of the State Department Policy Paper was a meeting held in the Ramallah Refugee Office representing some 500 refugees from Jordan and Palestine, as well as a member of the Arab Higher Commission, landowners, and businessmen who were authorized "to negotiate on behalf of the refugees in all matters concerning them."[57] Their meetings with Israeli officials did not yield any meaningful results.

Israel's position on the refugee question remained at the root of U.S. criticism through March and early April. Ethridge grew increasingly bitter and unprepared to remain silent before the "abortion of justice and humanity to which I do not want to be mid-wife; complete destruction of all faith in an international organization and creation of a very dangerous flame against U.S. in this part of world."[58]

The U.S. delegate to the PCC declared that Jews were prepared to conduct separate negotiations with Arab states but were unwilling to cooperate with the PCC on the internationalization of Jerusalem or the question of repatriation. His conclusions were severe.

> Jews have no respect for Commission or Arab states and having been born with sword seem convinced they can only grow with sword. Whatever merits of individual cases may be, Jews have acquired through armed force (1) western Galilee, (2) Jaffa, (3) most of Jerusalem, (4) all of territory between Jerusalem and Mediterranean including Arab towns and fields of Ramle, Lydda, Beersheba and (5) the Negev. Much of area was acquired during confused conditions of truce and periods between truce. With this background in mind and apparently realizing reluctance of UNGA or UNSC to take action, it seems unlikely Israel will cooperate with Commission unless UN and member states are willing jointly and separately to back UN instructions.[59]

Rusk and Acheson, who had become secretary of state in January 1949, met with Sharett several days later to review the question of Jerusalem and the refugees. Sharett indicated that Israel was still considering negotiations with Transjordan, but there was no concession possible on the refugee question.

Acheson described the 800,000 refugees as "the source of greatest immediate concern to the President."[60] He reminded Sharett of

UNGA Resolution 194 and its recommendation of refugee repatriation, recognizing "it can be understood that repatriation of all of these refugees is not a practical solution, nevertheless we anticipate that a considerable number must be repatriated if a solution is to be found."[61] He addressed a recurring theme in Israel's rejoinder on this question—namely, that repatriation be linked to a peace settlement—a position the United States rejected as it viewed the two problems as inextricably related.

Acheson suggested that Israel consider accepting "a portion, say a fourth, of the refugees eligible for repatriation."[62] Sharett replied by indicating that "Israeli experts" questioned the total number of refugees cited, suggesting that it was closer to 500,000 and 550,000, adding that "there were many local inhabitants who described themselves as refugees in order to obtain relief."[63] Moreover, Sharett maintained that the refugee question was the fault of the Arabs, as it had arisen as a result of their going to war against Israel. He then argued "that Israel had been willing to accept the presence of a large Arab minority within its territory, but that the situation is now completely changed." Repatriation "would disturb the homogeneity of Israeli areas," and he proposed that the refugees be resettled in Arab countries.[64]

As to territory, Sharett rejected the distinction between land allotted to Israel in the UN partition resolution of 1947, which the United States supported, and the land that Israel determined it required for its safety that was outside of the 1947 partition borders.

Acheson did not relent, conceding differences with respect to numbers of refugees but explaining that it was important to have some sense of the number of refugees Israel might consider repatriating for the PCC to progress, and additionally to be able to deal with Congress.[65] The secretary suggested that "initially repatriation might be to less critical areas from a security point of view and could be worked out so that it would not jeopardize the Israeli military position."[66]

Ethridge and Yalcin, the Turkish delegate who was now chair of the PCC, met with Ben-Gurion and aides twice in the course of the next few days, disclosing their familiar and incompatible positions. Prime Minister Ben-Gurion was willing to send representatives to meet alone or together with Arab representatives in a neutral place, such as Italy or Switzerland, but he "was unable to make any commitment regarding refugees prior to peace settlement during which question would be discussed and toward solution of which Israel would contribute what it could."[67] Ben-Gurion rejected the internationalization of Jerusalem, although he was prepared to consider the "international supervision of holy places," and he indicated his plans "to argue case before GA in September."[68]

Yalcin pointed out to Ben-Gurion that the PCC had been able to persuade Arabs not to make talks with Israel conditional on the solution of the refugee problem. He now turned to the Israeli leader requesting a "conciliatory statement on refugees without result."[69] In response,

> Ben-Gurion emphasized Arab states made war on Israel and that Palestine Arabs were invited by Arab states to fight Israel. Peace has not yet been achieved and it was not yet clear Arabs wished to live at peace. Israel was willing to contribute to solution of refugee problem. Such action would be in interest of justice and self-interest of Israel. It would depend, however on whether peaceful relations were established between Israel and Arab states.[70]

In addition, Ben-Gurion rejected the internationalization of Jerusalem because the UN had failed to protect it in May 1948 when "one hundred thousand Jews had been imperiled," due to destruction in the city.[71] Yalcin reminded Ben-Gurion that "Israel has always had world sympathy which has assisted Jews in reaching promised land. If Israel denies Arab rights, world opinion would be alienated. Israeli should not like Hitler, use methods incompatible with standards western civilization."[72] The prime minister's response was that

> Israel had been faithful to moral principles and reiterated Israel would make its contribution but that it depended on Arab states at time of peace settlement. Ben-Gurion emphatically denied Israel expelled any Arabs from Israeli territory and, with considerable emotion, stated "creation of refugee problem was organized plan by Arab states or British or both." He lamented the continuation of what he described as a "propaganda campaign magnifying refugee problem from 500,000 to 800,000, was being waged by those who had instigated Arab war against Israel.[73]

Ben-Gurion emphasized that settlement of Palestinian refugees in Arab states would be "more humane than in Israel."[74] While Ben-Gurion did not alter his position on repatriation, exceptions were made for Greek Catholic refugees who were to be allowed to remain in Israel, although they had infiltrated into the country.

Israeli records indicate that on June 22, 1949, the Israel foreign minister's office informed Israeli official Eliahu Sasson in Lausanne that

> Israel desires a similar arrangement with the Maronites, and it is proposed to intimate to Mubarak that he would be welcome to visit Israel, whereupon the Maronite churches in Israel would be ceremonially handed over to him and an arrangement on the Maronite refugees would be worked out. Political matters would also be discussed, and the visit would serve to silence criticism of Israel by the Catholic Church.[75]

As Ethridge was preparing his departure, he sent Acheson a surprisingly optimistic account. "We are beginning to see the beginning of the end," he wrote. "After nine weeks we have persuaded Arabs to sit down for peace talks with the Jews." Ethridge recognized that debate on Israel's admission to the UN might delay this process. Listing the armistice agreements that had either been signed or were in process, Ethridge conceded that the PCC was unable to find a solution for the refugee problem. But he believed that his partners in the PCC—Turkey and France, and even Britain—would go along with whatever plan the United States offered. Some analysts argued that the Arab position was not as unyielding as it appeared in official pronouncements. "What the Arab states wanted from Israel before engaging in negotiations was the acceptance of the refugees' *principle* right to return or receive compensation."[76]

Ben-Gurion invited Ethridge to meet with him before returning to the United States to clarify Israel's rejection of American proposals on refugees and land. He urged Washington to free itself of the British influence and to "develop Middle East economically and raise living standard throughout the area."[77] According to Ethridge, "Israel had no intention of relinquishing any part of Negev."[78] Further, according to Ben-Gurion, "if Egypt did not want Gaza because of refugees therein Israel would accept and permit those refugees to return to their homes."[79] George McGhee, in reviewing this period during his initiation into the refugee question, reported that Egypt rejected the proposal as it "did not want to be accused of trading land for refugees in overcrowded Egypt proper."[80] To this McGhee added that "perhaps they also felt they would end up with the refugees anyway, and lose the strip in the bargain."[81]

Ethridge reported that "Ben-Gurion made no reference to possible conciliatory statement by Israeli Government re refugees," proposing that "Palestinian and Israeli Arab refugees" be sent to Syria or Iraq, which he described as underpopulated.[82] Israel, according to this plan, would contribute to compensation for Arab refugees, providing technical assistance and allowing family reunification.

McGHEE, THE REFUGEE QUESTION, AND ISRAEL'S RESPONSE

While the U.S. continued to receive news of the efforts of Ethridge and other Palestine Conciliation Commission members, George McGhee was moving into his new position. McGhee presented the following "Plan of Action" in April.

> Agreement by Israel to repatriate at least 200,000 refugees, pursuant to the General Assembly Resolution, is considered a necessary precedent to any ultimate and satisfactory solution of the refugee problem. This is necessary to reduce the total to a number capable of assimilation on a self-supporting basis in the Arab countries within a reasonable time, and to provide a favorable atmosphere for assumption by the Arab states of the responsibilities involved in the resettlement.[83]

Continuing in circumspect language, McGhee referred to Israel's responsibility. In the light of

> large-scale preemption of Arab lands, housing and unemployment possibilities in Israel, primary attention should be directed to securing repatriation of refugees to those formerly predominantly Arab areas now under Israeli military occupation which are outside

the boundaries of the Jewish state as defined in the resolution of November 29, 1947.[84]

McGhee calculated the total number of "Palestine refugees and destitute persons" currently receiving relief as 950,000, of whom 700,000 qualified as "bonafide displaced persons" who would be either resettled or repatriated.[85]

McGhee had no illusions as to their conditions or impact, or the state of Arab economies, which were by no means identical. He broke down the location of such refugees, indicating that "Arab Palestine" had the highest number with 630,000 refugees, followed by Lebanon with 131,000, Transjordan with 99,000, Syria with 85,000, and Iraq with 5,000.[86] As McGhee pointed out, "if Transjordan acquires all of Arab Palestine, including the Gaza strip, she will have on present figures 729,000 refugees, in comparison with an original population of 850,000."[87] The result would double the size of the artificial state that owed its existence to the British, as McGhee pointedly remarked.

Two important developments occurred in this period, one of which was not directly related to the armistice talks or the Lausanne Conference, but it could hardly have avoided influencing its course. On May 11, the UNGA considered Israel's admission to the United Nations. The United States was cosponsor of the resolution calling for Israel's admission, which passed by a vote of 37 in favor and 12 opposed, with 9 abstentions.[88]

On May 12, Mark Ethridge informed Secretary of State Acheson that a protocol had been agreed to by Israel and the PCC that opened the doors to Israeli talks with Arab delegates through the offices of the PCC. As Ethridge stated, the protocol included a "map showing [19]47 partition lines be used as base for territorial talks," which was accepted by Israel and Arab delegates.[89] The parties, including the Arab states that had previously not recognized the partition resolution, moved to accept the map. However, the protocol did not lead to significant breakthroughs beyond this.[90]

Despite the difficulties in the Israeli–Syrian armistice negotiations, Ethridge was persuaded that Syria, as well as Transjordan, should agree to admit some 400,000 Palestinian refugees, with outside assistance. Some progress might be in the offing if Israel agreed to "take 250,000 in addition to those already in Israel or final total of 400,000 which is less than number under 1947 partition plan."[91]

Planning continued, as well as recommendations for policies to deal with the refugee crisis, but they yielded little but frustration. A strongly worded statement was submitted to the Israeli prime minister by Acting Secretary of State James Webb, with the support of Acheson and Truman. The Israeli prime minister and foreign minister considered it the "strongest representation yet sent by U.S. to Israel."[92]

> The Govt of the U.S. is seriously disturbed by the attitude of Israel with respect to a territorial settlement in Palestine and to the question of Palestinian refugees, as set forth by the representatives of Israel at Lausanne in public and private meetings. According to Dr Eytan, the Israeli Govt will do nothing further about Palestinian refugees at the present time, although it has under consideration certain urgent measures of limited character. In connection with territorial matters, the position taken by Dr Eytan apparently contemplates not only the retention of all territory now held under military occupation by Israel, which is clearly in excess of the partition boundaries of Nov 29, 1947, but possibly an additional acquisition of further territory within Palestine.[93]

According to Webb's statement, the United States expected Israel to "offer territorial compensation for any territorial acquisition which it expects to effect beyond the foundations" established in the UN partition resolution.[94] Webb recalled U.S. support for Israel's creation "because they have been convinced of the justice of this aspiration."[95] The United States now relied on Israel to act on the refugee question and to desist from making excessive territorial claims. If it did not, Webb warned, "the U.S. Govt will respectfully be forced to the conclusion that a revision of its attitude toward Israel has become unavoidable."[96]

The statement elicited an equally sharp rejoinder from the Israeli prime minister who challenged the account of Israel's origins and reminded his critics of the failure of the UN and the United States to protect the new state from Arab assault. "Israel was established not on basis November 29 but on that of successful war of defense," the prime minister asserted.[97] Ben-Gurion then accused the Department of State of ignoring two basic facts in its attitude to Israel: (a) that the State of Israel had come into being not as a result of the Partition Plan, but owing to a victory in the field very costly in casualties and achieved with no aid either from the U.S. or from the U.N., and (b) that the Arab refugees were Israel's potential enemies and that their repatriation without a peace agreement would threaten Israel's security.[98]

The weeks that followed were marked by repeated U.S. criticisms of Israeli positions that, according to Washington, undermined the gains achieved by the armistice accords. Among Israeli critics was Elias Sasson, head of the Middle Eastern Department of the Foreign Ministry, who was "the only Oriental Jew of senior rank in the Foreign Ministry," which virtually guaranteed him second tier status in the Israeli policy elite.[99] In Sasson's words,

"the Jews think they can achieve peace without any price—either maximal or minimal." They want the Arabs to cede the territory occupied by Israel; to absorb all the refugees in the Arab states; to accept frontier modifications favorable to Israel to control Palestine, in the south, and in the Jerusalem area, to waive rights to their property in Israel in return for compensation to be assessed by the Israelis and to be paid over a period of years after peace agreements have been signed; to institute immediate diplomatic and economic relations with Israel, and so on, and so forth.

The Arabs, while acknowledging Israel as an established fact, are in no hurry to extend official recognition in view of the terms set by the Israelis.[100]

Sasson's remarkably candid analysis of the Egyptian and Arab positions continued, as he reported that the Egyptians were concerned that "recognizing Israel would strengthen not only the latter but also Jordan and Iraq, and would disturb the balance of power in the Arab world to the detriment of Saudi Arabia, Syria, Egypt and the Lebanon."[101] The Egyptian view, as related by Abd al-Mun'im, was that under the circumstances Egyptians would not move to recognize Israel until it had become sufficiently strong "militarily, economically and technologically to be able to withstand a separate or collective Israeli, Jordanian or Iraqi threat."[102] Sasson added that from an Egyptian perspective he felt "it was difficult to quarrel with this thesis."[103]

Sasson was one of the few officials, including those in the United States, to admit that Palestinians were neither consulted nor included in deliberations about their fate. As he pointed out, everyone "is exploiting their plight towards ends entirely unrelated to the refugees' aspirations."[104] Jordan and Syria were eager to obtain U.S. aid and assistance. Egypt, which was in control of Gaza and its thousands of Palestinian refugees, remained unmoved, and Sasson attributed this to the Egyptians' familiarity with "human suffering, poverty and high mortality in their own country."[105] Sasson, however, did not support repatriation. Instead, he favored refugee settlement in Arab countries, which he claimed offered "the best guarantee for a formal settlement to evolve into a true and lasting peace," albeit, one that did not prevent "Israel from using the refugees for positive action which would benefit both them and Israel."[106]

Sasson reported on a Palestinian proposal, according to which Israel would "annex the Arab parts of Palestine, conditional on readmission of about one hundred thousand refugees and conferment of administrative autonomy on these Arab areas."[107] There were other dimensions of the proposal. None found support.

In September 1949, Sasson sent a sober memorandum to Moshe Sharett in which he left few illusions as to how Arabs looked on Israel. As Shlomo Ben-Ami reported, by the fall of 1949, Sasson concluded that it was "the cherished dream of the Arabs to do away with the State of Israel altogether."[108] Unable to carry that out, the Arab world "opted for a realistic strategy" that consisted of attempting to reduce Israel's size and limit her regional economic impact.[109]

ETHRIDGE'S FINAL ASSESSMENTS

By mid-June, Mark Ethridge had come to his own dismal conclusions regarding the failure of Lausanne.

> If there is to be any assessment of blame for stalemate at Lausanne, Israel must accept primary responsibility. Commission members,

particularly U.S. Rep, have consistently pointed out to Prime Minister, Foreign Minister, and Israeli delegation that key to peace
is some Israeli concession on refugees. USDel prepared memo
months ago of minor concessions which could be made without
prejudice to Israel's final position, pointing out that such concessions would lay the basis for successful talks at Lausanne. Israel
has made minor concessions with reservations, but has steadfastly
refused to make important ones and has refused to indicate either
publicly or privately how many refugees she is willing to take back
and under what conditions. Israel's refusal to abide by the GA
assembly resolution, providing those refugees who desire to return
to their homes, etc., has been the primary factor in the stalemate.
Israel has failed even to stipulate under what conditions refugees
wishing to return might return; she has given no definition of what
she regards as peaceful co-existence of Arabs and Jews in Israel
and she consistently returns to the idea that her security would be
endangered; that she can not bear the economic burden and that
she has no responsibility for refugees because of Arab attacks upon
her. I have never accepted the latter viewpoint. Aside from her
general responsibility for refugees, she has particular responsibility
for those who have been driven out by terrorism, repression and
forcible ejection.[110]

Ethridge addressed Israel's territorial claims and the seizure of land
by force. On the contentious question of what to do with Gaza and the
Negev, Ethridge suggested that the former could become "a basis for
settlement of refugee problem to extent of Israel's responsibility and also
a basis for territorial settlement."[111] Ethridge thought that, in exchange
for Gaza, Israel could agree to some "concession in the Negev."

Gaza had become a destination for Palestinian refugees after Israeli
attacks on Lydda and Ramle, but the Israelis were not interested, at the
time, in the quid pro quo Ethridge suggested. However, the idea of Israel
incorporating Gaza was not entirely abandoned. In September 1949, the
British Foreign Office maintained that refugees in Gaza "should be permitted to return to any part of Israel where they had property or special
interests and they should be able to earn a livelihood and presumably
have full rights of citizenship."[112]

Ethridge's conclusion was a denunciation of Israel's policies toward Palestinian refugees. They revealed the state's moral and ethical failings, and they endangered Israel's future and the stability of the Middle East.

> Israel was state created upon an ethical concept and should rest upon an ethical base. Her attitude toward refugees is morally reprehensible and politically short-sighted. She has no security that does not rest in friendliness with her neighbors. She has no security that does not rest upon the basis of peace in the Middle East. Her position as conqueror demanding more does not make for peace. It makes for more trouble.[113]

Israelis and pro-Israeli supporters in the United States attributed the severe criticisms of Israeli policy to the victory of the pro-Arab elements of the State Department over White House circles. Such criticism was blamed for encouraging Arab intransigence toward Israel.

To contain U.S. pressure on Israel, in June 1949 the Israeli ambassador to the United Nations met with American representatives of the American Jewish Committee along with Jacob Blaustein, head of the U.S. oil company Amoco, and Simon Segal. According to Blaustein's report,

> It is important that the pro-Arab section of the State Department which again seems to have won the upper hand, Mr. Dean Rusk being the key person in the situation, should be frustrated and that the Jessup formula [to require Israel to cede or pay compensation for land outside that given by the UN partition plan], which only encourages the Arabs in their intransigence, should be abandoned.[114]

In another criticism of U.S. policy that echoed Israel's position, Saadia Touval maintained that Washington's emphasis on the refugee problem gave it prominence that worked to the Arabs' advantage. He argued that it effectively subordinated the question of the political settlement.[115]

Washington insiders such as David Niles, who was also concerned with U.S. pressure on Israel, "informed Ambassador Eban of Truman's thinking and advised that Israeli President Chaim Weizmann send the U.S. president a letter arguing Israel's perspective."[116] The plan was effective. Niles had been in touch with Weizmann in early June, and by the end of the month the Israeli president sent a long letter to Truman defining the Israeli position and reminding him that Israel had admitted more than 25,000 Palestinian refugees and was prepared to implement a family reunification plan. Israel was even prepared to work with Arab states in the mixed armistice commissions, but it would not endanger its independence or accept what it could not afford to do.

Weizmann declared:

> It was not the birth of Israel which created the Arab refugee problem, as our enemies now proclaim, but the Arab attempt to prevent that birth by armed force. These people are not refugees in the sense in which that term has been sanctified by the martyrdom of millions in Europe—they are part of an aggressor group which failed and which makes no secret of its intention to resume aggression. They left the country last year at the bidding of their leaders and military commanders and as part of the Arab strategic plan.[117]

Weizmann rejected accusations of illegal expansion beyond the 1947 boundaries, and he accused Arabs of having rejected the first truce. To this he added that Israeli action was a function of its self-protection, for without the land in question, Israel would be "defenseless." Giving up the corridor to Jerusalem, he argued, would expose the population to having "its water supply cut off and of being starved into submission."[118] Weizmann continued, pointing to the western Galilee:

> In exactly the same way, Western Galilee holds the key to the defense of Haifa and the Valley of Jezreel, while the Ramley area assures the safety of Tel Aviv from such menacing attacks as were launched upon it last year. None of these areas was ever allotted to any of the Arab States with which we are now negotiating. All of them are occupied by Israel legally under armistice agreements.[119]

The president of the Nation Associations, Freda Kirchwey, highly esteemed as a loyal supporter of Israel by Eliahu Epstein and Clark Clifford, wrote to President Truman to express alarm at what she described as "the desire of the Near Eastern Division of the State Department to defeat your policies on this question and to make as its own the vicious policy of Foreign Minister Bevin of Great Britain."[120] She informed the president that "there has come into our possession conclusive evidence that the State Department position has been inspired by the oil companies, and that there is active collusion among the oil companies, the State Department, and Great Britain."[121] Kirchwey accused U.S. oil companies, including ARAMCO and its vice president, of seeking to undo the partition plan and so informing Arab heads of state.

Clark Clifford attracted other supporters of Israel eager to reach the president. Governor Chester Bowles of Connecticut conveyed the complaints of Judge Joseph E. Klau, who depicted the State Department as prone to "anti-Israel and pro-Arab sentiments" that "permeate the entire operating staff of the Department's Middle Eastern divisions."[122]

In early July, the U.S. consul in Jerusalem submitted his dire observations of the deteriorating situation of the refugees, Israel's role, and Arab reaction. Burdett made no attempt to mask his observations of Palestinian conditions or Israeli policies. He reflected on the hardening of Arab positions and the "reaffirmation of their early conviction that it is impossible to do business with the Jews. The turning point and one of the principal causes of this change was the harsh terms exacted by Israel in the 'Triangle.'"[123]

As Burdett wrote, Palestinian refugees wanted, above all, to return home "regardless of the government in control."[124] They viewed themselves as "victims not only of the UN and Israel but of the failure of the other Arab States to live up to their boasts." Burdett described their situation, adding this warning: "Despondency, misery, lack of hope and faith, and destruction of former standards of values, make the refugees an ideal field for the growth of communism. Having lost everything, the rosy, although vacuous pictures of a Communist society are a strong temptation."[125]

Israel, as Burdett pointed out, was not prepared to admit any "appreciable number of refugees except, perhaps, in return for additional territory."[126] But Burdett went further, adding that "Israel eventually intends to obtain all of Palestine, but barring unexpected opportunities or internal crises will accomplish this objective gradually and without the use of force in the immediate future."[127] Israel did not fear U.S. pressure because it was "convinced of its ability to 'induce' the United States to abandon its present insistence on repatriation of refugees and territorial changes. From experience in the past, officials state confidently 'you will change your mind,' and the press cites instances of the effectiveness of organized Jewish propaganda in the U.S."[128]

Burdett predicted that the United States faced two options. U.S. officials would have to "employ the necessary punitive measures against Israel to force her to consent to a reduction in territory and repatriation of refugees." Barring such a policy, the United States would have to "liquidate the Palestine problem, formed on the premise that the refugees will not return and that no territorial changes will occur."[129]

The drift of policies that the State Department and the president recognized as unacceptable led first to the selection of Paul A. Porter as the U.S. member of the PCC after Ethridge's resignation. He was empowered to inform the Israeli government that the administration would consider withholding funds allocated to it if its position on repatriation and territory remained unchanged. The reference was to Israel's request for the $1 million loan from the Export-Import Bank, which was made shortly after independence.

Some movement on the refugee question began to occur by midsummer. Signs were conveyed to Israel that its neighbors "would accept that the majority of Palestinian refugees were resettled within their borders."[130] King Abdullah had earlier informed the PCC that he was prepared to do as much, provided he obtained aid. He informed the Israelis "that he would absorb all of the refugees on the West Bank if Israel would lend support to the annexation of this area to Transjordan."[131] Other Arab states also indicated a willingness to accept refugees provided assistance was offered.

On July 25, General John J. Hilldring, who was known to Israelis to be a reliable source of information on developments in the White House, sent the secretary of state a message informing him that the Israeli consul general in New York had come to see him to convey Israel's willingness to accept some 100,000 "Arab refugees," a figure that included those who were described as already having entered Israel illegally, but excluding any currently in Gaza.[132] This was followed several days later by a meeting between Israeli Ambassador Eliahu Elath, Uriel Heyd, the Israeli first secretary, and Rusk, McGhee, and Wilkins. This meeting was designed to further clarify this offer.[133]

Israeli records reveal that Sharett, unable to break the State Department's hold on Truman, contemplated concessions. He explored how the United States would react to a pledge to repatriate 100,000 refugees while maintaining sufficient distance from the idea to drop it if the U.S. reaction seemed unsatisfactory. Arthur Lourie asked General Hildring to sound out Truman on July 18. Truman indicated that he might support an offer of 100,000 if it promised to break the deadlock, but he forbade Hildring from repeating his words. Despite this admonition, Hilldring conveyed Truman's position to David Niles, who promptly informed Lourie, who immediately related the news to Sharett. Encouraged, Sharett formally offered to repatriate 100,000 refugees in exchange for a peace treaty.[134] The effort failed, but not without further alienating the State Department, which informed the CIA "that a source in the White House had divulged secret information to Israel."[135]

This was part of a more ambitious attempt to undermine State Department policies with respect to the refugees that had included an effort to replace Ethridge with a more sympathetic figure. In August the PCC sent a questionnaire to delegates at Lausanne that included the declaration that refugees allowed to return to Israel would become "ipso facto citizens of Israel and that no discrimination will be practiced against them both regarding civil and political rights and obligations imposed on them by law of land."[136] Of this and other declarations, including Truman's exchange with Israeli President Weizmann, nothing came to pass.

On August 13, Frazer Wilkins helped Truman draft a letter to Chaim Weizmann that conveyed his disappointment with the Israeli response to UNGA Resolution 194, adding that "the views of the Israeli Government may also be considered as failing to take into account the principles regarding territorial compensation advanced by the United States as indicated in our Aide-Memoire of June 24."[137] Further, on the basis of developments at Lausanne, Truman wrote,

one may conclude that the Arab representatives are prepared to enter into negotiations with the objective of achieving a peace settlement. This conclusion would appear to be reinforced by the Commission's communiqué of July 28, which reports that "the Arab delegations and the delegation of Israel have given express assurances regarding their intentions to collaborate with the Commission with a view to the definitive settlement of the Palestine problem and to the establishment of a just and permanent peace in Palestine."[138]

At the same time, Truman maintained that the Arab states were unwilling to engage Israel directly, as provided for in the UNGA resolution of December 11, 1948. He expressed the hope that negotiations held in Lausanne might make this possible, ignoring the bilateral encounters that had taken place between Israeli and Arab delegates. In addition, Truman appeared unaware that,

> in 1949 the Arabs did recognize Israel's right to exist, they were willing to meet face to face to negotiate peace, they had their conditions for making peace with Israel, and Israel rejected these conditions because they were incompatible not with her survival as an independent state but with her determination to keep all the territory she held and to resist the repatriation of the refugees.[139]

From an Israeli perspective, relations between the United States and Israel were extremely tense by the end of August. Ambassador Elath in his communications with Foreign Minister Sharett claimed that "the American Government is growing increasingly bellicose and Acheson is being steadily drawn into the compass of the policy of the military circles."[140] Elath stated that U.S. pressure on Israel was to be expected and, if it deemed necessary, would result in the United States forcing Israel "to abandon her neutrality and place herself entirely at the disposal of the U.S."[141]

But as Elath and Sharett and other Israeli figures understood, the issue was not only Israel's neutrality but her position on repatriation and territory. On both matters, Israel's delegate to the Lausanne Conference believed that Paul Porter, Mark Ethridge's replacement, was more amenable to Israeli interests. This was by no means the general view in Israeli circles, particularly as the Conciliation Commission was viewed as hostile to Israel and, by the end of September, was determined to bring the Palestine question to the General Assembly.

Sasson was in favor of the commission being dissolved because "it is evident that the Commission intends to refer the Palestine issue to the

Assembly and to characterize Israel there as extremist and as guilty of contributing to instability in the Middle East."[142] Sasson believed this would be followed by recommendations to the General Assembly that involved Israeli withdrawal from territory that would then be given to Syria, Egypt, and Jordan while the General Assembly proceeded to "ratify the annexation of the Arab parts of Palestine to Jordan."[143]

Sasson's solution was that Israel not participate in the forthcoming New York session of the Conciliation Commission, thus making it clear that Israel rejected its proposals as representing the interests of the three powers whose delegates sat on the commission and not the United Nations. Sasson denounced Lausanne as

> seeking simultaneous solutions to the refugee, territorial and peace issues, [that] would of necessity be inimical to Israel's interests: Israel would be required to make concessions unacceptable to her, the Arabs would harden their positions and the path to permanent peace would become still longer and more tortuous.[144]

U.S. Ambassador to Israel James McDonald was frankly depressed by what he sensed was his marginalization in the policymaking establishment. McDonald was convinced that Washington did not pay sufficient attention to Israel's situation, and Mark Ethridge was frustrated by what he viewed as Israel's relentless intransigence. Both McDonald and Ethridge were puzzled, frustrated, and even embittered by U.S. policy, leading them to question its nature and purpose.

McDonald's encounter with Secretary of Defense Louis Johnson in the late summer of 1949 shed some light on that policy. As the defense secretary observed, Washington regarded Israel as useful from a strategic point of view, but Johnson thought it ought to do something more on the subject of refugees. Johnson said no more on this occasion, but on May 16, 1949, his views of Israel's importance to U.S. security in the Middle East were clearly articulated. They would not have comforted Ethridge, but they might well have consoled McDonald.

13

The View from the Pentagon and the National Security Council

Indeed, it was not the view of the secretary of defense alone but the views of the Joint Chiefs of Staff (JCS) with respect to Israel that contributed to defining U.S. policy in the aftermath of Israel's independence, marking a new phase of U.S. policy in the Middle East. Created under Franklin D. Roosevelt (FDR) to advise the president on matters related to "the strategic direction of the armed forces of the United States," the JCS continued to play an important role in postwar U.S. policy.[1]

In 1947, when the question of partition was being discussed and disputed in Washington, the Joint Chiefs of Staff were on record as opposed to such a policy. Their position was that it "would prejudice United States strategic interests in the Near and Middle East" to the extent that "United States influence in the area would be curtailed to that which could be maintained by military force."[2] Further, they warned of its impact on the states of the region, as well as on the Soviet Union, whose influence they predicted would increase if the United States endorsed partition. With the deterioration of conditions in Palestine following passage of the UNGA partition resolution, the alternative option of trusteeship was under discussion. The JCS were again consulted as to the forces that would be necessary to carry out such a policy.

The trusteeship option did not go beyond discussion, as has been detailed in previous chapters. Instead, it was the events of May 14, 1948, (Israel's declaration of independence and the departure of Britain from Palestine) that affected U.S. policy. More specifically, the performance of the Israeli military compelled reconsideration of the Palestinian situation by the U.S. military as well as by the Department of State.

The JCS conceded that Israel's emergence had altered the balance of power in the region, which led to another concern—namely, the influence of the USSR in the new state. Attention was now focused on securing Israel's pro-western and pro-American orientation as a prelude to integrating it into U.S. regional policy. This objective overruled other dimensions of U.S. policy, such as the prior emphasis on obtaining Israeli agreement to carry out UNGA Resolution 194, with its recommendations with respect to refugees, territory, and Jerusalem. Neither the JCS nor the State Department explicitly abandoned the policy, but the reassessment was accompanied by a purposeful lessening of pressure on the Israeli government with respect to compliance with the UN resolution. The result gave rise to accusations of confusion and contradictions in U.S. policy from those both within and outside of the policy framework. It was neither.

What, then, was behind these developments?

DEFINING U.S. INTERESTS IN ISRAEL

Throughout 1948 and 1949, the Defense Department focused on the importance of maintaining the pro-western orientation of the oil-producing states and ensuring U.S. access both to their oil and to U.S. defense arrangements, as in the case of the Dhahran base in Saudi Arabia. Israel's emergence did not lead to a break in contractual relations between the oil producing regimes and U.S. oil companies. But Israel's emergence did alter the dynamics of power in the region, and this affected but did not disrupt Arab relations with the United States.[3]

As officials of the Defense Department reconsidered their earlier critical assessment of partition and statehood in the wake of Israel's independence, they concluded that the new state merited recognition of its sovereignty and military capacity, which they judged to be second to that of Turkey in the Middle East, which rendered it useful in U.S. regional planning.

Such calculations were offset by concern with Israel's political orientation, and specifically its neutralist stance toward the USSR. The origins of Israel's position were understood in terms of the Israeli concerns regarding Soviet Jewry's emigration and the continuation of the Soviet Union's fuel exports to Israel. But U.S. priorities rested on turning Israel away from the Soviet Union and toward the United States and the West.

In July 1948, the Joint Strategic Plans Committee issued a report whose purpose was to determine whether the Joint Chiefs of Staff believed the United States and its allies were capable of protecting U.S. oil interests in the Middle East. In the event of war, the JCS stated that "the Allies do not at present have the capability of securing the Middle East oil resources initially in the event of hostilities. Allied forces can deny the use of this oil to the enemy and can later regain these resources as additional Allied forces become available for deployment."[4]

Radical changes in the region altered this assessment within a matter of months. In a memorandum from the chief of staff of the U.S. Air Force to the Joint Chiefs of Staff on "U.S. Strategic Interest in Israel," the Air Force stated that the balance of power had dramatically changed due to Israel's emergence as a new state in the region. The U.S. military recognized Israel's value in terms of oil and defense and the exclusion of the USSR from the Middle East.[5]

The March 7, 1949, memorandum by the chief of staff of the U.S. Air Force described the situation in the Middle East in the following terms.

(2) Existing Joint Chiefs of Staff policy on this subject appears now to have been overtaken by events. The power balance in the Near and Middle East has been radically altered. At the time the state of Israel was forming, numerous indications pointed to its extremely short life in the face of Arab League opposition. However, Israel has now been recognized by the United States and the United Kingdom, is likely soon to become a member of the United Nations, and has demonstrated by force of arms its right to be considered the military power next after Turkey in the Near and Middle East.[6]

Then, remarking on Britain's past role in the "strategically important area of Palestine," the Air Force chief of staff concluded that the United States was now poised to benefit from its support of Israel.

(3) The strategically important area of Palestine constituted an important British base in the recent past, and presumably remains of

strategic importance although lost to British control. The possibility exists that, as the result of its support to Israel, the United States might now gain strategic advantages from the new political situation. At a minimum, it appears that the United States should pursue a vigorous policy aimed at preventing any accrual of military advantages to the USSR in Israel.[7]

This statement leaves the erroneous impression that the British accepted their loss of Palestine, which they could not afford to do given their regional interests and Palestine/Israel's central location. Aside from recognizing Israel's military superiority, the British continued to appreciate the importance of Palestine's location in a region where their military and political power remained significant, such as in Egypt and Iraq. Both British and American military planners considered that the area of Palestine, now partitioned, "would become either a key battleground or at the very least, an area through which their vital communications would have to pass."[8] So far as the British were concerned, "in an emergency, Britain would need to deploy its (and later Commonwealth) troops, with all their logistic support systems, through and on Israeli territory, without any hindrance from the local armed forces or population."[9]

That option presented major problems in light of Britain's past relations with Jewish forces in Palestine and its long-standing opposition to the establishment of the Jewish state. Such considerations interfered with the possibility, entertained by some British officials, of establishing a British base in Israel.[10] Many years later, Kenneth Condit's official history of the U.S. Joint Chiefs of Staff recounted the view of General Vandenberg.

Israel, he said, had emerged as an independent state and as a military power in the Middle East second only to Turkey. It was possible that the United States, as a result of its support of Israel, might gain strategic advantages in the Middle East that would offset the effects of the decline of British power in that area. He requested, therefore, that the JCS restudy U.S. strategic objectives with regard to Israel and prepare a new statement of JCS views to be transmitted to the Department of State.[11]

What rapidly emerged from these evaluations was the Defense Department's desire to ensure Israel's pro-western, pro-American orientation. In the days and weeks that followed, other questions concerning U.S. policy were raised by prominent U.S. policymakers, including questions related to Israel's expansion and rejection of repatriation.

CONTRARY VOICES ON U.S. POLICY AND PURPOSE

The memorandum by the chief of staff of the U.S. Air Force that was issued on March 7, 1949, called for a policy toward Israel designed to ensure that the USSR gained no advantage in that country. In mid-March, the secretary of state was asked by Israel to consider training Israeli forces. The United States turned down, this request although: it reflected a level of trust incompatible with the severity of U.S. criticism of Israel's rejection of the recommendations of UNGA Resolution 194.

On March 16, 1949, Secretary of State Acheson took note of Israel's request for "permission to send a certain number of officers to the United States for training. Giving such permission could be one way of encouraging Israel towards a Western orientation."[12]

Several days later, the "top secret" page in the Rusk–McClintock papers on Palestine of March 19, 1949, opened with the statement that no changes were to be made with respect to boundaries "without Israel's free consent." This was followed by the observation that Israel's territorial claims were to be kept within the prescribed limits of the November 29, 1947, UNGA Resolution 181. But the reminder that no changes were to be made without Israel's approval was an example of U.S. deferral to Israel. It was similar to the approach recommended by Lovett in discussing the U.S. position on territorial changes concerning Israel in late November 1948. As Lovett calculated at the time, the change in regional conditions occasioned by Israel's emergence necessitated a corresponding change in U.S. policy.

In the midst of these developments, Assistant Secretary of State for United Nations Affairs Dean Rusk sent Dean Acheson explicit suggestions in anticipation of Acheson's meeting with Sharett. Rusk reported that, according to Ethridge, "without pressure placed by the United States on Israel there can be no good result from the work of his Commission."[13] The expectation, then, was that the secretary of state would apply the necessary pressure. What likelihood was there that the Israeli government would yield to such pressure?

Rusk identified the three issues Acheson was to raise with Sharett: issues bearing on territory, refugees, and Jerusalem. Acheson was also urged to follow along the lines presented by Philip Jessup, then U.S. representative at the United Nations. Restating the U.S. position, Rusk urged that "Israel should make appropriate territorial compensation for any territory it seeks to retain beyond that allotted to the Jewish state by the November 29 resolution."[14] On the question of Jerusalem, Acheson was to remind the Israeli official that "the United States Government firmly supports the principle of the internationalization of the Jerusalem area, as recommended by the General Assembly resolutions of November 29, 1947 and December 11, 1948."[15] On refugee repatriation, Rusk stated that

> the United States Government is deeply concerned by the problem represented by the 800,000 Palestine refugees. The United States is counting heavily upon Israel to play a major role in the solution of this problem, not only in offering financial assistance in the resettlement of these refugees who do not desire to return to Israel, but also in the repatriation to Israel of a substantial number of the refugees.[16]

On April 5, Acheson repeated Washington's position on the refugee question to Foreign Minister Sharett, indicating the president's concern. On April 9, Acheson received a telegram from the U.S. delegate to the Palestine Conciliation Committee (PCC) complaining of Israel's position. On April 20, it was Ethridge who sent news of the Israeli prime minister's rejection of the U.S. and UN positions. These efforts yielded no tangible results.

Throughout this period, other communications between Washington and Tel Aviv had an entirely different cast. Israeli records indicate that Major General William J. Donovan, "former head of the U.S. Office of Strategic Services, visited Israel in April 1949."[17] There were other visitors, including John Hilldring and Franklin Roosevelt Jr., then a U.S. congressman, who visited in the early summer. It is not the private visits but those of the military that are most of interest. Major General Donovan was clearly interested in the Israeli/Palestinian question. In the winter of 1948, when Eliahu Epstein was circulating the Jewish Agency's notes, Donovan was identified as being among those who had expressed an interest in seeing them.

At the end of April, another response to Israel's request for technical assistance came, this time from the chief of naval operations. On April 27, 1949, the chief of naval operations sent the Joint Chiefs of Staff a memorandum on the provision of technical assistance to Israel. It was prefaced by the statement that to date there had not been a formal policy statement on Israel: "an expression by the Joint Chiefs of Staff of their views with respect to that country is appropriate, and should be made available to the Secretary of State."[18] The declassified copy of this memorandum contained both a voided page and a "corrected" text, which revealed different formulations of the same statement of objectives. The voided paragraph is worth considering for its greater precision:

> Because of United States strategic interests in Israel, it would be desirable for her orientation toward the United States to be fostered and for her military capability to be such as to make her useful as an ally in the event of war with our most probable enemy. Most [difficult to read] of these points justify favorable consideration of eventual establishment of a United States military mission to Israel.[19]

The sanitized version of the same passage was abridged as follows:

> Because of United States strategic interests, it would be desirable to foster the orientation of Israel toward the United States. This may justify favourable consideration of eventual establishment of a United States military mission in Israel.[20]

In practice, the U.S. military opposed the presence of a military mission in Israel at this stage, much as it was wary of providing technical assistance, arguing that it was unnecessary and undesirable lest it embroil the United States in the ongoing Arab–Israeli conflict.

> From the military point of view, however, establishment of a military mission to Israel would be inadvisable until after conditions with respect to Israel and the Arab League have become so stabilized that risk of further conflict in that area is remote, otherwise, the United

States would be exposed to the possibility of overt involvement in Jewish-Arab conflict.

It appears that the Israeli Army is not now in dire need of any foreign technical assistance in its organization and training. Further, our strategic interests in the Middle East would unquestionably suffer if Israel should become involved in a resumption of the armed conflict with her neighbors after our establishment of a military mission there.[21]

Despite their reservations, the U.S. military's positive view of Israel remained: "the Joint Chiefs of Staff have recognized that United States policy toward Israel is one of friendly support."[22] Moreover, the question of military assistance was offered strictly from a military point of view and "without specific knowledge as to what the limits of present governmental policy may be."[23] Those limits had been amply clarified, as discussion in the first part of this chapter makes clear.

MAY 16, 1949, SECRETARY OF DEFENSE: U.S. STRATEGIC OBJECTIVES IN ISRAEL

On May 16, 1949, close to the first anniversary of Israeli independence, the Joint Chiefs of Staff issued a major reassessment of its policy toward Israel, leaving no doubt as to its appreciation of the new state's role in U.S. Middle East policy.

The Joint Chiefs of Staff prepared a "Study of United States Strategic Objectives in Israel," which led Defense Secretary Louis Johnson to recommend that the National Security Council (NSC) undertake to reexamine its own policy toward Israel. Johnson had replaced former Defense Secretary James Forrestal, who—as others in the Defense Department as well as the State Department—had been opposed to U.S. support for the partition of Palestine and additionally opposed to its role in domestic politics. The May 16 JCS statement was issued in a very different environment.

Johnson's memorandum to the NSC described the JCS study as resting on certain views concerning the Eastern Mediterranean and the Middle East that have a "bearing on United States strategic interests in the new State of Israel."[24] First among them was the axiomatic assertion of the importance of the region to U.S. security, and allied to it was the assurance of the exclusion of the USSR.[25]

Israel's strategic importance was defined in terms of its location, military capacity including bases, and political orientation. Discounted as a major base area, it was viewed positively in light of its airfields and air bases, as well as its harbor in Haifa and its experienced military; the latter was key to the revised assessment of Israel's role in U.S. policy.

First, then, was the question of location.

> The direct land routes (road and rail) between Turkey and the Cairo-Suez area pass through Israeli territory. In addition, the main land routes from the Caspian area of the USSR and from Iraq, Iran, and Saudi Arabia to Egypt and the Levant pass through or near Israel's territory, as do the pipelines from the Middle East oil areas to the Mediterranean. Israel controls the land approaches to the Cairo-Suez area from the east, the border between Israel and Egypt being about one hundred and fifty miles east of the Suez Canal.[26]

Second, was the question of bases. Although the U.S. military did not envision Israel as the location of a major base, as the secretary of defense argued, Israel did possess

> a fine, but small, artificial harbor at Haifa, and an excellent, although limited system of well-developed airfields and air bases. In our hands, these air installations would be most useful in the interdiction of the lines of communication from the USSR to the Middle East oil resources with medium and short-range aircraft.[27]

Israel was unprepared to give Washington any guarantees with respect to military bases, although in the winter of 1949 Israeli Foreign Minister Moshe Sharett explained to U.S. Supreme Court Judge Felix Frankfurter that given Israel's ties to U.S. Jewry there was no cause for alarm. Sharett claimed that "the very existence of U.S. Jewry affords such a guarantee, for Israel would never imperil her ties with the five million American Jews."[28]

The U.S. military recognized that "the new State of Israel has close ties with the United States because of our large and influential Jewish minority and is geographically well separated from Soviet-dominated countries."[29] The JCS conceded that "Israel's foreign policy can at present be considered pro-Western although not necessarily anti-Soviet. However, Israel's policy is one of neutrality in the 'cold war.' "[30] What reassured the JCS was that "Israel's leaders have stated privately that their sympathies lie with the West but that for the present it is necessary for Israel publicly to assume a 'neutral' position," the explanation rested in Israel's dependence on Soviet support at the UN and to ensure Jewish emigration from the Soviet bloc.[31]

It was Sharett who, in June, invited Andrei Gromyko, deputy to the foreign minister in the USSR and head of the Soviet delegation at the UN, to visit Israel. Such a visit, he observed, "will serve to refute Soviet charges of Israeli pro-western orientation arising from frequent reciprocal American-Israeli visits."[32] The same visit, if known to U.S. officials, would serve to confirm their fears with respect to Israeli–Soviet relations.

Third, and perhaps most important in the JCS reevaluation of Israel's strategic importance, was the designation of its military force as potentially critical to U.S. policy in the region. The description of Israel's "indigenous military forces, which have had some battle experience," and which could be important in any attempt to establish control over the Eastern Mediterranean and Middle East, was key to the U.S. military's reevaluation.[33] In the face of a Soviet attempt to "secure or neutralize the oil facilities of the Middle East and to operate against the Cairo-Suez base area," Israel's position and its forces would be critical.

> From the viewpoint of tactical operations, Israel's territory and its indigenous military forces, which have had some battle experience, would be of importance to either the Western Democracies or the USSR in any contest for control of the Eastern Mediterranean-Middle East area. It is estimated that in such a contest the USSR has the capability, and would probably attempt to secure or neutralize the oil facilities of the Middle East and to operate against the Cairo-Suez base area. The final line of strong defensive possibilities for the defense of the Cairo-Suez area is at the Jordan rift. Should Israel ally herself with the Western Democracies in the event of war with the USSR, full advantage could be taken of defensive positions in

that country and of Israel's forces for the defense of the Cairo-Suez area and for land operations to defend or to recapture the Middle East oil facilities. The cooperation of Israel would be of considerable assistance to the Western Democracies in meeting maximum Soviet capabilities in the Palestine area. Israel, as an ally or a friendly neutral, would enable the United States to use the Cairo-Alexandretta railway for a limited time for the shipment of supplies to Turkey. Israel as an unfriendly neutral would deny us these advantages.[34]

Fourth was the emphasis on the importance of resolving Anglo-American differences and coordinating policy with the British. To this was added the possibility of promoting the formation of a NATO-like pact, which would include Turkey, Greece, Israel, and possibly Arab states, irrespective of Arab opposition. Reasons were plainly cited. Despite anticipated Arab opposition due to Israel's presence, "the strategic location and military strength of the latter make it almost mandatory that Israel be a member, providing the participation of Saudi Arabia and Iran is not precluded by such action, if the pact is aimed to resist Soviet aggression."[35]

The May 16 memorandum by Secretary of Defense Johnson to the National Security Council's executive secretary left no doubt about the defense secretary's appreciation of Israel's potential in a U.S. regional strategy. Johnson understood that criticism of Israeli policies on the refugee question did not preclude support for other dimensions of U.S.–Israeli relations. As Johnson had told James McDonald in their casual encounter when the U.S. ambassador was in Washington, "Israel is important strategically and we must support her. But they ought to try to take some more refugees in."[36]

At the end of May, however, James Webb, the acting secretary of state, delivered a message of severe criticism concerning Israeli policies to Tel Aviv, which elicited a similarly strong reply from the Israeli prime minister. Such critical exchanges would continue in the coming weeks. In mid-June, Acheson asked the secretary of defense for his assessment of the refugee problem in terms of "US military and strategic interests in the Near East."[37]

Johnson conveyed the views of the Joint Chiefs of Staff, and those of the national military establishment. Their concern was a function of "the strategic importance of the Middle East to the U.S. and its security interests."[38] Oil and war were at the heart of U.S. planning, and oil required friendly relations with Arab oil producing states. In this context, the refugee problem was seen as a source of instability and political insecurity.

Johnson's pronouncements were similar to those of his predecessor, James Forrestal, who had informed the chair of the House Committee on Foreign Affairs in January 1949 that the military was in full support of State Department policy on aiding Palestinian refugees. At the time, Forrestal had pointed to previous reports from Brigadier General William Riley, U.S.M.C., who was assigned as the chief of staff of UN Mediator Ralph Bunche, as additional evidence of the thinking of highly placed members of the U.S. military on the refugee question. The military was concerned with the destabilizing potential of the refugee situation and called for assistance to alleviate their condition.[39]

In August 1949, the Defense Department supported the State Department's approval of arms sales to Israel and Arab states, which had hitherto been prohibited by UN agreement. In consideration of the armistice agreements signed by Israel and Lebanon, Egypt, and Syria, the Security Council concluded that the existing truce arrangements were to be superseded by arms sales to the states concerned. The State Department followed suit, and export licenses were subsequently granted.

Washington was aware of Israel's reliance on Czech arms, which some argue determined the outcome of the first phase of the 1948 war.[40] The State Department was also aware of Israeli efforts to obtain arms from other Eastern European states and from the Soviet Union itself. Israel had turned to the USSR for military assistance in the fall of 1948, when Israeli military attaché Yohanan Ratner met with Soviet General Serev to request Soviet military manuals and the possibility of Soviet training of Israeli officers. This was followed by the Israeli request to purchase German war materiel captured by Soviet troops during the war. At the time, Ivan Bakulin, head of the Department of Middle and Near Eastern Countries of the Soviet Ministry of Foreign Affairs, counseled against such a transfer, reminding the Israelis of the UN embargo.[41]

One year later, on October 4, 1949, the Israelis again turned to Bakulin, this time with the request "that I.D.F. officers in certain branches be allowed to study the organization of the Red Army."[42] In response to the "notion that the I.D.F. was to be organized on the American model," Sharett's reply was "inconceivable at G.H.Q.," which he proceeded to explain. Aside from the obvious differences between the U.S. and Israeli military, Sharett emphasized "the combination of agricultural work with military training, and of centrally based striking forces with a peripheral belt of defensive settlements."[43]

Condit's account indicates "that Israel wanted to hire a limited number of U.S. Army reserve or retired regular officers as advisers in military organization to the Israeli Army."[44] The JCS opposed it at the time as inappropriate given existing tensions and the risk of war between Israel and the Arab states.

In early April 1950, the U.S. Munitions Board claimed that Israel had lately been requesting "not only surplus munitions in commercial channels, but many items of the most advanced types in use by the U.S. Forces."[45] A list followed.[46] In a report at the end of the same month by the Joint Strategic Plans Committee, the United States defined its position on arms shipment to Israel as including only that considered "necessary to help Israel maintain internal order and provide for legitimate defense."[47]

On May 5, 1950, the JCS opposed the release to Israel of the equipment listed by the Munitions Board as being in excess of the state's legitimate requirements for defense.[48]

THE NATIONAL SECURITY COUNCIL, OCTOBER 1949

Six months after the Joint Chiefs of Staff issued their report affirming the importance of Israel to U.S. policy, the National Security Council followed suit. "A Report to the President by the National Security Council on United States Policy Toward Israel and the Arab States," issued October 17, 1949, was approved by the president on October 20.[49] Its purpose was to "define and assess the policy which the United States should follow toward Israel and the Arab States, with particular reference to problems arising out of the recent hostilities in Palestine."[50]

In its comprehensive survey, the NSC reviewed the history of the conflict and ensuing UN resolutions, affirming U.S. support for Israel's independence while criticizing its policies on boundaries and refugee repatriation. Recognizing the stark imbalance of power in the area, the

NSC attributed Arab weakness to the absence of effective political leadership, aggravated by the perpetuation of the Palestine conflict and a preoccupation with military as opposed to economic development.

Without comment, the NSC statement compared the size of the area of Palestine assigned to the Jewish zone by UNGA Resolution 181 with that for Palestinian Arabs. In so doing, it recognized the extent to which Israel had expanded its territorial control since the initial UN partition resolution, and its impact on the number of Palestinian refugees.

4a. The area of the Jewish State as contemplated under the General Assembly resolution was approximately 5,600 square miles, the area of the Arab state 4,400 square miles. The proposed population of the Jewish State was approximately 550,000 Jews and 500,000 Arabs; that of the Arab state, 745,000 Arabs and 10,000 Jews; and that of Jerusalem, 100,000 Arabs and 100,000 Jews.

b. At the present time, the total area of Palestine under Israeli control or military occupation is estimated at 7,750 square miles. The present population of Israel consists of approximately 800,000 Jews and 70,000 to 100,000 Arabs. Jewish immigrants have been entering Israel at the rate of 25,000 monthly since May 15, 1948.

c. As a result of the hostilities, some 700,000 Palestinian Arabs fled or were expelled from Israeli-controlled territory. They took refuge in areas of Palestine under Arab military occupation and in the neighboring Arab states. The Palestinian Arabs, together with the Arab populations of the independent Arab states of the Near East, number about 35,000,000.[51]

The NSC reviewed the U.S. response to these developments in its support of the UN cease fire of May 29, 1948; the UN truce of July 15, 1948; the creation of the UN Relief and Works Agency (UNRWA) in November 1948; and the PCC. It echoed State Department pronouncements on repatriation and compensation, describing the Israeli government as "intensely nationalistic" and under pressure from its "extremist elements," which rendered the prospect of compromise unlikely.

U.S. officials came to suspect that the Israeli government exploited the threat of extremist actions in its exchanges with Washington. Israel's threatening response to the possibility of a Syrian–Iraqi union was one such case. It arose in conversation between George McGhee and Eliahu Elath as the latter warned that such an event could lead to "grave internal repercussions in Israel. The extremist elements might well regard the union as justification for action by Israel to annex Eastern Palestine. The Government, which would be extremely hard pressed by the extremists, would be placed in a most difficult position."[52] According to the U.S. record, the Israeli foreign minister informed the U.S. ambassador to Israel that if any such union occurred "it would be idle [to] pursue peace objectives when surrounded by an earthquake."[53]

In a mid-November exchange between U.S. and British officials on the subject, the British explained that the post–World War I "territorial settlement" was responsible for "artificial territorial divisions which have been continuously resented."[54] The result was a desire for union that was linked to overall reform, which the UK did not want to appear to be blocking. McGhee claimed to agree but let it be known that the United States opposed a Syrian–Iraqi union as inauspicious and untimely. Was he deferring to Israel's warnings?

The October 1949 NSC report called attention to the striking contrast between Israeli and Arab economic conditions and prognoses for development. It was candid in attributing Israel's advanced technical skills to western, especially U.S., assistance and in predicting that the absence of comparable assistance to Arab states would contribute to exacerbating the tension between Israel and its neighbors. In addition, it pointed to Israel's long-term dependence on western assistance to enable it to cope with its immigration program, which risked leading it to expand beyond its current borders.

As in the case of the Defense Department, the NSC praised the new state's military:

> Israel's military establishment, although small, is a relatively modern and effective fighting machine which has proved itself adequate to resist the poorly equipped, ill-trained and badly led armies of the Arab League states in the course of recent hostilities and to occupy considerable territory beyond that awarded under the partition plan. It can be expected that the future effectiveness of the Israeli Army will increase with the implementation of current plans for training and reorganization.[55]

In turning to the Arab states, the NSC pointed to "competing nationalisms and personal and dynastic rivalries" that rendered them vulnerable to "extremist elements and the imposition of authoritarian and unrepresentative forms of government."[56] The assessment linked these conditions to inadequate development, which had been aggravated by the Palestinian problem. As the report's authors understood, until there was a solution of the Palestine problem, Arab regimes would be obliged to put their resources and efforts into shoring up their military sectors, ignoring the urgent economic and social needs of the countries involved.

The NSC report acknowledged the extensive role of the United Kingdom in the past, but it said nothing about British or French responsibility for blocking economic development, or for providing inferior military equipment, as in the case of the British in Egypt. At the same time, Washington supported continued French colonial control in North Africa. U.S. officials were keenly aware of the desire on the part of Arab regimes for closer relations with Washington, which was compatible with the U.S. objective of promoting "the resumption of commercial intercourse within and through the area, uninterrupted flow of petroleum products, and uninhibited operation of and access to internal and international surface and air transport facilities."[57]

Before its concluding remarks, the NSC report addressed the U.S. role, pointing out that "U.S. policy toward Israel and the Arab states will be an important factor in determining whether they can be stimulated to constructive actions in their own behalf to provide the basis for a stable and progressive political structure and a balanced and viable economy."[58] Reiterating previous U.S. positions with respect to Israel and the repatriation of Palestinian refugees, territorial expansion, compensation, and the internationalization of Jerusalem, the NSC report underscored the risks of jeopardizing U.S. regional interests in the absence of accord on these critically important issues.

Against this background, the NSC underlined the value of economic development and the opportunities it offered for the region's people "above the level at which social revolution is a recurring threat."[59]

U.S. ASSESSMENT OF ISRAEL'S PLACE IN
U.S. STRATEGY BETWEEN 1948 AND 1949

As early as July 1948, on the basis of his calculations of Israel's "strong military position," Philip Jessup, then acting U.S. representative at the United Nations, concluded that it "could become a force operating to our own advantage and to advantage of Arab countries."[60] But it was the implications of the new state's military prowess that clearly interested Jessup and others who were convinced of the importance of the region in the context of overall U.S. oil interests.

Within a matter of months, the chief of staff of the U.S. Air Force had conceded that Israel's emergence had altered the power balance in the region. Reflecting on the changed perception of the new state's viability, he observed that Israel "has demonstrated by force of arms its right to be considered the military power next after Turkey in the Near and Middle East."[61] Some six weeks later, the chief of naval operations sent a message to the JCS urging them to make their views with respect to Israel known to the secretary of state. The JCS memorandum discussed earlier referred to Israel's military capability as making "her useful as an ally in the event of war with our most probable enemy."[62]

On May 16, Secretary of Defense Louis Johnson submitted a memorandum to the executive secretary of the National Security Council, Sidney Souers, on U.S. strategic interests in Israel.[63] Included in it was the JCS study on U.S. strategic objectives in Israel, which explicitly connected Israel's role as an ally to "Western Democracies" with the protection of oil. This statement identified Israel's territory and military forces as potentially useful in the event of war with the Soviet Union, in which case "full advantage could be taken of defensive positions in that country and of Israel's forces for the defense of the Cairo-Suez area and for land operations to defend or to recapture the Middle East oil facilities."[64]

By the spring of 1949, the Defense Department concluded that the new state, which was well situated and endowed with an impressive military-political cadre, justified its inclusion in the postwar U.S. regional order, whose purpose was to protect U.S. interests in the eastern Mediterranean and the Middle East.

The Joint Chiefs of Staff's reassessment of Israel in 1949 cannot be interpreted as evidence that the JCS envisioned a "special relationship" with Israel at this date. What it signified was recognition of the potential value, in terms of U.S. strategy, of a state whose origins had initially aroused opposition due to the fear that U.S. support would imperil access to oil. Its reconsideration was in the context of U.S. calculations with respect to the overall assessment of the "U.S. Strategic Position in the Eastern Mediterranean and Middle East," in which the exclusion of communist and Soviet penetration into Greece, Turkey, and Iran was paramount.

In this framework, there was a clear understanding that lack of resolution of the continuing conflict between Jews and Arabs risked jeopardizing U.S. interests.[65] To further qualify the nature of U.S. support for Israel at this stage, it is important to recall that by the end of 1949 Washington had provided Israel with a $100 million loan from the Export-Import Bank.

Insofar as arms were concerned, Israel's principal supplier of military assistance in this period was France.

Washington's assistance to Israel grew in the decade of the 1950s, from $35.1 million in 1951 to an economic grant of $73.6 million in 1953, to $85 million in 1958, and to $126.8 million in 1966—a figure that included $90 million in military loans.

In 1968, after the Six Day War, U.S. assistance reached $196.5 million.[66] In that year, the U.S. replaced France as Israel's military supplier. "[T]he Johnson Administration, with strong support from Congress, approved the sale of Phantom aircraft to Israel, establishing the precedent for U.S. support for Israel's qualitative military edge over its neighbors."[67] Seven years later "Israel became the largest recipient of U.S. foreign assistance," and in the period from 1971 to 2008, U.S. annual aid to Israel was on the order of $2.6 billion, "two-thirds of which has been military assistance."[68]

14

The Israeli–U.S. Oil Connection and Expanding U.S. Oil Interests

Did U.S. policy toward Israel undermine U.S. oil companies operating in Saudi Arabia and the Gulf, as many feared it would? An informed observer of "The Militarization of the Middle East," Max Holland, stated the problem as follows: "As the 1940s drew to a close, these two funda-mental—yet seemingly contradictory—aims of U.S. policy were thus in place: access to oil, and support for Israel. It would fall to U.S. policy-makers to juggle these interests and keep them from colliding."[1]

No such collision occurred. Contrary to what many in the State and Defense departments feared, the risks to U.S. oil interests as a result of U.S. support for Israel proved to be misplaced. In fact, U.S. oil company activity expanded after May 1948. The communication and understand-ing developed between Jewish Agency officials and U.S. oil execu-tives, including the director of the Oil and Gas Division of the Interior Department, had long-term repercussions, as is described in part II on the "oil connection."

U.S. oil companies suffered far less than did other U.S. commercial or cultural operations in the Middle East. The period following Israel's emergence proved to be one of expansion, not contraction, for the U.S. oil industry. Indeed, U.S. sources predicted "that the oil companies are in a position to recover lost ground in the Near East sooner than U.S. Government or other private interests."[2] In 1949, the so-called Seven Sisters dominated the global petroleum industry.

The outstanding characteristic of the world's petroleum industry is the dominant position of seven international companies. The seven companies that conduct most of the international oil business include five American companies—Standard Oil Co. (New Jersey), Standard Oil Co. of California, Socony-Vacuum Oil Co., Inc., Gulf Oil Corp., and The Texas Co.—and two British-Dutch companies—Anglo-Iranian Oil Co. Ltd., and the Royal Dutch Shell group. Apart from Mexico and Russian controlled countries, these seven companies control directly or indirectly most of the world's petroleum business.[3]

In 1952 the International Petroleum Cartel reported that the cartel with its Seven Sisters "owned 65 percent of the world's estimated crude-oil reserves. . . . Outside the United States, Mexico, and Russia, these seven companies, in 1949, controlled about 92 percent of the estimated crude reserve."[4] In addition, the same seven companies "accounted for more than one-half of the world's crude production . . . about 99 percent of output in the Middle East, over 96 percent of the production in the Eastern Hemisphere, and almost 45 percent in the Western Hemisphere."[5] Refining was controlled by the same companies.

At the end of 1949, the U.S. minister to Saudi Arabia informed the secretary of state that the tension that had marked U.S.–Saudi relations as a result of U.S. support of Israel had eased considerably. As Maurice Jr. Labelle points out, "once the first Arab-Israeli war concluded, the two states formulated a stronger partnership," one that was deterred neither by Truman's support of Israel nor Saudi support for the Arab League stance in defense of Palestine.[6]

Less than a year after Israel's creation, ARAMCO was pursuing access to offshore rights in the Gulf and making sure the Dhahran air base in Saudi Arabia was in good repair. U.S. military objectives were to have access to "telecommunications and airbase facilities in Aden, Hadhramaut, Oman, Trucial Oman, Socotra Island and Asmara; air and naval base facilities at Massaua; air and advanced ship repair facilities in Aden; advanced base facilities at Bahrein."[7]

Negotiating offshore oil rights was a major concern for U.S. oil companies, ARAMCO chief among them given its privileged position in Saudi Arabia. Such concern was supported by the Department of State with an understanding that British oil and commercial interests were similarly involved. In January 1949, there was talk in the State Department and among oil executives of dividing the Persian Gulf between the UK, ARAMCO, and the United States, with the understanding that the Saudis would not stand in the way while awaiting clarification of the ownership of offshore oil, including the thirteen islands off the Saudi coast. Raymond Hare, deputy director of the Office of Near Eastern and African Affairs, disclosed that U.S. Ambassador to Iran John C. Wiley warned it was important "that no proclamations or publicity were put out on this subject."[8]

ARAMCO's legal team was in charge. Its legal counsel, Judge Manley Hudson, offered the Saudis consideration of a "decree concerning Persian Gulf subsoil and sea bed but also decrees concerning islands in the Gulf and the territorial waters of Saudi Arabia."[9] Such decrees recognized that these islands were under Saudi ownership.

There was action on other oil fronts as well. U.S. officials had long indicated interest in establishing a U.S. Consulate in Kuwait, despite British fears of being displaced. There were also Anglo-American discussions concerning the status of the Haifa refinery, which had been closed since being taken over by Israel. The British estimated that "the failure to reopen the refinery would represent a drain on the UK's dollar resources amounting to $50 million a year."[10]

Several months after Israel's independence, the director of the Oil and Gas Division of the Interior Department, Max W. Ball, noted in his diary that two CIA officers had come to discuss the

> best means of making National Intelligence Surveys (NIS) showing basic oil facts about each country in the world, 103 of them. Tentative decision that MPAC (?) should be asked to designate man to work on each of about 20 principal countries with man in OGD paid for by CIA to supervise and edit.[11]

At the end of the month, representatives of major U.S. petroleum agencies met to discuss how to obtain oil company assistance for the intelligence project and concluded that the best approach was to work directly with U.S. and British companies operating in the area. Whether they included the study of the mobilization of labor across the oil industry in the Middle East is unclear, but this information would not have been difficult to obtain.[12]

Max Ball returned to his private practice as an oil geologist in 1951, following his resignation as head of the Oil and Gas Division of the Department of the Interior. Working with his son Douglas, Ball agreed to write a report on the possibilities of oil prospecting in Palestine for the Israeli government.

Ball had remained in touch with his son-in-law Ray Kosloff, who had returned to Israel in the spring of 1949 when offered a position as "Petroleum Director and Adviser to the Ministry of Finance." He later served on the Executive Committee of Delek, Israel's oil company, becoming "Israel's influential Oil Adviser."[13] In the spring of 1951, Max Ball provided his son-in-law, then head of Delek, with the names of those who might be helpful in making Venezuelan oil available for the Haifa refinery.[14]

Kosloff's appointment coincided with Israel's search for a reliable source of fuel, a constant subject of concern among Israeli policymakers in the early years of the state's existence. Increasingly, the government in Tel Aviv sought alternative sources of oil that would lessen its dependence on U.S. and British oil companies that were unable, or unwilling, to persuade Arab regimes to allow the flow of oil to Israeli ports. The result was that Israel turned to the Soviet Union and then to the "Iranian market which was to become its principal source of fuel provision for many years."[15]

In the interim, the following took place. Beginning as a ban on ships flying Israeli flags, the maritime Arab blockade was broadened in 1949 to prohibit third-party vessels from carrying contraband war materials— arms and oil—to Israel. Closure of the Suez Canal to oil bound for Israel reduced operations at the Haifa refinery, and soon it was closed. The financial implications for Israel's oil imports were considerable. Direct and indirect damages to the Israeli economy from oil boycott actions in the period 1948 to 1951 were estimated at $23 million. In the period from 1951 to 1955, damages amounted to $44 million.[16]

Despite the Arab boycott, Uri Bialer observed that "agreements with AIOC, Shell, Socony Vacuum and Standard Oil of New Jersey" were made, offering Israel opportunities "in the general directions envisaged by Kosloff and others."[17] Was Max Ball responsible for indicating these directions? Earlier he had attempted to introduce Eliahu Elath (then Epstein) to some of the major oil company executives, among them Terry Duce of ARAMCO. When Kosloff returned to Washington, having decided to leave the United States and settle in Israel, Ball arranged for him to meet a number of figures in the oil industry. Among those Kosloff met was Walter Levy, known to be friendly to Israel.

On May 18, 1949, Ball contacted "Phil Kidd of ARAMCO to try to arrange for Kosloff to see Terry Duce in New York next week," which was not possible as the vice president of ARAMCO was on the west coast.[18] "Charlie Harding, Ditto Bert Hull. All of them are attending an ARAMCO directors' meeting in California. Duke Curtice of Conorado is in Venezuela."[19]

On May 13, 1949, Ball "took Ray [Kosloff] and Charlie Raynor to lunch at the Cosmos Club. Charlie is Washington manager of American Independent Oil Co. We talked about the oil possibilities of Palestine."[20] Raynor proved to be less than enthusiastic, however, as he made clear to Ball several days later when he called to report that "American Independent has about all it can handle in the Middle East with its neutral zone concession and that he doesn't think therefore they could tackle anything in Israel."[21] Ball does not appear to have been deterred.

In the summer of 1949, Ball met with Israeli officials through Eliahu Elath, including the economic adviser in the Israeli Embassy, Mr. Witkon. Ball referred to an unidentified memo written by Ray Kosloff, but there is no indication of what it contained. At the same time, he advised Elath and Witkon about developments taking place in international oil, noting that the cartel was giving way to competition among the major players.

> I told them I thought competition among the 8 principal producers and vendors of crude end products in the Middle East had replaced the former cartel arrangements and marketing agreements and gave them my evidence for the belief. I recommended pursuing policies that would create the maximum competition in both exploration and distribution, and most particularly in distribution, with anti-trust laws against price fixing and restraint of trade and with no distributor, public or private, given either a monopoly or a favored position. I recommend, in other words, that the government not go into the distribution business.

I agreed to sound out Charlie Harding, Stewart Coleman, and Terry Duce to see whether the time has yet come (which it had not the last time I talked to them) when they feel that they can have informal talks with the representatives of Israel without endangering their operations in Arab countries.[22]

Ball continued to try to arrange meetings between the oil men he knew and Israeli officials such as Eliahu Elath when they were in the United States. These efforts did not mature because most of the oil executives were unprepared to enter into such engagements at this stage.[23]

When Ball met with Terry Duce of ARAMCO, Duce agreed to meet with Elath but pointed out that "they [ARAMCO] would not dare build a line across Israel, that in fact their permit to build the line across Saudi Arabian territory contains a stipulation that the line will not cross Jewish territory."[24] But Duce had a suggestion for Israel—namely, that it investigate natural gas, which was to be found in the area. This may have been among the topics Duce discussed with Elath when the two met, thanks to Ball's arrangements, at "Mr. Elath's apartment at the Shoreham at 4:00pm Wednesday afternoon for a drink and a discussion."[25]

Ball received an invitation to visit Israel through the intercession of his son-in-law, Ray Kosloff, which he eventually accepted with his son and associate, Douglas Ball. In the summer of 1950, the two went to Israel with their families. Between July 18 and August 31, Max Ball compiled information to use in his assessment of Israel's oil prospects, which he prepared at the request of the Israeli government.[26] Ball assisted in writing the petroleum laws for Israel and for Turkey. The following year, Kosloff reported that the Israeli Embassy had received "numerous inquiries from oil men indicating a disposition to spend money on oil exploration in Israel."[27]

Interest emerged from another source as well. In 1951, Joel D. Wolfsohn, who was then assistant secretary of the interior and had worked with the American Jewish Committee as its European director, met with Ball to discuss the possibilities of stockpiling oil in several locations in Israel.[28] Ball had met with Wolfsohn in April 1948, at which time he had talked about Palestine with him and Tex Goldschmidt, who was in charge of a committee dealing with foreign aid.[29] Wolfsohn asked Ball if he and his son would be willing to present their study of Israeli oil prospects "before a meeting of technical employees of Interior some time in the future."[30] The reference was to the Department of the Interior, Ball's home base. Ball accepted the invitation.

At the end of May, Wolfsohn and Ball were again in discussion on the stockpiling issue, in preparation for a presentation to David Ben-Gurion and Israeli geologists. Ball reported that Wolfsohn thought it likely that

> the United States would fill, say 7 million barrels of storage in Israel if Israel would supply the storage capacity in reasonably bomb-proof form. I told them that despite the tendency of many people to shrug off the idea I thought storage in a suitable underground cavern feasible, and that if a suitable cavern could not be found an artificial cavern could be created for little cost, if there is a market for the limestone.[31]

Throughout this period, Ball continued to work on the Israeli report, which generated considerable interest among Israeli officials, including Ben-Gurion, who inquired as to its status when he met Ball at the reception held in Washington in honor of Israel's third anniversary. Ball and his son continued to consult with Kosloff and high-level Israeli officials. In the summer of 1951 Kosloff turned to Ball, "asking whether I [Ball] could help to get Israel 12,000 to 20,000 barrels of aviation gasoline."[32] Ball concluded that it would be appropriate for such matters to be handled by someone else, but he remained involved.

In May 1951, Israeli Prime Minister Ben-Gurion organized a meeting in Chicago on oil development in Israel, to which he invited Ball, who was preparing a draft of the Petroleum Act for Israel. The Chicago meeting took precedence. Its purpose, as Ben-Gurion explained, was "to discuss the possibility of getting American oil men interested in Israeli oil exploration and development."[33] Nothing came of the Chicago meeting, but it stimulated interest and led Ball to recommend that Israel clarify its conditions for such exploration. The former director of the Oil and Gas Division persisted in the attempt to interest American oilmen in both the Petroleum Act and "in doing some wildcatting."[34]

In the interim, Ball won the approval of Teddy Kollek, who was working closely with Ben-Gurion. Ball observed that Kollek "liked the letters

I sent to about ten independents and majors asking if they would be willing to read and comment on the draft Petroleum act."[35] Kollek also approved the "background information" on Israel that Ball included in his report.[36]

In an article in the *Global Jewish News Source* on May 11, 1951, Ball indicated that the

> possibilities of finding oil in Israel are good enough to warrant explo-
> ration. Mr Ball surveyed Israel and reported each of the "geologic
> provinces has oil possibilities" and that the most promising are the
> Negev, the foothill belt of Judas the coastal plain, and the Dead Sea-
> Wadi Araba rift valley.[37]

Ball's optimistic prediction appeared to be the partial fulfillment of a pronouncement by the directors of the Industrial Institute of Israel who, in 1949, predicted the growth and development of the Israeli economy in a series of Industrial Survey reports. The board of directors included a range of American corporate leaders whose views evoked those of the Nathan, Gass, and Creamer study of 1946. That work had described Zionist development as benefiting Jews as well as Arabs. Three years later, Ralph Friedman, who identified himself as an industrialist, sur-veyed the economic conditions of the new state and offered recommen-dations for its development to the directors of the Industrial Institute of Israel. He concluded his remarks with the observation that,

> despite mountainous difficulties, the leaders of Israel believe (and I
> agree with them) that this new little state has a chance for greatness,
> possessed as it is of a strategic location and of a population gifted
> with talents, education, imagination, and with a driving ambition to
> become a peaceful example of material progress of moral force in
> that large and very backward part of the world.[38]

On November 9, Friedman wrote to Clark Clifford with informa-tion he had sent the finance minister of Israel. It included a list of those "versed in finance, industry and commerce who would be available to study, consult on and in general to encourage the flow of capital from this country to the State of Israel."[39] As Friedman observed, "Israel with our help, may in the years to come represent a western outpost and anchor in the whole Near East."

Michael J. Cohen reminded readers "that in issuing the Balfour Declaration in November 1917, the British had gone to great lengths, and to no small degree of subterfuge, in order to install the Jews in Palestine, largely so that they might guard the British position at the Suez Canal."[40] U.S. policy in Palestine was not analogous to that of Great Britain in World War 1. Washington did not "install the Jews in Palestine," and until May 1948 most U.S. officials engaged in policy related to Palestine were convinced that both partition and a Jewish state were undesirable and virtually impossible to implement without the use of force.

Israel's emergence obliged U.S. officials to reconsider the regional balance of power and to revise their views of Israel, whose military capacity they now deemed to be second to that of Turkey in the region. Once perceived as a liability in the context of U.S. regional interests, after independence Israel emerged as an asset. Washington then moved to ensure Israel's orientation was toward the United States and the West, a prerequisite to its integration into the U.S. regional strategy. This same process led U.S. officials to reduce their pressure on Israel to comply with the recommendations of UNGA Resolution 194, notably on the repatriation of the Palestinian refugees, the adjudication of boundaries, and the internationalization of Jerusalem. The decision to defer to Israel on these core issues signified Washington's subordination of the Palestine Question, and its legitimation of Israel's use of force in its policy toward the Palestinians to calculations of US interest.

This revised U.S. policy toward Israel and Palestine represented "the end" of one phase of U.S. policy—which had been marked by support for UNGA Resolution 194—and the "beginning" of another, whose consequences are with us today.

PART VI

In Place of a Conclusion

Reflections on Discovery,
Denial, and Deferral

To those aiming to make sense of U.S. policy, confronting the foundations of U.S. policy in the Middle East in the troubled years from 1945 through 1949 offers a guide to the perplexed. The records reviewed and uncovered in the preceding pages reveal a policy designed to ensure the extraordinary conjuncture of wealth and power in a country untouched by the last war, and endowed with the means to assure its dominance in anticipation of the next. The present study analyzes the primacy of the petroleum order in relation to the evolution of the "Palestine question" and challenges the long-standing claims that U.S. policy toward Israel exposed U.S.-based international oil operations to potentially fatal risks. The pragmatism of U.S. oil companies and the extent to which oil company operations expanded despite U.S. support for Israel have been demonstrated.

In this framework the question of Palestine emerged in 1945 as "the most important and urgent" in an environment marked by the blight of war and the despair of refugees. The failures of immigration reform and the racist nativism that accompanied it strengthened those who sought admission to Palestine.

For U.S. policymakers, the fateful choice in the immediate postwar years appeared to be support for Zionist objectives in Palestine, as opposed to support for U.S. interests in the Middle East. Underlying these alternatives was the dominant assumption that support for the first would critically undermine Arab support for U.S. oil companies, while support for the second would doom Europe's refugees. In practice,

Washington's support for partition and, eventually, Jewish statehood did not undermine U.S. oil company access to the prized resources of the Arab East.

Little known in the history of Jewish Agency efforts to affect U.S. decision making on partition was the encounter between the Jewish Agency representative in the U.S., Eliahu Epstein, and Max Ball, director of the Oil and Gas Division of the U.S. Interior Department. Their meeting opened the door to the unlikely "oil connection" revealed in these pages. As important as it was, that connection in no way mollified the violent effects of partition in Palestine. Nor did it hide the bitter struggle over the consequences of the transformation of Palestine with respect to the fate of Jerusalem, the definition of boundaries, or the increasing numbers of refugees. The refugees became a major concern of U.S. officials, who feared the pressure of caring for such a large number of refugees would lead to the destabilization and radicalization of the Middle East.

In the period immediately following the end of the Second World War, the State Department was preoccupied with ensuring that the United States had access to and control over the petroleum resources of the Arab East. Keenly aware of the indispensability of petroleum to defense, U.S. officials were also aware of the inseparability of oil from the larger context of political problems affecting the region. The months between November 1947 and passage of UNGA Resolution 181 supporting the partition of Palestine and Israel's declaration of independence in May 1948 were defined by escalating violence.

As the preceding chapters have shown, the elite policymakers in Washington were aware of the deteriorating conditions in Palestine. Developments on the ground, which led to the flight and expulsion of Palestinians who rapidly became refugees, were described by U.S. consuls. By the winter of 1948, U.S. policymakers were prepared to abandon their support of partition in favor of a temporary UN trusteeship over Palestine. Instead, they accepted the results of the vigorous and effective lobbying spearheaded by the Jewish Agency's representative in the U.S., Eliahu Epstein, who, with his insider allies, succeeded in reversing the prevailing opposition to partition. With President Truman's move to offer de facto recognition of the new state immediately after Israel's declaration of independence, there followed the radical shift in orientation of U.S. officials from a critical opposition to partition and statehood and toward unqualified support for Israeli sovereignty.

Major U.S. officials, however, remained formally committed to promoting a consensual accord over the conflict over Palestine. In the process, they also remained committed to persuading the Provisional Government of Israel (PGI) to accept the repatriation of Palestinian refugees, as recommended by UN resolutions, culminating in UNGA Resolution 194 of December 11, 1948. Official U.S. pronouncements attest to the extent of U.S. support for Palestinian refugee repatriation and Washington's seemingly unwavering criticism of Israel's rejection of the same. As the later chapters show, however, U.S. policy was shaped primarily by calculations of force, which ultimately led Washington to legitimize Israel's reliance on military force in its determination of boundaries and refugee policy.

The trajectory of U.S. policy in these years can be expressed as a three-part process: from *discovery* to *denial* to *deferral*. Each phase of policy exposed changes in direction that were not always mutually exclusive. A chronological sketch accompanied by official pronouncements sharply demarcates these turnings from acknowledgment to criticism to accommodation.

The *discovery phase* includes U.S. recognition of the importance of the Palestine question in 1945; the U.S. commitment to a policy of consensus and binationalism at the time of the Anglo-American Committee of Enquiry in 1946; Washington's increasing awareness of Zionist objectives in Palestine during passage of the UN partition resolution (UNGA Resolution 181); and the Jewish Agency's refusal to accept the U.S. recommendation of a truce in Palestine several weeks prior to Israel's declaration of independence in 1948.

The *denial phase* corresponds to the period following Israel's declaration of independence on May 14, 1948, when U.S. officials criticized the PGI's position on the origin and treatment of Palestinian refugees. In accord with UN resolutions, Washington endorsed Palestinian refugee repatriation and resolution of issues bearing on territorial expansion and the future of Jerusalem, as set out in UNGA Resolution 194, December 11, 1948. The critical reports of Israeli indifference to and rejection of these UN resolutions can be found in statements by Philip Jessup, Secretary of State George C. Marshall, the U.S. ambassador to London, and the CIA in the period from July to October 1948.

The *deferral phase* is marked by the gradual movement of U.S. officials such as the Joint Chiefs of Staff and the defense secretary toward accommodation and deference to Israeli policies. Collectively, they argued in favor of diminishing pressure on Israel to accept policies it considered unacceptable in an effort to ensure the Jewish state's western orientation. The justification for this turn in U.S. policy revolved around calculations that Israel would be useful in U.S. strategic planning for the Middle East.

However, as the National Security Council emphasized in October 1949, the failure to resolve the refugee problem remained a cause of concern, lest it lead to the radicalization and destabilization of the entire region. The result was increasing emphasis on the role of economic development in dealing with the refugee question in an attempt to blunt the disparity in economic and political development between Israel and the Arab states.

Consider the following chronology and accompanying pronouncements.

1. DISCOVERY

May 1945

A State Department report on U.S. economic policy in the Middle East warned of "grave difficulties" to come.

> Of all the political problems which call for solution in this area the Palestine question is probably the most important and urgent at the present time. Unless our attitude in regard to it be clarified in a manner which will command the respect and as far as possible the approval of the peoples of the Middle East, our Middle East policy will be beset with the gravest difficulties.[1]
>
> [I]t was understood that "the successful implementation of our general economic policy in the Middle East is closely related to the success which we achieve in the political field."[2]
>
> In that context, the authors identified the Palestine question as critical, indicating that they recognized it to be a British concern primarily. However, they added, "we favor a just and reasonable solution, at the proper time, after consultation with all interested parties."[3]

In the summer of 1945, President Truman sent Earl G. Harrison as his envoy to the Displaced Persons camps. Harrison's report sharply criticized the army's treatment of the Jewish survivors.

1946

Following the Harrison report, the British pressed for a joint "Anglo-American Committee of Enquiry," which followed in 1946. Its diverse, often discordant members offered critical observations about both Jews and Arabs, calling for Palestine to be "a country in which the legitimate national aspirations of both Jews and Arabs can be reconciled, without either side fearing the ascendancy of the other."[4] The committee's report called for trusteeship under UN auspices.

1946

Gordon Merriam, then chief of the Division of Near Eastern Affairs of the State Department, agreed with the president's support for the admission of 100,000 refugees to Palestine based on the findings of the Harrison report. But Merriam also called for an international response to the refugee problem, reform in U.S. immigration policy, and granting independence to Palestine.

(1) Palestine is an A Mandate. As such, it was to be prepared for independence. Were it not for the complication of the Jewish National Home, it would be independent today, as all the other A mandates have become. Arabs and Jews live there and must, sooner or later, come to some sort of a political agreement based on a minimum of mutual confidence and give-and-take, if they are to govern Palestine.

Merriam also insisted on the importance of consensus as the basis of policy.

Otherwise we should violate the principle of self-determination which has been written into the Atlantic Charter, the Declaration of the United Nations, and the United Nations Charter—a principle that is deeply embedded in our foreign policy. Even a United Nations determination in favor of partition would be, in the absence of such consent, a stultification and violation of UN's own charter.[5]

1946

Evan M. Wilson, an American staff member of the Anglo-American Committee, reflected in later years that

> we in the [State] Department had reason to be aware of the force of the Zionist drive toward a Jewish state, we continued until the end of 1946, at least, to think in terms of a compromise solution in Palestine. We thought there should be a solution under which, in the words of the Anglo-American Committee of Inquiry, Jew would not dominate Arab and Arab would not dominate Jew. In other words, we were thinking of a bi-national state long after the conflict between the parties had become so complete, and their oppositions so intractable, as to put this out of the question. As men who tried to be reasonable, we thought that it should be possible to achieve a compromise, but the hard fact was that neither of the two parties in the dispute wanted a compromise; the depth of the nationalistic feeling on both sides precluded this.[6]

1947

On the eve of the United Nations General Assembly passage of the partition resolution (UNGA Resolution 181), the recently established Central Intelligence Agency prepared its assessment of partition.

> In the long run no Zionists in Palestine will be satisfied with the territorial arrangements of the partition settlement. Even the more conservative Zionists will hope to obtain the whole of the Nejeb [Negev], Western Galilee, the city of Jerusalem, and eventually all of Palestine. The extremists demand not only all of Palestine but Transjordan as well. They have stated that they will refuse to recognize the validity of any Jewish government which will settle for anything less, and will probably undertake aggressive action to achieve their ends.[7]

The CIA's warnings were echoed in State Department reports that questioned the UNGA partition resolution's recommendations, and Secretary of State Marshall received reports of accelerating violence in Palestine.

1948

In early May, Robert McClintock, assistant to Dean Rusk, reported on the Jewish Agency's refusal to accept Washington's proposed truce, which he interpreted as evidence that it was

> the intention of the Jews to go steadily ahead with the Jewish separate state by force of arms. While it is possible that Arab acceptance of our proposal might place the Jewish Agency in such a position vis-a-vis public opinion that it would have to go through the motions of looking for a truce, it seems clear that in light of the Jewish military superiority which now obtains in Palestine, the Jewish Agency will prefer to round out its State after May 15 and rely on its armed strength to defend that state from Arab counterattack.[8]

2. DENIAL

1948

Israel declared its independence on May 14, 1948. Washington followed with de facto recognition of the new state, and U.S. officials affirmed its sovereignty. Concern continued with regard to Israel's denial of responsibility for, and treatment of, Palestinian refugees.

Philip Jessup, acting U.S. representative at the UN, sent Secretary of State Marshall Israel's official position on the subject of Palestinian refugees on July 27, 1948.

> The Government of Israel must disclaim any responsibility for the creation of this problem. The charge that these Arabs were forcibly driven out by Israel authorities is wholly false; on the contrary, everything possible was done to prevent an exodus which was a direct result of the folly of the Arab states in organizing and launching a war of aggression against Israel. The impulse of the Arab

civilian population to migrate from war areas, in order to avoid being involved in the hostilities, was deliberately fostered by Arab leaders for political motives. They did not wish the Arab population to continue to lead a peaceful existence in Jewish areas, and they wished to exploit the exodus as a propaganda weapon in surrounding Arab countries and in the outside world. This inhuman policy has now faced the governments concerned with practical problems for which they must assume full responsibility.[9]

In successive communications through August 1948, Secretary of State Marshall, Dean Rusk, the CIA, and the U.S. ambassador to London expressed their views on the Palestinian refugee question.

1948

On August 13, 1948, Secretary of State Marshall sent the U.S. Embassy in London his impressions of the UN mediator's views on Israeli policies on land and refugees. According to Marshall, "Bernadotte thinks that Jews should be given valuable lands in western Galilee which they now hold by virtue of military conquest but in return for this acquisition should permit Arabs to take over most of Negev."[10]

Marshall agreed with Bernadotte on the refugee question.

With ref to economic, political military factors in connection with return Arab refugees to Israel, we appreciate security considerations governing PGI attitude but believe that under supervision Mediator substantial number refugees so desiring could be permitted gradually return their homes and resume occupations without prejudicing maintenance internal security Israel. From economic viewpoint, Israel now demonstrating ability absorb large numbers European DPs [Displaced Persons] monthly. It would therefore be unfortunate for PGI, by continuing refuse permit Arab repatriation, to create impression that assimilation Jewish immigrants was taking place at expense former Arab inhabitants Israel. From political standpoint, PGI action to permit gradual return Arab refugees would provide Arabs with tangible assurance of PGI desire establish cooperative relations with Arab states on long range basis.

We consider overall solution Arab refugee problem intrinsic to final settlement Palestine problem, but believe increasingly critical nature refugee problem makes it essential that at least partial return of refugees should be permitted for those so desiring prior to achievement final settlement. Moreover, we believe PGI assistance in alleviating situation would substantially improve chances securing early peaceful settlement Palestine problem. Conversely, PGI failure to cooperate by partial repatriation refugees might create difficulties for 265,000 Jews permanently residing Arab states.[11]

Marshall also expressed the State Department's concern about Israel's adoption of "a more aggressive attitude in Palestine."[12]

The Department has noted evidence of hostility of Israelis in Palestine towards the military observers serving under Count Bernadotte; the inflammatory speeches of the Israeli Foreign Minister, Mr. Shertok, with regard to alleged "rights" of Israel in Jerusalem; the military occupation by Israel of much of the Jerusalem area; and the refusal of the Israeli military governor in Jerusalem to cooperate with Count Bernadotte in discussions regarding the demilitarization of Jerusalem. The Department has likewise noted increasing evidence of systematic violations of the United Nations truce by the forces of Israel, including forward movement of Israeli forces from agreed truce positions, continued sniping and firing against Arab positions; and conclusive evidence of the organized transport of arms shipments to Palestine from France, Italy and Czechoslovakia. Furthermore, the Israeli Foreign Minister has officially proclaimed that Israel will not accept, pending negotiation of a final peace settlement, the return of the approximately 300,000 Arab inhabitants of that part of Palestine now comprising the Jewish State who fled from their homes and are now destitute in nearby Arab areas.[13]

1948

At the end of August, Dean Rusk, the director of the Office of UN Affairs, sent Truman's views on the refugee issue to acting Under Secretary Robert Lovett. According to the president, as part of this government's diplomatic participation in securing a peaceful settlement of the Palestine problem, it urges upon the Provisional Government of Israel and other governments concerned the need for repatriating Arab and Jewish refugees under conditions which will not imperil the internal security of the receiving states.[14]

1948

In response to the secretary of defense's request, on August 31, 1948, the CIA issued an evaluation of "Possible Developments from the Palestine Truce." It described the refugee situation, saying,

the most serious population upheaval since the termination of World War II, has been the exodus of Palestinian Arabs from Israeli-held areas. The Arab refugees, conservatively estimated at 330,000, exceed in number the Jewish DP's in Europe. The Arab countries have neither the economic resources nor the political stability to absorb such large numbers of destitute refugees. Israel's decision not to allow the refugees to return to their homes has greatly exacerbated Arab bitterness against the Jews.[15]

1948

On September 1, Marshall once again turned to Israeli policies and the refugee question in his exchange with U.S. Ambassador McDonald.

Arab refugee problem is one which, as you quote PGI as saying, did develop from recent war in Palestine but which also began before outbreak of Arab-Israeli hostilities. A significant portion of Arab refugees fled from their homes owing to Jewish occupation of Haifa on April 21–22 and to Jewish armed attack against Jaffa April 25. You will recall statements made by Jewish authorities in Palestine promising safeguards for Arab minority in areas under Jewish control. Arab refugee problem is one involving life or death of some 300,000 people. The leaders of Israel would make a grave miscalculation if they thought callous treatment of this tragic issue could pass unnoticed by world opinion. Furthermore, hatred of Arabs for Israel engendered by refugee problem would be a great obstacle to those peace negotiations you say PGI immediately desires.

In the light of the foregoing I do not concur in your conclusion that "Jewish emphasis on peace negotiations now is sounder than present US and UN emphasis on truce and demilitarization and refugees."[16]

1948

In October, the U.S. ambassador in London sent the following message to Washington, urging that it be shown to the chair of the Senate Foreign Relations Committee.

Palestine situation is probably as dangerous to our national interests as is Berlin. The danger of the latter has been played up in the headlines. The danger (not the situation) of the former has been ignored in the headlines. I have sometimes thought that this concealment of the danger in Palestine has permitted the Soviet to play her game in the Middle East without attracting attention.[17]

1949

On May 28, 1949, acting Secretary of State James Webb sent the U.S. Embassy in Israel the following note "classified secret" to be delivered to David Ben-Gurion. It addressed the question of refugees as well as territorial expansion.

The Govt of the US is seriously disturbed by the attitude of Israel with respect to a territorial settlement in Palestine and to the question of Palestinian refugees, as set forth by the representatives of Israel at Lausanne in public and private meetings. According to Dr Eytan, the Israeli Govt will do nothing further about Palestinian refugees at the present time, although it has under consideration certain urgent measures of limited character. In connection with territorial matters, the position taken by Dr Eytan apparently contemplates not only the retention of all territory now held under military occupation by Israel, which is clearly in excess of the partition boundaries of Nov

29, 1947, but possibly an additional acquisition of further territory within Palestine.[18]

1949

In mid-June 1949, Mark Ethridge, U.S. delegate to the Palestine Conciliation Commission (PCC), submitted to the secretary of state his evaluation of the reasons for the failure of the Lausanne Conference. The aim of the conference had been to develop a permanent settlement as the step following the armistice agreements previously signed by Israel and its neighbors.

> If there is to be any assessment of blame for stalemate at Lausanne, Israel must accept primary responsibility. Commission members, particularly U.S. Rep, have consistently pointed out to Prime Minister, Foreign Minister, and Israeli delegation that key to peace is some Israeli concession on refugees. USDel prepared memo months ago of minor concessions which could be made without prejudice to Israel's final position, pointing out that such concessions would lay the basis for successful talks at Lausanne. Israel has made minor concessions with reservations, but has steadfastly refused to make important ones and has refused to indicate either publicly or privately how many refugees she is willing to take back and under what conditions. Israel's refusal to abide by the GA assembly resolution, providing those refugees who desire to return to their homes, etc., has been the primary factor in the stalemate. Israel has failed even to stipulate under what conditions refugees wishing to return might return; she has given no definition of what she regards as peaceful co-existence of Arabs and Jews in Israel and she consistently returns to the idea that her security would be endangered; that she can not bear the economic burden and that she has no responsibility for refugees because of Arab attacks upon her. I have never accepted the latter viewpoint. Aside from her general responsibility for refugees, she has particular responsibility for those who have been driven out by terrorism, repression and forcible ejection.[19]

Ethridge continued:

> Israel was state created upon an ethical concept and should rest upon an ethical base. Her attitude toward refugees is morally reprehensible and politically short-sighted. She has no security that does not rest in friendliness with her neighbors. She has no security that does not rest upon the basis of peace in the Middle East. Her position as conqueror demanding more does not make for peace. It makes for more trouble.[20]

Former Israeli diplomat and minister of Foreign Affairs Shlomo Ben-Ami maintained that no statesman in Israel in 1948 or later "would conceive of peace based on the massive repatriation of Palestinian refugees as an offer the Jewish state could accept and yet survive. The ethos of Zionism was twofold: it was about demography—gathering the exiles in a stable Jewish state with as small an Arab minority as possible—and land."[21]

Did U.S. policymakers understand this? In 1982, Seth Tillman, a member of the Senate Foreign Relations Committee's professional staff and its Subcommittee on Near Eastern and South Asian Affairs, offered his impression of the applicability of the principle of self-determination to Palestine. He concluded that there was "no way to reconcile Zionism with the self-determination of an established population."[22] U.S. officials recognized the incompatibility to which Tillman pointed in their earliest discussions of developments in Palestine, yet they persisted in supporting consensus and compromise, even as they failed to achieve either.

They also understood Ben-Ami's description of the "ethos of Zionism," and they eventually deferred to Israeli policies, endorsing the transfer—that is, the expulsion of Palestinians—in conformity with Israel's objective of creating a homogeneous community. In the spring of 1949, however, the acting secretary of state explained Truman's admonition of Ben-Gurion on the basis of U.S. adherence to the PCC as well as to UN principles. U.S. policy in support of repatriation, he explained, was based on the principles of UNGA Resolution 194, urging "substantial repatriation" to be initiated on a "reasonable scale which would be well within the numbers to be agreed in a final settlement."[23]

Was implementation of such policies, even in the symbolic terms Mark Ethridge had urged, inconceivable? Or was it deemed unnecessary in light of the conviction that Washington would not enforce its principles in the face of domestic pressure or other considerations?

Israeli pressure on U.S. officials during the November 1948 U.S. election campaign appears to have been a factor in the president's policy statements. But it was part of a larger matrix of considerations that reflected changes in U.S. calculations of policy toward Israel and Palestine, which had become evident within months of its independence, as U.S. officials reconsidered their earlier assessments of Israel. The result was an appreciation of the new state's military capacity and a commitment to ensure its political orientation toward the United States and the West, leading to a deliberate lessening of U.S. pressure on Israel to comply with the UN resolutions. The result gave rise to a policy of deferral, in which U.S. officials were instructed to seek Israeli approval when considering changes in policy.

3. DEFERRAL

1948

On July 1, 1948, Philip Jessup, who was then U.S. special delegate to the United Nations, argued the case for withholding pressure on Israel on the basis of the strategic importance of Palestine/Israel. Jessup's argument revolved around three points. First:

> From the strategic viewpoint we assume that Palestine, together with the neighboring countries is a major factor presumably in any future major conflict this region would be of vital importance to US as a potential base area and with respect to our lines of communication. Presumably also the oil resources of the area are considered vital. It is our feeling that this last point may not perhaps have been dealt with adequately and frankly enough in official and public discussion of the Palestine question.
>
> From the economic viewpoint it is probable that with the exception of oil our trade and other economic relations with Palestine and the other Near East countries are not directly of any substantial

importance. Indirectly, however, the economic stability and develop-ing prosperity of Palestine and the Middle East area under peaceful conditions could make a very substantial contribution to the eco-nomic recovery of the world generally and thus contribute to the economic welfare of the US. With respect to oil, we recognize that the oil supply from the area is of great importance in the European recovery program. Were it not for this factor, however, and the stra-tegic importance of oil, we should probably not allow the economic importance of this commodity to condition our judgment substantially with regard to Palestine.[24]

Second, Israel was in a stronger position than had been anticipated, probably including by its own leaders.

Israel is also in strong military position, perhaps stronger than they thought they might be. From point of view of numbers, organiza-tion, discipline and efficiency they are more than a match for most of Arab states put together. Abdullah has only very effective force on Arab side and effectiveness of this force is almost undoubtedly due to British elements. Israel has been successful in holding its own positions and beyond this has established effective control of western Galilee.[25]

Third, Jessup reasoned that, under the circumstances, it was desirable to ensure Israel's westward orientation, which meant lessening Wash-ington's pressure on Tel Aviv to comply with UNGA resolutions to avert its reliance on the USSR.

If in process of negotiation PGI is pushed too hard to accept arrange-ments intolerable from their point of view, [it] seems clear that this will increase its difficulties in dealing with Communist-inspired dis-sident elements and will also force it to rely more extensively on Russian support.[26]

By withholding such pressure, which Jessup interpreted as treating Israel fairly, "it [Israel] could become a force operating to our own advantage and to advantage of Arab countries."[27] Given his positive assessment of Israel's military position, the change in policy that Jessup recommended was clearly designed to enhance U.S. strategic capacity.

1948

At the beginning of September, in correspondence with U.S. Ambassador McDonald, George Marshall indicated that he thought the Provisional Government of Israel wanted both territory allotted to it in UNGA Resolution 181 and "such additional territory as is now under military occupation by Israeli forces, including the rich area of western Galilee and a portion of Jerusalem."[28]

Here Marshall departed from the tenor of his preceding remarks, indicating that he agreed that Israel "should have boundaries which will make it more homogeneous and well integrated than the hourglass frontiers drawn on the map of the November 29 Resolution."[29] In sum, Marshall accepted Israel's objectives with respect to territory, justifying his position in terms of the merits of Israel's desire for a "more homogeneous" entity.

1948

In the midst of the presidential campaign in November, which Democrats feared would result in a Republican upset and a victory for Thomas Dewey, President Truman adopted the deferral code in his description of U.S. policy on territorial issues. As Lovett explained on November 10, "in plain language, the President's position is that if Israel wishes to retain that part of Negev granted it under Nov 29 resolution, it will have to take the rest of Nov 29 settlement which means giving up western Galilee and Jaffa."[30] But Truman added that changes to the UNGA resolution of November 29, 1947, "should be made only if fully acceptable to the State of Israel."[31] Here, then, was an expression of deferral to Israel. It was followed by others.

Meanwhile, the president indicated his support for borders that satisfied the requirements of a homogeneous state, which meant one with a majority determined by the Israeli government.

1949

The March 7, 1949, memorandum by the chief of staff of the U.S. Air Force described the situation in the Middle East in the following terms:

> (2) Existing Joint Chiefs of Staff policy on this subject appears now to have been overtaken by events. The power balance in the Near and Middle East has been radically altered. At the time the state of Israel was forming, numerous indications pointed to its extremely short life in the face of Arab League opposition. However, Israel has now been recognized by the United States and the United Kingdom, is likely soon to become a member of the United Nations, and has demonstrated by force of arms its right to be considered the military power next after Turkey in the Near and Middle East.[32]

1949

On April 27, 1949, the chief of naval operations sent the Joint Chiefs of Staff a memorandum on the provision of technical assistance to Israel. It was prefaced by the statement that to date there had not been a formal policy statement on Israel; hence, "an expression by the Joint Chiefs of Staff of their views with respect to that country is appropriate, and should be made available to the Secretary of State."[33] The declassified copy of this memorandum contained both a "voided" page and a "corrected" text, which revealed different formulations of the same objectives. The voided paragraph is more precise:

> Because of United States strategic interests in Israel, it would be desirable for her orientation toward the United States to be fostered and for her military capability to be such as to make her useful as an ally in the event of war with our most probable enemy. Most [difficult to read] of these points justify favorable consideration of eventual establishment of a United States military mission to Israel.[34]

The sanitized version of the same passage was abridged as follows:

> Because of United States strategic interests, it would be desirable to foster the orientation of Israel toward the United States. This may

justify favorable consideration of eventual establishment of a United States military mission in Israel.[35]

1949

On May 16, 1949, approximately one year after Israel's independence, the secretary of defense sent a memorandum to the executive secretary of the National Security Council with several observations concerning Israel. The first was on the merits of its location:

> The direct land routes (road and rail) between Turkey and the Cairo-Suez area pass through Israeli territory. In addition, the main land routes from the Caspian area of the USSR and from Iraq, Iran, and Saudi Arabia to Egypt and the Levant pass through or near Israel's territory, as do the pipelines from the Middle East oil areas to the Mediterranean. Israel controls the land approaches to the Cairo-Suez area from the east, the border between Israel and Egypt being about one hundred and fifty miles east of the Suez Canal.[36]

Secretary Johnson's second statement dealt with Israel's bases. The secretary maintained that Israel possessed

> a fine, but small, artificial harbor at Haifa, and an excellent, although limited system of well-developed airfields and air bases. In our hands, these air installations would be most useful in the interdiction of the lines of communication from the USSR to the Middle East oil resources with medium and short-range aircraft.[37]

DEFERRAL AND DEVELOPMENT

1949

On October 17, 1949, the National Security Council issued its report to the president on U.S. policy toward Israel and the Arab states. Citing Israel's superior, though small, military establishment, the NSC report indicated that Israel had been able to "occupy considerable territory beyond that awarded under the partition plan."[38] The NSC additionally compared the expanded area of Palestine currently under Israeli control with that designated under UNGA Resolution 181. To this it added evidence of changes in population, observing the following: "As a result of hostilities, some 700,000 Palestinian Arabs fled or were expelled from Israeli-controlled territory. They took refuge in areas of Palestine under Arab military occupation and in the neighboring Arab states."[39]

The NSC report reviewed U.S. policies toward Palestine and Israel, acknowledging that compromise was unlikely given the "intensely nationalistic" character of the Israeli regime and its "extremist elements."[40] Despite these conditions, Israel enjoyed a relative comparative advantage in terms of development due to its receipt of U.S. assistance. The NSC report warned, however, that the absence of a solution of the Palestinian refugee problem would further the disparity between Israeli military capacity and that of its neighbors, and further distort the economic as well as the political development of Arab regimes.

The president had earlier recognized the value of dealing with the refugee problem as one of development when he named George McGhee to be in charge of refugee development programs. In the fall of 1949, the NSC report underlined the dangerous predicament of the Arab world, in which the absence of "capable and progressive leadership" emphasized the urgency of providing assistance that would raise living standards "above the level at which social revolution is a recurring threat."[41]

Three years later, Washington confronted the Egyptian revolution of 1952, the opening call of a new chapter in the political development of the Middle East in which Palestine remained "the most important and urgent [issue] at the present time," as U.S. officials had discovered in 1945.

Reflecting on the course and consequences of U.S. policy as it evolved from discovery to denial and deferral in the years from 1945 to 1949, is not only an exercise in uncovering past history. It is an attempt at understanding its connection with a troubled present. Toward this end, examining the intertwined histories in which U.S. policy continues to play a critical role is an essential step in reclaiming the history and responsibility that many have been dying to forget.

Notes

INTRODUCTION: OPEN SECRETS

1. The opening pages of this Introduction originally appeared under the title "Gaza, 1948 and U.S. Policy," in Israeli Occupation Archive (IOA) (www .Israeli-Occupation.org), http://www.israeli-occupation.org/2014-08-25/irene -gendzier-gaza-1948-and-us-policy/.

2. Glenn Greenwald, "Cash, Weapons and Surveillance: The U.S. Is a Key Party to Every Israeli Attack," *The Intercept*, no. 885, Aug. 4, 2014.

3. Among the revelations that appeared in the *Wall Street Journal* was that on July 20, in the midst of the fighting in Gaza, the "Israel's Defense Ministry asked the U.S. for a range of munitions, including 120mm mortar shells and 40mm illuminating rounds, which were already kept stored at a pre-positioned weapons stockpile in Israel. The request was approved through military channels three days later but not made public. Under the terms of the deal the Israelis used U.S. financing to pay for $3 million in tank rounds." Adam Entous, "Gaza Crisis: Israel Outflanks the White House on Strategy," *Wall Street Journal* online, Aug. 13, 2014, http://online.wsj.com /articles/u-s-sway-over-israel-on-gaza-at-a-low-1407979365.

4. William R. Polk, "Gaza and the Struggle for Palestine: Historical Background" (Pt 1.a), *Informed Comment*, blog by Juan Cole, Aug. 10, 2014, www .juancole.com/2014/08/palestine.

5. Beryl Cheal, "Refugees in the Gaza Strip, December 1948–1950," *Journal of Palestine Studies* 18, no.1 (Autumn 1988): 138–157.

6. As quoted in Ethan Bronner, "Israel, Battlefield Altered, Takes a Tougher Approach," *New York Times*, Nov. 17, 2012, A1.

7. Donna Nevel, "The Problem in Gaza Is not Hamas," *Tikkun Daily*, Aug. 14, 2014.

8. Steven Erlanger, "Israel Is Trapped in a War That Never Ended as Instability Persists at Home," *New York Times*, Aug. 16, 2014, A10.

9. "Kerry Is Right about Netanyahu's Unnecessary Jewish State Demand," editorial, *Ha'aretz*, Mar. 16, 2014.

10. Paul A. Silverstein and Ussama Makdisi, *Memory and Violence in the Middle East and North Africa* (Bloomington: Indiana University Press, 2006), 1.

11. Eugene L. Rogan and Avi Shlaim, eds., *The War for Palestine, Rewriting the History of 1948* (Cambridge, UK: Cambridge University Press, 2001), 1.

12. Irene Gendzier, "What the US Knew and Chose to Forget in 1948 and Why It Matters in 2009," *Znet*, Jan. 22, 2009; and Gendzier, "The Risk of Knowing," in "Academic Freedom and Intellectual Activism in the Post-9/11 University," ed. E. Carvalho and D. Downing, special issue, *Works and Days* 51/52, 53/54, 26–27(2008–09): 323–338.

13. See Ian Black, "Remembering the Nakba: Israeli Group Puts 1948 Palestine Back on the Map," *Guardian*, May 2, 2014.

14. Frank E. Manuel, *The Realities of American-Palestinian Relations* (Washington, DC: Public Affairs Press, 1949); and Howard Sachar, *A History of Israel, from the Rise of Zionism to Our Time* (New York: Knopf, 1976).

15. Michael T. Benson, *Harry S. Truman and the Founding of Israel* (Westport, Ct.: Praeger, 1997); Arnold Offner, *Another Such Victory: President Truman and the Cold War, 1945–1953* (Stanford: Stanford University Press, 2002).

16. Ussama Makdisi, *Faith Misplaced, The Broken Promise of U.S.-Arab Relations: 1820–2001* (New York: Public Affairs, 2010); Seth Tillman, *The United States in the Middle East* (Bloomington: Indiana University Press, 1982); see also Allis Radosh and Ronald Radosh, *A Safe Haven: Harry S. Truman and the Founding of Israel* (New York: HarperCollins, 2009).

17. Peter L. Hahn, *Caught in the Middle East, U.S. Policy Toward the Arab-Israeli Conflict, 1945–1951* (Chapel Hill: University of North Carolina Press, 2004), Part 1, chap. 3; Melvyn Leffler, "In Conclusion, Searching for Synthesis," in *Harry S. Truman, the State of Israel, and the Quest for Peace in the Middle East*, ed. Michael J. Devine (Kirksville, Mo.: Truman State University Press, 2009), 131; and John B. Judis, *Genesis, Truman, American Jews, and the Origins of the Arab-Israeli Conflict* (New York: Farrar, Strauss and Giroux, 2014).

18. Michael J. Cohen, "Truman's Recognition of Israel, the Domestic Factor," in *Harry S. Truman, the State of Israel, and the Quest for Peace in the Middle East*, ed. Michael J. Devine (Kirksville, Mo.: Truman State University Press, 2009); Cohen, *Truman and Israel* (Berkeley: University of California Press, 1990); Cohen, "The Genesis of the Anglo-American Committee on Palestine,

November 1945: A Case Study in the Assertion of American Hegemony," *The Historical Journal* 22, no. 1 (1979): 185–207, 204; John Snetsinger, *Truman, the Jewish Vote, and the Creation of Israel* (Stanford: Hoover Institution Press, 1974); and Ritchie Ovendale, *The Origins of the Arab-Israeli Wars*, 2nd ed. (New York: Longman, 1992); and Douglas Little, *American Orientalism: The United States and the Middle East Since 1945*, 3rd ed. (Chapel Hill: University of North Carolina Press, 2002).

19. Personal communication cited in Rashid Khalidi, *Resurrecting Empire: Western Footprints and America's Perilous Path in the Middle East* (Boston: Beacon, 2005), 127.

20. Among those that illustrate these trends of a new international and/or transnational scholarship are Michael J. Hogan, "The 'Next Big Thing': The Future of Diplomatic History in a Global Age," *Diplomatic History* 28, no. 1 (Jan. 2004): 1–21; Akira Iriye, "The Transnational Turn," *Diplomatic History* 31, no. 3 (June 2007): 373–376; and Peter L. Hahn, "The View from Jerusalem: Revelations about U.S. Diplomacy from the Archives of Israel," *Diplomatic History* 22, no. 4 (Fall 1998): 509–532. See also Donald Neff, "U.S. Policy and the Palestinian Refugees," *Journal of Palestine Studies* 18, no. 1 (Autumn 1988): 96; Fred H. Lawson, "The Truman Administration and the Palestinians," *Arab Studies Quarterly* 12 (Winter/Spring 1990): 43–65; Michael Ottolenghi, "Harry Truman's Recognition of Israel," *The Historical Journal* 47, no. 4 (2004): 963–988.

21. Ussama Makdisi, "After Said: The Limits and Possibilities of a Critical Scholarship of U.S.-Arab Relations," *Diplomatic History* 38, no. 3 (June 2014): 657–684.

22. See Robert Vitalis, "The Noble American Science of Imperial Relations and Its Laws of Race Development," *Comparative Studies in Society and History* 52, no. 4 (2010): 909–938; Kees van der Pijl, *The Discipline of Western Supremacy, Modes of Foreign Relations and Political Economy*, vol. 3 (London: Pluto Press, 2014).

23. See introductory remarks by Avi Shlaim to his analysis of "The Debate About 1948," in *The Israel/Palestine Question, Rewriting Histories*, ed. Ilan Pappé (New York: Routledge, 1999), 171.

24. "'No Common Ground': Joseph Massad and Benny Morris Discuss the Middle East," *History Workshop Journal* 53 (2002): 205–216, http://www.jstor.org/stable/4289780.

25. Nur-eldeen Masalha, "On Recent Hebrew and Israeli Sources for the Palestinian Exodus, 1947–1949," *Journal of Palestine Studies* 18, no. 1 (Autumn 1988): 134.

26. Joel Beinin, "Forgetfulness for Memory: The Limits of the New Israeli History," *Journal of Palestine Studies* 34, no. 2 (Winter 2005): 10.

1. THE PRIMACY OF OIL

1. David Painter, "Oil and the American Century," *Journal of American History* 99, no. 1 (2012): 24; see also Painter, "Supply, Demand and Security: The Cold War and the Transition from Coal to Oil," International Economic History Conference, Helsinki, Finland, Aug. 2006.

2. Taken from the title of Tony Judt's book, *Postwar: A History of Europe Since 1945* (New York: Penguin, 2005).

3. Perry Anderson, "Imperium and Concilium," *New Left Review* 83 (Sept.-Oct. 2013): 22.

4. The meaning and usage of the term "Displaced Persons," referring to postwar Europe, is discussed by Bob Moore in his review of Gerard Daniel Cohen, *In War's Wake: Europe's Displaced Persons in the Postwar Order*, *American Historical Review* 117, no. 5 (2012): 1656–1657.

5. John A. Loftus, "Petroleum in International Relations," *Department of State Bulletin* 13, no. 319 (Aug. 5, 1945): 173.

6. Ibid.

7. Ibid., 175.

8. Philip H. Burch Jr., *Elites in American History* (New York: Holmes and Meier, 1980), 109.

9. Ibid.

10. Anderson, "Imperium and Concilium," 42.

11. Michael J. Cohen, "William A. Eddy, the Oil Lobby and the Palestine Problem," *Middle Eastern Studies* 30, no. 1 (1994): 166–180.

12. "The Department: Petroleum Division," *Department of State Bulletin* 10, no. 249 (Apr. 1, 1944): 303.

13. Max W. Ball, "Fueling a Global War, an Adventure in Statecraft," *Ohio Journal of Science* 45, no. 1 (Jan. 1945): 38.

14. Ibid.

15. Ibid., 34.

16. Ralph K. Davies, United States Department of the Interior, Oil and Gas Division, Papers of Ralph K. Davies, Harry S. Truman Library, Dec. 12, 1946.

17. Ibid.

18. Harold F. Williamson, Ralph L. Andreano, Arnold R. Daum, and Gilbert C. Klose, *The American Petroleum Industry, 1809–1959, The Age of Energy* (Evanston, Ill.: Northwestern University Press, 1963), 754; for more extensive discussion of the "formidable task" involved in the mobilization of the oil industry in this period, see pages 747–762.

19. Ibid., 755.

20. Cited in "Multinational Oil Corporations and U.S. Foreign Policy— Report to the Committee on Foreign Relations," United States Senate, by the

Subcommittee on Multinational Corporations (Washington, D.C.: U.S. Government Printing Office, Jan. 2, 1975), 6. It was also in 1944 that the California Arabian Standard Oil Company became known as ARAMCO, the Arabian American Oil Company.

21. Herbert Feis, *Petroleum and American Foreign Policy* (Stanford, Calif.: Food Research Institute, Stanford University, Mar. 1944), 54.

22. Ibid., 62.

23. Ibid., 43.

24. Robert Engler, *The Politics of Oil* (Chicago: University of Chicago Press, 1961), 271.

25. Ibid., 291.

26. Ibid.

27. Feis, *Petroleum and American Foreign Policy*, 29.

28. "The Ambassador in the Soviet Union to the Secretary of State," *Foreign Relations of the United States* 5 (Feb. 28, 1947): 636.

29. "Foreign Petroleum Policy of the United States," *Foreign Relations of the United States* 5 (Apr. 11, 1944): 28.

30. Ibid., 29.

31. Ibid.

32. Lloyd C. Gardner, *Three Kings, The Rise of an American Empire in the Middle East after World War II* (New York: New Press, 2009), 33.

33. "The Secretary of State to the Ambassador in the United Kingdom (Winant)," *Foreign Relations of the United States* 5 (Oct. 17, 1944): 666.

34. "The Secretary of War (Stimson) to the Secretary of State," *Foreign Relations of the United States* (Oct. 27, 1944): 748.

35. Ibid., 750–751.

36. "The Minister Resident in Saudi Arabia (Moose) to the Secretary of State," *Foreign Relations of the United States* (Mar. 29, 1944): 678–679.

37. "Memorandum by Colonel John W. Bowen of the War Department General Staff," *Foreign Relations of the United States* (Nov. 22, 1944): 669.

38. "Report by the Ad Hoc Committee of the State-War-Navy-Coordinating Committee," *Foreign Relations of the United States* 8 (Feb. 22, 1945): 852.

39. "The Secretary of the Navy (Forrestal) to the Secretary of State," *Foreign Relations of the United States* 5 (Dec. 11, 1944): 755.

40. "The Minister in Saudi Arabia (Eddy) to the Secretary of State," *Foreign Relations of the United States* 8 (Aug. 8, 1945): 944.

41. Ibid.

42. Annex 1, Draft Memorandum to President Truman, prepared by Chief of the Division of Near Eastern Affairs (Merriam) and submitted to the Director of the Office of Near Eastern and African Affairs (Henderson) early in August 1945, attached to "Memorandum by the Under Secretary

of State (Acheson) to the Secretary of State," *Foreign Relations of the United States* 8 (Aug. 1945): 45.

43. Ibid., 46.

44. Ibid.

45. Draft Memorandum to President Truman, included in "Report by the Coordinating Committee of the Department of State," *Foreign Relations of the United States* 8 (May 2, 1945): 45.

46. Ibid., 46.

47. Statement is by William Quandt in his Introduction to Evan M. Wilson, *A Calculated Risk, the U.S. Decision to Recognize Israel* (Covington, Kt.: Clerisy Press, 2008), 13.

48. All references to the exchange between Parker and Merriam are based on an interview with Gordon Merriam of July 7, 1990, by Richard Parker, and sent to the author in 1992.

49. Ibid.

50. Robert Vitalis, "Aramco World: Business and Culture on the Arabian Oil Frontier," in *Counter-Narratives, History, Contemporary Society, and Politics in Saudi Arabia and Yemen,* ed. Madawi al-Rasheed and Robert Vitalis (New York: Palgrave, Macmillan, 2004), 152.

51. "Draft Memorandum to President Truman," *Foreign Relations of the United States* 8 (May 2, 1945): 46.

52. Ibid., 45.

53. Ibid., 47.

54. Robert Vitalis, "Black Gold, White Crude: An Essay on American Exceptionalism, Hierarchy, and Hegemony in the Gulf," *Diplomatic History* 26, no. 2 (Spring 2002): 190.

55. "Policy of the United States Toward the Arab Principalities of the Persian Gulf and the Gulf of Oman," Memorandum Prepared in the Department of State, *Foreign Relations of the United States* 7 (Mar. 15, 1946): 67.

56. "Visit of the Regent of Iraq to the United States," *Foreign Relations of the United States* 8 (May 28, 1945): 586.

57. Ibid.

58. "Concern of the United States for Ensuring American Participation in the Development of Petroleum Resources in the Near East," *Foreign Relations of the United States* 8 (May 29, 1945): 49.

59. Irene L Gendzier, *Notes from the Minefield,* 2nd ed. (New York: Columbia University Press, 2006), 22.

60. U.S. Senate, Multinational Oil Corporations and U.S. Foreign Policy, 49.

61. "Policy of the United States toward the Arab Principalities of the Persian Gulf and the Gulf of Oman," *Foreign Relations of the United States* 7 (Mar. 15, 1946): 68.

62. William Engdahl, *A Century of War, Anglo-American Oil Politics and the New World Order*, 2nd ed. (London: Pluto, 1992), 93.

63. For a clear and valuable discussion of the issues at stake in the controversy over AIOC that led to the 1953 coup, see Ervand Abrahamian, *The Coup, 1953, the CIA, and the Roots of Modern U.S.-Iranian Relations* (New York: New Press, 2013).

64. Roger Owen and Sevket Pamuk, *A History of Middle East Economies in the Twentieth Century* (Cambridge, Mass.: Harvard University Press, 1999), 69.

65. Joel Beinin, *Workers and Peasants in the Modern Middle East* (Cambridge, UK: Cambridge University Press, 2001), 117.

66. Ibid., 126.

67. Ibid.

68. Ibid., 126–127.

69. Zachary Lockman, *Comrades and Enemies, Arab and Jewish Workers in Palestine, 1906–1948* (Berkeley: University of California Press, 1996), 332.

70. Beinin, *Workers and Peasants*, 124.

71. Ibid., 125.

72. Joel Beinin, *Was the Red Flag Flying There? Marxist Politics and the Arab-Israeli Conflict in Egypt and Israel, 1948–1965* (Berkeley: University of California Press, 1990), 43.

73. Malek Abisaab, "'Unruly' Factory Women in Lebanon, Contesting French Colonialism and the National State, 1940–1946," *Journal of Women's History* 16, no. 3 (2004): 65.

74. Hanna Batatu, *The Old Social Classes and the Revolutionary Movements of Iraq* (Princeton, N.J.: Princeton University Press, 1978), 623.

75. Ibid.

76. Marion Farouk-Sluglett and Peter Sluglett, "The Social Classes and the Origins of the Revolution," in *The Iraqi Revolution of 1958, the Old Social Classes Revisited*, ed. R. A. Fernea and William R. Louis (New York: I. B. Tauris, 1991), 127.

77. Owen and Pamuk, *A History of Middle East Economies*, 87.

78. Robert Vitalis, *America's Kingdom, Mythmaking on the Saudi Oil Frontier* (Stanford, Calif.: Stanford University Press, 2006), 22. A brief account of "labor organizations in the American petroleum industry" appears as the Appendix in *The American Petroleum Industry*, ed. Williamson et al., 827–845.

79. Vitalis, *America's Kingdom*, 25; Timothy Mitchell, *Carbon Democracy, Political Power in the Age of Oil* (London: Verso, 2011).

80. Vitalis, *America's Kingdom*, 95.

81. Figures cited in the Mulligan papers, named for William E. Mulligan, a longtime ARAMCO public relations officer and archivist for the period

1946–1978, in *Inside the Mirage, America's Fragile Partnership with Saudi Arabia*, Thomas W. Lippman (Boulder, Colo.: Westview Press, 2004), 79.

82. Ibid., 80–81.

83. Laurent Rucker, *Staline, Israel et les Juifs* (Paris: Presses Universitaires de France, 2001), 62–63, 63 nt.1.

84. Ibid., 63–64, where Rucker describes this exchange but points to its divergent interpretations. In Laurent Rucker, "Moscow's Surprise: The Soviet–Israeli Alliance of 1947–1949," Cold War International History Project, Working Paper 46 (Washington, D.C.: Woodrow Wilson International Center for Scholars, n.d.), 2, different figures are given. There, Weizmann is reported to have said that "if half a million Arabs could be transferred, two million Jews could be put in their place." For an earlier version of this article, see Laurent Rucker, "The Unexpected Alliance: USSR and Israel during the 1940s," in Ruskii Vopross, Russia and Jewish World, http://www.ruskiivopros.com/print.phd.php?id=77.

85. Benny Morris, *The Birth of the Palestine Refugee Problem Revisited* (Cambridge, UK: Cambridge University Press, 2004), 52–53.

86. See Rucker, "Moscow's Surprise," 14, and Rucker, *Staline, Israel et les Juifs*, 93, for a discussion of the Soviet position on bi-nationalism in this period.

87. Ervand Abrahamian, *Iran between Two Revolutions* (Princeton, N.J.: Princeton University Press, 1982), 210.

88. Painter, "Oil and the American Century," 113.

89. Barin Kayaoglu, "Cold War in the Aegean, Strategic Imperatives, Democratic Rhetoric: The United States and Turkey, 1945–1952," *Cold War History* 9, no. 3 (Aug. 2009): 325.

90. Melvyn Leffler, *A Preponderance of Power, National Security, the Truman Administration, and the Cold War* (Stanford, Calif.: Stanford University Press, 1992), 125.

91. Joyce and Gabriel Kolko, *The Limits of Power: The World and United States Foreign Policy, 1945–1954* (New York: Harper and Row, 1972), 235.

92. Ibid., 345–346.

2. THE PALESTINE QUESTION: 1945

1. "Report by the Coordinating Committee of the Dept of State, Annex," *Foreign Relations of the United States* 8 (May 2, 1945): 37.

2. Evan M. Wilson, *A Calculated Risk: The U.S. Decision to Recognize Israel* (Covington, Ky.: Clerisy Press, 2008), 39. Originally published under the title *Decision on Palestine: How the U.S. Came to Recognize Israel* (Stanford, Calif.: Hoover Institution Press, 1979).

3. Rashid Khalidi, *Resurrecting Empire: Western Footprints and America's Perilous Path in the Middle East* (Boston: Beacon Press, 2004), 185 n. 61.

4. William Roger Louis, *The British Empire in the Middle East, 1945–1951* (New York: Oxford University Press, 1988), 421–422.

5. Evan M. Wilson, "The Palestine Papers, 1943–1947," *Journal of Palestine Studies* 2, no. 4 (Summer 1973): 34–35.

6. Jerry N. Hess, "Oral History Interview with George M. Elsey," Harry S. Truman Library, July 7, 1970, 325.

7. Richard D. McKinzie, "Oral History Interview with Loy W. Henderson," Harry S. Truman Library, June 14, 1973, 30.

8. Ibid.

9. Michael J. Cohen, *Truman and Israel* (Berkeley: University of California Press, 1990), chap. 5; Wilson, *A Calculated Risk*, chap. 3; Peter L. Hahn, *Caught in the Middle East, U.S. Policy toward the Arab-Israeli Conflict* (Chapel Hill: The University of North Carolina Press, 2004), 26–28.

10. Nahum Goldmann, *The Autobiography of Nahum Goldmann: Sixty Years of Jewish Life* (New York: Holt, Rinehart and Winston, 1969), 232–233. For additional information, see Peter L. Hahn, "The View from Jerusalem: Revelations about U.S. Diplomacy from the Archives of Israel," *Diplomatic History* 22, no. 4 (Fall 1998): 513.

11. Louis, *The British Empire*, 424.

12. Cohen, *Truman and Israel*, 77.

13. Hahn, *Caught in the Middle East*, 27.

14. Michael T. Benson, *Harry S Truman and the Founding of Israel* (Westport Conn.: Praeger, 1997), 83.

15. David S. Wyman and Rafael Medoff, *A Race against Death, Peter Bergson, America, and the Holocaust* (New York: New Press, 2002), 152–153.

16. All citations attributed to Merriam are drawn from an unpublished interview conducted by Richard Parker in 1990 and sent to the author in 1992.

17. Ibid.

18. Memorandum Prepared in the Department of State, "Palestine: Form of Government" (A Summary), *Foreign Relations of the United* 8 (Jan. 30, 1945): 684.

19. "Palestine: Form of Government," 684.

20. "Palestine: Immigration," 685.

21. Ibid., 686.

22. Ibid.

23. "Lieutenant Colonel Harold B. Hoskins to the Deputy Director of the Office of Near Eastern and African Affairs (Ailing)," *Foreign Relations of the United States* 8 (Mar. 5, 1945): 691.

24. "President Truman to the Amir Abdullah of Trans-Jordan," *Foreign Relations of the United States* 8 (May 17, 1945): 707.

25. "Memorandum of Conversation by Mr. Evan M. Wilson of the Division of Near Eastern Affairs," *Foreign Relations of the United States* 8 (June 27, 1945): 714.

26. Ibid., 715.

27. Ibid.

28. "Memorandum by the Director of the Office of Near Eastern and African Affairs (Henderson) to the Secretary of State," *Foreign Relations of the United States* 8 (Aug. 24, 1945): 730.

29. Ibid., 728.

30. Ibid., 727–728.

31. Ibid., 728.

32. Ibid.

33. Ibid.

34. Ibid.

35. Ibid., Annex 2, 733.

36. Ibid.

37. "Memorandum by the Chief of the Division of Near Eastern Affairs (Merriam)," *Foreign Relations of the United States* 8 (Aug. 31, 1945): 735.

38. Harry S. Truman, *Memoirs, Years of Trial and Hope,* Vol. 2 (Garden City, N.Y.: Doubleday, 1956), 136.

39. "President Truman to the British Prime Minister (Attlee)," *Foreign Relations of the United States* 8 (Aug. 31, 1945): 738.

40. Melvyn I. Urofsky, *American Zionism from Herzl to the Holocaust* (New York: Anchor, 1976), 369. See the comprehensive analysis by John B. Judis, *Genesis, Truman, American Jews, and the Origins of the Arab/Israeli Conflict* (New York: Farrar, Straus and Giroux, 2014).

41. Urofsky, *American Zionism,* 377.

42. David Ben-Gurion, *Israel: A Personal History* (London: New English Library, 1972), 54.

43. Arnold A. Offner, *Another Such Victory* (Stanford, Calif.: Stanford University Press, 2002), 277.

44. The letter of Nov. 26, 1945, from Jacob Blaustein of the American Jewish Committee to Secretary of State Byrnes, is in the James McDonald Papers, Box 7, folder 617, in the Columbia University Rare Book and Manuscript Library, Butler Library, 6th floor, 535 West 114th St., New York, N.Y. 10027.

45. Peter Grose, *Israel in the Mind of America* (New York: Knopf, 1983), 197.

46. Report of Earl G. Harrison to President Truman, "The Treatment of Displaced Jews in the United States Zone of Occupation in Germany," included in Truman's Letter Regarding the Harrison Report and the Treatment of Displaced Jews, Sept. 29, 1945, White House Release, Jewish Virtual Library, 10, http://www.jewishvirtuallibrary.org/jsource/Holocaust/truman_.

47. Ibid., 7.

48. Yosef Grodzinsky, *In the Shadow of the Holocaust* (Monroe, Maine: Common Courage Press, 2004), 56–57.

49. Ibid., 57.

50. Ibid.

51. Gilbert Achcar, "The Arab-Israeli War of Narratives," *openDemocracy*, Apr. 19, 2010, http://www.opendemocracy.net.

52. Arno J. Mayer, *Why Did the Skies Not Darken?* (New York: Pantheon, 1988), 165.

53. David S. Wyman, *Paper Walls, America and the Refugee Crisis, 1938–1941* (New York: Pantheon, 1968), 33.

54. David McBride, "American Nativism and Common Misperceptions: How the Displaced Persons Issue Influenced America's Palestine Policy, 1945–1948," *Eras Journal* 7 (June 27, 2010): 1.

55. Noam Chomsky, *The Fateful Triangle: The United States, Israel and the Palestinians* (Cambridge, Mass.: South End, 1999), 91–92, 170 n. 10.

56. Grodzinsky, *In the Shadow of the Holocaust*, 167.

57. Stephen Green, *Taking Sides, America's Secret Relations with a Militant Israel* (New York: William Morrow, 1984), 48–51, 261 n. 2–3. Green cites "Secret" intelligence reports from the Office of the Director of Intelligence, OMGUS, for the periods Jan. 10 and July 3, 1948, in Publications File, Records of the Document Library Branch, Office of the Assistant Chief of Staff G-2, Record Group 319, National Archives.

58. "The Secretary of State to the Embassy in Egypt," *Foreign Relations of the United States* 5, part 2 (June 25, 1938): 1149.

59. Grodzinsky, *In the Shadow of the Holocaust*, 163.

60. Ibid., 225.

61. Ibid., 223. Grodzinsky offers figures to illustrate the "Migration patterns of Jewish DPS, 1945–1951" in the Allied occupation zones. Out of a total of 333,000, 140,000 or 42 percent migrated to Palestine; 120,000 or 36 percent went to the United States; 20,000 or 6 percent went to South America; 15,000 or 4.5 percent went to Canada; 10,000 or 3 percent went to Australia; some 20,000 or 6 percent remained in Germany; and another 8,000 or 2.5 percent remained in Europe. For difficulties involved in arriving at reliable calculations, see pages 222–224.

62. "The Consequences of the Partition of Palestine," Central Intelligence Agency, Nov. 28, 1947, 17, http://www.foia.cia.gov/browse_docs_full.asp.

63. Gilbert Achcar, *The Arabs and the Holocaust* (New York: Metropolitan, 2009), chap. 4; see the discussion by Achcar of "liberal westernizers" in the Arab world, his citation of the work of Lebanese intellectuals and nationalists, including Joseph Achcar, 36; the studies of Egyptian intellectuals and Syrian

nationalists by Gershoni and Ayalon, 37–41; and the views of Palestinian opponents of Naziism and fascism, 41–46.

64. Mohamed Hassanein Heikal, "Reflections on a Nation in Crisis, 1948,"
Journal of Palestine Studies 18, no. 1 (Autumn 1988): 113.

65. Interview with Eric Rouleau, St Jean de Quentin, June 2010.

66. Heikal, "Reflections on a Nation in Crisis, 1948," 115.

67. Achcar, *The Arabs and the Holocaust,* 41.

68. Ibid., 45.

69. Ibid.

70. Cohen, *Truman and Israel,* 126.

71. McKinzie, "Oral History Interview with Loy W. Henderson," 29.

72. Goldmann, *The Autobiography of Nahum Goldmann,* 232.

73. Cohen, *Truman and Israel,* 126.

74. "Oral History Interview with Loy W. Henderson," McKinzie, 29.

75. Dean Acheson, *Present at the Creation: My Years in the State Department*
(New York: Norton, 1969), 172.

76. Louis, *The British Empire,* 398. The descriptions of the British members
of the committee are taken from Louis's discussion.

77. "Preface to Report of the Anglo-American Committee of Enquiry," regard-
ing the problems of European Jewry and Palestine, Apr. 20, 1946, Lausanne.
London, His Majesty's Stationery Office (henceforth identified as Anglo-American
Committee). For informative analyses of the Anglo-American Committee, see
J. C. Hurewitz, *The Struggle for Palestine* (New York: Norton, 1950); Louis, *The
British Empire;* Amikam Nachmani, *Great Power Discord in Palestine: The Anglo-
American Committee of Inquiry into the Problems of European Jewry in Palestine,
1945–1948* (London: Frank Cass, 1986); Susan Lee Hattis, *The Bi-National Idea in
Palestine during Mandatory Times* (Haifa, Israel: Shikmona, 1970).

78. Anglo-American Committee, "Preface to Report of the Anglo-American
Committee of Enquiry," 39.

79. Ibid., 40.

80. Ibid., 41.

81. Ibid., 34–35.

82. Ibid., 35.

83. Ibid., 27.

84. Noam Chomsky, *Peace in the Middle East? Reflections on Justice and
Statehood* (New York: Pantheon, 1974), 83.

85. Ibid.

86. Anglo-American Committee, "Preface to Report of the Anglo-American
Committee of Enquiry," 35.

87. From Nahla Abdo and Nira Yuval-Davis, "Palestine, Israel and the
Zionist Settler Project," as cited in *Unsettling Settler Societies, Articulations of*

Gender, Race, Ethnicity and Class, ed. D. Stasuilis and N. Yuval-Davis (Thousand Oaks, Calif.: Sage, 1995), 298.

88. Anglo-American Committee, "Preface to Report of the Anglo-American Committee of Enquiry," 29.

89. Ibid., 31.

90. Ibid.

91. "Eliahu Epstein to Robert Lovett," in Files of Clark Clifford, Harry S. Truman Library, Aug. 3, 1948.

92. Testimony of Robert Nathan, in Hearing Before the Anglo-American Committee of Inquiry, Washington, D.C., State Department Building, Jan. 7, 1946. Ward and Paul, Electreporter, Inc., Official Reporters, 1760 Pennsylvania, Ave. N.W., Washington, D.C.

93. Robert R. Nathan, Oscar Gass, and Daniel Creamer, *Palestine: Problem and Promise, an Economic Study* (Washington, D.C.: Public Affairs Press, American Council on Public Affairs, 1946), 5.

94. Ibid., 13.

95. I am grateful to John Justin Hayden for giving me access to his thesis, *1946: A Revisionist Thesis on Canada and Palestine,* American University of Beirut, Department of Political Studies and Public Administration, 2011, Canada.

96. Anglo-American Committee, "Preface to Report of the Anglo-American Committee of Enquiry," 1.

97. Ibid., 7.

98. Ibid., 4.

99. Wilson, *A Calculated Risk*, 294.

100. Ibid., 187.

101. Cited in Allis Radosh and Ronald Radosh, *A Safe Haven: Harry S Truman and the Founding of Israel* (New York: Harper, 2009), 118.

102. Hurewitz, *The Struggle for Palestine*, 257–258.

103. "The Ambassador in the United Kingdom (Harriman) to the Secretary of State," *Foreign Relations of the United States* 7 (July 24, 1946): 652.

104. Acheson, *Present at the Creation*, 175.

105. Ibid., 176.

106. "Memorandum by the Assistant Chief of the Division of Near Eastern Affairs (Wilson)," *Foreign Relations of the United States* 7 (Sept. 5, 1946): 693.

107. Truman's statement was included in his Oct. 3 communication to British Prime Minister Attlee, *Foreign Relations of the United States* 7 (Oct. 3, 1946): 701–703; see also Cohen, *Truman and Israel*, 143–146.

108. Wilson, *A Calculated Risk*, 197, and Cohen, *Truman and Israel*, 144.

109. Goldmann, *The Autobiography of Nahum Goldmann*, 235. On Truman's recognition of Israel, see John Snetsinger, *Truman, the Jewish Vote, and the Creation of Israel* (Stanford, Calif.: Hoover Institution Press, 1974); Michael

Ottolenghi, "Harry Truman's Recognition of Israel," *Historical Journal* 47, no. 4 (2004): 963–988; Bruce J. Evensen, "The Limits of Presidential Leadership: Truman at War with Zionists, the Press, Public Opinion and His Own State Department over Palestine," *Presidential Studies Quarterly* 23, no. 2 (Spring 1993): 269–287.

110. Wilson, *A Calculated Risk,* 199–200.

111. Ibid., 199.

112. Ibid.

113. "Memorandum by the Chief of the Division of Near Eastern Affairs (Merriam) to the Director of the Office of Near Eastern and African Affairs (Henderson)," *Foreign Relations of the United States* 7 (Dec. 27, 1946): 733.

114. Ibid., 733–734.

115. Ibid., 734.

116. Ibid.

117. Wilson, *A Calculated Risk,* 209.

118. Dec. 27, 1946, Memorandum, 732, note at bottom of page.

119. "Aspects of Thinking in the Department of State on Political and Economic Policies of the United States in the Near and Middle East," *Foreign Relations of the United States* 7 (1946): 1.

120. Ibid., 4.

121. Ibid.

3. THE CRITICAL YEAR: 1947

1. "The Under-Secretary of State (Acheson) to the Director of the Office of Near Eastern an African Affairs (Henderson)," *Foreign Relations of the United States* 5 (Feb. 15, 1947): 1048.

2. "'The Pentagon Talks of 1947' Between the United States and the United Kingdom Concerning the Middle East and the Eastern Mediterranean," *Foreign Relations of the United States* 5 (1947): 544–545. For a critical view of Anglo-American relations in the Persian Gulf in the 1940s, see Simon Davis, "The Persian Gulf in the 1940s and the Question of an Anglo-American Middle East," *History* 95, no. 317 (Jan. 2010): 64–88.

3. Loy Henderson's talk was covered by Bertram F. Linz, "*Watching Washington,*" *The Oil and Gas Journal* (Nov. 22, 1947): 5. See the papers of Max W. Ball, Harry S. Truman Library, Box 1.

4. Ibid.

5. Michael T. Benson, *Harry S. Truman and the Founding of Israel* (Westport, Conn.: Praeger, 1997), 78.

6. David S. Painter, "Oil and the American Century," *Journal of American History* 99, no. 1 (June 2012): 5.

7. Taken from the introductory paper on the Middle East submitted informally by the United Kingdom representative, included under the heading of the "Substance of Response of the Acting Secretary to the British Ambassador, at the First Meeting on October 16, 1947," in "'The Pentagon Talks of 1947,'" *Foreign Relations of the United States* 5 (1947): 569. Note that the title "Acting Secretary" sometimes appears as "Under-Secretary."

8. "Memorandum by Mr. Fraser Wilkins of the Division of Near Eastern Affairs," *Foreign Relations of the United States* 5 (Jan. 14, 1947): 1004.

9. Ibid., 1005.

10. "The Secretary of State to the Embassy in the United Kingdom," *Foreign Relations of the United States* 7 (Jan. 15, 1947): 1006 n. 1.

11. "Memorandum of Conversation by the Under Secretary of State (Acheson)," *Foreign Relations of the United States* 7 (Jan. 31, 1947): 1010.

12. "The Consul General at Basel (Sholes) to the Secretary of State," *Foreign Relations of the United States* 7 (Dec. 30, 1946): 737. For an analysis of "The Paradox of American Zionism," see John B. Judis, *Genesis* (New York: Farrar, Straus and Giroux, 2014), part 2.

13. Shlomo Ben-Ami, *Scars of War, Wounds of Peace: The Israeli-Arab Tragedy* (New York: Oxford University Press, 2007), 13.

14. "Memorandum of Conversation by the Assistant Chief of the Division of Near Eastern Affairs (Wilson)," *Foreign Relations of the United States* 7 (Sept. 5, 1946): 693.

15. "The Secretary of State to the Embassy in the UK," *Foreign Relations of the United States* 5 (Jan. 15, 1947): 1012.

16. Ibid., 1013.

17. Ibid.

18. J. C. Hurewitz, *The Struggle for Palestine* (New York: Norton, 1950), 290.

19. Ibid., 265.

20. William Roger Louis, *The British Empire in the Middle East, 1945–1951* (New York: Oxford University Press, 1988), 462.

21. Walid Khalidi, ed., *From Haven to Conquest* (Beirut, Lebanon: Institute for Palestine Studies, 1971), 680.

22. Ibid., 662. Section 11, "Relief of Jewish Refugees and Displaced Persons," in "Binationalism not Partition."

23. Ibid., 677.

24. Ilan Pappé, *The Ethnic Cleansing of Palestine* (Oxford, England: Oneworld, 2006), 34.

25. Khalidi, *From Haven to Conquest*, 677.

26. Ibid., 681.

27. Gilbert Achcar, *The Arabs and the Holocaust* (New York: Metropolitan, 2009), 49.

28. As cited in Evan Wilson, *Decision on Palestine, How the U.S. Came to Recognize Israel* (Stanford, Calif.: Hoover Institution Press, 1979), 118. Henderson's entire memo is included in this work on pages 117–121.

29. Ibid., 121.

30. Ibid., 120.

31. Ibid.

32. Richard D. McKinzie, Oral History Interview with Loy W. Henderson, Harry S. Truman Library, 43.

33. Ibid.

34. Ibid.

35. Ibid., 28.

36. Ibid.

37. See John Judis's reference to the idea of "transfer" in the Peel Commission Report, as well as Ben-Gurion's views of transfer in Judis, *Genesis*, 116–117. For the idea of transfer in Zionist thinking before 1948, see Benny Morris, *The Birth of the Palestinian Refugee Problem Revisited* (Cambridge, UK: Cambridge University Press, 2004), chap. 3 and chap. 5; Nur Masalha, *Expulsion of the Palestinians: The Concept of "Transfer" in Zionist Political Thought, 1882–1948* (Beirut, Lebanon: Institute for Palestine Studies, 1992), and *The Politics of Denial: Israel and the Palestinian Refugee Problem* (London, UK: Pluto, 2003), chap. 1.

38. Morris, *Birth of the Palestinian Refugee Problem*, 51–52.

39. Cited in Pappé, *Ethnic Cleansing*, 48.

40. Ibid., 49.

41. Morris, *Birth of the Palestinian Refugee Problem*, 43.

42. Israel Shahak, "The History of the Concept of 'Transfer' in Zionism," *Journal of Palestine Studies* 18, no. 3 (Spring 1989): 26.

43. Ibid., 28.

44. Ari Shavit, "Lydda, 1948," *The New Yorker*, Oct. 21, 2013, 46; and Ari Shavit, *My Promised Land: The Triumph and Tragedy of Israel* (New York: Spiegel & Grau, 2013).

45. Ari Shavit, "Survival of the Fittest," *Ha'aretz*, Jan. 8, 2004; see also Benny Morris, "We Must Defeat Hamas Next Time," *Ha'aretz*, July 30, 2014.

46. "Memorandum of Conversation by the Director of the Office of Near Eastern and African Affairs (Henderson)," included in "The Pentagon Talks of 1947," *Foreign Relations of the United States* 5 (Sept. 9, 1947): 498.

47. Ibid., 499.

48. Editorial Note before No. 31 (Main volume, p. 44). Refers to material that appears in the Companion Volume, *Political and Diplomatic Documents, December 1947–May 1948*, State of Israel, Israel State Archives, Jerusalem, 1979, 45.

49. Ilan Pappé, *The Making of the Arab-Israeli Conflict, 1947–1951* (New York: I. B. Tauris, 1951), 119.

50. See Avi Shlaim, "The Debate about 1948," in *The Israel/Palestine Question,* ed. Ilan Pappé (New York: Routledge, 1999), 183–186.

51. "The Pentagon Talks of 1947," *Foreign Relations of the United States* 5 (1947): 538.

52. Richard D. McKinzie, Oral History Interview with Loy W. Henderson, Harry S. Truman Library, 39.

53. Ibid.

54. Ibid., 40.

55. "Memorandum by Mr. Robert M. McClintock to the Under Secretary of State (Lovett)," *Foreign Relations of the United States* 5 (Oct. 20, 1947): 1190.

56. Ibid.

57. Ibid., 1191.

58. Ibid., 1191–1192.

59. Central Intelligence Agency, "The Current Situation in the Mediterranean and the Near East," *ORE* 52 (Oct. 17, 1947): 2; http://www.foia.cia.gov /browse_docs_full.asp.

60. Central Intelligence Agency, "The Current Situation in Palestine," *ORE* 49 (Oct. 20, 1947): copy no. 45, p. 1; http://www.foia.cia.gov/browse_docs.asp.

61. Ibid.

62. Oct., 10, 1947, JCS 1684/3, cited in Michael A. Palmer, *Guardians of the Gulf: A History of America's Expanding Role in the Persian Gulf, 1833–1992* (New York: Simon & Schuster, 1992), 55.

63. Richard D. McKinzie, Oral History Interview with Loy W. Henderson, 36–37.

64. Walter Millis, ed., *The Forrestal Diaries* (New York: Viking, 1951), 358.

65. McKinzie, Oral History Interview with Loy W. Henderson, 37.

66. Central Intelligence Agency, "The Consequences of the Partition of Palestine" (Nov. 28, 1947): 8; http://www.foia.cia.gov/browse_docs_full.asp.

67. Ibid., 8–9.

68. Ibid., 4.

69. Ibid.

70. Ibid., 5.

71. Ibid., 7. For another view of what occurred in Baghdad, see Achcar, *The Arabs and the Holocaust,* 99–103.

72. Central Intelligence Agency, "The Consequences of the Partition of Palestine," 13.

73. Ibid.

74. Ibid., 14.

75. Ibid., 13.

76. Ibid., 14.

77. Ibid., 10.

78. Ibid.

79. Ibid., 10.

80. Ibid., 12.

81. Shlaim, "The Debate about 1948," 294.

82. Khalidi, *From Haven to Conquest*, Appendix 8, "Note on Arab Strength in Palestine, Jan–15 May 1948," 860.

83. Ibid.

84. Ibid., Appendix lX-B, "The Arab Expeditionary Forces to Palestine, 15/5/48," 867.

85. Central Intelligence Agency, "The Consequences of the Partition of Palestine," 9.

86. Ibid., 1.

87. Ibid., 1, 17.

88. "Interest of the United States in the Security of the Eastern Mediterranean and the Middle East," *Foreign Relations of the United States* 5 (1948): 2.

89. UN General Assembly Resolution 181 (II), "Future Government of Palestine" UN GAOR, 2nd session, 128th plenary (Nov. 29, 1947), 131–132. See also UN Special Committee on Palestine (UNSCOP Palestine Report), General Assmbly Official Records, 2nd session, Supplement No. 11, September 3, 1947, UN Doc A/364, Vol. 1, p. 35. I am indebted to Susan M. Akram, "Myths and Realities of the Palestinian Refugee Problem: Reframing the Right of Return," in *Commemorating the Naksa, Evoking the Nakba* 8 (Spring 2008): 183–198. MIT Electronic Journal of Middle East Studies, http://web.mit.edu /cis/www,mitejmes.

90. Musa Budeiri, *The Palestine Communist Party, 1919–1948* (Chicago: Haymarket, 1979), 155–165; Joel Beinin, *Was the Red Flag Flying There?* (Berkeley: University of California Press, 1990), part 2.

91. Cited in Nafez Abdullah Nazzal, "The Zionist Occupation of Western Galilee, 1948," *Journal of Palestine Studies* 111, no. 3 (Spring 1974): 59.

92. Ibid., 59 n. 2.

93. Pablo de Azcarate, *Mission in Palestine, 1948–1952* (Washington, D.C.: Middle East Institute, 1966), 4.

94. Cited in Ben-Ami, *Scars of War*, 34.

95. Cited in Pappé, *Ethnic Cleansing*, 49.

96. Simha Flapan, *The Birth of Israel, Myths and Realities* (New York: Pantheon, 1987), 90.

97. Ibid.

98. Ibid.

99. Ibid.

100. "The Consul General at Jerusalem (Macatee) to the Secretary of State," *Foreign Relations of the United States* 5 (Dec. 31, 1947): 1322.

101. Ibid., 1323.

102. Ibid.

103. Cited in Uri Bialer, *Between East and West: Israel's Foreign Policy Orientation 1948–1956* (New York: Cambridge University Press, 1990), 173.

104. David McCullough, *Truman* (New York: Simon & Schuster, 1992), 604.

105. "Memorandum of Conversation, by Mr Fraser Wilkins of the Division of Near Eastern Affairs," *Foreign Relations of the United States* 5, part 2 (Jan. 6, 1948): 537.

106. Zachary Lockman, *Comrades and Enemies: Arab and Jewish Workers in Palestine, 1906–1948* (Berkeley: University of California Press, 1996), 351.

107. According to Ben-Gurion's diaries of Jan. 1948, "the strategic objective [of the Jewish forces] was to destroy the urban communities, which were the most organized and politically conscious sections of the Palestinian people. This was not done by house-to-house fighting inside the cities and towns, but by the conquest and destruction of the rural areas surrounding most of the towns. This technique led to the collapse and surrender of Haifa, Jaffa, Tiberias, Safed, Acre, Beit-Shan, Lydda, Ramleh, Majdal, and Beersheba." Cited in Flapan, *The Birth of Israel,* 92.

4. THE WINTER OF DISCONTENT: 1948

1. Editorial Note, *Foreign Relations of the United States* 5, part 2 (1948): 543.

2. David Mayers, *George Kennan and the Dilemmas of U.S. Foreign Policy* (New York: Oxford University Press, 1988), 249–261.

3. "Report by the Policy Planning Staff on Position of the United States with Respect to Palestine," *Foreign Relations of the United States* 5, part 2, Annex (Jan. 19, 1948): 548.

4. Ibid., 546–547.

5. "Memorandum by Mr. Samuel K.C. Kopper of the Office of Near Eastern and African Affairs," *Foreign Relations of the United States* 5, part 2, Annex 3 (Jan. 27, 1948): 564.

6. Ibid.

7. Ibid., 565.

8. Ibid.

9. Simha Flapan, *The Birth of Israel, Myths and Realities* (New York: Pantheon, 1987), 95.

10. "The Consul General at Jerusalem (Macatee) to the Secretary of State," *Foreign Relations of the United States* 5, part 2 (Feb. 9, 1948): 606.

11. Ibid.

12. Ibid., 607.

13. Ibid., 609.

14. Ibid., 611.

15. "The Consul General at Jerusalem, Secret, A-37," *Foreign Relations of the United States* 5, part 2 (Feb. 9, 1948): 612.

16. "The Consul General, A-35," *Foreign Relations of the United States* 5, part 2 (Feb. 9, 1948): 608.

17. Flapan, *The Birth of Israel*, 95.

18. "Memorandum by the Policy Planning Staff (PPS /21)," *Foreign Relations of the United States* 5, part 2 (Feb. 11, 1948): 619, 620.

19. Ibid.

20. Ibid., 625. See explanation in note 5.

21. Undated handwritten notes by Robert M. McClintock, *Foreign Relations of the United States* 5, part 2 (1948): 627; note indicates that this was prepared for the National Security Council meeting planned for Feb. 13, 1948.

22. Ibid., 628.

23. Ibid., 629.

24. "Draft Report prepared by the Staff of the National Security Council," *Foreign Relations of the United States* 5, part 2 (Feb. 17, 1948): 632.

25. Ibid.

26. Ibid., 633

27. Ibid., 633.

28. Department of State to President Truman, "Message to the President," *Foreign Relations of the United States* 5, part 2 (Feb. 1948): 638–639. There is a discrepancy in dating this message. Note 1 on page 637 indicates that the text is dated Feb. 23, but it refers to the message being transmitted to the president two days earlier.

29. Ibid., 640.

30. Ibid.

31. Ibid.; see 637 n. 1.

32. In the papers of Clark N. Clifford, "Top Secret" [Draft], "The Position of the United States with Respect to Palestine," Harry S. Truman Library, Feb. 17, 1948.

33. Forrest C. Pogue, *George C. Marshall: Statesman* (New York: Viking, 1987), 359.

34. "Report by the Policy Planning Staff, PPS/23," *Foreign Relations of the United States* 5, part 2 (Feb. 24, 1948): 656.

35. "Possible Developments in Palestine, Report by the Central Intelligence Agency," *Foreign Relations of the United States* 5, part 2 (Feb. 28, 1948): 666 n. 1.

36. Ibid., 666.

37. Ibid., 672.

38. Ibid., 674.

39. Cited in William Roger Louis, *The British Empire in the Middle East, 1945–1951* (New York: Oxford University Press, 1988), 462.

40. Richard D. McKinzie, "Oral History Interview with Loy W. Henderson," Harry S. Truman Library, June 14, 1973, 39.

41. Michael J. Cohen, "Truman and the State Department: The Palestine Trusteeship Proposal, March 1948," *Jewish Social Studies* 43, no. 2 (Spring 1981): 167.

5. THE OIL CONNECTION

1. "J. Robinson to A. Lourie," Jan. 27, 1948 (No. 147), in *Political and Diplomatic Documents, December 1947–May 1948* (Jerusalem: Israel State Archives, 1979), 248.

2. See the discussion by Uri Bialer, *Between East and West: Israel's Foreign Policy Orientation 1948–1956* (New York: Cambridge University Press, 2008), part 1; and Zohar Segev, "Struggle for Cooperation and Integration," *Middle Eastern Studies* 42, no. 5 (2006): 827–828.

3. "Memorandum of Conversation, by the Under-Secretary of State," *Foreign Relations of the United States* 5, part 2 (Feb. 21, 1948): 642.

4. Ibid., 646.

5. Ibid.

6. Ibid.

7. Avi Shlaim, *The Politics of Partition* (New York: Columbia University Press, 1990), 11. Shlaim cites Eliahu Elath (Epstein) as among the group of Jewish Arabists that included Reuven Shiloah, Aharon Cohen, Yaacov Shimoni, and Elias Sasson; on Eliahu Epstein, see Philip Khoury, *Syria and the French Mandate: The Politics of Arab Nationalism, 1920–1945* (Princeton, N.J.: Princeton University Press, 1987), 548–552.

8. Eliahu Elath, *Israel and Elath: The Political Struggle for the Inclusion of Elath in the Jewish State* (London: Weidenfeld and Nicolson, 1966), 18.

9. Clark Clifford (with Richard Holbrooke), *Counsel to the President: A Memoir* (New York: Random House, 1991), 18.

10. See the Freda Kirchwey Papers at the Schlesinger Library on the History of Women in America, Radcliffe Institute, Harvard University, including the Apr. 19, 1948, Letter to Gael Sullivan of the Democratic National Committee.

11. See Peter L. Hahn, "The Influence of Organized Labor on U.S. Policy Toward Israel, 1945–1967," in *Empire and Revolution: The U.S. and the Third World Since 1945*, ed. Peter L. Hahn and Mary Ann Heiss (Columbus: Ohio State University Press, 2001), 162.

12. "Petroleum Administration for War," Ralph K. Davies Papers, Harry S. Truman Library, Apr. 5, 1946.

13. J. E. Jones, "Oil Exploration in the Western U.S.," *The Mossadegh Project,* MohammadMossadegh.com, Aug. 9, 1951.

14. Max W. Ball, "Petroleum in the European Recovery Program," *The Mines Magazine,* 13, included in papers of Max W. Ball, Harry S. Truman Library, Box 2, May 1948.

15. Max W. Ball, "Government for the People," I.P.A. of A. Monthly, presentation before the American Petroleum Institute, Chicago, Ill., 28 in papers of Max W. Ball, Harry S. Truman Library, Box 2, Nov. 11, 1948.

16. Ibid.

17. Ball, "Petroleum in the European Recovery Program," 13.

18. Ibid.

19. Hon. Dewey Short, cited in "Report of Investigation of Petroleum in Relation to National Defense," conducted by the Special Subcommittee on Petroleum Committee on Armed Services, House of Representatives (Washington, D.C.: U.S. Government Printing Office, Jan. 20, 1948), 15.

20. See Nathan J. Citino, "The Rise of Consumer Society: Postwar American Oil Policies and the Modernization of the Middle East," 14th International Economic History Congress, Helsinki 2006, Session 118, 14.

21. Ibid., Session 24, 69, 77.

22. Bialer, *Between East and West,* 85.

23. Ibid., 128.

24. "Max W Ball to Mr Paul Glowa," in papers of Max W. Ball, Harry S. Truman Library, Box 2, Mar. 13, 1948.

25. "Personal Diary," in papers of Max W. Ball, Harry S. Truman Library, Box 2.

26. Ibid., Oct. 14, 1948.

27. "Report on Investigation of Special Subcommittee on Petroleum," in *Report of Investigation of Petroleum in Relation to National Defense,* conducted by the Special Subcommittee on Petroleum Committee on Armed Services, House of Representatives (Washington, D.C.: U.S. Government Printing Office, 1948), no. 263.

28. Testimony by James Terry Duce, Petroleum for National Defense, House of Representatives, Committee on Armed Services, Special Subcommittee on Petroleum, Feb. 2, 1948, 204.

29. Ibid., 203.

30. Ibid.

31. Ibid., 207.

32. Cited in Edward W. Chester, *United States Oil Policy and Diplomacy: A Twentieth Century Overview* (Westport, Conn: Greenwood Press, 1983), 240.

33. Ibid.

34. Ibid., 207–208.

35. Ibid., 211.

36. Ibid.

37. Ibid., 216.

38. Ibid.

39. Robert R. Nathan, Oscar Gass, and Daniel Creamer, *Palestine: Problem and Promise, An Economic Study* (Washington, D.C.: Public Affairs Press, American Council on Public Affairs, 1946), 5; and see discussion in chap. 1, "Problems and Economic Potentialities."

40. See "Consultation of Jewish Agency staff and advisers (Washington, 3 February 1948)," Feb. 4, 1948 (No. 173), in *Political and Diplomatic Documents, December 1947–May 1948* (Jerusalem: Israel State Archives, Ahva Press, 1979), 294–297. See also Peter Grose, *Israel in the Mind of America* (New York: Alfred A. Knopf, 1983), 265–266.

41. Grose, *Israel in the Mind of America*, 265.

42. Ibid., 267.

43. Companion Volume No. 162, *Political and Diplomatic Documents, December 1947–May 1948* (Jerusalem: State of Israel Archives, Ahva Press, 1979), 75.

44. Memorandum by Jewish Agency Office, "Note on Palestine Policy. Problem of Implementation" (No. 162), in *Political and Diplomatic Documents, December 1947–May 1948* (Jerusalem: State of Israel Archives, 1979), 273.

45. Ibid., 272.

46. "Memorandum by the Arab Section of the Jewish Agency's Political Department," Mar. 1, 1948 (No. 239), in *Political and Diplomatic Documents, December 1947–May 1948* (Jerusalem: State of Israel Archives, 1979), 402.

47. Grose, *Israel in the Mind of America*, 267.

48. "Personal Diary," in papers of Max W. Ball, Box 2, Feb. 13, 1948.

49. Ibid., Feb. 14, 1948.

50. "Memorandum for M. Shertok (New York)," Feb. 18, 1948 (No. 210), in *Political and Diplomatic Documents, December 1947–May 1948* (Jerusalem: State of Israel Archives, 1979), 354. Gideon Ruffer (aka Gideon Rafael) is identified as an adviser to the Jewish Agency delegation at the United Nations in the Index of the Companion Volume of *Political and Diplomatic Documents, December 1947–May 1948*, 211. "Kosloff" is the transliteration of Israel Koslov's name as it appears in U.S. sources.

51. "Personal Diary," in papers of Max W. Ball, Box 2.

52. Ibid.

53. "Memorandum for M. Shertok (New York)," 18 February 1948, 354.

54. Ibid., 354–355.

55. Bialer, *Between East and West*, 24.

56. "Memorandum for M. Shertok (New York)," 355.

57. Robert Vitalis, *America's Kingdom: Mythmaking on the Saudi Oil Frontier* (Stanford, Calif.: Stanford University Press, 2006), 82–84.

58. "Memorandum for M. Shertok (New York)," 355.

59. Cited in Irvine Anderson, *Aramco, The U.S. and Saudi Arabia* (Princeton, N.J.: Princeton University Press, 1961), 185.

60. Cited in Vitalis, *America's Kingdom,* 119; see also 104, 118, and chap. 4, "The Wizards of Dhahran," for further discussion and evidence of a dimension of ARAMCO's activities not previously available.

61. "Memorandum for M. Shertok (New York)," 355.

62. Ibid.

63. Ibid.

64. Ibid., 356.

65. Ibid.

66. Ibid., 357.

67. "Personal Diary," in papers of Max W. Ball, Box 2, Apr. 27, 1949.

68. "Memorandum for M. Shertok (New York)," 357.

69. Ibid.

70. Bialer, *Between East and West,* 32.

71. "Personal Diary," in papers of Max W. Ball, Box 2, Feb. 20, 1948.

72. "Personal Diary," in papers of Max W. Ball, Box 1, Jan. 14, 1948.

73. Robert Vitalis, "Black Gold, White Crude: An Essay on American Exceptionalism, Hierarchy, and Hegemony in the Gulf," *Diplomatic History* 26, no. 2 (Spring 2002): 205.

74. Ibid., 205–206. See Kirchwey to Clark Clifford, June 18, 1948, and enclosures, RG 59 890E6363/6–2248.

75. "Personal Diary," in papers of Max W. Ball, Box 1, Mar. 10, 1948.

76. "E. Epstein to members of the Jewish Agency Executive," Mar. 17, 1948 (No. 281), in *Political and Diplomatic Documents, December 1947–May 1948* (Jerusalem: State of Israel Archives, 1979), 469.

77. Ibid., 470.

78. Ibid., 471.

79. Ibid.

80. Ibid.

81. Ibid.

82. Citino, "The Rise of Consumer Society," 13.

83. Ibid.

84. "The Minister in Saudi Arabia (Childs) to the Secretary of State," *Foreign Relations of the United States* 5, part 2 (Mar. 13, 1948): 719.

85. Central Intelligence Agency, "The Consequences of the Partition of Palestine," *ORE* 55 (Nov. 28, 1947): 9.

The quoted phrase in the title of part III is taken from the "Draft Memorandum by the Director of the Office of United Nations Affairs (Rusk) to the Under Secretary of State (Lovett)," *Foreign Relations of the United States* 5, part 2 (May 4, 1948): 894. The memorandum was drafted by Robert McClintock, but according to U.S. sources it was not sent.

6. THE TRANSFORMATION OF PALESTINE

1. Pablo de Azcarate, *Mission in Palestine 1948–1952* (Washington, D.C.: Middle East Institute, 1966), 32.

2. "Draft Memorandum by the Director of the Office of United Nations Affairs (Rusk) to the Under Secretary of State (Lovett)," *Foreign Relations of the United States* 5, part 2 (May 4, 1948): 894.

3. Ibid., 894–895.

4. Ibid., 895.

5. Ilan Pappé, *The Making of the Arab-Israeli Conflict, 1947–1951* (New York: I. B. Tauris, 1994), 85. See Pappé's comprehensive review of Plan Dalet in Ilan Pappé, *The Ethnic Cleansing of Palestine* (London: Oneworld, 2006), chap. 5, "The Blueprint for Ethnic Cleansing: Plan Dalet."

6. Avi Shlaim, *The Iron Wall, Israel and the Arab World* (New York: Norton, 2000), 31.

7. Simha Flapan, *The Birth of Israel, Myths and Realities* (New York: Pantheon, 1987), 93.

8. Benny Morris, *The Birth of the Palestinian Refugee Problem Revisited* (New York: Cambridge University Press, 2004), 164. See Joel Beinin's rejoinder and review in "No More Tears: Benny Morris and the Road Back from Liberal Zionism," *Middle East Report* 34 (Spring 2004): 8.

9. Morris, *Birth of the Palestinian Refugee Problem Revisited,* 164.

10. See a critical examination of Benny Morris's arguments in Norman Finkelstein, *Image and Reality of the Israel-Palestine Conflict,* 2nd ed. (New York: Verso, 2003), chap. 3, "Borne of War, Not by Design," 80–87.

11. Walid Khalidi, "Plan Dalet: Master Plan for the Conquest of Palestine," *Journal of Palestine Studies* 18, no. 1 (October 1988): 30. This was the first comprehensive analysis and translation of Plan Dalet to appear in English.

12. Walid Khalidi, "The Arab Perspective," in *The End of the Palestine Mandate,* ed. William Roger Louis and Robert Stookey (Austin: University of Texas Press, 1986), 127.

13. Ibid.

14. Finkelstein, *Image and Reality,* xiv.

15. Israel Shahak, "A History of the Concept of 'Transfer' in Zionism," *Journal of Palestine Studies* 18, no. 3 (Spring 1989): 23.

16. Benny Morris, *The Birth of the Palestinian Refugee Problem, 1947–1949* (New York: Cambridge University Press, 1987), 25.

17. Nur Masalha, *The Politics of Denial, Israel and the Palestinian Refugee Problem* (London: Pluto, 2003), 24; and by the same author, *Expulsion of the Palestinians: The Concept of "Transfer" in Zionist Political Thought, 1882–1948* (Washington, D.C.: Institute for Palestine Studies, 1992).

18. Masalha, *The Politics of Denial*, 25.

19. Ari Shavit, "Survival of the Fittest? An Interview with Benny Morris," *Ha'aretz*, Jan. 8, 2004.

20. Ibid.

21. As reported in Morris, *Birth of the Palestinian Refugee Problem Revisited*, 53.

22. Benny Morris, "The Harvest of 1948 and the Creation of the Palestinian Refugee Problem," *Middle East Journal* 40, no. 4 (Autumn 1986): 677.

23. Ibid., 678.

24. Ibid., 679. Italics added. See discussion of the Transfer Committee in Morris, *The Birth of the Palestinian Refugee Problem, 1947–1949*, 135–138.

25. Simha Flapan, "The Palestinian Exodus of 1948," *Journal of Palestine Studies* 16, no. 4 (Summer 1987): 10.

26. Hillel Cohen, *Army of Shadows*, trans. by Haim Watzman (Berkeley: University of California Press, 2008), 232–233, and 309 n. 7, citing Haganah Archives as well as those of the Israel Defense Forces. Cohen writes: "An unconfirmed Arab source reported a day before the attack on Deir Yasin that the people of the village and of 'Ayn Karem were asked to host *mujahidin* (Arab fighters). The latter agreed, but the former refused and argued that they are in a peaceful relationship with their Jewish neighbors and the presence of foreigners would disturb it."

27. "The Consul at Jerusalem (Wasson) to the Secretary of State," *Foreign Relations of the United States* 5, part 2 (Apr. 13, 1948): 817.

28. Jacques de Reynier, "Deir Yassin," in *From Haven to Conquest: Readings in Zionism and the Palestine Problem Until 1948*, 2nd ed., ed. Walid Khalidi (Washington, D.C.: Institute for Palestine Studies, 1987), 764.

29. Masalha, *The Politics of Denial*, 32–33. In a letter published in the *New York Times* on Dec. 4, 1948, a group of radical American Jews denounced the events of Deir Yassin and the party responsible for it. They similarly denounced the then current visit to the United States of Menachem Begin, leader of the "Freedom Party," "a political party closely akin in its organization, methods, political philosophy and social appeal to the Nazi and Fascist parties. It was formed out of the membership and following of the former Irgun Zvai Leumi, a terrorist, right-wing, chauvinist organization in Palestine."

30. Benny Morris, *1948: The First Arab-Israeli War* (New Haven, Conn.: Yale University Press, 2008), 128.

31. Ibid.

32. Ibid.

33. James G. McDonald, *My Mission in Israel 1948–1951* (New York: Simon and Schuster, 1951), 174–175.

34. Ibid., 175.

35. Flapan, *The Birth of Israel*, 94.

36. Tom Segev, *1949: The First Israelis* (New York: Free Press, 1986), 89.

37. "Memorandum by the Director of the Office of Near Eastern and African Affairs (Henderson) to the Acting Secretary of State (Lovett)," *Foreign Relations of the United States* 5, part 2 (Apr. 9, 1948): 804.

38. "The Acting Secretary of State to the Consulate General at Jerusalem," *Foreign Relations of the United States* 5, part 2 (Apr. 10, 1948): 811.

39. Ibid.

40. Ibid., n. 2.

41. "C. Weizmann to President Truman (Washington)," *Israeli Documents December 1947–May 1948* (Apr. 9, 1948): 590.

42. "The Acting Secretary of State to the Embassy in Egypt," *Foreign Relations of the United States* 5, part 2 (Apr. 10, 1948): 812.

43. Menachem Begin, *The Revolt* (New York: Dell, 1977), 225. (Originally published in 1951.)

44. Flapan, *The Birth of Israel*, 94.

45. "The Consul at Jerusalem (Wasson) to the Secretary of State," *Foreign Relations of the United States* 5, part 2 (Apr. 22, 1948): 842–843.

46. Walid Khalidi, "The Fall of Haifa Revisited," *Journal of Palestine Studies* 37, no. 3 (Spring 2008): 46.

47. Khalidi, "The Arab Perspective," 129.

48. Donald Neff, "U.S. Policy and the Palestinian Refugees," *Journal of Palestine Studies* 18, no. 1 (Autumn 1988): 96.

49. Ibid.

50. Beinin, "No More Tears," 2.

51. Flapan, "The Palestinian Exodus of 1948," 4; see also Major R. D. Wilson, "The Battle for Haifa, April 21–22, 1948," in *From Haven to Conquest*, 771–774; Walid Khalidi, "Special Feature: The Fall of Haifa Revisited," *Journal of Palestine Studies* 37, no. 3 (Spring 2008): 30–58.

52. Khalidi, "Special Feature: The Fall of Haifa Revisited," 41–42.

53. Flapan, "The Palestinian Exodus of 1948," 5.

54. Flapan, *The Birth of Israel*, 89.

55. "Editorial Note," *Foreign Relations of the United States* 5, part 2 (1948): 838–839.

56. "Lippincott, Haifa to Secretary of State," Palestine Reference Files of Dean Rusk and Robert McClintock, 1947–1949, Record Group 59, National Archives and Records Service (Washington, D.C.: General Services Administration, 1981), Apr. 24, 1948, reel 10, no. 8955.

57. Mustafa Abbasi, "The Fall of Acre in the 1948 Palestine War," *Journal of Palestine Studies* 39, no. 4 (Summer 2010): 24.

58. Wilson, "The Battle for Haifa," 774.

59. "The Consul at Haifa (Lippincott) to the Secretary of State," *Foreign Relations of the United States* 5, part 2 (June 23, 1948): 1138.

60. Ibid.

61. Cited in Morris, *Birth of the Palestinian Refugee Problem Revisited,* 310.

62. Ibid., 310–311.

63. Zachary Lockman, *Comrades and Enemies: Arab and Jewish Workers in Palestine, 1906–1948* (Berkeley: University of California Press, 1996), 351.

64. "The Ambassador in the United Kingdom (Douglas) to the Secretary of State," *Foreign Relations of the United States* 5, part 2 (June 18, 1948): 1123.

65. "The Secretary of State to the Embassy in the United Kingdom," *Foreign Relations of the United States* 5, part 2 (June 22, 1948): 1132.

66. Ibid., 1133.

67. Ibid.

68. "Memorandum by the Assistant Chief of the Petroleum Division (Moline)," *Foreign Relations of the United States* 5, part 1 (Sept. 10, 1948): 42.

69. Ibid.

70. Uri Bialer, *Oil and the Arab-Israeli Conflict, 1948–1963* (New York: St. Martin's, 1999), 35.

71. See "Editorial Note," *Foreign Relations of the United States* 5, part 1 (1948): 67.

72. Amiram Cohen, "US Checking Possibility of Pumping Oil from Northern Iraq to Haifa, via Jordan," *Ha'aretz,* Aug. 25, 2003.

73. Ed Vuillamy, "Israel Seeks Pipeline for Iraqi Oil," *The Guardian* (London), Apr. 19, 2003.

74. "The Ambassador in Egypt (Tuck) to the Secretary of State," *Foreign Relations of the United States* 5, part 2 (Apr. 26, 1948): 863.

75. See Rashid Khalidi, "The Palestinians and 1948: The Underlying Causes of Failure," in *The War for Palestine: Rewriting the History of 1948,* 2nd ed., Eugene Rogan and Avi Shlaim (New York: Cambridge University Press, 2007), 30; and see also Rashid Khalidi, *The Iron Cage: The Story of the Palestinian Struggle for Statehood* (Boston: Beacon, 2006), chap. 4.

76. Michael Palumbo, *The Palestinian Catastrophe: The 1948 Expulsion of a People From Their Homeland* (Boston: Faber and Faber, 1987), 89.

77. Ibid., 87.

78. Ibid., 88.

79. From the American Legation, Beirut, cover letter by Lowell Pinkerton to Acheson dated Apr. 11, 1949, included in Irene Gendzier, "The Memorandum Submitted to the Government of the United States of America," by the Jaffa and District Inhabitants Council," *Journal of Palestine Studies* 18, no. 3 (Spring 1989): 97.

80. Ibid, 103.

81. Ibid., 102.

82. Ibid., 104.

83. Ibid., 105.

84. Ibid., 107.

85. Ibid., 99; and see Morris, *Birth of the Palestinian Refugee Problem Revisited*, 321.

86. Palumbo, *The Palestinian Catastrophe*, 92.

87. Morris, *Birth of the Palestinian Refugee Problem Revisited*, 219.

88. The agreement is included in Gendzier, "The Memorandum Submitted to the Government of the United States of America," 99.

89. "Instructions to the Arab Population by the Commander of the Haganah, Tel-Aviv District," May 13, 1948, is included in the agreement of May 13, 1948, in Gendzier, "The Memorandum Submitted to the Government of the United States of America," 100.

90. Ibid.

91. Ibid.

92. Ibid., 104; see under the category of "Submissions."

93. Ibid.

94. Cited in Segev, *1949*, 75.

95. Morris, *Birth of the Palestinian Refugee Problem Revisited*, 220; Jon Kimche, *Seven Fallen Pillars* (London: Secker and Warburg, 1953), 234.

96. Morris, *Birth of the Palestinian Refugee Problem Revisited*, 221.

97. Cited in Pappé, *The Ethnic Cleansing in Palestine*, 204.

98. Ibid., 206. In an interview of Gen. (Reserves) Mordechai Gur by Alex Fishman that appeared in *Al-Hamishmar* on May 10, 1978, the general addressed the question of looting of Palestinian property by the IDF in his remarks to a skeptical reporter. He referred to the case of Haifa. "When you tell people, who were raised on the ethics of 'Thou shalt not kill!' 'Go to war and kill the enemy'—then everything else is permitted. The minute you overturn the moral code, what can a man do." In response to the interviewer's questions about who identified the enemy, and what of a civilian population, Gur replied, "in Jaffa there once was a civilian population or was there not? In Haifa was there a hostile civilian population or was there not? Did they leave one apartment untouched or unlooted?" I am grateful to the late Israel Shahak for this interview.

99. Ibid., 205.

100. Ibid., 103.

7. TRUCE AND TRUSTEESHIP

1. "The Secretary of State to the United States Representative at the United Nations (Austin)," *Foreign Relations of the United States* 5, part 2 (Mar. 5, 1948): 681.

2. Ibid., 697.

3. John Snetsinger, *Truman, The Jewish Vote, and the Creation of Israel* (Stanford, Calif.: Hoover Institution Press, 1974), 86; see also the views of Defense Secretary Forrestal, as reported in Walter Millis, ed., *The Forrestal Diaries* (New York: Viking, 1951), 387. For a contrasting interpretation, see Melvyn P. Leffler, "National Security and U.S. Foreign Policy," in *Origins of the Cold War*, 2nd ed., ed. Melvyn P. Leffler and David S. Painter (New York: Routledge, 2005), 23; and Melvyn P. Leffler, *A Preponderance of Power, National Security, the Truman Administration and the Cold War* (Stanford, Calif.: Stanford University Press, 1992), chap. 5 and chap. 6.

4. "Memorandum by the President's Special Counsel (Clifford) to President Truman," *Foreign Relations of the United States* 5, part 2 (Mar. 8, 1948): 695.

5. Ibid., 691.

6. "Memorandum by Mr. Samuel K. C. Kopper to the United States Representatives at the United Nations (Austin)," *Foreign Relations of the United States* 5, part 2 (Mar. 14, 1948): 724.

7. Ibid.

8. Ibid., 725.

9. Avi Shlaim, "Britain and the Arab-Israeli War of 1948," *Journal of Palestine Studies* 16, no. 4 (Summer 1987): 55. For the most comprehensive account of this relationship and its evolution, see the work of Avi Shlaim, *Collusion Across the Jordan* (New York: Columbia University Press, 1988).

10. "Memorandum by the Legal Adviser (Gross) to the Director of the Office of United Nations Affairs (Rusk)," *Foreign Relations of the United States* 5, part 2 (Mar. 19, 1948): 748.

11. "Editorial Note," *Foreign Relations of the United States* 5, part 2 (1948): 748–749, includes reference to the critical position of Dan Kurzman, author of *Genesis 1948* (Cleveland, Ohio: New American Library/World Publishing Company, 1970), who claimed that "President Truman telephoned to Secretary Marshall at San Francisco on March 20 and instructed him to issue a statement making it clear that trusteeship had not been proposed as a substitute for partition but had simply been suggested as a temporary measure to fill the political vacuum in Palestine until partition could be affected" (748). Truman's statement, however, indicated only that trusteeship was regarded as a temporary measure.

12. Oral History Interview with Loy W. Henderson by Richard D. McKinzie, Harry S. Truman Library, 41.

13. "Memorandum by the Director of the Executive Secretariat (Humelsine) to the Secretary of State," *Foreign Relations of the United States* 5, part 2 (Mar. 22, 1948): 749.

14. Ibid., 750.

15. "Memorandum Prepared in the Office of Near Eastern and African Affairs," *Foreign Relations of the United States* 5, part 2 (n.d.): 756. Footnote indicates that this memorandum was transmitted by Henderson to Marshall "with his memorandum of March 24."

16. Department of State, "Draft Trusteeship Agreement for Palestine With the United Nations as the Administering Authority," *Foreign Relations of the United States* 5, part 2 (Apr. 2, 1948): 778–796.

17. For analysis of what came to be known as the minority report, see Walid Khalidi, "Binationalism not Partition," in *From Haven to Conquest: Readings in Zionism and the Palestine Problem Until 1948,* 2nd ed., ed. Walid Khalidi (Washington, D.C.: Institute for Palestine Studies, 1987), 645–699, and more specifically, the pages relevant to the "Principles underlying the constitution of a unitary State in Palestine," 687–690. The original text of Subcommittee 2 can be found in A/AC.14/32 and Add. 1.

18. Department of State, "Draft Trusteeship Agreement for Palestine," 779.

19. Ibid., 780. For a comparison with "Principles underlying the constitution," see Khalidi, *From Haven to Conquest,* 688. See Shira Robinson's study, *Citizen Strangers: Palestinians and the Birth of Israel's Liberal Settler State* (Stanford, Calif.: Stanford University Press, 2013), especially chap. 3.

20. Department of State, "Draft Trusteeship Agreement for Palestine," 781. The UN committee principles recommended constitutional recognition of the use of Hebrew as a "second language in areas in which they [the Jews] are in a majority." See Khalidi, *From Haven to Conquest,* 688.

21. Department of State, "Draft Trusteeship Agreement for Palestine," 789.

22. "The Acting Secretary of State to Certain Diplomatic and Consular Offices," *Foreign Relations of the United States* 5, part 2 (Apr. 18, 1948): 832 n. 2.

23. "Editorial Note," 776.

24. "Memorandum by the Joint Chiefs of Staff to President Truman," *Foreign Relations of the United States* 5, part 2 (Apr. 4, 1948): 799.

25. "The Secretary of Defense (Forrestal) to the Secretary of State," *Foreign Relations of the United States* 5, part 2 (Apr. 19, 1948): 832.

26. Ibid.

27. Abba Eban, *An Autobiography* (New York: Random House, 1977), 103; and William Roger Louis, *The British Empire in the Middle East, 1945–1951* (New York: Oxford University Press, 1984) 514–515 and n. 4.

28. April 15, 1948, Secretary of State from Chaim Weizmann, included in The Palestine Reference Files of Dean Rusk and Robert McClintock, 1947–1949. Record Group 59, National Archives and Records Service, General Services Administration, Washington 1981. Reel 10, no. 449. Also in "The United States Representatives of the United States (Austin) to the Secretary of State," *Foreign Relations of the United States* 5, part 2 (Apr. 15, 1948): 823.

29. "The United States Representatives of the United States (Austin) to the Secretary of State," 823.

30. Ibid., 824.

31. "The Ambassador in Egypt (Tuck) to the Secretary of State," *Foreign Relations of the United States* 5, part 2 (Apr. 18, 1948): 830–831.

32. "The Acting Secretary of State to Certain Diplomatic and Consular Offices," *Foreign Relations of the United States* 5, part 2 (Apr. 18, 1948): 832 n. 2.

33. "Memorandum by the Director of the Office of Near Eastern and African Affairs (Henderson) to the Under Secretary of State (Lovett)," *Foreign Relations of the United States* 5, part 2 (Apr. 22, 1948): 840.

34. "Memorandum by the Director of the Office of Near Eastern and African Affairs (Henderson) to the Under Secretary of State (Lovett)," *Foreign Relations of the United States* 5, part 2 (Apr. 23, 1948): 854.

35. No such map is included in the declassified documents of the period.

36. "The United States Representative at the United Nations (Austin) to the Secretary of State," *Foreign Relations of the United States* 5, part 2 (Apr. 27, 1948): 864 no. 2.

37. See Walter Laqueur, *A History of Zionism* (New York: Schocken, 1972), 467, 552; for a discussion of the view of the American Jewish Committee on Palestine and Zionism, see Cyrus Adler and Aaron M. Margalith, *With Firmness in the Right: American Diplomatic Action Affecting Jews, 1840–1945* (New York: American Jewish Committee, 1946), 450–452.

38. "The United States Representative at the United Nations (Austin) to the Secretary of State," *Foreign Relations of the United States* 5, part 2 (Apr. 25, 1948): 858.

39. "The United States Representative at the United Nations (Austin) to the Secretary of State," *Foreign Relations of the United States* 5, part 2 (Apr. 22, 1948): 849.

40. "Memorandum of Conversation, by the Director of the Office of Near Eastern and African Affairs (Henderson)," *Foreign Relations of the United States* 5, part 2 (Apr. 26, 1948): 859.

41. Ibid.

42. "Memorandum by the Director of the Office of Near Eastern and African Affairs (Henderson) to the Under Secretary of State (Lovett)," *Foreign Relations of the United States* 5, part 2 (Apr. 22, 1948): 840.

43. Ibid.

44. Ibid., 841.

45. Ibid.

46. "The United States Representative at the United Nations (Austin) to the Secretary of State," *Foreign Relations of the United States* 5, part 2 (Apr. 27, 1948): 867 n. 3.

47. "Mr. Moshe Shertok to Secretary of State," *Foreign Relations of the United States* 5, part 2 (Apr. 29, 1948): 876 n. 2.

48. "The United States Representative at the United Nations (Austin) to the Secretary of State," *Foreign Relations of the United States* 5, part 2 (Apr. 29, 1948): 873 n. 1.

49. "Memorandum of Conversation, by the Director of the Office of United Nations Affairs (Rusk)," *Foreign Relations of the United States* 5, part 2 (Apr. 30, 1948): 878.

50. "Moshe Shertok to Hon. George S. Marshall," in papers of Clark M. Clifford, Harry S. Truman Library, Apr. 29, 1948.

51. "Memorandum of Conversation, by the Director of the Office of United Nations Affairs (Rusk)," *Foreign Relations of the United States* 5, part 2 (Apr. 30, 1948): 878.

52. See Louis, *The British Empire*, 514–515.

53. Ibid., 515.

54. "The United States Representative at the United Nations (Austin) to the Secretary of State," *Foreign Relations of the United States* 5, part 2 (Apr. 30, 1948): 880.

55. Ibid.

56. "The Secretary of State to the Embassy in the United Kingdom," *Foreign Relations of the United States* 5, part 2 (Apr. 27, 1948): 865.

57. Pablo de Azcarate, *Mission in Palestine 1948–1952* (Washington, D.C.: Middle East Institute, 1966), 22.

58. "The Consul General at Jerusalem (Wasson) to the Secretary of State," *Foreign Relations of the United States* 5, part 2 (May 3, 1948): 889.

59. "The Secretary of State to the Consulate General at Jerusalem," *Foreign Relations of the United States* 5, part 2 (May 1, 1948): 882 n. 2.

60. "The United States Representative at the United Nations (Austin) to the Secretary of State," *Foreign Relations of the United States* 5, part 2 (Apr. 30, 1948): 880.

61. "The Consul General at Jerusalem (Wasson) to the Secretary of State" (May 3, 1948): 889.

62. Ibid., 890.

63. Ibid.

64. Ibid., 891.

65. Nur Masalha, *The Politics of Denial: Israel and the Palestinian Refugee Problem* (London: Pluto, 2003), 32.

66. "The Secretary of State to the Embassy in the United States," *Foreign Relations of the United States* 5, part 2 (May 3, 1948): 891.

67. "Mr. Moshe Shertok to the Director of the Office of United Nations Affairs (Rusk), at Washington," *Foreign Relations of the United States* 5, part 2 (1948): 893.

68. "Draft memorandum by the Director of the Office of United Nations Affairs (Rusk) to the Under Secretary of State (Lovett)," *Foreign Relations of the United States* 5, part 2 (May 4, 1948): 894.

69. Ibid.

70. Ibid., 894–895.

71. Ibid., 895.

72. Ibid.

73. Ibid.

74. Ibid., 895 n. 3 (continued on 896).

75. See discussion of Magnes's visit to Washington in Louis, *The British Empire in the Middle East,* 519.

76. May 4, 1948, "Memorandum of Conversation, by the Secretary of State," *Foreign Relations of the United States* 5, part 2 (May 4, 1948): 902.

77. Ibid.

78. Ibid., 903.

79. Ibid.

80. Ibid., 904.

81. Ibid.

82. "The United States Representative at the United Nations (Austin) to the Secretary of State," *Foreign Relations of the United States* 5, part 2 (May 4, 1948): 905.

83. Ibid.; see 905 n. 1 for the qualifications proposed by McClintock.

84. "Transcript of Remarks Made by Mr. Dean Rusk in Conversation by Telephone With Mr. Jessup and Mr. Ross," *Foreign Relations of the United States* 5, part 2 (May 11, 1948): 965.

85. Ibid., 967.

86. Ibid.

87. Ibid.

88. Ibid.

89. Ibid., 968.

90. "Editorial Note," 906.

91. "Memorandum by Mr. John E. Horner," *Foreign Relations of the United States* 5, part 2 (May 4, 1948): 899.

92. Ibid.

93. Ibid., 900.

94. Ibid., 900–901.

95. Ibid., 901.

96. Cited in Statement (with handwritten date, May 9, 1948, included) that appears under the file titled "Palestine: Recognition of the Jewish State, May 7, 1948," in the papers of Clark M. Clifford, Harry S. Truman Library.

97. Ibid., 3.

8. RECOGNITION AND RESPONSE

1. "Memorandum of Conversation by Secretary of State (drafted by McClintock)," *Foreign Relations of the United States* 5, part 2 (May 12, 1948): 972–976. See also Richard Holbrooke, "President Truman's Decision to Recognize Israel," *Jerusalem Viewpoints*, no. 563 (May 1, 2008).

2. "A. Lourie to M. Shertok," *Political and Diplomatic Documents, Dec 1947–May 1948*, Israel State Archives (May 11, 1948): 776. The precise wording is: "Crum [Bartley Crum] saw President yesterday, returned fairly optimistic. Clifford advised we go firmly forward with planned announcement of State, has definite impression President considering recognition. Meanwhile understand Lovett, Rusk, doing utmost against /us/."

3. David Ben-Gurion, *Israel: A Personal History* (New York: New English Library, 1971), 273.

4. Ibid., 274.

5. "Palestine," in papers of Clark M. Clifford, Harry S. Truman Library, May 11, 1948.

6. Ibid., no. 1, 1.

7. Ibid., 2.

8. Ibid.

9. "For Mr Clifford: Supplemental Memo on (1) The Arab States; (2) British Investment in Jewish Palestine," internal date April 8, 1948; see also letter from Palestine Economic Corporation addressed to Max Lowenthal. Both are in papers of Clark M. Clifford, Harry S. Truman Library. In addition, see Clark Clifford, *Counsel to the President: A Memoir* (New York: Random House, 1991), 3–25.

10. Ibid.

11. "Memorandum of Conversation by Secretary of State (drafted by McClintock)," *Foreign Relations of the United States* 5, part 2 (May 12, 1948): 973.

12. Ibid.

13. Ibid., 974.

14. Ibid. See also William Roger Louis, *The British Empire in the Middle East, 1945–1951* (New York: Oxford University Press, 1984), 527.

15. "The Secretary of State to Certain Diplomatic Offices," *Foreign Relations of the United States* 5, part 2 (May 13, 1948): 984.

16. "The Consul at Jerusalem (Wasson) to the Secretary of State," *Foreign Relations of the United States* 5, part 2 (May 13, 1948): 985.

17. Ibid.

18. Ibid.

19. Jonathan Daniels, *The Man of Independence* (Philadelphia: Lippincott, 1950), 320.

20. "Memorandum of Conversations by the Under Secretary of State (Lovett)," *Foreign Relations of the United States* 5, part 2 (May 17, 1948): 1007.

21. Clifford and Holbrooke, "President Truman's Decision to Recognize Israel," 8; Clifford with Richard Holbrooke, *Counsel to the President,* 18–25. See also "The Agent of the Provisional Government of Israel (Epstein) to President Truman," *Foreign Relations of the United States* 5, part 2 (May 14, 1948): 989 n. 2, which refers to a George Elsey note that "C M C [Clifford] spent the afternoon getting arrangements made, including arrangement that Epstein would send in the request to U.S. Gov't for recognition."

22. "The Agent of the Provisional Government of Israel (Epstein) to President Truman," *Foreign Relations of the United States* 5, part 2 (May 14, 1948): 989.

23. Ibid.

24. Simha Flapan, *The Birth of Israel, Myths and Realities* (New York: Pantheon, 1987), 35.

25. Ibid.

26. Baruch Kimmerling, *Politicide: The Real Legacy of Ariel Sharon* (London: Verso, 2003), 25.

27. "The Secretary of State to Mr Eliahu Epstein, at Washington," *Foreign Relations of the United States* 5, part 2 (May 14, 1948): 992.

28. "Memorandum by the Director of the Office of Near Eastern and African Affairs (Henderson) to the Under Secretary of State (Lovett)," *Foreign Relations of the United States* 5, part 2 (May 16, 1948): 1002.

29. Cited in Tom Segev, *1949: The First Israelis* (New York: The Free Press, 1986), xviii.

30. Ibid.

31. Shlomo Ben-Ami, *Scars of War, Wounds of Peace* (London: Oxford University Press, 2007), 37.

32. "Editorial Note," includes the June 13, 1974, letter by Dean Rusk to the Historical Office recalling the events at the UN on May 14, *Foreign Relations of the United States* 5, part 2 (1948): 993.

33. Ibid.

34. Ibid.

35. Ibid.

36. "The United States Representative at the United Nations (Austin) to the Secretary of State," *Foreign Relations of the United States* 5, part 2 (May 19, 1948): 1013.

37. Ibid.

38. "The United States Representative to the United Nations (Austin) to the Secretary of State," *Foreign Relations of the United States* 5, part 2 (May 15, 1948): 997.

39. Douglas Little, "Gideon's Band: America and the Middle East," *Diplomatic History* 18, no. 4 (Fall 1994): 520.

40. Douglas Little, *American Orientalism* (London: I. B. Tauris, 2002), 87.

41. Consider some of the following analyses of postwar U.S. policy toward Israel that include discussions of Truman's decision to recognize Israel. This is not a complete list of works addressing this subject. Justus D. Doenecke, "Principle and Expediency: The State Department and Palestine, 1948," *Journal of Libertarian Studies* 2, no. 4 (1978): 343–356, offers a critical assessment of *Foreign Relations of the United States* 5, part 2, and Truman's decision to recognize Israel. Peter L. Hahn, *Caught in the Middle East: U.S. Policy Toward the Arab-Israeli Conflict, 1945–1961* (Chapel Hill: The University of North Carolina Press, 2004), 26–31, provides a broad review of the varied explanations offered by historians for Truman's decisions. The following contribute to our understanding of the range of explanations offered for the president's decision: Clark Clifford and Richard Holbrooke, "President Truman's Decision to Recognize Israel"; *The Jerusalem Viewpoints* series included in Clifford and Holbrooke, *Counsel to the President*; Michael J. Cohen, *Truman and Israel* (Berkeley: University of California Press, 1990), chap. 12; W. Brands, *Inside the Cold War: Loy Henderson and the Rise of the American Empire, 1918–1961* (New York: Oxford University Press, 1991), chap. 12; Noam Chomsky, *The Fateful Triangle* (Cambridge, Mass.: South End Press, 1999), 94–98; Michael Ottolenghi, "Harry Truman's Recognition of Israel," *Historical Journal* 47, no. 4 (2004): 963–988; Lawrence Davidson, "Truman the Politician and the Establishment of Israel," *Journal of Palestine Studies* 39, no. 1 (Summer 2010); David McCullough, *Truman*, 613–620; John Snetsinger, *Truman, the Jewish Vote, and the Creation of Israel* (Stanford, Calif.: Hoover Institution Press, 1974); Melvyn Leffler, "Searching for Synthesis," in *Harry S. Truman, the State of Israel, and the Quest for Peace in the Middle East*, ed. Michael J. Devine (Kirksville, Mo.: Truman State University Press, 2009); "Oral History Interview with George M. Elsey," in Harry S. Truman Library, Feb. 1974, vol. 11, 212–477; J. C. Hurewitz, *The Struggle for Palestine* (New York: Norton, 2008), 322–323; Little, "Gideon's Band," 513–541; Louis, *The British Empire*, 528; Arnold A. Offner, *Another Such Victory* (Stanford, Calif.: Stanford University Press, 2002), 275, 298; Evan M. Wilson, *Decision on Palestine: How the U.S. Came to Recognize Israel* (Stanford, Calif.: Hoover Institution Press,

1979), 149; Zvi Ganin, *Truman, American Jewry and Israel, 1945–1948* (New York: Holmes & Meier, 1979); Peter Grose, *Israel in the Mind of America* (New York: Schocken, 1984); Michael T. Benson, *Harry S. Truman and the Foundation of Israel* (Westport, Conn.: Praeger, 1997); Kenneth R. Bain, *March to Zion: United States Policy and the Founding of Israel* (College Station: Texas A&M University Press, 2000); Michelle Mart, *Eye on Israel: How America Came to View Israel as an Ally* (Albany: State University of New York Press, 2006); Yaacov Bar-Siman-Tov, "A 'Special Relationship,'" *Diplomatic History* 22, no. 2 (Spring 1993): 231–262.

42. Cohen, *Truman and Israel*, 277.

43. Ibid.

44. Louis, *The British Empire*, 528.

45. Hahn, *Caught in the Middle East*, 40–41.

46. Avi Shlaim, *The Iron Wall: Israel and the Arab World* (New York: Norton, 2000), 34.

47. Zeev Maoz, *Defending the Holy Land: A Critical Analysis of Israel's Security and Foreign Policy* (Ann Arbor: The University of Michigan Press, 2006), 4.

48. Shlaim, *The Iron Wall*, 35.

49. Flapan, *The Birth of Israel*, 198.

50. Ibid.

51. Ibid., 198–199.

52. Ilan Pappé, *The Making of the Arab-Israeli Conflict, 1947–1951* (New York: I. B. Tauris, 1994), 137.

53. "The Minister in Lebanon (Pinkerton) to the Secretary of State," *Foreign Relations of the United States* 5, part 2 (May 16, 1948): 1003.

54. Mohamed Hassanein Heikal, "Reflections on a Nation in Crisis, 1948," *Journal of Palestine Studies* 18, no. 1 (Autumn 1988): 117.

55. "Nasser's Memoirs of the First Palestine War," translated and annotated by Walid Khalidi, *Journal of Palestine Studies* 2, no. 2 (Winter 1973): 8.

56. Ibid., 10.

57. Ibid.

58. "Summary of Testimony by Amnon Neumann, Zochrot" (June 17, 2010), 1. http://zochrot.org/index.php?id=844.

59. Ibid., 2.

60. Ibid.

61. Rashid Khalidi, "The Palestinians and 1948," in *The War for Palestine*, ed. Eugene L. Rogan and Avi Shlaim (New York: Cambridge University Press, 2001), 14.

62. As cited in Ilan Pappé, *The Ethnic Cleansing of Palestine* (London: Oneworld, 2006), 132.

63. Khalidi, "The Palestinians and 1948," 14.

64. Walid Khalidi, ed., *All That Remains: The Palestinian Villages Occupied and Depopulated by Israel in 1948* (Washington, D.C.: Institute for Palestine Studies, 1992), xx, 585. For a comprehensive review of how this figure was arrived at, consult the Preface.

65. Benny Morris, *The Birth of the Palestinian Refugee Problem, 1947–1949* (New York: Cambridge University Press, 1987), 221.

66. Ibid., 121.

67. Ibid., 122.

68. Mustafa Abbasi, "The Fall of Acre in the 1948 Palestine War," *Journal of Palestine Studies* 39, no. 4 (Summer 2010): 7.

69. Ibid., 14.

70. Ibid., 21.

71. "Statement Made by Ambassador Austin Before the Security Council on May 17, 1948," *Foreign Relations of the United States* 5, part 2 (May 17, 1948): 1009.

72. Ibid., 1010.

73. "Text presented by Count Bernadotte at Rhodes," *Foreign Relations of the United States* 5, part 2 (June 28, 1948): 1153.

74. Ibid., 1153–1154.

75. Pappé, *The Making of the Arab-Israeli Conflict*, 149.

76. Avi Shlaim, *Collusion Across the Jordan: King Abdullah, the Zionist Movement, and the Partition of Palestine* (New York: Columbia University Press, 1988), 261.

77. Pappé, *The Making of the Arab-Israeli Conflict*, 140.

78. "The Consul at Jerusalem (Wasson) to the Secretary of State," *Foreign Relations of the United States* 5, part 2 (May 22, 1948): 1030.

79. Ibid.

80. The U.S. Representative to the UN informed the president of the UN Security Council of the attack on Wasson on May 22, 1948. S/771, Telegram dated 22 May 1948 from the Representative of the United States Addressed to the President of the Security Council.

81. *New York Post,* June 8, 1948, posted the following account: "Home of the Brave: America's Sorry Record in Failing to Protect Flag or Citizen Abroad Since Nov.," http://www.varchive.org/obs/480608.htm. The *New York Times,* which initially repeated the story, retracted it, suggesting that it was unlikely that Wasson knew who had attacked him. See Stephen Green, *Taking Sides* (New York: William Morrow, 1984), 33.

82. Pablo de Azcarate, *Mission in Palestine 1948–1952* (Washington, D.C.: Middle East Institute, 1966), 90–91.

83. Ibid., 91.

84. Richard D. McKinzie, "Oral History with Stuart W. Rockwell," Harry S. Truman Library, July 8, 1976, 4. A later interview with Stuart Rockwell as well

as Robert B. Houghton, who was reported to have been in the hospital at the same time as Wasson, appears in Green, *Taking Sides,* 33, 260 n. 19.

85. Ibid., 5.

86. Evan M. Wilson, *A Calculated Risk: The U.S. Decision to Recognize Israel* (Covington, Ky.: Clerisy Press, 2008), 275.

87. "The Vice Consul at Jerusalem (Burdett) to the Secretary of State," *Foreign Relations of the United States* 5, part 2 (May 29, 1948): 1075.

88. "Memorandum by the Director of the Office of Near Eastern and African Affairs (Henderson) to the Secretary of State," *Foreign Relations of the United States* 5, part 1 (May 26, 1948): 15.

89. "The Minister in Saudi Arabia (Childs) to the Secretary of State," *Foreign Relations of the United States* 5, part 2 (June 25, 1948): 1147.

90. Ibid.

91. Maurice Jr. Labelle, "'The Only Thorn': Early Saudi-American Relations and the Question of Palestine, 1945–1949," *Diplomatic History* 35, no. 2 (April 2011): 281.

92. "The Charge in Egypt (Patterson) to the Secretary of State," *Foreign Relations of the United States* 5, part 2 (June 30, 1948): 1159.

93. Ibid.

94. "The Vice Consul at Jerusalem (Burdett) to the Secretary of State," *Foreign Relations of the United States* 5, part 2 (June 25, 1948): 1145.

95. Ibid.

9. RECONSIDERING U.S. POLICY IN PALESTINE

1. "Memorandum by Mr. Gordon P Merriam, Member of the Policy Planning Staff, to Staff Members," *Foreign Relations of the United States* 5, part 2 (July 15, 1948): 1222.

2. "The Acting United States Representative at the United Nations (Jessup)," *Foreign Relations of the United States* 5, part 2 (July 1, 1948): 1182.

3. Richard D. McKinzie, "Oral History Interview with Loy W. Henderson," Harry S. Truman Library, June 14, 1973, 42. Henderson's account is confirmed in David McCullough, *Truman* (New York: Simon & Schuster, 1992), 620.

4. McKinzie, "Oral History Interview with Loy W. Henderson," 42.

5. Ibid.

6. "Memorandum of Conversation by the Director of the Office of Near Eastern and African Affairs (Henderson)," *Foreign Relations of the United States* 5, part 2 (June 6, 1948): 1100.

7. Ibid.

8. "The Ambassador to the United Kingdom (Douglas) to the Secretary of State," *Foreign Relations of the United States* 5, part 2 (June 19, 1948): 1125.

9. "The Secretary of State to the Embassy in the United Kingdom," *Foreign Relations of the United States* 5, part 2 (June 22, 1948): 1134.

10. "The Vice Consul at Jerusalem (Burdett) to the Secretary of State," *Foreign Relations of the United States* 5, part 2 (June 8, 1948): 1105.

11. "The Secretary of State to the Embassy in the United Kingdom," *Foreign Relations of the United States* 5, part 2 (June 22, 1948): 1133–1134.

12. Ibid., 1134.

13. "Memorandum by Mr. Robert McClintock," *Foreign Relations of the United States* 5, part 2 (June 23, 1948): 1135. See asterisk at bottom of page referring to the Republican Party Platform for 1948, which McClintock noted, repeating its claim, that it had been the "first to call for the establishment of a free and independent Jewish Commonwealth," to which he added that the Democratic Party Platform would "undoubtedly include equivalent references to the State of Israel."

14. "Memorandum by Mr. Robert McClintock to the Director of the Office of United Nations Affairs (Rusk)," *Foreign Relations of the United States* 5, part 2 (July 1, 1948): 1177.

15. Ibid.

16. "Memorandum by Mr. Robert McClintock," *Foreign Relations of the United States* 5, part 2 (June 23, 1948): 1135.

17. Ibid., 1136.

18. Ibid.

19. Ibid.

20. Ibid., 1137.

21. Ibid., 1136.

22. Ibid., 1137.

23. Ibid.

24. Ibid., 1136.

25. Ibid., 1137.

26. "The Acting United States Representative at the United Nations (Jessup) to the Secretary of State," *Foreign Relations of the United States* 5, part 2 (June 30, 1948): 1161.

27. "The Acting United States Representative at the United Nations (Jessup) to the Secretary of State," *Foreign Relations of the United States* 5, part 2 (July 1, 1948): 1183.

28. Ibid.

29. "The Acting United States Representative of the United Nations (Jessup) to the Secretary of State," *Foreign Relations of the United States* 5, part 2 (June 30, 1948): 1165–1166.

30. Ibid., 1163.

31. Avi Shlaim, *Collusion Across the Jordan: King Abdullah, the Zionist Movement, and the Partition of Palestine* (New York: Columbia University Press, 1988), 326.

32. Nafez Nazzal, "The Zionist Occupation of Western Galilee, 1948," *Journal of Palestine Studies* 3, no. 3 (Spring 1974): 58–76.

33. Rashid Khalidi, *Palestinian Identity: The Construction of Modern National Consciousness* (New York: Columbia University Press, 1997), 190–191.

34. "The Acting United States Representative at the United Nations (Jessup) to the Secretary of State," *Foreign Relations of the United States* 5, part 2 (July 1, 1948): 1185.

35. "The Acting United States Representative at the United Nations," *Foreign Relations of the United States* 5, part 2 (June 30, 1948): 1165.

36. Ibid., 1170.

37. Ibid., 1169.

38. "The Acting United States Representative at the United Nations (Jessup) to the Secretary of State," *Foreign Relations of the United States* 5, part 2 (July 1, 1948): 1182.

39. Ibid., 1183.

40. Ibid.

41. Ibid., 1184.

42. Ibid., 1184.

43. Ibid., 1183.

44. Ibid., 1181.

45. Ibid., 1184.

46. Ibid., 1183.

47. Ibid., 1184.

48. Ibid.

49. Robert R. Nathan, Oscar Gass, and Daniel Creamer, *Palestine: Problem and Promise* (New York: Public Affairs, 1948), 39.

50. Cited in Shlaim, *Collusion Across the Jordan,* 343.

51. "The Acting United States Representative at the United Nations (Jessup) to the Secretary of State," *Foreign Relations of the United States* 5, part 2 (July 1, 1948): 1184.

52. "Memorandum by Mr. Robert M. McClintock to the Director of the Office of United Nations Affairs (Rusk)," *Foreign Relations of the United States* 5, part 2 (July 1, 1948): 1172.

53. Ibid.

54. David Mayers, *George Kennan and the Dilemmas of US Foreign Policy* (New York: Oxford University Press, 1988), 253.

55. Ibid.

56. "Memorandum by the Director of Central Intelligence (Hillenkoetter) to President Truman," *Foreign Relations of the United States* 5, part 2 (July 8, 1948): 1200.

57. "Report by the Central Intelligence Agency," *Foreign Relations of the United States* 5, part 2 (July 27, 1948): 1242.

58. Ibid., 1245.

59. Ibid.

60. Ibid., 1244.

61. Ibid., 1245.

62. The reference was to the Map of the Military Situation of 18 July 1948, accompanying the "Report by the Central Intelligence Agency," *Foreign Relations of the United States* 5, part 2 (July 27, 1948): 1241.

63. Ibid., 1244.

64. Ibid.

65. Ibid.

66. Avi Shlaim, *The Politics of Partition: King Abdullah, the Zionists, and Palestine 1921–1951* (New York: Oxford University Press, 1990), 205.

67. Benny Morris, "In '48, Israel Did What It Had to Do," Commentary, *Los Angeles Times*, Jan. 26, 2004. Reporting on the *Ha'aretz* interview Benny Morris had given to Ari Shavit, Morris claimed that "after looking afresh at the events of 1948 and at the context of the whole Arab-Zionist conflict from its inception in 1881 until the present day—I find myself as convinced as ever that the Israelis played a major role in ridding the country of tens of thousands of Arabs during the 1948 war, but I also believe their actions were inevitable and made sense. Had the belligerent Arab population inhabiting the areas destined for Jewish statehood not been uprooted, no Jewish state would have arisen, or it would have emerged so demographically and politically hobbled that it could not have survived. It was an ugly business. Such is history."

68. Benny Morris, *The Birth of the Palestinian Refugee Problem, 1947–1949* (Cambridge, UK: Cambridge University Press, 1987), 208–209.

69. Ibid., 209.

70. "Report by the Central Intelligence Agency," *Foreign Relations of the United States* 5, part 2 (July 27, 1948): 1245.

71. Ibid., 1242.

72. Ibid., 1247.

10. THE PALESTINE REFUGEE PROBLEM

1. For a comprehensive account of Palestinian refugee archives, see Salim Tamari and Elia Zureik, eds., *Reinterpreting the Historical Record: The Uses of Palestinian Refugee Archives for Social Science Research and Policy Analysis* (Beirut: Institute for Palestine Studies, 2001).

2. "The Consul General at Jerusalem (MacDonald) to the Secretary of State," *Foreign Relations of the United States* 5, part 2 (June 27, 1948): 1151.

3. Benny Morris, *The Birth of the Palestinian Refugee Problem, 1947–1949* (New York: Cambridge University Press, 1987), 204.

4. Ibid.

5. Cited in Benny Morris, *The Birth of the Palestinian Refugee Problem Revisited* (New York: Cambridge University Press, 2004), 322.

6. Many Israelis changed their name after the declaration of Israel's independence; thus Moshe Shertok took the name Sharett and Eliahu Epstein became Eliahu Elath. U.S. officials used the old as well as the new names interchangeably during this time.

7. Avi Shlaim, *Collusion Across the Jordan: King Abdullah, the Zionist Movement, and the Partition of Palestine* (New York: Columbia University Press, 1988), 491.

8. Nur Masalha, *The Politics of Denial: Israel and the Palestinian Refugee Problem* (Sterling, Va.: Pluto, 2003), 30.

9. Spiro Munayyer, "The Fall of Lydda," *Journal of Palestine Studies* 27, no. 4 (1997/1998): 96; see also Masalha, *The Politics of Denial*, 29.

10. See Munayyer, "The Fall of Lydda," for an apologetic account of the atrocities committed; see also *Ha'aretz* journalist Ari Shavit, "A Massacre in Palestine," *The New Yorker*, Oct. 21, 2013, 46, in which Shavit justified the events as "a crucial phase of the Zionist revolution, and they laid the foundation for the Jewish state." Shavit develops this thesis in *My Promised Land: The Triumph and Tragedy of Israel* (New York: Spiegel & Grau, 2013).

11. "The Acting United States Representative at the United Nations (Jessup) to the Secretary of State," *Foreign Relations of the United States* 5, part 2 (July 27, 1948): 1248. See also Ilan Pappé, ed., *The Israel/Palestine Question* (New York: Routledge, 1999), part IV, "The New History of the 1948 War," and the articles by Avi Shlaim, Benny Morris, and Nur Masalha.

12. Amnon Kapeliuk, "New Light on the Israeli-Arab Conflict and the Refugee Problem and Its Origins," *Journal of Palestine Studies* 16, no. 3 (1987): 21.

13. James G. McDonald, *My Mission in Israel 1948–1951* (New York: Simon and Schuster, 1951), 175.

14. Ibid.

15. Ibid.

16. Ibid., 176.

17. Ibid.

18. Ibid.

19. "Possible Developments From the Palestine Truce," Central Intelligence Agency (Aug. 31, 1948): 3; http:www.foia.cia.gov/browse_docs_full.asp.

20. Ibid.

21. "The Charge in Egypt (Patterson) to the Secretary of State," *Foreign Relations of the United States* 5, part 2 (Aug. 7, 1948): 1295.

22. Ibid.

23. Ibid.

24. Ibid., 1296.

25. Ibid.

26. Ibid.

27. Ibid.

28. "The Secretary of State to the Embassy in the United Kingdom," *Foreign Relations of the United States* 5, part 2 (Aug. 13, 1948): 1309.

29. "The Secretary of State to the Legation in Lebanon," *Foreign Relations of the United States* 5, part 2 (Aug. 20, 1948): 1333; in addition to the agencies cited in "The Secretary of State to the Embassy in the United Kingdom," *Foreign Relations of the United States* 5, part 2 (Aug. 14, 1948): 1311.

30. Morris, *The Origin of the Palestinian Refugee Problem, 1947–1949*, 150.

31. "The Secretary of State to the Embassy in the United Kingdom," *Foreign Relations of the United States* 5, part 2 (Aug. 13, 1948): 1309.

32. "The Secretary of State to the Embassy in the United Kingdom," *Foreign Relations of the United States* 5, part 2 (Aug. 14, 1948): 1311.

33. Susan M. Akram, "Myths and Realities of the Palestinian Refugee Problem: Reframing the Right of Return," in "Commemorating the Naksa, Evoking the Nakba," *MIT Electronic Journal of Middle East Studies* (Spring 2008): 186. Elia Zureik, "The Palestinian Refugee Problem: Conflicting Interpretations," *Global Dialogue* 4, no. 3 (Summer 2002): 93.

34. "Memorandum by the Secretary of State to President Truman," *Foreign Relations of the United States* 5, part 2 (Aug. 16, 1948): 1313.

35. Ibid., 1313–1314.

36. Ibid., 1314.

37. Ibid.

38. "Memorandum by the Director of the Office of United Nations Affairs (Rusk) to the Under Secretary of State (Lovett)," *Foreign Relations of the United States* 5, part 2 (Aug. 20, 1948): 1331.

39. Ibid., 1331–1332.

40. Ibid., 1332.

41. Ibid.

42. Tom Segev, *1949, The First Israelis* (New York: Free Press, 1986), 86.

43. James McDonald, *My Mission in Israel*, 189.

44. "The Secretary of State to the Special Representative of the United States in Israel (McDonald)," *Foreign Relations of the United States* 5, part 2 (Aug. 31, 1948): 1364.

45. "The Secretary of State to the Special Representative of the United States in Israel (McDonald)," *Foreign Relations of the United States* 5, part 2 (Sept. 1, 1948): 1367.

46. Ibid.

47. Ibid.

48. Ibid., 1367–1368.

49. Ibid., 1368.

50. "The Secretary of State to the Embassy in the United Kingdom," *Foreign Relations of the United States* 5, part 2 (Sept. 1, 1948): 1369.

51. "Memorandum of Conversation Prepared in the Office of the Special Representative of the United States in Israel," *Foreign Relations of the United States* 5, part 2 (Sept. 7, 1948): 1377.

52. "The Consul General at Jerusalem (MacDonald) to the Secretary of State," *Foreign Relations of the United States* 5, part 2 (Sept. 8, 1948): 1383.

53. Ibid.

54. Ibid.

55. "The Ambassador in the United Kingdom (Douglas) to the Secretary of State," *Foreign Relations of the United States* 5, part 2 (Sept. 9, 1948): 1384.

56. "The Special Representative of the United States in Israel (McDonald) to the Secretary of State," *Foreign Relations of the United States* 5, part 2 (Sept. 9, 1948): 1385.

57. Ibid.

58. Seth P. Tillman, *The United States in the Middle East: Interests and Obstacles* (Bloomington: Indiana University Press, 1982), 58–59.

59. Ibid., 175.

60. "The Consul General at Jerusalem (MacDonald) to the Secretary of State," *Foreign Relations of the United States* 5, part 2 (Sept. 17, 1948): 1412.

61. Ibid., 1413 n. 1.

62. "The Acting Secretary of State to Certain Diplomatic and Consular Offices," *Foreign Relations of the United States* 5, part 2 (Sept. 21, 1948): 1415.

63. "Mr. Robert M. McClintock to Mr. Dean Rusk, at Paris," *Foreign Relations of the United States* 5, part 2 (Sept. 30, 1948): 1439.

64. "The Ambassador to Egypt (Griffis) to the Secretary of State," *Foreign Relations of the United States* 5, part 2 (Sept. 15, 1948): 1398.

65. Ibid.

66. Ibid.

67. "Progress Report of the United Nations Mediator in Palestine," *Foreign Relations of the United States* 5, part 2 (1948): 1403.

68. Ibid.

69. Ibid.

70. Ibid., 1403–1404.

71. Ibid.

72. Ibid., 1405–1406.

73. Ibid., 1406.

74. Dana Adams Schmidt, "Blankets Needed by Arab Refugees," *New York Times*, Oct. 19, 1948, 5.

75. Progress Report of the United Nations Mediator in Palestine, *Foreign Relations of the United States* 5, part 2 (1948), 1403.

76. Ibid.

77. Walid Khalidi, ed., *All That Remains: The Palestinian Villages Occupied and Depopulated by Israel in 1948* (Washington, D.C.: Institute for Palestine Studies, 2006), xxxi.

78. Ibid., xxxii.

79. Ibid.

80. Ibid.

81. Ibid.

82. See the project organized by the Israeli NGO Zochrot, Towards a Common Archive: Reframing the Roots of Palestine and Israel, at http://zochrot .org/en/press/54591; see also the Truth Commission on the Responsibility of Israeli Society for the Events of 1948–1960 in the South at http://zochrot.org /en/keyword/45528.

11. THE STATE DEPARTMENT ON THE RECORD

1. Victor Kattan, *From Coexistence to Conquest: International Law and the Origins of the Arab-Israeli Conflict, 1891–1949* (London: Pluto, 2009), 218.

2. "The Secretary of State to the Acting Secretary of State," *Foreign Relations of the United States* 5, part 2 (Oct. 15, 1948): 1481.

3. "The Secretary of State to the Acting Secretary of State," *Foreign Relations of the United States* 5, part 2 (Oct. 16, 1948): 1481.

4. Ibid., 1482.

5. Ibid.

6. Stian Johansen Tiller and Hilde Henriksen Waage, "Powerful State, Powerless Mediator: The United States and the Peace Efforts of the Palestine Conciliation Commission, 1949–1951, *International History Review* 33, no. 3 (Sept. 2011): 501–524.

7. "The Secretary of State to the Acting Secretary of State," *Foreign Relations of the United States* 5, part 2 (Oct. 16, 1948): 1482–1483.

8. Ibid., 1483.

9. "The Special Representative of the United States to Israel (McDonald) to President Truman," *Foreign Relations of the United States* 5, part 2 (Oct. 17, 1948): 1486.

10. Ibid.

11. Ibid.

12. "The Ambassador in the United Kingdom (Douglas) to the Acting Secretary of State," *Foreign Relations of the United States* 5, part 2 (Nov. 12, 1948): 1571.

13. "The Ambassador in the United Kingdom (Douglas) to the Acting-Secretary of State," *Foreign Relations of the United States* 5, part 2 (Oct. 29, 1948): 1531.

14. Ibid., 1532.

15. Ibid.

16. Ibid.

17. Ibid.

18. "The Acting Secretary of State to the Secretary of State, at London," *Foreign Relations of the United States* 5, part 2 (Oct. 30, 1948): 1533.

19. Ibid., 1534.

20. Ibid.

21. "E. Elath to M. Sharett (Paris)," *Documents on the Foreign Policy of Israel, October 1948–April 1949*, vol. 2 1984 (Oct. 30, 1948): 74.

22. "The Acting Secretary of State to the Secretary of State, at London," *Foreign Relations of the United States* 5, part 2 (Oct. 31, 1948): 1535.

23. Benny Morris, *The Birth of the Palestinian Refugee Problem Revisited* (New York: Cambridge University Press, 2004), 468.

24. Michael Palumbo, *The Palestinian Catastrophe: The 1948 Expulsion of a People from Their Homeland* (London: Faber & Faber, 1987), xiii–xiv.

25. Ibid., xiv.

26. Morris, *The Birth of the Palestine Refugee Problem Revisited*, 469, and 495 n. 45 where Morris claims that "this report, and others like it, were most probably based on rumours than first-hand accounts or investigation."

27. Palumbo, *The Palestinian Catastrophe*, xiv. See also the work of Sara Roy, *Gaza Strip: The Political Economy of De-Development* (Washington, D.C.: Institute for Palestine Studies, 1995), 65, and *Failing Peace: Gaza and the Palestinian Israeli Conflict* (London: Pluto, 2006).

28. Beryl Cheal, "Refugees in the Gaza Strip, December 1948–1950," *Journal of Palestine Studies* 18, no. 1 (Autumn 1988): 138.

29. Roy, *Gaza Strip*, 67.

30. Ilan Pappé, *The Making of the Arab-Israeli Conflict, 1947–1951* (New York: I. B. Tauris, 1994), 174.

31. Morris, *Origins of the Palestine Refugee Problem Revisited*, 481.

32. Ibid., 492.

33. Air Force Captain E. J. Zeuty's presence is cited in Palumbo, *The Palestinian Catastrophe*, 163.

34. "Memorandum of Conversation, by the Acting Secretary of State," *Foreign Relations of the United States* 5, part 2 (Nov. 10, 1948): 1563.

35. Ibid.

36. Ibid.

37. Ibid.

38. Ibid.

39. "Note by Comay, Paris #142, Note On United States Visit 6th to 13th November 1948," *Documents in the Foreign Policy of Israel* 2 (Nov. 15, 1948): 181.

40. "Mr. Wells Stabler to the Acting Secretary of State," *Foreign Relations of the United States* 5, part 2 (Nov. 9, 1948): 1557.

41. "The Acting Secretary of State to the Secretary of State, at Paris," *Foreign Relations of the United States* 5, part 2 (Nov. 10, 1948): 1565.

42. Ibid.

43. Ibid.

44. Ibid.

45. "The Acting Secretary of State to the Legation in Lebanon," *Foreign Relations of the United States* 5, part 2 (Nov. 11, 1948): 1569.

46. Ibid.

47. Ibid., 1570 n. 2.

48. "Memorandum of Conversation, by the Acting Secretary of State," *Foreign Relations of the United States* 5, part 2 (Dec. 21, 1948): 1677 n. 4.

49. "The Minister in Lebanon (Pinkerton) to the Acting Secretary of State," *Foreign Relations of the United States* 5, part 2 (Dec. 16, 1948): 1670.

50. Ibid.

51. "The Secretary of State to the Acting Secretary of State," *Foreign Relations of the United States* 5, part 2 (Nov. 15 [16], 1948): 1595.

52. "The Secretary of State to the Acting Secretary of State," *Foreign Relations of the United States* 5, part 2 (Nov. 16, 1948): 1594.

53. "Memorandum by Mr. Robert M. McClintock to the Acting Secretary of State," *Foreign Relations of the United States* 5, part 2 (Nov. 17, 1948): 1598.

54. Ibid.

55. Ibid., 1600.

56. Ibid., 1601.

57. "The Acting Secretary of State to the United States Delegation at Paris," *Foreign Relations of the United States* 5, part 2 (Nov. 22, 1948): 1622.

58. Ibid.

59. "The Acting Chairman of United States Delegation at Paris (Dulles) to the Secretary of State," *Foreign Relations of the United States* 5, part 2 (Nov. 29, 1948): 1636.

60. "President Truman to the President of the Provisional Government of Israel (Weizmann)," *Foreign Relations of the United States* 5, part 2 (Nov. 29, 1948): 1633.

61. Ibid., 1633–1634.

62. "The Acting Secretary of State to the Embassy in the United Kingdom," *Foreign Relations of the United States* 5, part 2 (Dec. 1, 1948): 1639.

63. Ibid.

64. "Mr Wells Stabler to the Acting Secretary of State," *Foreign Relations of the United States* 5, part 2 (Dec. 6, 1948): 1647 n. 1.

65. "The First Secretary of Embassy in the United Kingdom (Jones) to the Director of the Office of Near Eastern and African Affairs (Satterthwaite)," *Foreign Relations of the United States* 5, part 2 (Dec. 8, 1948): 1650.

66. Ibid., 1651.

67. United Nations General Assembly, A/RES/212 (111), Nov. 19, 1948.

68. Ibid.

69. "The Acting Secretary of State to the United States Delegation at Paris," *Foreign Relations of the United States* 5, part 2 (Dec. 7, 1948): 1648.

70. United Nations General Assembly A/RES/194 (111), Dec. 11, 1948.

71. Salim Tamari and Elia Zureik, eds., *Reinterpreting the Historical Record: The Uses of Palestinian Refugee Archives for Social Science Research and Policy Analysis* (Beirut: Institute for Palestine Studies, 2001), 3.

72. Ibid, 5.

73. "The Acting Secretary of State to Certain Diplomatic and Consular Offices," *Foreign Relations of the United States* 5, part 2 (Dec. 29, 1948): 1697.

74. Nur Masalha, *The Politics of Denial: Israel and the Palestinian Refugee Problem* (Sterling, Va.: Pluto, 2003), 75.

75. "The Acting Secretary of State to Certain Diplomatic and Consular Offices," *Foreign Relations of the United States* 5, part 2 (Dec. 29, 1948): 1696 n. 1.

76. "Editorial Note," *Foreign Relations of the United States* 6 (1949): 688.

77. Ibid.

78. Ibid.

79. Ibid.

80. Ibid., 688–689.

81. Ibid., 688.

82. See John Judis, *Genesis: Truman, American Jews, and the Origins of the Arab–Israeli Conflict* (New York: Farrar, Strauss & Giroux, 2014), part 11, part 111.

12. THE PCC, ARMISTICE, LAUSANNE, AND PALESTINIAN REFUGEES

1. Walter Mills, ed., *The Forrestal Diaries* (New York: Viking, 1951), 124.

2. "Mr. John C. Ross to the Secretary of State," *Foreign Relations of the United States* 6 (Jan. 4, 1949): 610.

3. "Memorandum by Mr. Samuel K. C. Kopper to Mr. Mark F. Ethridge," *Foreign Relations of the United States* 6 (Jan. 27, 1949): 703.

4. Ibid., 704.

5. "Proposed Representations to Government of Israel on Armistice Negotiations with Egypt," Dean Rusk Reference Book, January 16–April 1949, *The Palestine Reference Files of Dean Rusk and Robert McClintock, 1947–1949*, reel 7, National Archives, RG 59, Film S 1040 (Feb. 4, 1949).

6. Tom Segev, *1949: The First Israelis* (New York: Free Press, 1986), 8.

7. Ilan Pappé, *The Making of the Arab-Israeli Conflict, 1947–1951* (New York: I. B. Tauris, 1994), 179.

8. Cited in Segev, *1949*, 8.

9. Ibid., 659.

10. "Tel Aviv (McDonald) to Secretary of State," *The Palestine Reference Files of Dean Rusk and Robert McClintock, 1947–1949*, no. 88 (Feb. 3, 1949).

11. Ibid.

12. "The Consul at Jerusalem (Burdett) to the Secretary of State," *Foreign Relations of the United States* 6 (Mar. 10, 1949): 814.

13. "The Consul at Jerusalem (Burdett) to the Secretary of State," *Foreign Relations of the United States* 6 (Feb. 8, 1949): 736.

14. Ibid., 737.

15. Ibid., 738 n. 3.

16. "Jerusalem (Burdett) to Secretary of State," *The Palestine Reference Files of Dean Rusk and Robert McClintock, 1947–1949*, no. 216 (Mar. 11, 1949).

17. "Mr Wells Stabler to the Secretary of State," *Foreign Relations of the United States* 6 (Mar. 12, 1949): 824.

18. Pappé, *The Making of the Arab-Israeli Conflict, 1947–1951*, 190.

19. Ibid., 189. The "Little Triangle" was described in Pappé's work as including "Wadi Ar'ara (Ara nowdays), its immediate surroundings and the road which runs through it connecting the two Israeli towns of Afula in the valley and Hadera on the coast."

20. "The Consul at Jerusalem (Burdett) to the Secretary of State," *Foreign Relations of the United States* 6 (Apr. 8, 1949): 900.

21. Shlaim, *Collusion Across the Jordan*, 427.

22. "New York (Austin) to Secretary of State," Dean Rusk Reference Book, January 16–April 1949, *The Palestine Reference Files of Dean Rusk and Robert McClintock, 1947–1949*, reel 7, no. 356 (Mar. 17, 1949).

23. Avi Shlaim, *Collusion Across the Jordan: King Abdullah, the Zionist Movement, and the Partition of Palestine* (New York: Columbia University Press, 1988), 391.

24. "E. Sasson and Z. Liff (Lausanne) to Sharett, 31 May 1949 (15:00)," *Documents on the Foreign Policy of Israel*, Companion Volume, 4, no. 46 (May–Dec. 1949): 31–32.

25. "Memorandum of Conversation by the Secretary of State," *Foreign Relations of the United States* 6 (Mar. 4, 1949): 790.

26. Ibid.

27. "The Consul at Jerusalem (Burdett)," *Foreign Relations of the United States* 6 (Mar. 14, 1949): 825. The opening of this "Top Secret" "Urgent" communique indicated that it was written "for Acheston's eyes only from Ethridge."

28. See Joshua Landis, "Early U.S. Policy Toward Palestinian Refugees: The Syria Option," in *The Palestinian Refugees: Old Problems—New Solutions*, ed. Joseph Ginat and Edward J. Perkins (Norman: University of Oklahoma Press, 2001), 77–87.

29. Benny Morris, "A Second Look at the 'Missed Peace,' or Smoothing Out History: A Review Essay," *Journal of Palestine Studies* 24, no. 1 (Autumn 1994): 81; and Itamar Rabinovich, *The Road Not Taken* (New York: Oxford University Press, 1991), chap. 3.

30. "The Minister in Syria (Keeley) to the Secretary of State," *Foreign Relations of the United States* 6 (July 19, 1949): 1235.

31. "M. Sharett: Guidelines for Israeli Missions Abroad," *Documents on the Foreign Policy of Israel*, Companion Volume, 4 (July 25, 1949): 79.

32. Ibid.

33. Ibid.

34. Ibid.

35. Avi Shlaim, *The Iron Wall: Israel and the Arab World* (New York: Norton, 2001), 51.

36. Shlaim, *Collusion Across the Jordan*, 428.

37. J. C. Hurewitz, *The Struggle for Palestine* (New York: Norton, 1950), 319.

38. Shlaim, *Collusion Across the Jordan*, 492.

39. Benny Morris, *The Birth of the Palestinian Refugee Problem, 1947–1949* (New York: Cambridge University Press, 1987), 261–262.

40. "Jerusalem (Burdett) to Secretary of State," *The Palestine Reference Files of Dean Rusk and Robert McClintock, 1947–1949*, reel 7, no. 82, RG 59 Film S 1040 (Jan. 29, 1949).

41. "Policy Paper Prepared in the Department of State," *Foreign Relations of the United States* 6 (Mar. 15, 1949): 837.

42. "Memorandum by Mr. Robert M. McClintock," *Foreign Relations of the United States* 6 (Jan. 11, 1949): 640.

43. "The Acting Secretary of State in Certain Diplomatic Missions in the American Republics," *Foreign Relations of the United States* 6 (Jan. 18, 1949): 677.

44. "The Secretary of State to Consulate General of Jerusalem," *Foreign Relations of the United States* 6 (Mar. 11, 1949): 818.

45. For a valuable overview of McGhee's role and the plan he was to oversee, in principle, see Peter Hahn, *Caught in the Middle East: U.S. Policy Toward the Arab–Israeli Conflict, 1945–1961* (Chapel Hill: North Carolina University Press, 2004), 102–108.

46. Ibid.

47. "Policy Paper Prepared in the Department of State, Palestine Refugees," *Foreign Relations of the United States* 6 (Mar. 15, 1949): 828, and see n. 5.

48. The 800,000 figure is cited in "Memorandum of Conversation, by the Secretary of State," *Foreign Relations of the United States* 6 (Apr. 5, 1949): 891; see also "Memorandum by the Coordinator on Palestine Refugee Matters (McGhee) to the Secretary of State," *Foreign Relations of the United States* 6 (Apr. 22, 1949): 935.

49. "Policy Paper Prepared in the Department of State, Palestine Refugees," *Foreign Relations of the United States* 6 (Mar. 15, 1949): 828.

50. Ibid., 830–831.

51. Ibid.

52. Ibid., 837.

53. Ibid., 838.

54. For a recent exposé of the severe limits of coverage of the Israeli–Palestinian conflict in the *New York Times*, see Howard Friel and Richard Falk, *Israel–Palestine on Record* (New York: Verso, 2007).

55. Peter Hahn, "The View from Jerusalem: Revelations About U.S. Diplomacy from the Archives of Israel," *Diplomatic History* 22, no. 4 (Fall 1998): 516.

56. "Top Secret, Palestine," *The Palestine Reference Files of Dean Rusk and Robert McClintock, 1947–1949*, reel 7, RG 59 Film S 1040 (Mar. 19, 1949).

57. Shlaim, *Collusion Across the Jordan*, 489.

58. "Control 11599, from Beirut, Ethridge (signed Pinkerton) to Secretary of State," *The Palestine Reference Files of Dean Rusk and Robert McClintock, 1947–1949* (Mar. 29, 1949).

59. "Control 12738, Beirut (signed Pinkerton) to Secretary of State," *The Palestine Reference Files of Dean Rusk and Robert McClintock, 1947–1949* (Mar. 31, 1949).

60. "Memorandum of Conversation, by the Secretary of State," *Foreign Relations of the United States* 6 (Apr. 5, 1949): 891.

61. Ibid.

62. Ibid.

63. Ibid., 892.

64. Ibid., 893.

65. Ibid.

66. Ibid.

67. "Control 3618, Incoming Telegram To Secretary of State," NARG 59 Film S 1040, #M1175, Dean Rusk Reference Book, January 16–April 1949, *The Palestine Reference Files of Dean Rusk and Robert McClintock, 1947–1949*, reel 7 (Apr. 9, 1949).

68. Ibid.

69. Ibid.

70. Ibid.

71. Ibid.

72. Ibid.

73. Ibid.

74. Ibid.

75. "Bureau of the Minister of Foreign Affairs (Tel Aviv) to E. Sasson (Lausanne)," *Documents on the Foreign Policy of Israel*, Companion Volume, 4 (June 22, 1949): 53.

76. Stian J. Tiller and Hidle H. Waage, "Powerful States, Powerless Mediator: The United States and the Peace Efforts of the Palestine Conciliation Commission, 1949–51," *International History Review* 33, no. 3 (Sept. 2011): 507.

77. "The Consul at Jerusalem (Burdett) to the Secretary of State," *Foreign Relations of the United States* 6 (Apr. 20, 1949): 925.

78. Ibid., 926.

79. Ibid., 926–927.

80. See discussion of this and related issues in George McGhee, *Envoy to the Middle World: Adventures in Diplomacy* (New York: Harper & Row, 1983), 36.

81. Ibid.

82. "The Consul at Jerusalem to the Secretary of State," *Foreign Relations of the United States* 6 (Apr. 20, 1949): 926.

83. "Memorandum by the Coordinator on Palestine Refugee Matters (McGhee) to the Secretary of State," *Foreign Relations of the United States* 6 (Apr. 22, 1949): 935–936.

84. Ibid., 836.

85. Ibid., 935.

86. Ibid.; see information under distribution of refugees and destitute persons as estimated by Palestine Conciliation Commission, at bottom of page.

87. "Memorandum by the Coordinator on Palestine Refugee Matters (McGhee) to the Secretary of State," *Foreign Relations of the United States* 6 (Apr. 22, 1949): 938.

88. "Editorial Note," *Foreign Relations of the United States* 6 (1949): 995–996.

89. "Mr. Mark F. Ethridge to the Secretary of State," *Foreign Relations of the United States* 6 (May 12, 1949): 998.

90. See discussion of these events in Hahn, *Caught in the Middle East*, 87.

91. "The Minister in Switzerland (Vincent) to the Secretary of State," *Foreign Relations of the United States* 6 (May 16, 1949): 1014.

92. "The Ambassador in Israel (McDonald) to the Secretary of State," *Foreign Relations of the United States* 6 (May 29, 1949): 1075.

93. "The Acting Secretary of State to the Embassy in Israel," *Foreign Relations of the United States* 6 (May 28, 1949): 1072.

94. Ibid., 1073.

95. Ibid.

96. Ibid., 1074.

97. "The Ambassador in Israel (McDonald) to the Secretary of State," *Foreign Relations of the United States* 6 (May 29, 1949): 1075.

98. Yemina Rosenthal, "Editorial Note," *Documents on the Foreign Policy of Israel,* Companion Volume, 4 (May–Dec. 1949): 30.

99. Shlaim, *Collusion Across the Jordan,* 473. See also Shlaim's discussion of Sasson's views of the overall Israeli position at this period, 474–476.

100. "E. Sasson (Lausanne) to S. Divon," *Documents on the Foreign Policy of Israel,* Companion Volume, 4 (June 16, 1949): 48. Note that the quotation marks in the text are as they appear in the Israeli documents. The remainder of the citation is a summary of Sasson's position.

101. Ibid.

102. Ibid.

103. Ibid.

104. Ibid., 49.

105. Ibid.

106. Ibid.

107. Ibid.

108. Shlomo Ben-Ami, *Scars of War, Wounds of Peace: The Israeli–Arab Tragedy* (New York: Oxford University Press, 2006), 53.

109. Ibid.

110. "The Ambassador in France (Bruce) to the Secretary of State," *Foreign Relations of the United States* 6 (June 12, 1949): 1124. The opening line of this communique marked "Top Secret" is "From Ethridge."

111. Ibid.

112. "The British Embassy to the Department of State," *Foreign Relations of the United States* 6 (Sept. 1, 1949): 1345.

113. "The Ambassador in France (Bruce) to the Secretary of State," *Foreign Relations of the United States* 6 (June 12, 1949): 1125. See note 110 above for an indication of Ethridge's authorship of statement.

114. Cited from the papers of Jacob Blaustein in Abba A. Solomon, *The Speech, and Its Context* (Baltimore, Md.: American Jewish Committee, 2011), 143.

115. Saadia Touval, *The Peace Brokers: Mediators in the Arab-Israeli Conflict, 1948–1979* (Princeton, N.J.: Princeton University Press, 1982), 92.

116. Hahn, "The View from Jerusalem," 513.

117. "Weizmann to Truman, in President's Secretary's File," in Papers of Harry S. Truman, Harry S. Truman Library, June 24, 1949.

118. Ibid.

119. Ibid.

120. "Freda Kerchwey to the Hon. Harry S. Truman," in Papers of Clark M. Clifford, Harry S. Truman Library, June 19, 1948.

121. Ibid.

122. "Judge Joseph E. Klau, Hartford, Conn., sent by Governor Chester Bowles to Clark M. Clifford," in Papers of Clark M. Clifford, Harry S. Truman Library, June 27, 1949.

123. "The Consul at Jerusalem (Burdett) to the Secretary of State," *Foreign Relations of the United States* 6 (July 6, 1949): 1203.

124. Ibid., 1204.

125. Ibid.

126. Ibid.

127. Ibid., 1205.

128. Ibid.

129. Ibid.

130. Tiller and Waage, "Powerful State, Powerless Mediator," 513.

131. Ibid.

132. "Major General John H. Hilldring to the Secretary of State," *Foreign Relations of the United States* 6 (July 25, 1949): 1250.

133. "Memorandum of Conversation, by the Deputy Under-Secretary of State (Rusk)," *Foreign Relations of the United States* 6 (July 28, 1949): 1264.

134. Hahn, "The View from Jerusalem," 515.

135. Ibid.

136. "Mr Stuart W. Rockwell to the Secretary of State," *Foreign Relations of the United States* 6 (Aug. 15, 1949): 1313.

137. "President Truman to President Weizmann, at Rehevoth, Israel," *Foreign Relations of the United States* 6 (Aug. 13, 1949): 1307.

138. Ibid., 1306–1307.

139. Shlaim, *Collusion Across the Jordan,* 488.

140. "E. Elath (Washington) to M. Sharett," *Documents on the Foreign Policy of Israel, May–December 1949,* Companion Volume, 4 (Aug. 30, 1949): 158.

141. Ibid.

142. "E. Sasson (Jerusalem) to M. Sharett," *Documents on the Foreign Policy of Israel, May–December 1949,* Companion Volume, 4 (Sept. 28, 1949): 199.

143. Ibid.

144. Ibid., 200.

13. THE VIEW FROM THE PENTAGON AND THE NATIONAL SECURITY COUNCIL

1. As described in the Foreword to Kenneth W. Condit, *The History of the Joint Chiefs of Staff: The Joint Chiefs of Staff and National Policy, 1947–1949,* Vol. 2

(Washington, D.C.: Office of Joint History, Office of the Chairman of the Joint Chiefs of Staff, 1996), v. David A. Armstrong, director for Joint History, has pointed out that "inasmuch as the text has not been considered by the Joint Chiefs of Staff, it must be construed as descriptive only and does not constitute the official position of the Joint Chiefs of Staff on any subject" (vi).

2. Ibid., 43.

3. See the valuable discussion of U.S.–Saudi relations throughout this period in Maurice Jr. Labelle, "'The Only Thorn': Early Saudi-American Relations and the Question of Palestine, 1945–1949," *Diplomatic History* 35, no. 2 (Apr. 2011): 257–281.

4. "Report of the Joint Strategic Plans Committee to the Joint Chiefs of Staff on Military Viewpoint Regarding the Eastern Mediterranean and Middle East Area," *Records of the Joint Chiefs of Staff*, 1887/1 (July 19, 1948): 5–6.

5. Peter L. Hahn, *Caught in the Middle East: U.S. Policy Toward the Arab-Israeli Conflict, 1945–1961* (Chapel Hill: University of North Carolina Press, 2004), 70; Michael J. Cohen, *Fighting World War Three from the Middle East: Allied Contingency Plans, 1945–1954* (London: Frank Cass, 1997), 195–199.

6. "Memorandum by the Chief of Staff, U.S. Air Force to the Joint Chiefs of Staff on U.S. Strategic Interest in Israel," enclosure in *Records of the Joint Chiefs of Staff*, part 2, 1948–1953 [sect B], the Middle East, film A 368 (B), reel 2 (Mar. 7, 1949): 181.

7. Ibid.

8. Cohen, *Fighting World War Three*, 196.

9. Ibid.

10. Ibid., 207–208.

11. Condit, *The History of the Joint Chiefs of Staff*, 55.

12. "The Secretary of State to the Embassy in Iraq," *Foreign Relations of the United States* 6 (Mar. 16, 1949): 844.

13. "Memorandum by the Assistant Secretary of State for United Nations Affairs (Rusk) to the Secretary of State," *Foreign Relations of the United States* 6 (Mar. 29, 1949): 880.

14. Ibid., 881.

15. Ibid. See also discussion of U.S.–Israeli exchanges and policy toward Jerusalem in Hahn, *Caught in the Middle East*, chap. 8.

16. Ibid.

17. "M. Sharett (Tel Aviv) to M. Namir (Moscow)," *Documents on the Foreign Policy of Israel*, Companion Volume, 4 (June 27, 1949): 59.

18. "Memorandum by the Chief of Naval Operations to the Joint Chiefs of Staff on United States Strategic Interest in Israel," *Records of the Joint Chiefs of Staff*, 1684/30, part 2, 1948–1953 [sect B], the Middle East, film A 368 (B), reel 2 (Apr. 27, 1949).

19. Ibid., 98.

20. Ibid.; note that both voided and sanitized pages are numbered identically.

21. Ibid.

22. Ibid., 99.

23. Ibid.

24. "Memorandum by the Secretary of Defense (Johnson) to the Executive Secretary of the National Security Council (Souers)," *Foreign Relations of the United States* 6 (May 16, 1949): 1012.

25. Ibid., 1012.

26. Ibid., 1010.

27. Ibid.

28. "Meeting: M. Sharett–F. Frankfurter (Washington, 15 December 1949)," *Documents on the Foreign Policy of Israel,* Companion Volume, 4 (Dec. 15, 1949): 300.

29. "Memorandum by the Secretary of Defense (Johnson) to the Executive Secretary of the National Security Council (Souers)," *Foreign Relations of the United States* 6 (May 16, 1949): 1011.

30. Ibid.

31. Ibid.

32. "M. Sharett (Tel Aviv) to M. Namir (Moscow)," *Documents on the Foreign Policy of Israel,* Companion Volume, 4 (June 27, 1949): 158–159.

33. "Memorandum by the Secretary of Defense (Johnson) to the Executive Secretary of the National Security Council (Souers)," *Foreign Relations of the United States* 6 (May 16, 1949): 1011.

34. Ibid.

35. Ibid.

36. James G. McDonald, *My Mission in Israel, 1948–1951* (New York: Simon and Schuster, 1951), 189.

37. "The Secretary of Defense (Johnson) to the Secretary of State," *Foreign Relations of the United States* 6 (June 14, 1949): 1134.

38. Ibid.

39. "The Secretary of Defense (Forrestal) to the Chairman of the House Committee on Foreign Affairs (Bloom)," *Foreign Relations of the United States* 6 (Jan. 25, 1949): 697–698.

40. Laurent Rucker, *Staline, Israel et les Juifs* (Paris: PUF, 2001), 172.

41. Ibid., 139–140.

42. "M. Sharett (Tel Aviv) to M. Namir (Moscow)," *Documents on the Foreign Policy of Israel,* Companion Volume, 4 (Oct. 4, 1949): 209.

43. Ibid.

44. Condit, *The History of the Joint Chiefs of Staff,* 57.

45. "Munitions Board, Memorandum for the Joint Chiefs of Staff," enclosure in *Records of the Joint Chiefs of Staff,* 1684 (Apr. 5, 1950): 34.

46. Ibid., Appendix. JCS 1684/39 contains the following list: "List of Arms Required by the Government of Israel for Defensive Purposes": 50 machine guns 250 ground and aircraft; 40 mm antiaircraft guns 30; 90 mm antiaircraft guns with radar control and PF ammunition 36; 76.2 mm or 90 mm antitank guns 48; 76.2 mm or 90 mm antitank self-propelled guns M10 20; 105 mm Howitzers 36; 155 mm Howitzers 18; 105 mm Howitzers self-propelled M7 12; M4 tanks with 76.2 mm guns (Sherman) 45; M24 tanks 18; M38 or M8 armored cars 90; 75 mm recoilless rifles 100; 5 inch aircraft rockets 10,000; 4.5 inch ground to ground rockets 25,000; 24 barreled launchers; field artillery 25; jet fighters 18; radar and communication equipment, details of which will follow.

47. "Report by the Joint Strategic Plans Committee to the Joint Chiefs of Staff on United States Policy Toward Arms Shipments to the Near East." *Records of the Joint Chiefs of Staff,* 1684/42, film A, 368B, reel 2 (Apr. 28, 1950).

48. Condit, *The History of the Joint Chiefs of Staff,* 58.

49. "Report by the National Security Council," *Foreign Relations of the United States* 6 (Oct. 17, 1949): 1440. Also available as NSC 47/2, NSC Registry (Permanent Files), Oct. 17, 1949, "A Report to the President by the National Security Council on United States Policy Toward Israel and the Arab States." All references in the citations that follow are to the *Foreign Relations of the United States* edition cited here.

50. Ibid., 1430.

51. Ibid.

52. "Memorandum of Conversation, by the Assistant Secretary of State for Near Eastern, South Asian, and African Affairs (McGhee)," *Foreign Relations of the United States* 6 (Oct. 18, 1949): 1441.

53. Ibid., 1441 n. 3.

54. "Statement by the United States and the United Kingdom Groups, Discussion on Arab Unity," *Foreign Relations of the United States* 6 (Nov. 15, 1949): 69.

55. "Report by the National Security Council," *Foreign Relations of the United States* 6 (Oct. 17, 1949): 1434.

56. Ibid.

57. Ibid., 1438.

58. Ibid., 1436.

59. Ibid.

60. "The Acting United States Representative at the United Nations (Jessup) to the Secretary of State," *Foreign Relations of the United States* 6 (July 1, 1948): 1184.

61. "Memorandum by the Chief of Staff, U.S. Air Force to the Joint Chiefs of Staff on U.S. Strategic Interest in Israel," enclosure in *Records of the Joint Chiefs of Staff,* part 2, 1948–1953 [sect B], the Middle East, film A 368 (B), reel 2 (Mar. 7, 1949): 181.

62. "Memorandum by the Chief of Naval Operations to the Joint Chiefs of Staff on United States Strategic Interest in Israel," *Records of the Joint Chiefs of Staff,* 1684/30, part 2, 1948–1953 [sec B], the Middle East, film A 368 (B), reel 2 (Apr. 27, 1949): 98.

63. "Memorandum by the Secretary of Defense (Johnson) to the Executive Secretary of the National Security Council (Souers)," *Foreign Relations of the United States* 6 (May 16, 1949): 1009.

64. Ibid., 1010.

65. "Memorandum by the Politico-Military Adviser in the Bureau of Near Eastern, South Asian, and African Affairs (Robbertson)," *Foreign Relations of the United States* 6 (Nov. 14, 1949): 56. See also Gabriel Kolko, *The Politics of War: The World and United States Foreign Policy, 1943–1945* (New York: Pantheon Books, 1958), chap. 8; and Joyce Kolko and Gabriel Kolko, *The Limits of Power: The World and United States Foreign Policy, 1945–1954* (New York: Harper & Row, 1972), chap. 8.

66. These figures come from Jeremy M. Sharp, "U.S. Foreign Aid to Israel," *Congressional Research Service (CRS) Report for Congress* (Jan. 2, 2008): CRS-19.

67. Ibid., CRS-15.

68. Ibid.

14. THE ISRAELI–U.S. OIL CONNECTION AND EXPANDING U.S. OIL INTERESTS

1. Max Holland, *The Militarization of the Middle East* (Philadelphia: Peace Education Division, American Friends Service Committee, 1983), 2.

2. "Memorandum by the Acting Director of the Office of Near Eastern and African Affairs (Hare) to the Under Secretary of State (Lovett)," *Foreign Relations of the United States* 5, part 1 (Aug. 25, 1948): 40.

3. International Petroleum Cartel, "Staff Report to the Federal Trade Commission," released through Subcommittee on Monopoly of Select Committee on Small Business (Washington, D.C.: U.S. Senate 83rd Congress, 2nd session, 1952), 2. Page numbers are from online version, chap. 11, "Concentration of Control of the World Petroleum Industry"; http://www.mtholyoke.edu/acad/Petroleum/ftc22.htm.

4. Ibid., 2–3.

5. Ibid., 4.

6. Maurice Jr. Labelle, "'The Only Thorn': Early Saudi-American Relations and the Question of Palestine, 1945–1949," *Diplomatic History* 35, no. 2 (Apr. 2011): 279.

7. "Memorandum by the Joint Chiefs of Staff," *Foreign Relations of the United States* 5, part 1 (Aug. 10, 1948): 245.

8. "Memorandum of Conversation by Mr Richard H Sanger of the Division of Near Eastern Affairs," *Foreign Relations of the United States* 6 (Jan. 5, 1949): 91.

9. "Memorandum of Conversation, by Mr Richard H Sanger of the Division of Near Eastern Affairs," *Foreign Relations of the United States* 6 (Jan. 25, 1949): 98.

10. Ibid.

11. Papers of Max W. Ball, Harry S. Truman Library, July 7, 1948, Box 2.

12. Consider the following sources: Hanna Batatu, *The Old Social Classes and the Revolutionary Movements of Iraq* (London: Saqi, 2004); Petter Nore and Terisa Turner, eds., *Oil and Class Struggle* (London: Zed, 1980); Ervand Abrahamian, *Iran Between Two Revolutions* (Princeton, N.J.: Princeton University Press, 1982); Marion Farouk-Sluglett and Peter Sluglett, "Labor and National Liberation: The Trade Union Movement in Iraq, 1920–1958," *Arab Studies Quarterly* 5, no. 2 (Spring 1983); Zachary Lockman, *Comrades and Enemies: Arab and Jewish Workers in Palestine, 1906–1948* (Berkeley: University of California Press, 1996); Fawaz Traboulsi, *A History of Modern Lebanon* (London: Pluto, 2007); Joel Beinin, *Workers and Peasants in the Modern Middle East* (Cambridge, Mass.: Cambridge University Press, 2001); Joel Beinin and Zachary Lockman, *Workers on the Nile: Nationalism, Communism, Islam, and the Egyptian Working Class, 1882–1954* (Princeton, N.J.: Princeton University Press, 1988); and Malek Abisaab, "'Unruly' Factory Women in Lebanon: Contesting French Colonialism and the National State, 1940–1946," *Journal of Women's History* 16, n. 3 (2004). Also see Malek Abisaab, "Militant Women of a Fragile Nation" (unpublished manuscript), which provides an extensive analysis of the role of Lebanese women in the history of the Lebanese labor movement with special attention to women workers in tobacco factories.

13. Uri Bialer, *Oil and the Arab-Israeli Conflict, 1948–1963* (New York: St. Martin's, 1999), 128, 85.

14. "Diary," Papers of Max W. Ball, New York, Harry S. Truman Library, Box 2, Mar. 12, 1951.

15. Bialer, *Oil and the Arab-Israeli Conflict*, 96.

16. Ibid., 92.

17. Ibid., 93.

18. "Diary," Papers of Max W. Ball, Washington, Harry S. Truman Library, Box 2, May 12, 1949, 175.

19. Ibid.

20. Ibid., May 13, 1949, 176.

21. Ibid., May 16, 1949, 178.

22. Ibid., Aug. 1, 1949, 176.

23. Ibid., Aug. 3, 1949, 175.

24. Ibid., Aug. 4, 1949.

25. Ibid., Aug. 8, 1949.

26. Ibid., July 18–Aug. 31, 1950.

27. Ibid., Mar. 11, 1951, 190.

28. Ibid., Feb. 28, 1951, Mar. 8, 1951, May 1, 1951.

29. "Diary," Papers of Max W. Ball, Washington, Harry S. Truman Library, Box 2, Apr. 16, 1948.

30. "Diary," Papers of Max W. Ball, Washington, Harry S. Truman Library, Box 2, May 1, 1951.

31. "Diary," Papers of Max W. Ball, Washington, Harry S. Truman Library, Box 2, May 21, 1951.

32. "Diary," Papers of Max W. Ball, Washington, Harry S. Truman Library, Box 2, Aug. 30, 1951.

33. "Diary," Papers of Max W. Ball, Washington, Harry S. Truman Library, Box 2, May 27, 1951.

34. "Diary," Papers of Max W. Ball, Washington, Harry S. Truman Library, Box 2, June 26, 1951.

35. "Diary," Papers of Max W. Ball, Washington, Harry S. Truman Library, Box 2, July 12, 1951.

36. "Diary," Papers of Max W. Ball, Washington, Harry S. Truman Library, Box 2, Dec. 22, 1951.

37. "Oil Possibilities in Israel Reported by American Expert: Explorations Considered," *JTA,* May 11, 1951. More recently, the subject of Israel drilling for oil was once again in the headlines: "Israel to Drill for Oil in the West Bank," *Al Jazeera,* Nov. 4, 2013; http:www.aljazeera.com/indepth/features/2013/11/Israel-drill-oil-west-bank-20131114571416794.html.

38. "Ralph Friedman to Directors of the Industrial Institute of Israel," Files of Clark M. Clifford, Harry S. Truman Library, Sept. 20, 1949.

39. "Ralph Friedman to Clark Clifford," Files of Clark M. Clifford, Harry S. Truman Library, Nov. 9, 1949.

40. Michael J. Cohen, *Fighting World War Three from the Middle East: Allied Contingency Plans, 1945–1954* (New York: Routledge, 1997), 96.

REFLECTIONS ON DISCOVERY, DENIAL, AND DEFERRAL

1. "Report by the Coordinating Committee of the Dept. of State, Annex," *Foreign Relations of the United States* 8 (May 2, 1945): 37.

2. Ibid.

3. Ibid., 35 n. 2.

4. "Report of the Anglo-American Committee of Enquiry regarding the problems of European Jewry and Palestine, Lausanne" (London: His Majesty's Stationery Office, Apr. 20, 1946), 4.

5. Ibid.

6. Evan M. Wilson, *A Calculated Risk: The U.S. Decision to Recognize Israel* (Cincinnati, Ohio: Clerisy Press, 2008), 294.

7. Central Intelligence Agency, "The Consequences of the Partition of Palestine" (Nov. 28, 1947): 8; http://www.foia.cia.gov/browse_docs_full.asp.

8. "Draft Memorandum by the Director of the Office of United Nations Affairs (Rusk)," *Foreign Relations of the United States* 5, part 2 (May 4, 1948): 894.

9. "The Acting United States Representative at the United Nations (Jessup) to the Secretary of State," *Foreign Relations of the United States* 5 (July 27, 1949): 1248.

10. "The Secretary of State to the Embassy in the United Kingdom," *Foreign Relations of the United States* 5, part 2 (Aug. 13, 1948): 1309.

11. "The Secretary of State to the Embassy in the United Kingdom," *Foreign Relations of the United States* 5, part 2 (Aug. 14, 1948): 1311.

12. "Memorandum by the Secretary of State to President Truman," *Foreign Relations of the United States* 5, part 2 (Aug. 16, 1948): 1313.

13. Ibid., 1313–1314.

14. "Memorandum by the Director of the Office of United Nations Affairs (Rusk) to the Under Secretary of State (Lovett)," *Foreign Relations of the United States* 5, part 2 (Aug. 20, 1948): 1331.

15. Central Intelligence Agency, "Possible Developments from the Palestine Truce" (Aug. 31, 1948): 3; http:www.foia.cia.gov/browse_docs_full.asp.

16. "The Secretary of State to the Special Representative of the United States in Israel (McDonald)," *Foreign Relations of the United States* 5, part 2 (Sept. 1, 1948): 1367.

17. "The Ambassador in the United Kingdom (Douglas) to the Acting Secretary of State at London," *Foreign Relations of the United States* 5, part 2 (Oct. 30, 1948): 1532.

18. "The Acting Secretary of State to the Embassy in Israel," *Foreign Relations of the United States* 6 (May 28, 1949): 1072.

19. "The Ambassador in France (Bruce) to the Secretary of State," *Foreign Relations of the United States* 6 (June 12, 1949): 1124; opening indicates Mark Ethridge as author.

20. Ibid., 1125.

21. Shlomo Ben-Ami, *Scars of War, Wounds of Peace: The Israeli-Arab Tragedy* (Oxford: Oxford University Press, 2007), 50.

22. Seth P. Tillman, *The United States in the Middle East: Interests and Obstacles* (Bloomington: Indiana University Press, 1982), 58–59.

23. "The Acting Secretary of State to the Embassy in Israel," *Foreign Relations of the United States* 6 (May 28, 1949): 1073.

24. "The Acting United States Representative at the United Nations (Jessup) to the Secretary of State," *Foreign Relations of the United States* 5, part 2 (July 1, 1948): 1181.

25. Ibid., 1183.

26. Ibid., 1184.

27. Ibid.

28. "The Secretary of State to the Special Representative of the United States in Israel (McDonald)," *Foreign Relations of the United States* 5, part 2 (Sept. 1, 1948): 1367.

29. Ibid., 1367–1368.

30. "The Acting Secretary of State to the Secretary of State, at Paris," *Foreign Relations of the United States* 5, part 2 (Nov. 10, 1948): 1566.

31. Ibid., 1565.

32. "Memorandum by the Chief of Staff, US Air Force to the Joint Chiefs of Staff on US Strategic Interest in Israel" [enclosure]. *Records of the Joint Chiefs of Staff,* part 2, 1948–1953 [sect B], the Middle East, film A 368 (B), reel 2 (Mar. 7, 1949): 181.

33. "Memorandum by the Chief of Naval Operations to the Joint Chiefs of Staff on United States Strategic Interest in Israel," *Records of the Joint Chiefs of Staff,* part 2, 1948–1953 [sect B], the Middle East, film A 368 (B), reel 2 (Apr. 27, 1949).

34. Ibid., 98.

35. Ibid.; note that both voided and sanitized pages are numbered identically.

36. "Memorandum by the Secretary of Defense (Johnson) to the Executive Secretary of the National Security Council (Souers)," *Foreign Relations of the United States* 6 (May 16, 1949): 1009–1010.

37. Ibid., 1010.

38. "Report by the National Security Council," *Foreign Relations of the United States* 6 (Oct. 17, 1949): 1434.

39. Ibid., 1431.

40. Ibid., 1433.

41. Ibid., 1435.

Index

Carter, Jimmy, 3
Central Intelligence Agency (CIA),
331*n*63; on Arab League, 110;
McClintock and Palestine, 67–78;
oil and, 295; Palestine assessed by,
68–73, 88–89; Palestinian refugees
and, 202–3, 205–6, 312; on
partition, 310–11; in Saudi Arabia,
13; secret information leaks and,
272; U.S. policy on Palestine and,
197–200
Chamoun, Camille, 138
children, 72; Jewish refugees, 36;
Palestinian refugees, 127–28, 177,
210–11, 222; violence and, 77,
120–21, 123, 222
Childs, J. Rives, 12–13, 110, 178–79
China, 142, 257
Chizik, Yitzak, 136
Christians, 17, 26–27, 48–49, 237;
Arabs, 198, 253; Greek Catholics,
261; Maronites, 249, 253, 261;
relief organizations, 208
CIA. *See* Central Intelligence Agency
Citino, Nathan, 109
citrus industry, 49, 133
Cizling, Aharon, 226
Clayton, William L., 4
Clifford, Clark, 21, 25, 211,
300, 359*n*2, 360*n*21; Butler
memorandum and, 85–87;
influence, 50, 94, 111, 270,
361*n*41; Israel's independence and,
166, 169; May 12 debate and, 159,
160–62, 163, 185; partition and,
138, 155, 156–58, 162
Cohen, Aharon, 345*n*7
Cohen, Gerard Daniel, 328*n*4
Cohen, Hillel, 350*n*26
Cohen, Michael J., 50, 90, 168, 301
Comay, Michael, 227–28
Communist Party: Iraq, 18;
Palestine, 17

Condit, Kenneth W., 278, 380*n*1
Connelly, Matthew, 159
Consolidated Refineries, 16
control. *See* power
corporations, 69, 268; Palestine
Economic Corporation, 161;
power shared between U.S. and,
7–8, 10, 12–15, 101; U.S. oil policy
influenced by, 3–9
costs, oil and security, 13. *See also*
finances
coup, in Syria, 250
*The Coup, 1953, the CIA, and the
Roots of Modern U.S.-Iranian
Relations* (Abrahamian), 331*n*63
Creamer, Daniel, 45, 195, 300
Crick, Wilfred, 41
Crossman, Richard, 41, 45
Crum, Bartley C., 41, 359*n*2
Curtice, Duke, 297
Czechoslovakia, 61, 170, 210, 223–24,
286, 313

Daniel, Jonathan, 163
Danin, Ezra, 66, 119
Davies, Ralph K., 5–6, 99
Dawayma massacre, 226
Dayan, Moshe, 253
debate, of May 12, 159–64
deferral. *See* Middle East, U.S.
policy on
Deir Yassin massacre: context,
115, 129, 137, 153, 204, 350*n*26;
denounced, 252, 350*n*29; Wasson
on, 120–25, 151
Dekanozov, V., 20
democracy, dictatorships and, 13
Democratic Party, 365*n*13
denial. *See* Middle East, U.S.
policy on
de Reynier, Jacques, 121
development. *See* Middle East, U.S.
policy on

Fascism, 39, 41, 350n29
Fawzi Bey, Mahmoud, 139, 142, 144–45, 215
Feis, Herbert, 6–7, 8
Feisal (Prince of Saudi Arabia), 145, 147, 149
finances: banks, 161, 210, 212, 249, 271, 292; Haifa refinery, 295; market percentages, 7; oil and security costs, 13; Palestinian refugees and, 208, 235, 237–38, 253; partition, 74; U.S. and Israel, 212, 292; for weapons sales, 325n3. *See also* economy
Firestone Rubber Company, 69
Fishman, Alex, 353n98
Flapan, Simha, xix, 116, 117, 125, 165, 170
flight, truth about, 125–26. *See also* Haifa; refugees, Palestinian
"A Foreign Oil Policy for the United States," 6–7
"Foreign Petroleum Policy of the United States," 8
Foreign Relations of the United States (FRUS), xx, 84
"Form of Government." *See* trusteeship
Forrestal, James, 4, 10, 58, 96, 141, 225; on Ethridge, 243; with strategic objectives in Israel, 286
France, 11–12, 17, 142, 210, 261
Frankfurter, Felix, 69, 283
Friedman, Ralph, 300–301
FRUS. *See* Foreign Relations of the United States
Futuwwa, 72

Galili, Israel, 166
Gass, Oscar, 45, 99, 195, 300
Gaza, xiii–xv, 267; Egypt in, 244–45, 266; Palestinian refugees in, 226; weapons and, 325n3
Genesis (Judis), 340n37

Genesis 1948 (Kurzman), 354n11
genocide, 199, 205, 226
geography, prime oil-production areas, 8, 13–14
Germany, 35–38, 161, 335n61. *See also* Nazis
Glubb, John Bagot (Sir), 139
Goldmann, Nahum, 19, 25, 27, 28, 41; AAC and, 50; trusteeship and, 147, 153
Goldschmidt, Tex, 298
Grady, Henry, 79
Great Britain: Arab-Israeli conflict and, 26; Bahrein Petroleum Company, Ltd., 12, 13; Haifa and, 125; Morrison-Grady plan and, 31, 48–50; oil expansion and, 8–9, 14; Palestine and, 23, 26, 29, 30–33, 35, 44, 53–54, 58, 61, 89, 118, 169, 185, 190, 208–9, 276, 277–78; partition and, 81; Peel Commission Report (1937), 64, 118, 187, 190, 340n37; truce and, 245–46; trusteeship and, 26, 52–53, 84; U.S. State Department and warnings from, 224–26; White Paper (1939), 32–33, 35, 190
Greece, 22, 30, 157, 192, 261
Grew, Joseph, 27, 28
Griffis, Stanton, 223
Grodzinsky, Yosef, 335n61
Gromyko, Andrei, 284
Grose, Peter, 34, 101
Gross, Ernest A., 79, 85, 139
Gruenther, Alfred (Major General), 84–85
Guatemala, 61
guerrilla warfare, Arabs with, 72, 81–82
Gulf Exploration Company, 14
Gulf Oil Corp., 294
Gur, Mordechai (General), 353n98
Gurney, Henry (Sir), 131–32

Haber, William, 38
Haganah, 78; characterization of, 42, 71–72, 81–82, 88, 150–51; numbers, 72; Palestinian refugees and, 204; Plan Dalet and, 115–36; recruitment, 37–38
Hahn, Peter L., xvii, 25, 94, 168, 327n20, 361n41
Haifa: flight from, 121, 124–25, 213; Lippincott and, 125–31; population of Arabs in, 127–28; refinery, 78, 103, 129–31, 295–96; violence in, 126–28
Hambros Bank, 161
Harding, Charlie, 106, 107, 297
Harriman, W. Averell, 4, 49, 99
Harrison, Earl G., 34–35, 168; AAC and, 41; Palestinian refugees and, 309
Harrison Report: Jewish immigration and Holocaust, 31–40; Palestine and, 35–36
Hart, Parker, 12
Hashomer Hatzair, 39, 43
Hayden, John Justin, 337n95
Heikal, Mohamed Hassanein, 39, 171
Henderson, Loy, xxi, 12, 20, 22, 41; Deir Yassin and, 122–23; Israel's independence and, 166; on Jewish immigration, 64; Merriam and, 50, 51, 53; Palestine and, 24–25, 28–30, 54; partition and, 57–60, 62–64, 69, 78–79, 82, 85, 88–90; transfer and, 184; trusteeship and, 144, 145–46; UNSCOP and, 67; U.S. policy on Palestine and, 184–86
Heyd, Uriel, 271
Hilldring, John J. (General), 271–72
The History of the Joint Chiefs of Staff (Condit), 380n1
Hitler, Adolf, 90
Hogan, Michael J., 327n20

Holbrooke, Richard, 361n41
Holland, Max, 293
Holocaust. *See* refugees, Jewish
Holton, George V., 15
Horner, John, 155, 157
Hoskins, Harold B. (Lt. Colonel), 24
Houghton, Robert B., 363n84
Hourani, Albert, 45, 46
House of Representatives, U.S., 96–101
Hudson, Manley, 295
Hull, Bert, 297
Hull, Cordell, 9
Hurewitz, J. C., xviii, 60, 251–52
al-Husayni, Jamal, 45
Husseini, Abdul Kader, 81, 120–21
al-Husseini, Amin (Haj), 66, 81, 93, 121, 139, 157
al-Husseini, Fawzi, 43
Hutcheson, Joseph C., 41

Ibn Muammar, Abd al-Aziz, 18
Ibn Saud (King of Saudi Arabia): Israel's independence and, 178; trusteeship and, 139, 152; U.S. corporations and, 12–13, 101; U.S. military and, 9–11
Ickes, Harold, 4, 5, 6, 25, 26, 95, 96
IDF. *See* Israel Defense Forces
Ikhwan al Muslimin (Muslim Brotherhood), 71, 72, 171
illegal immigration, 46–47, 128
imbalance. *See* populations
immigration: children with, 36; Holocaust and Jewish, 27, 31–40, 46, 54, 64, 68, 335n61; illegal, 46–47, 128; legislation, 36, 37; Morrison-Grady plan and, 49–50; Palestine and Jewish, 27, 30–33, 35, 37–40, 64, 190; trusteeship and, 141, 147–48; White Paper (1939), 32–33, 35, 190

land, 368*n*10; boundaries, 220–24, 227–31, 233–34, 236–38, 244–45, 257–59, 288; citrus industry and, 49, 133; expansion, xv, 208, 269, 315–16; Gaza, xiii–xv, 226, 244–45, 266–67, 325*n*3; "Little Triangle," 248, 270, 375*n*19; Plan Dalet and, 120, 133, 165; population-land ratio, 74, 134, 211, 288; "seven basic premises," 215–19; transfer policy and, 27, 43, 45, 211, 274; trusteeship and, 141–42

Lausanne Conference (1949), xvii, 241, 243, 250, 253–54; Ethridge on, 252, 316–17; Shlaim on, 252

laws. *See* legislation

League for Victory (V League), 20

Leahy, William, 142

leaks, secret information, 272

Lebanon, 11, 39, 128, 197, 206; boundaries and, 230–31; Israel and, 248–49, 286; labor strikes in, 17–18; Maronites, 249, 253, 261; Palestinian refugees and, 236, 263; partition and, 74

Leffler, Melvin, xvii

Leggett, Frederick (Sir), 41

legislation: immigration, 36, 37; oil, 299–300

Lehman, Herbert, 256

Levantine Coast, 8

Levy, Walter, 297

Liberia, 69

Libya, 27

Lie, Trygvie, 167

Liff, Zalman, 249

Lippincott, Aubrey, Haifa and, 125–31

Little, Douglas, 168

"Little Triangle," 248, 270, 375*n*19

Litvinov, Maxim, 20

Lodge, Henry C., 256

Loftus, John, 3–4

Long, Breckinridge, 33

looting, 353*n*98

Louis, William Roger, 23–24, 168

Lourie, Arthur, 272

Lovett, Robert A., xxi, 4, 63, 279, 320, 359*n*2; boundaries and, 220–24, 227–30, 234; Butler memorandum, 83–85, 87; Deir Yassin and, 122; Great Britain's warning and, 224–25; May 12 debate and, 159–62, 163–64; Palestinian refugees and, 207–15, 232–33, 235, 236–37, 253, 254, 314; partition and, 58, 69, 82, 88, 92–93; truce and, 244, 245–46; trusteeship and, 138, 140, 144, 146, 147, 151, 155, 156; U.S. policy on Palestine and, 186, 196

Lowenthal, Max, 25, 138, 160–61, 169

Macatee, Robert B., xxi; partition and, 76–77; on violence, 80–82

Magnes, Judah (Rabbi), 43, 60, 145, 188; AAC and, 45; Deir Yassin and, 122–23; trusteeship and, 153–55

Maisky, Ivan, 19–20, 119

Malik, Charles, 138, 249–50

Manningham Buller, Reginald, 41

Mardam Bey, Jamil, 178

Margalit, Abraham, 135–36

market percentages, 7

Maronites, 249, 253, 261

Marshall, George C., xxi, 22, 24, 120, 354*n*11; boundaries and, 220–24; Butler memorandum and, 83, 85; Great Britain's warning and, 224; on Haifa refinery, 129–30; Israel's independence and, 165, 167, 169, 320; on Jewish immigration, 38; May 12 debate and, 159, 160–62; Palestinian refugees and, 201, 207–16, 231–33, 238, 312–15;

partition and, 58, 76; transfer and, 184; trusteeship and, 137, 140, 144–51, 153–54; U.S. policy on Palestine and, 185, 196

Masalha, Nur-eldeen, xix

massacres. *See* Dawayma massacre; Deir Yassin massacre

Massad, Joseph, xix–xx

May 12 debate. *See* independence, Israel's

McBride, David, 37

McClintock, Robert M., xxi, 344*n*21, 365*n*13; Butler memorandum and, 83–84; CIA and Palestine, 67–78; on Jewish Agency, 311; May 12 debate and, 159; Palestinian refugees and, 216, 232, 238, 253; partition and, 79, 88; on Plan Dalet, 115–16; transfer and, 184; trusteeship and, 138, 140, 146–52, 155; UNSCOP and, 67–68; U.S. policy on Palestine and, 186–88, 196–97

McCloy, John, 4

McDonald, James G., 41, 121, 285; influence, 274; Israel's admission to UN and, 233; Palestinian refugees and, 201, 204–5, 208, 211–14, 220, 222–23, 314–15; relief organizations and, 223; truce and, 246

McGhee, George, 12, 323; Egypt and, 262; October 1949 NSC report and, 288–89; with Palestinian refugees and Israel's response, 262–66, 271; resettlement plan and, 254

McKinzie, Richard D., 63, 176–77, 184

media: Deir Yassin in, 350*n*29; Palestinian refugees ignored by, 256; in Soviet Union, 8; weapons sales in, 325*n*3

mediators. *See* United Nations

Meir, Golda (Myerson, Golda), 45, 66, 77, 128–29

merger, ARAMCO, 14–15

Merriam, Gordon P., xxi, 238, 330*n*48, 333*n*16; on Arab-Israeli conflict, 50–54; Jewish refugees and, 32; oil policy and, 11–15; Palestine and, 24, 25–28, 30–31, 50–54, 309–10; partition and, 78, 79; U.S. policy on Palestine and, 183, 184

Mexico, 294

Middle East: Arab-Israeli relations and, xiii–xxii, 6, 7, 11; Israel's power in, 291, 319; Merriam on, 11–15; postwar views of, 16–19; prime oil-production areas in, 8, 13–14; studies, xviii–xx; U.S. Air Force assessment on, 277–78, 321; U.S. State Department on, 308–9

Middle East, U.S. policy on: deferral and development, 308, 322–23; denial, 307, 311–22; discovery, 307, 308–11; explanation of, 305–8

migration. *See* refugees, Jewish

military, Israeli. *See* Irgun Zvai Leumi; Israel Defense Forces; Stern Gang

military, U.S.: Air Force, 9–10, 277–78, 321; Army, 11; Butler memorandum and, 84–86; Israel and, 279, 281–82, 286–87, 292; JCS and, xxii, 239, 275–78, 282–84, 287, 291, 321–22, 380*n*1; Navy, 10, 97; NSC and, xxii, 25, 83–84, 86, 239, 275–92, 321–22, 344*n*21, 380*n*1; oil interests, xv, 7–11, 16, 21; Palestinian refugees and, 254; in Saudi Arabia, 9–15, 294; SWNCC, 10; trusteeship and, 142; weapons sales, 325*n*3, 383*n*46

military groups, Arabs, 72–73, 80, 81, 88, 197–98

Mobil, 15

Moore, Bob, 328*n*4

Morgenthau, Henry, 34

Morris, Benny, xix, xx, 134, 340*n*37; on Arab-Israeli conflict, 199, 367*n*67, 372*n*26; Dawayma massacre and, 226; Palestinian refugees and, 202; on Plan Dalet, 117; transfer and, 65, 118–20

Morris, Ernest L., 37

Morrison, Robert (Lord), 41

Morrison-Grady plan, 31, 48–50

Mossadegh, Mohammed, 14, 15, 21

Mulligan, William E., 331*n*81

Munayyer, Spiro, 203

Murphy, Frank, 69

Murray, Wallace S., 24, 132

Muscat, 14

Muslim Brotherhood (Ikhwan al Muslimin), 71, 72, 171

Myerson, Golda. *See* Meir, Golda

My Promised Land: The Triumph and Tragedy of Israel (Shavit), 368*n*10

Najjada, 72

Najjar, Orayb Aref, 39–40

Nakhleh, Isa, 82

name changes, with independence, 202, 368*n*6

Nashashibi, Azmi, 214

Nasser, Gamal Abdel, 172

Nathan, Robert, 45, 99, 195, 300

National Liberation League, 17

National Petroleum Council, 5, 7

National Petroleum War Service Committee, 7

National Security Agency (NSA), xiii

National Security Council (NSC), 25, 83–84, 86, 275, 344*n*21; on IDF, 289; Israel's place in U.S. strategy (1948–1949), 290–92, 321–22; JCS and, xxii, 239, 275–78, 282–84, 287, 291, 321–22, 380*n*1; October 1949 report, 287–90; policy and purpose,

pros and cons, 279–82; U.S interests in Israel, 276–79; U.S. strategic objectives in Israel, 282–87

Navy, U.S., 10, 97

El Nazer, Salah Effendi, 134

Nazis, 127; Holocaust and, 35, 36, 39–40, 41, 46; Jews with Nazi-like behavior, 121, 226, 350*n*29; support for, 40

Near East Division. *See* State Department, U.S.

Neff, Donald, 125

Netherlands, 61

Nevel, Donna, xiv

Niles, David, 25, 40–41, 50, 69, 94; boundaries and, 228; May 12 debate and, 159; Palestinian refugees and, 268, 272

Nitze, Paul H., 4

Nixon, Richard, 3

Nokrashi Pasha, 139

Norstad, Lauris (Major General), 142

North Africa, 9, 16, 62, 103, 150, 161, 290

NSA. *See* National Security Agency

NSC. *See* National Security Council

Nuri Pasha, 14

Office of Near Eastern and African Affairs. *See* State Department, U.S.

Office of Petroleum Coordinator, 4, 5, 6

Office of Strategic Services (OSS), 13, 23

offshore oil rights, 294–95

OGD. *See* Oil and Gas Division

oil: AIOC, 14, 15, 21, 98, 250, 331*n*63; antitrust and, 6, 15; ARAMCO, 10, 12–15, 18–19, 97, 104, 108, 110–11, 294–95, 297, 298, 328*n*20; Ben-Gurion and, 299; CIA and, 295; embargo, 296; employment, 18, 129, 331*n*78; expansion, 8–9, 14–15, 18, 97, 328*n*20; Gulf Oil Corp., 294; Haifa

refinery, 78, 103, 129–31, 295–96;
Kuwait Oil Company, 14, 250;
legislation, 299–300; offshore oil
rights, 294–95; OPEC, 18; PAW,
4–6; petroleum, 4–8, 12–14,
18, 78, 103, 129–30, 294; prime
oil-production areas, 8, 13–14;
private ownership of, 7, 293–94;
security costs, 13; Seven Sisters,
293–94; Socony-Vacuum Oil
Company, 12, 98, 106–7, 250, 294,
296; Soviet Union and, 19–22, 73,
101; Standard Oil Company, 95,
98, 106, 250, 294, 296; Standard
Oil Company of California, 6,
13, 98, 294, 328n20; TAPLINE,
97, 105, 250; U.S. military with
interests in, xv, 7–11, 16, 21; U.S.
with worldwide control of, 4–5, 7,
10–15, 98, 293–94
Oil and Gas Division (OGD), 5–6, 94
oil connection: ARAMCO and, 297,
298; Ball, Max, and, 93–99, 101–
12, 295–300; Bevin and, 109; Duce
and, 93, 95, 96, 97–99, 106, 109,
110, 297; Elath and, 93, 94, 96, 99,
101–12, 297–98; House hearings
on oil and national defense,
96–101; Israel and, xx–xxi, 91–96,
293–302; Jewish Agency and,
91–96, 306; Kosloff, Ray, and,
93, 95–96, 101, 102, 297–99; U.S.
and, xx–xxi, 92–96, 293–302; U.S.
policy on Palestine and, 99–101
oil policy, U.S.: Arab-Israeli conflict
and, xvi–xxii, 6, 7, 11, 57–58,
80, 85, 193–94, 285–86, 319;
corporations influencing, 3–9;
Loftus with, 3–4; Merriam and,
11–15; Middle East, postwar, 16–
19; Saudi Arabia and, 3, 8, 9–15;
Soviet Union in Middle East,
19–22; U.S. Justice Department
influenced by, 6

Oman, 8, 14, 98, 294
OPEC, 18
organizations, relief. *See* relief
organizations
OSS. *See* Office of Strategic Services
Oumanski, Konstantin, 19
Owen, Roger, 16
Oxnam, Bromley, 154

Painter, David, 58
Palestine, xvii, 3, 4, 300, 340n37;
AAC report (1946), 31, 40–48,
309; as "anomalous situation,"
151–55; Arab Liberation Army,
73, 80; "cancerous situation" in,
143–46; CIA and, 67–78, 88–89,
197–200, 202–3, 205–6, 312;
Towards a Common Archive and,
xvi, 219, 371n82; Communist
Party, 17; Gaza, xiii–xv, 226,
244–45, 266–67, 325n3; Great
Britain and, 23, 26, 29, 30–33, 35,
44, 53–54, 58, 61, 89, 118, 169,
185, 190, 208–9, 276, 277–78;
Harrison Report and, 35–36;
Henderson and, 24–25, 28–30,
54; Israel's transfer policy and,
xiv, 20, 64–65, 118–19, 121, 236,
332n84, 367n67; Jewish Agency
and, 27, 28; Jewish immigration
and, 27, 30–33, 35, 37–40, 64, 190;
labor strikes in, 16–17; May 12
debate, 159–64; with McClintock
and CIA, 67–78; Merriam and,
24, 25–28, 30–31, 50–54, 309–10;
Middle East studies and, xviii–xx;
Morrison-Grady plan, 31, 48–50;
Truman and, 26, 27–29, 31–32,
40–41, 48, 60, 354n11; UNSCOP,
31–32, 58, 61–62, 67; U.S. State
Department and, 25–31; White
Paper (1939), 32–33, 35, 190. *See
also* Arab-Israeli conflict; refugees,
Palestinian

The Politics of Partition (Shlaim),
345*n*7
Polk, William R., xiii
populations: Arab military groups,
73, 88; Arabs in Haifa, 127–28;
Haganah, 72; imbalance, 59, 62,
64–65, 74, 89, 173; Palestinian
refugees, 198, 203–4, 206, 210,
218, 226, 236–38, 255, 257,
258–59, 263, 271, 314, 377*n*48;
Plan Dalet and, 118; population-
land ratio, 74, 134, 211, 288; Stern
Gang, 72. *See also* immigration;
transfer policy, Israel
Porter, Paul A., 271, 273
*Postwar: A History of Europe Since
1945* (Judt), 328*n*2
Potofsky, Jacob S., 228
power: Abdullah and, 319; Middle
East and Israel's, 291, 319; with
oil worldwide under U.S. control,
4–5, 7, 10–15, 98, 293–94; U.S.
and corporations with shared,
7–8, 10, 12–15, 101
private ownership, of oil, 7, 293–94
Proskauer, Joseph M., 50, 144–45
Provisional Government of Israel
(PGI): Haifa refinery and, 129–31;
Palestinian refugees and, 206, 209,
253, 307; U.S. policy on Palestine
and, 192, 194
Qatar, 8, 13, 14, 97
Quandt, William, 12, 330*n*47
Quwwatli, Shukri, 250
Rabin, Yitzhak, 199
racism: anti-Semitism, 33, 54, 63;
against Arabs, 121; ARAMCO
and, 104; with immigration and
Holocaust, 33, 54
Rayner, Charles, 12
Raynor, Charlie, 297
recruitment. *See* Haganah; Irgun Zvai
Leumi

refinery. *See* Haifa
refugees, Jewish, 19, 23; children,
36; as Displaced Persons, 31, 33,
37, 46, 328*n*4, 335*n*61; Haganah
and, 37–38; with Holocaust and
immigration, 27, 31–40, 46, 54,
64, 68, 335*n*61; Irgun Zvai Leumi
and, 37–38, 42–43; migration
patterns, 335*n*61
refugees, Palestinian, xiii–xv, xx, xxii,
12, 250, 340*n*37; Bernadotte and,
202, 206–19, 221; boundaries,
Jerusalem, and, 220–24; children,
127–28, 177, 210–11, 222; CIA
and, 202–3, 205–6, 312; Ethridge
and, 257–59, 261–63, 266–74, 280;
expulsion and flight, 65, 75–76,
115, 121–22, 124–26, 132–33,
172–73, 198–99, 203–4, 213,
226–27, 229, 247, 255, 311–16,
322–23; finances, 208, 235, 237–
38, 253; Haifa, 125–31; Israel's
independence and, 171, 307;
Jaffa, 131–36; Lovett and, 207–15,
232–33, 235, 236–37, 253, 254,
314; Marshall with, 201, 207–16,
231–33, 238, 312–15; McGhee
and Israel's response, 262–66, 271;
media's ignoring of, 256; origins,
125, 201–7; partition and, xxi, 15,
30, 50, 55, 57–66, 68–96, 99–101,
113, 115–40, 155–58, 162, 169,
174–75, 183, 207, 213, 233, 255,
275, 279, 288, 306–7, 310–11,
320, 323, 345*n*7; populations,
198, 203–4, 206, 210, 218, 226,
236–38, 255, 257, 258–59, 263,
271, 314, 377*n*48; repatriation
for, xiv, 119, 133, 175, 201–2,
204, 205, 209, 211, 215, 218, 221,
222, 236, 243, 245–46, 252–56,
259, 272, 276, 279, 280, 301,
307, 317; resettlement plan, 254;

refugees (*continued*)
  Rusk and, 206–16, 232, 233, 254,
    258, 268, 271, 280, 314; "seven
    basic premises" and, 215–19;
    transfer policy and, 64–65; UN
    Resolution 212 and, 235; U.S. State
    Department and, 231–39, 254–62,
    309; with villages destroyed, xvi,
    65, 76, 81–82, 117, 119, 120–21,
    125, 129, 131, 151, 173–74, 218,
    256
Regie de Tabacs, 17
relief organizations, 208, 223,
  226–27, 235–36. *See also* United
  Nations
repatriation: rejection of, 119,
  133, 201–2, 204, 209, 211, 215,
  222, 252–56, 259, 280; UNGA
  Resolution 194, xiv, 175, 205, 218,
  221, 236, 243, 245–46, 254–55,
  259, 272, 276, 279, 301, 307, 317
Republican Party, 365n13
resettlement plan, 254
Resolution 181. *See* partition; United
  Nations General Assembly
  Partition Plan
Resolution 186. *See* United Nations
Resolution 194. *See* repatriation;
  United Nations General Assembly
  Partition Plan
Resolution 212. *See* United Nations
Revercomb, Chapman, 37
Riley, William (Brigadier General), 286
Robinson, Jacob, 91
Rockwell, Stuart W., 176–77, 363n84
Rogan, Eugene, xv
Roman Catholics, 261
Roosevelt, Eleanor, 99
Roosevelt, Franklin D., 4, 14;
  immigration and Holocaust,
  32–33; JCS and, 275
Rosen, Pinhas, 166
Rosenman, Samuel I., 25, 148

Ross, John C., 155, 244
Rouleau, Eric, 39
Roumania, 8
Royal Dutch Shell group, 294, 296
Rucker, Laurent, 332n84
Ruffer, Gideon, 101–2, 347n50
Rusk, Dean, 63, 67, 279–80, 359n2;
  Israel's admission to UN and,
  233; Israel's independence and,
  166–67; May 12 debate and, 160;
  Palestinian refugees and, 206–16,
  232, 233, 254, 258, 268, 271, 280,
  314; partition and, 78, 79, 85;
  truce and, 244; trusteeship and,
  144, 146–52, 155–56; U.S. policy
  on Palestine and, 196
Russia, 8, 35, 294. *See also* Soviet
  Union

Sabath, A. J., 256
Safwat, Ismail (General), 125
sales, weapons, 223–24, 286, 325n3,
  383n46
Sasson, Elias, 189, 246, 345n7;
  Palestinian refugees and, 265–66,
  273–74; Plan Dalet and, 119
Sasson, Elihau, 66, 261
Satterthwaite, Joseph C., 234–35,
  244
Saudi Arabia, 197; CIA in, 13;
  employment in, 18–19; Palestinian
  refugees and, 238; partition and,
  74, 75; trusteeship and, 145, 147,
  149; U.S. military in, 9–15, 294;
  U.S. oil policy and, 3, 8, 9–15
Savitz, Joseph, 256
Schmidt, Dana Adams, 218
secret information, leaks, 272
security, 13. *See also* National
  Security Agency; National
  Security Council
Segal, Simon, 268
self-determination, 51, 63, 215

"seven basic premises," UN and, 215–19

Seven Sisters, 293–94

Shaarawi, Huda, 39

Shahak, Israel, 118, 353n98

Sharett, Moshe (Shertok, Moshe), 45, 59, 102, 106, 189, 279, 283; AHC misrepresented by, 93, 140; boundaries and, 227; IDF and, 286–87; Israel's independence and, 159–62; name change and, 202, 368n6; Palestine policy and oil connection, 99, 100; Palestinian refugees and, 201–3, 205, 207, 209, 214, 232, 247, 258–59, 266, 272, 273, 280; partition and, 92–93; Soviet Union and, 284; transfer policy and, 64, 65, 118; truce and, 247, 251; trusteeship and, 140–42, 147–48, 151–52; U.S. State Department and, 225

Shavit, Ari, 118, 367n67, 368n10

Shertok, Moshe. *See* Sharett, Moshe

Shiloah, Reuven, 345n7

Shimoni, Yaacov, 345n7

Shlaim, Avi, xv, xix, 72–73, 198, 345n7; with Israel's independence and violence, 169–70; Lausanne Conference (1949), 252; Plan Dalet and, 116–17; truce and, 248; U.S. policy on Palestine and, 189

Short, Dewey, 95, 98

Shuqayri, Ahmed, 46

Silver, Abba Hillel (Rabbi), 32, 59

Simon, Julius, 161

Singleton, John (Sir), 41

Six Day War, 292

Snyder, John W., 4

Socony-Vacuum Oil Company, 12, 98, 106–7, 250, 294, 296

Sophoulis, Themistoklis, 22

Souers, Sidney W. (Admiral), 142, 291

Soviet Union, 8, 14; Arab-Israeli conflict and, 19–22, 193, 223; Israel and, 284; oil and, 19–22, 73, 101; partition and, 68–69; transfer policy and, 119; Turkish-Soviet Friendship Treaty (1925), 21; UNGA Partition Plan and, 74

Sprinzak, Yosef, 203

Stabler, Wells, 228–29, 234, 247–48

Standard Oil Company, 95, 98, 106, 250, 294, 296

Standard Oil Company of California, 6, 13, 98, 294, 328n20

State Department, U.S.: ARAMCO run as replica of, 13; changes in, 24–25; Great Britain's warning and, 224–26; Jewish refugees, 32; on Middle East, 308–9; Near East Division, 23, 25–26, 29, 30, 59, 82, 92; Office of Near Eastern and African Affairs, 24; Palestine, 25–31; Palestinian refugees and, 231–39, 254–62, 309; refugees, boundaries, and Jerusalem, 220–24; U.S. Consul in Jerusalem and, 226–27; Washington, Beirut, and Tel Aviv, 227–31

State-War-Navy Coordinating Committee (SWNCC), 10

Stern Gang, 43, 179; capabilities, 68, 88, 122, 216; characterization, 72, 81–82, 192; Deir Yassin massacre and, 120–21

Stettinius, Edward, 4, 26

Stevenson, Adlai, 99

Stimson, Henry, 9, 99

strategies: IDF objectives, 343n107; Israel's place in U.S. strategy (1948–1949), 290–92, 321–22; U.S. objectives in Israel, 282–87

Stratton, William, 37

strikes, labor, 16–19, 104

Suez Canal, 80, 283, 284–85, 301, 322

violence: assassinations, 176–79, 215–16; Ben-Gurion and, 75–76, 77, 126; bombings, 80, 82, 199; Butler memorandum and, 87; children and, 77, 120–21, 123, 222; genocide, 199, 205, 226; in Haifa, 126–28; Israel's independence and, 169–74; massacres, 115, 120–25, 129, 137, 151, 153, 204, 226, 252, 350n26, 350n29; partition and, 71–78, 80–82, 88

Vitalis, Robert, 13

V League. *See* League for Victory

Vyshinskii, Andrei, 20

Wadsworth, George, 68, 118

wages, 16–19

Washington, DC, 227–31

Wasson, Thomas C., xxi, 228, 363n84; assassination of, 176–79; on Deir Yassin massacre, 120–25, 151; Israel's independence and, 162–63, 175–76; trusteeship and, 143, 150–51, 158

Watzman, Haim, 350n26

weapons: embargo, 256; Gaza and, 325n3; IDF, xv, 287, 325n3, 383n46; sales, 223–24, 286, 325n3, 383n46

Webb, James, 264, 285, 315–16

Wehba, Hafiz (Sheikh), 149

Weisgal, Meyer W., 34

Weitz, Josef, 65

Weitz, Yosef, 119

Weizmann, Chaim, 19–20, 34, 143, 205, 332n84; AAC and, 45; Palestinian refugees and, 269, 272; partition and, 59, 93–94, 137, 140; transfer policy and, 64, 119; Truman and, 233–34,

268–69, 272–73; trusteeship and, 148

Welles, Sumner, 99, 228

West Bank, 248, 271

White Paper (1939), 32–33, 35, 190

Wiley, John C., 295

Wilkins, Fraser, 59, 78, 82, 92, 139; May 12 debate and, 159; Palestinian refugees and, 271, 272

Wilson, Evan M., 330n47; AAC and, 47–48, 310; Merriam and, 50–51; Palestine and, 24, 26, 27, 28, 53

Wise, Stephen S. (Rabbi), 19, 25, 26, 32, 37

Witkon, Moshe, 297

Wolfsohn, Joel D., 298–99

women, with labor strikes, 17–18

World Jewish Congress, 25

World War II: economy after, 3; with Jewish immigration and Holocaust, 27, 31–40, 46, 54, 64, 68, 335n61; Saudi Arabia with oil after, 3, 8, 9–15; U.S. as plutocracy after, 3–10, 12–15, 270

World Zionist Organization, 25

Yadin, Y. (General), 120

Yalcin, Husayn Jahed, 243, 252, 259–60

Yale, William, 24, 26, 30–31

Yemen, 74, 161, 246

Yom Kippur statement, 49–50

Yugoslavia, 61, 138

Zaim, Husni, 250

Zeuty, E. J., 227

Zionism: AAC's rejection of, 46–47; influence, 249; partition and, 59, 70, 91–96; transfer policy and, 65; World Zionist Organization, 25

Zochrot, xvi, 219, 371n82

Zureik, Elia, 236